Seamus Heaney

For my dear friend Kyle Irwin, who was brought back from the dead.
Deo Soli Gloria.

Seamus Heaney
An Introduction

Richard Rankin Russell

EDINBURGH
University Press

Edinburgh University Press is one of the leading university presses in the UK. We publish academic books and journals in our selected subject areas across the humanities and social sciences, combining cutting-edge scholarship with high editorial and production values to produce academic works of lasting importance. For more information visit our website: edinburghuniversitypress.com

© Richard Rankin Russell, 2016

Edinburgh University Press Ltd
The Tun – Holyrood Road
12(2f) Jackson's Entry
Edinburgh EH8 8PJ

Typeset in 10.5/13 Adobe Sabon by
Servis Filmsetting Ltd, Stockport, Cheshire

A CIP record for this book is available from the British Library

ISBN 978 1 4744 0165 4 (hardback)
ISBN 978 1 4744 0167 8 (webready PDF)
ISBN 978 1 4744 0166 1 (paperback)
ISBN 978 1 4744 0168 5 (epub)

The right of Richard Rankin Russell to be identified as the author of this work has been asserted in accordance with the Copyright, Designs and Patents Act 1988, and the Copyright and Related Rights Regulations 2003 (SI No. 2498).

Contents

Acknowledgments	vi
Legend	ix
Introduction	1
1. Life and Contexts	6
2. Burrowing and Bogs: Early Poems, *Death of a Naturalist*, *Door into the Dark*, *Wintering Out*, *North*	29
3. Reading the Ground and the Sky: *Field Work*, *Station Island*, *The Haw Lantern*	90
4. Radiance: *Seeing Things*, *The Spirit Level*, *Electric Light*	142
5. Return: *District and Circle*, *Human Chain*, and Late Uncollected Poetry	190
6. Prose, Drama, and Translations	233
Primary Works by Seamus Heaney	260
Annotated Bibliography of Selected Critical Books, Book Chapters, Interviews, and Essay Collections	266
Works Cited	272
Index	286

Acknowledgments

Seamus Heaney was consistently kind and thoughtful in his correspondence with me. I am grateful for his incredible generosity, his courage, and for his life's work.

A research leave from Baylor University's College of Arts and Sciences in Fall of 2014 enabled much thinking, researching, and writing. I am very grateful to the university's committee on research leaves and to Dean Lee Nordt of the College of Arts and Sciences for that time and funding and for his support of my work, and to Baylor President Ken Starr and my former chair in the Baylor English Department, Dianna Vitanza, for their confirmation and recognition of my work.

My current chair in English, Kevin Gardner, graciously provided funding at a crucial late stage of this project.

Many thanks also go to my former Provost, David Lyle Jeffrey, and former chair in English, Maurice Hunt, for reducing my teaching load several years ago so that I might have more time for scholarship. I especially appreciate Professor Hunt's friendship and sustained support of my life and career.

The Centennial Professor Committee at Baylor awarded me the 2012 Baylor Centennial Professor Award in May, 2012, which enabled me to conduct research in the Heaney collections at Emory and Chapel Hill and helped me purchase Heaney material for my classroom and scholarly use. Additional thanks go to the Baylor Class of 1945, which funds the Centennial Professor Award.

Professor Kevin Young gave very helpful information about the holdings on Heaney, including those in the Seamus Deane Collection, and also to the members of staff at Emory's Manuscript, Archive, and Rare Book Library for their assistance during my time there in May, 2012.

Hearty thanks to Seamus Heaney for permission to quote from his archival material at Emory University's Manuscripts, Archives, Rare Books Library, and from his estate and Faber and Faber for permission to quote from his archival material at Ireland's National Library and from the uncollected poems I cite.

All other permissions from Heaney's poetry are covered by the principle of Fair Use in academic publications.

Thank you to Peter Fallow, editor of Gallery Press, for permission to cite from Gallery's edition of Heaney's *Crediting Poetry* and from his *The Last Walk*.

I am very thankful to the two outside readers, whose comments and suggestions were most helpful.

Many thanks to Jackie Jones, Edinburgh University Press's Acquisitions Editor, for a thorough, thoughtful, and speedy publishing process, and to Adela Rauchova, who did a wonderful job as the book's Assistant Commissioning Editor. Additional thanks to the other staff members of Edinburgh University Press, especially Managing Desk Editor James Dale, for their help in cover design, publicity, editing, proofreading, and other work on my book.

I offer grateful thanks to my mentor, Weldon Thornton, at the University of North Carolina, Chapel Hill, who exemplified how to be an excellent father and husband, scholar, and teacher.

I am grateful to my undergraduate and graduate students at Baylor University for their own thoughts on Seamus Heaney's poetry, prose, and drama over the years, which have aided my own understanding. Most recently, I would single out the graduate students in my graduate seminar on Auden, Walcott, and Heaney in the Spring of 2014, who created particularly congenial and rigorous classroom environments and helped me think differently and better about Heaney.

I am grateful to the many friends who have offered encouragement during the writing of this book, which I began before Seamus Heaney's untimely death:

George Lensing, University of North Carolina, Chapel Hill; Bryan Giemza, University of North Carolina, Chapel Hill; Marilynn Richtarik, Georgia State University; Bernard O'Donoghue, Oxford University; Peter Fallon, Loughcrew, Ireland; Joe Heininger, Dominican University; Marie Heaney, Dublin;

My church family at Redeemer Presbyterian in Waco, Texas;

My past and present Baylor colleagues the late James Barcus, Mona Choucair, Mike DePalma, Julia Daniel, Alex Engebretson, Luke Ferretter, Sarah Ford, Joe Fulton, Greg Garrett, Clement Goode,

Maurice Hunt, Joshua King, the late Ann Miller, Coretta Pittman, Lisa Shaver, Betsy Vardaman, and William Weaver, all of whom make the Baylor English Department and Baylor University the best kind of home for me;

My family in Tennessee, Paul L. Russell, Rachel Diggs, Marjorie, Herb, and Vincent Levy, and my family in North Carolina, Tim and Glenda Gray, Gretta and John Kubis.

As always, my deepest and most heartfelt gratitude must go to my wife, Hannah Russell, and my two sons, Connor and Aidan—they are my North, my South, my East, my West.

Legend

Multiple presses have published Heaney's primary works and thus the pagination of these works differs from edition to edition; all these are cited in full in the Primary Bibliography. These editions are the ones cited parenthetically throughout the study.

CP   *Crediting Poetry*. Loughcrew, Ireland: Gallery Press, 1996 rpt. of 1995 edn.
CT   *The Cure at Troy: A Version of Sophocles' Philoctetes*. New York: Noonday, 1990.
DC   *District and Circle*. New York: Farrar, Straus & Giroux, 2006.
DD   *Door into the Dark*. London: Faber & Faber, 1969.
DN   *Death of a Naturalist*. London: Faber & Faber, 1966.
EL   *Electric Light*. New York: Farrar, Straus & Giroux, 2001.
FW   *Field Work*. New York: Noonday, 1979.
HC   *Human Chain*. New York: Farrar, Straus & Giroux, 2010.
HL   *The Haw Lantern*. London: Faber & Faber, 1987.
N   *North*. London: Faber & Faber, 1975.
SI   *Station Island*. London: Faber & Faber, 1984.
SL   *The Spirit Level*. London: Faber & Faber, 1996.
SS   *Stepping Stones: Interviews with Seamus Heaney*, conducted by Dennis O'Driscoll. New York: Farrar, Straus & Giroux, 2008.
ST   *Seeing Things*. New York: Noonday, 1991.
TLW   *The Last Walk: Translations from the Italian of Giovanni Pascoli*, with paintings and drawings by Martin Gale. Loughcrew, Ireland: Gallery Press, 2013.
WO   *Wintering Out*. London: Faber & Faber, 1972.

Introduction

Seamus Heaney's 2013 poem, "On the Gift of a Fountain Pen," provides an appropriate starting point for this critical introduction to his work since it encapsulates his central concern—the role of the writer. In pondering his vocation, Heaney has always worried about his obligation to others—not just readers, but also to the general public—and this poem vocalizes that worry ably. Moreover, he seems also to fear a drying-up of inspiration here. Drawing on John Keats's "When I Have Fears that I May Cease to Be," he opens by musing, "Now that your pen is in my hand / And I have fears / That poems may cease to be."[1] No one could have known, but less than nine months after writing these words, the poet himself would cease to be, felled by a heart condition on August 30, 2013. Heaney's loss to the republic of poetry, to literature, to the world itself, is inestimable, and only time will tell what his absence portends for those who care about literature. But, as a number of his admirers noted after his death, his words survive, living on and sustaining us. One of these admirers, Neil Corcoran, an outstanding critic of his work—and Heaney often drew the best critics of his time to that work—argued in his obituary for *The Guardian* that

> For all the strength of personality manifest in Heaney's life, it is . . . to the poetry that we will return. This is always, as it were, a life altogether elsewhere; and the elsewhere in Heaney is characteristically the life of memory, and specifically the memory of his childhood place, the townlands of his origins whose Irish names—Anahorish, Broagh, Toome, Mossbawn, Bellaghy—are now such an indelible part of English-language poetry, as are their accents, rhythms, and people. There is a real sense in which his poetry is permanent homesickness, as the place is returned to again and again, but always with a difference, until its topography becomes the register of an immensely complex psychological, emotional, cultural and political terrain; until the place has become . . . in the title of one of Heaney's collections of lectures, the "place of writing."[2]

"The place of writing" signifies the complicated ways in which Heaney's home region is intertwined with his notion of writing. Place and writing, for him, are both real and imagined, written and oral, a permanent record and a palimpsest written over repeatedly by generations of inhabitants.

To return to "On the Gift of a Fountain Pen," itself characteristically in conversation with earlier Heaney poems, including his signature poem "Digging," collected in *Death of a Naturalist* (1966) and a series of poems from *Human Chain* (2010), we see how his fascination with the material conditions of writing, including its tools, have long been wedded to his anxiety about the ethical dimension of writing, particularly to questions of audience. The poet asks in stanza two of "On the Gift," "What of the years / Of every other obligation / Imposed and undertaken?," an admission of the heavy toll his legendary generosity at helping others has taken on him. He continues, "All that 'Do unto others / As you would have done unto you'? / Mistaken? Virtue?" Typically for Heaney, he wonders whether he has done the right thing in meeting so many of these obligations. Were these mistakes or did they exemplify virtue on his part? Characteristically, he concludes, "Yes and no. I dip and fill / And start again, doubts / Or no doubts. Heigh-ho."[3] When he read this poem on March 4, 2013, at Baylor University, he uttered "Heigh-ho" in a weary tone, as if to indicate how exhausting meeting his commitments had been for him, and then looked up and smiled. This candid self-questioning of his very hard work conducted outside of his own personal and poetic life remains one of his enduring and endearing qualities. I think, however, he would not have had it any other way.

In his 1979 poem, "Casualty," Heaney urges, "Question me again," to his fisherman friend, Louis O'Neill, who was blown up during a curfew other members of the local Catholic community observed in the wake of the Bloody Sunday murders of January 30, 1972 (FW 24). And the poet's ability, even desire, to put himself in the role of being questioned repeatedly—by himself and others—signifies his great interest in, and commitment to, the ethics of writing. Now that Heaney's career has run its course, there remain questions worth asking about it that this study pursues: How to account for the remarkable consistency of this self-questioning throughout his career even as the honors, including the 1995 Nobel Prize, mounted? How and why, in an age of decreasing literacy and particularly, given such a lack of interest in poetry, has Heaney's work stayed so popular? Estimates of the sales of his poetry volumes in Britain suggest that they account for two-thirds to 70 percent of all poetry sold there annually. What are his individual poems, volumes, dramas, and translations that have become part of the canon of English and Irish literature? In his obituary for Heaney, Corcoran indicates that his intense interest in place names has already become part of the landscape of our literature—that they are now "an indelible part of English-language poetry." And there are many other touchstones of Heaney's work that live on the tongues of his readers and are still quoted in various literary and political contexts.

The Northern Ireland-born Heaney was, at the time of his death, the most well-known and beloved poet in the world. The day he died, his passing was the number one trending topic on Twitter. Even before he won the Nobel Prize, his work generated extended, often appreciative reviews in leading periodicals and even more startling sales figures. His poetry consistently outsells the combined poets on the Faber list (including T. S. Eliot) by a factor of ten to one. Heaney's introduction to the Old English epic *Beowulf* has become a standard one, featured in the *Norton Anthology of English Literature*, and his work is always included in anthologies of Irish and British writing. It also appears regularly on the leaving examinations for high-school students in Britain and Ireland and features on the curriculum in English departments globally. One measure of the Irish public's great love for him and his poetry occurred a year and a half after his death when his untitled third sonnet from "Clearances" in *The Haw Lantern* that begins "When all the others were away at mass" was chosen Ireland's best loved poem of the last one hundred years.[4]

Two of the best critical considerations of Heaney's work, Neil Corcoran's *The Poetry of Seamus Heaney: A Critical Study* (1998) and Helen Vendler's *Seamus Heaney* (1998), are now badly out of date. Thus they cannot consider the three original poetry collections that follow *The Spirit Level* (1996)—*Electric Light* (2001), *District and Circle* (2006), *Human Chain* (2010)—or *The Last Walk* (2013), comprised of Heaney's versions of poems by the Italian poet Giovanni Pascoli. Nor do they treat some of the essays published in *Finders, Keepers: Selected Prose* (2002) or Heaney's adaptation of Sophocles' *Antigone, The Burial at Thebes* (2004). Despite its date, a more recent introduction, Andrew Murphy's *Seamus Heaney* (3rd edition, 2010), does not cover Heaney's *oeuvre* after his 1999 translation of *Beowulf*, which also includes his "autobiography," *Stepping Stones*, consisting of revealing interviews with fellow Irish poet Dennis O'Driscoll. Therefore, there is no current critical introduction to Heaney that discusses not only the biography and the context of his life and work, but also his major work throughout his career, including his late uncollected poems, as the current study does.

This book enables students of Heaney ranging from general readers, through high school, college, and graduate students, along with specialists in his work, to gain a clearer understanding of his life, contexts, major works, and secondary criticism on him. Moreover, rather than reading Heaney solely through either, say, a New Critical framework or a postcolonial one—as valuable as these methods can be—this study will instead consistently feature the sort of historically attentive close readings of the poems they deserve. Rather than appropriating Heaney to a particular national identity or literary tradition, the entire study assumes that he is an inherently transnational writer grounded in the culture and literature of his native Northern Ireland but conversant with British, Irish, American, Asian, and Eastern European cultural and literary traditions. This assumption clarifies Heaney's remarkable ability to inhabit various regions, cultures, even politics, and presents him as the world writer that he really is.

A special focus of this study, as mooted above, concerns Heaney's intense engagement with the act of writing itself, from his self-conscious declaration to wield his pen as did his father and grandfather their shovels in "Digging"; through his later explorations of concepts such as the "frontier of writing" in his essay and poem that draw on this phrase reveal; to one of his last poems, "On the Gift of a Fountain Pen," which fears the end of his poetry. No self-conscious postmodernist that perceives signifiers floating free of their signified, Heaney nonetheless has consistently sought to meditate upon the process and act of writing in his work and by so doing, offer it as a great moral force with the potential to hold a space for our concentration, as he claims it does in his essay "The Government of the Tongue."

Chapter 1 addresses the salient aspects of Heaney's life as a minority Catholic in majority Protestant Northern Ireland in the 1940s and 1950s, his teaching career, and the arc of his literary career, along with the various contexts of his work. Chapters 2 through 5, the heart of the study, analyze Heaney's accomplishments in poetry. These chapters privilege extended close readings of the major poems. The sixth and final chapter considers other genres such as his prose criticism, translations, and drama. Another section lists Heaney's primary works in different genres and includes an annotated critical bibliography of selected books and essays. The final section contains the Works Cited pages.

The cover of this study features a graffito that was painted on some buildings in Dublin after Heaney's death: "Don't Be Afraid." This exhortation is the English translation of Heaney's last words (in Latin) that he texted to his wife before he died: "*Noli timere.*" As a poet supremely concerned with suffering in the twentieth century, Heaney nonetheless often affirmed joy through solidarity with other human beings. A signature poem that captures for him poetry's role in keeping us courageous and joyful is W. H. Auden's "In Memory of W. B. Yeats." Writing about the last two couplets of that poem that conclude with an invitation to praise, Heaney argues that these "emphatically rhymed and confidently metrical" lines make the poem a "rallying cry that celebrates poetry for being on the side of life, and continuity of effort, and enlargement of the spirit."[5] Never saccharine, always attuned to man's capacity for depravity, Heaney's work nonetheless similarly affirms life, including the life of the spirit. And so this study finally explores and charts that affirmation through its close engagement with his artful words.

Notes

1. Heaney, "On the Gift of a Fountain Pen."
2. Corcoran, "Seamus Heaney Obituary," n.p.
3. Heaney, "On the Gift of a Fountain Pen."
4. "Seamus Heaney Poem Chosen as Ireland's Best-Loved," n.p.
5. Heaney, "New Staves," 6.

Chapter 1

Life and Contexts

Stirrings: 1939–1968

Seamus Heaney's work vacillates restlessly between the demand for solitude by the artistic self and the lure of communal intimacy, a dialectic captured most memorably in his 1979 elegy "Casualty," which begins by praising the solitude of a dead friend, an eel fisherman, moves to an appreciation of the Catholics murdered on Bloody Sunday, and then concludes in solitude again by recalling a fishing trip he took with the slain fisherman, Louis O'Neill. Somewhat surprisingly for one who "in the early 1970s . . . surely did identify with the Catholic minority,"[1] he rejects what he perceives as the "swaddling band" of collective comfort endemic to the nationalist community in Northern Ireland before and during the "Troubles" in favor of the solitary life of O'Neill (FW 22). And yet the way in which he quietly registers his outrage at the murdered civil rights marchers in the poem signifies his real sense of being part of that community and its particular problems and strengths as well. He learned to value both solitude and community as a child in Northern Ireland. This chapter concentrates especially on Heaney's rural, Catholic upbringing and on the public reaction to his passing, the latter of which signifies how well he spoke to the human condition through his apologia for poetry. Readers wishing to know Heaney's own sense of his rich life story are directed to his articulate and nuanced book-length interview with Dennis O'Driscoll that took place over the course of eight years, *Stepping Stones: Interviews with Seamus Heaney*.[2]

Born into a large but relatively financially secure farming family, Heaney "grew up," as he has said in "Terminus," "in between"—in between English and Irish culture, in between his native English tongue and the vestiges of the Irish language embedded in his culture (HL 5). He has discussed how as a child delivering milk at night to the next house down the road enabled him to straddle the confluence of a series of geographical, municipal, and diocesan boundaries as he crossed the Sluggan, a small stream:

> [T]his water was part of a long drain or stream that marked the boundary between the townland of Tamniarn and the townland of Anahorish, as well as the boundary between the parish of Bellaghy and the parish of Newbridge, and then ... the boundary between the diocese of Derry and the archdiocese of Armagh ... Every day on my road to and from school I crossed and recrossed the Sluggan, and every time my sense of living on two sides of a boundary was emphasized. I never felt the certitude of belonging completely in one place ... .[3]

And yet this in-betweenness came to paradoxically signify his sure linguistic, geographic, and cultural foundations.

Despite being marginalized as part of the Catholic minority in the majority-Protestant Northern Irish state, formed in 1920 by the Government of Ireland Act with its own Unionist-dominated Parliament that opened in 1921, Heaney was sheltered from much of the overt discrimination directed toward Catholics by his immersion in a family that his wife Marie has characterized as "utterly together, like an egg contained within the shell, without any quality of otherness, without the sense of loss that this otherness brings."[4] He recalled "The clean-swept floor, the closed doors that let the heat gather, the shut-in safety of the kitchen," an atmosphere that was "huddled and snug" (*SS* 13). Heaney's formative years enabled him to be part of a close-knit local community on two family farms. He believed that "The really valuable thing about my childhood was the verity of the life I lived within the house and the sense of trust that I had among the people on the ground."[5] That verity and trust grounded his locally inflected poetry.

In these communities, he imbibed the rhythms of rural life in the 1940s and early- to mid-1950s, then watched and lamented as they ebbed away. The reference to the young Wordsworth "drinking in" nature from Book I of *The Prelude* is deliberate.[6] Heaney often made clear the salutary influence of the English Romantic poet.[7] Like Wordsworth, whose seminal childhood moments, Heaney notes, "were not only the foundation of his sensibility, but the clue to his fulfilled identity,"[8] he returned repeatedly to his own childhood, finding it a stable source of values and traditions, but also discovering it generating horrors such as rats in "An Advancement of Learning," a "rat-grey fungus" in "Blackberry-Picking," and drowned kittens in "The Early Purges" (*DN* 6–7, 8, 11). Even his family barn felt dangerous to him at times, as he recalled: "I was always afraid in its dark heat that something was going to jump out of its corners—a rat, an owl, anything."[9] He too was "fostered alike by beauty and by fear," a phrase that features as part of an epigraph from Book I of *The Prelude* for Heaney's sequence "Singing School" from his 1975 volume *North* (qtd in N 56). Unlike Wordsworth, however, who had written his greatest poetry, save *The Prelude*, by the age of 37, Heaney wrote memorable, moving, even magnificent poetry his entire career. Although childhood remained a crucial aspect of his poetry, he consistently found ways to enlarge that original world by steeping himself in the work of many world poets—including Yeats, Dante, Joyce, Eliot, Hardy, Frost, and a series of Eastern European poets—many of whom lived through times as troubled or more so than his own and who were both eyewitnesses to trauma and apologists for poetry.

Seamus Justin Heaney was born April 13, 1939, on the family farm, Mossbawn, in the townland of Tamniarn near Castledawson, in southern County Derry, Northern Ireland, to Patrick and Margaret Heaney. He was the oldest of nine children, a total of seven boys and two girls. His father's uncles and his father were all cattle dealers. He observed that "the Scullion uncles" who reared his father in "The Wood" (another family farm), whose parents had died young "were prosperous old boys, and so he'd always lived on land and owned land, was always on a social par with the smallholders and the not so small," noting further that "He would have considered himself a cut above 'the men of no property,' whereas there was something in my mother that identified with the working class and the laboring class" (*SS* 28). Elsewhere, Heaney spoke of his father as "a creature of the archaic world, really," noting further, "He would have been entirely at home in a Gaelic hill-fort."[10]

His mother, on the other hand, "was more a creature of modernity. Her people lived in the village of Castledawson, which was in some respects a mill village."[11] Heaney further pointed out, "I suppose you could say my father's world was Thomas Hardy and mother's D. H. Lawrence. Castledawson was that kind of terrace-house village, spic-and-span working class." He recalled her being steeped in her McCann family's penchant for order and polish, but has suggested as well that the McCanns "had a strong sense of justice and civil rights and they were great arguifiers. They genuinely and self-consciously relished their own gifts for contention and censoriousness," while his father's people felt that "Argumentation, persuasion, speech itself ... seemed otiose and superfluous to them. It had to do with their rural background, with the unspoken Gaelic thing that was still vestigially there."[12] Understandably, just as Heaney's own great facility with conversation and argumentation must have been influenced by the McCanns' emphasis on such verbal facility, his simultaneous appreciation of silence and quiet understanding, seen in his poems about taciturn rural craftsmen, likely stemmed from his immersion in this quieter world of the Scullions and Heaneys.

Heaney's Mossbawn functioned to him as a manifestation of what Mircea Eliade, a religious thinker whose classic work *The Sacred and the Profane* the poet was later to read while writing his volume *Station Island* (*SS* 309), has termed "sacred space." As Eliade remarked, "the religious experience of the nonhomogeneity of space is a primordial experience, homologizable to a founding of the world."[13] Heaney has written about his primordial sense of occupying the center of the world by chanting the word *omphalos* to open his autobiographical essay "Mossbawn":

> I would begin with the Greek word, *omphalos*, meaning the navel, and hence the stone that marked the centre of the world, and repeat it, *omphalos, omphalos, omphalos,* until its blunt and falling music becomes the music of somebody pumping water at the pump outside our back door.[14]

His perception of himself as being at the *omphalos* as a child recalls Eliade's contention that the "nonhomogeneity of space" is "the break effected in space that allows the world to be constituted, because it reveals the fixed point, the central axis for all future orientation."[15] Heaney's Mossbawn became just this "central axis" that continued to orient him throughout his life and poetic career. For instance, in "The Toome Road," the speaker sees British Army troops deployed as part of the conflict in Northern Ireland that he compares to domineering Roman charioteers, but as the poem concludes, he affirms that "It stands here still, stand vibrant as you pass, / The invisible, untoppled omphalos" (*FW* 15). His wife Marie stated that "All he's ever wanted to do was go back," and Heaney's powerful and enduring sense of home colors all of his work.[16]

The language that he uses elsewhere in his essay about Mossbawn, "the first place," could have come from Genesis, especially in a passage suffused with light:

> I have a sense of air, of lift and light, when this comes back to me. Light dancing off the shallows of the Moyola River ... Light changing on the mountain itself ... Light above the spire, away at Magherafelt. Light frothing among the bluebells on Grove Hill.[17]

Heaney's recognition of this sacred space accords with what he termed Wordsworth's belief that he was "visited by sensations of immensity, communing with a reality he apprehended beyond the world of the senses, and he was therefore naturally inclined to accept the universe as a mansion of spirit rather than a congeries of matter."[18]

The child in rural Ulster created his little world anew, "consecrating it" as Eliade claims all members of archaic societies do.[19] And make no mistake about it: Heaney's childhood was essentially archaic, pre-electric, powered by horse-drawn carts and buggies, with no indoor toilets, a stable for the animals attached to the house, and without any running water except for that cosmic community pump and rainwater the family could collect. Speaking about this rural milieu, he remarked, "What with thatch and well water and horse-drawn vehicles and horse ploughs and so on, when I look back on it, there's a strong sense that it belonged in another age, really."[20]

In addition to consecrating Mossbawn in this ancient, cosmic sense, Heaney was born into a specifically Irish Catholic milieu that indelibly shaped his worldview. He has said that while he is attracted to Yeats's visionary powers, "I'm much closer to the fundamentally Catholic mysticism in Kavanagh" (*SS* 318). Moreover, he pointed out that

> far from being deprived of religion in my youth, I was oversupplied. I lived with, and to some extent lived by, divine mysteries: the sacrifice of the Mass, the transubstantiation of bread and wine into the body and blood of Christ, the forgiveness of sin, the resurrection of the body and the life of the world to come, the whole disposition of the cosmos from celestial to infernal, the whole supernatural population, the taxonomy of virtues and vices and so on. (318)

Neil Corcoran has argued that along with confessions, Mass-going, recitation of the family rosary, and catechism, Heaney would have practiced "numerous small pieties of a now virtually extinct phase of Irish Catholicism, which supplied almost the whole context for an ordinary life."[21] And Heaney himself recalled, "there were always religious magazines like the *Far East* and the *Messenger*" in his household while he was growing up.[22]

Being born into such a world gave him two important advantages in becoming a poet: he tended to see the entire world as a miracle, and, just as important, he was steeped in a faith that valued symbolism and ritual and contemplation, all qualities that would enable him to begin opening himself to the mysteries of poetry eventually. He positively commented about the relationship between Catholicism and language, observing, "The vocabulary of the language: We live in it; it lives in us. There are cathedrals of possibility that you're walking around in."[23] Eamon Duffy, an expert on medieval English and Irish Catholicism, has recalled that being raised an Irish Catholic in the 1950s made him realize that "the religion of my childhood had a good deal in common with the symbolic world of the late Middle Ages."[24] Heaney suggested that if you take a poetic point of view, a Catholic childhood and adolescence puts you right at the center of a radiant universe. From the moment you begin to be aware, you [realize you] are a cell of the whole shimmering fabric . . . and nothing you do is without significance."[25]

Robert Welch even identified "the entire inclination of Catholic thinking" as "sacramental," and thus argues that it "reverences profoundly all the minute activities of life and the flesh."[26] Heaney's imagination remained sacramental in this sense and he consistently recognized "the value in making this thing, here and now, other."[27] This outlook manifested itself in his consistent poetic rendering of ordinary objects extraordinary; in Heaney's hands, the thing itself moves and shimmers with a life of its own.[28]

Heaney's parents grew up in "an era when the [Catholic] Church was thriving, directing, often controlling and nearly always educating," with priests who "place[d] a strong emphasis on the values of the farm society" and rejected urban life.[29] The Heaneys' farm life would thus have been thoroughly endorsed by the Church and privileged as a locus for Catholic moral development and the religious training of children. Moreover, in the years leading up to the poet's birth, Catholicism throughout the island of Ireland, on both sides of the border, reached an apogee with the Eucharistic Congress held in Dublin during 1932. He even remembered that there was "a kind of little shrine picture" hanging on the wall of his childhood home "to commemorate the Eucharistic Congress in Dublin in 1932" (SS 11). The congress "was an occasion for Catholic triumphalism on both sides of the border," and "Many Catholic streets in towns throughout the north [Northern Ireland] were bedecked with bunting, and mini-altars were erected at which people gathered nightly for the recitation of the rosary and other prayers."[30] But the poet noted that his own family members

> were quiet, watchful, oblique, sly. There was a great element of respectability. I think . . . they had been debilitated by a certain "churchiness." I think that the dominant Protestant ethos affected them. The other was the clerical influence tending toward respectability.[31]

Catholics in Northern Ireland were united by virtue of their being in the minority of the new state of Northern Ireland, in which Protestants dominated every aspect of life and often gerrymandered cities such as Derry/Londonderry where they were in the minority but managed to contrive it so they still had a majority on the city council. Writing in the mid-1990s, one Jesuit priest who grew up in Belfast has noted that beginning with the Ulster Plantation of the early seventeenth century that displaced many Catholics and brought in English and Scottish Protestant settlers to take their place, the Catholic community in the north of Ireland, then later Northern Ireland, was "bereft of political power and economic security, and with a gradual erosion of the cultural *mores* dependent on these factors, the community had only Catholicism left to preserve its identity," and thus that "an attachment to the idea of Catholicism and the recognition of a sense of belonging to a wider religious community gave a cohesion to Ulster Catholics which, arguably, they have never lost."[32] The very lack of power Catholics held in Northern Ireland thus contributed to an astonishing sense of cohesiveness—recall Heaney's "swaddling band" phrase from "Casualty." His and his close family's culture, faith, and nationalist politics were all intertwined with and encompassed by Ulster Catholicism, particularly since the Catholic Church was historically a refuge for the minority in Northern Ireland where they could be free from overt and covert acts of discrimination visited upon them officially and unofficially by many, but certainly not all, Protestants in Northern Ireland.

Yet the development of Heaney's ecumenism, perhaps even more so than his Catholicism, has come to be seen as a central feature of his poetry. Certainly some of his marked ecumenism must have emerged from his years spent at the local Anahorish School, a "mixed" school with both Protestants and Catholics attending. Another originary place, Anahorish confirmed the value of education for the young boy and was a secure and safe place away from his close-knit family during the week.

In the spring of 1954, after the death in February of 1953 of his brother Christopher, whom the poet elegized in "Mid-Term Break," the Heaneys moved to "The Wood" several miles from Mossbawn. Heaney mentioned that the family relocated because his father inherited the farm at The Wood "when his uncle Hughie died, round about 1952 or 53. The second [reason] was . . . that there was a bad feeling about staying on so close to the road where Christopher was killed . . ." (*SS* 22). His "father's heart had always been in The Wood," though, because of his rearing there (*SS* 22).

Heaney never felt as close to that farm as he did Mossbawn and in fact, his first sundering from his family had already come with his matriculation at St Columb's College, Derry City, in 1951. He recalled that "The sword of sorrow swung widely on the day I went as a boarder to St Columb's College," remembering that as he stood watching his parents leave he was "brimming with grief. Unblaming, unavailing grief. A space that was separate and, for sure, not a little sorrowing" (*SS* 32, 33). St Columb's was a Catholic school that also boasts as alumni the playwright Brian Friel, the critic and writer Seamus Deane, and the politician John Hume. Especially as the eldest child in the family, much was expected of the young Seamus. Heaney boarded there during the school year for the next six years until he went to Queen's University, Belfast, in 1957. While at St Columb's, Heaney was drilled in the English literary classics and his love of Keats and Hopkins, among other writers, stems from his immersion in their work at the time.

In attending Queen's, Heaney was an early beneficiary of the 1947 Education Act that introduced grants for so-called "third-level education" and helped many students from less well-off backgrounds attend university as the first in their families to do so. Once he entered university, "the experience of University was religiously alienating, as the folk Catholicism of home met the sophistications and skepticism of the secular—or at any rate the Protestant—academy." In Belfast, "Heaney and his Catholic contemporaries found themselves ... at one level members of the Chaplaincy Sodality, being urged to daily communion, and in another part of the same building analyzing Joyce's blasphemous manipulation of the ideas and imagery of Catholicism."[33] Indeed, Heaney himself pointed out that "Part of the mission of the young graduate in my time was to secularize yourself, you know? I meant to Joycify yourself if possible. Any literary reading of the twentieth century leads to that challenge to faith."[34] Joyce's example was a powerful one and Heaney would return to it in his essays and poems often, invoking, for instance, a passage from *A Portrait of the Artist as a Young Man* as an epigraph to "The Wool Trade" from *Wintering Out* and famously meeting Joyce's shade at the end of the middle and titular section of his volume *Station Island*.[35] Joyce has always stood powerfully for both artistic independence and a delight in words for Heaney and moreover, while Joyce's affection always ran to his native city of Dublin, he nonetheless modeled a fidelity to place that Heaney has never wavered from in his lasting allegiance to his rural home ground.

In the first lyric from "Out of This World," his poetic tribute to the Polish poet Czesław Miłosz, Heaney's speaker reflects on his loss of faith in language that is likely autobiographical: "There was never a scene / when I had it out with myself or with another. / The loss occurred off stage." "And yet," the speaker continues, "I cannot / disavow words like 'thanksgiving' or 'host' / or 'communion bread.' They have an undying / tremor and draw, like well water far down" (*DC* 45). This passage captures Heaney's wistful attitude toward his childhood and adolescent Catholic faith. He experienced no violent denunciation of Irish Catholicism like Joyce's protagonist Stephen Dedalus does in his novel *A Portrait of the Artist as a Young Man*; instead, his faith slowly ebbed away but its seminal words nonetheless continued to convey an indelible power to him. While he was at Queen's University, Heaney remembered, "The doctrinal observance, the practicing Catholicism, it just went," hastening to add, "Definitely I have what you'd call a Catholic imagination insofar as I found it difficult and unnecessary to deconstruct the shape received, that is, of a here and now and a big Otherwise, elsewhere."[36] Over time, he did, however, come to feel constrained by his religious upbringing, noting that "The blueprint for the spirit and the feelings which Irish Catholicism offered my generation was bound to become a straitjacket."[37] Yet he consistently evinced a marked spirituality that deepened over time and remains indebted not so much to doctrines of Catholicism but to its ability to inspire imaginative worlds beyond our ken.

During his time at Queen's, Heaney began publishing poems in literary magazines under the pen name of "Incertus," but he had not yet decided to become a poet. After graduating with a first class degree in English literature, he took a teachers' training course at St Joseph's College of Education in Andersonstown, West Belfast, from 1961 to 1962, when he began reading other poets such as Patrick Kavanagh, John Hewitt (from Northern Ireland), Gerard Manley Hopkins, and Ted Hughes in earnest. He reminisced that "in 1962 the current began to flow" when he read Hughes's "View of a Pig" from his volume *Lupercal* in the Belfast public library and was so inspired that he wrote two poems that "were Hughes pastiches almost."[38] That same year, his reading of Patrick Kavanagh's anti-pastoral "The Great Hunger" from his volume *Soul for Sale* also "gave me this terrific breakthrough from English literature into home ground."[39] In 1962–3, he taught at St Thomas's Intermediate School in Ballymurphy, another working-class Catholic area of Belfast.

The real turning point for his career as a writer occurred when he joined Queen's University English lecturer Philip Hobsbaum's "Belfast Group" of writers in 1963 while he himself was lecturing at St Joseph's in English. Hobsbaum saw Heaney as his star to the chagrin of his fellow contemporary Michael Longley. Longley's work was already largely his own; Heaney still suffered confidence issues and Hobsbaum encouraged him both to write about his rural childhood, to "roughen up" and "hit the stride of living speech" (*SS* 40), and to immerse himself in the work of the so-called English "Movement" poets such as Philip Larkin. Heaney recollected too that "What you were seeing in action was the effect of poetry stored up within an individual's memory and the way it functioned as a shared value" (75), which quickly became a consistent hope for his own poetry throughout his career as he sought to evoke shared values across demarcations of class and religion. Although he never relied on rhyme the way Larkin did, this grounding in formalism enabled him to learn the different types of poetry, including the sonnet, which came to be one of his favorite forms, and, when necessary, to break from formalism with experiments in lineation and rhyme. By 1965, at Hobsbaum's instigation, Heaney's first chapbook, *Eleven Poems*, was published as part of the Belfast Festival.

The year 1966 was something of an *annus mirabilis* for Heaney since he published his first volume, *Death of a Naturalist*, that year and also got married to Marie Devlin, a County Tyrone native whom he had first met in October of 1962. In fact, the two events coalesced when he took Marie to the Faber offices on Russell Square in London on the first day of their honeymoon. He recalled meeting Larkin while there (*SS* 337). Heaney also took up the lectureship in English created by Hobsbaum's departure for Glasgow University in Scotland and began running Hobsbaum's Belfast Group, where he helped foster the poetic talents of the young Paul Muldoon, Frank Ormsby, Ciaran Carson, and Medbh McGuckian. *Death of a Naturalist* won the Geoffrey Faber Prize, the Somerset Maugham Award, the Cholmondeley Award, and the Eric Gregory Award for Young Writers, and Heaney became famous nearly overnight.

Strife: 1969–1991

While Heaney continued to teach at Queen's in the late 1960s, his sons Michael (1966) and Christopher (1968) were born. He became more confident in his poetic voice, publishing *Door into the Dark*, his second full volume, in 1969, which led the esteemed English critic Christopher Ricks to declare that it established Heaney as "the poet of muddy-booted blackberry-picking." The remark was not really meant to be pejorative: Ricks went on to praise Heaney's poetry for being "lovingly specific and specifically loving" in its evocation of the particular contours of rural life.[40] But events in Northern Ireland would put pressure on the poet to leave behind that carefully and sensuously evoked rural world of childhood and write directly about the growing conflict there. The fraught state of relations between Protestants and Catholics in the province was broken with the outbreak of the so-called "Troubles" by late 1968 with the October 5 attack on Catholic civil rights marchers in Derry by loyalists. An anguished Heaney, torn between his allegiance to his fellow Catholics and his commitment to poetry's independence, left for Berkeley, California in the fall of 1970, not returning to the North until September of 1971. The British Army, originally brought into the province in August of 1969 to protect Catholics from attacks by loyalists and by the largely Protestant Royal Ulster Constabulary, began the policy of internment that same year, whereby they scooped up many young Catholic men and interrogated them about their being members of the Irish Republican Army (IRA). Many who were not members joined the IRA during this period and after the horrific British Army shootings of unarmed Catholics in Derry (thirteen of whom died then and one later) on January 30, 1972, an atrocity that was later covered up by the Widgery Tribunal. Only in 2010, with the published report of the Saville Inquiry, were these civil rights marchers exonerated. When a bomb went off down the street from Marie and when Heaney received a death threat after the airing of a documentary about him, he resigned his lectureship at Queen's and the family moved south to County Wicklow, where they rented the primitive Glanmore Cottage from family friend and Canadian academic Anne Saddlemyer. He believed at the time that "The stakes were being raised to deadlier levels all the time," noting further, "People you knew [were] getting killed either by accident or at random or by deliberate targeting" (*SS* 119). He rejected the assertion that the violence made them leave the province, however, arguing that the year in Berkeley "gave me a sense that I could make a choice. I wasn't just on the conveyor belt. I could step off it. When we came back from Berkeley in 1971, I was ready to make the move and become a writer, as it were. America influenced me in taking the step to leave Queen's and go freelance." He also claimed that that in Belfast "I felt I was drinking too much"[41] and further, that he and Marie moved their family south to obtain better educational opportunities for their children. Finally, he said that "If you move south of the border it is seen as an abdication from Ulster, a running away . . . that's not true at all because I've been up to my neck in it," concluding, "I suppose the simple reason for the move was to clear my head, to clarify my mind."[42] But the violence and threatened violence must surely have played a role in this decision for artistic purposes as Heaney's last statement suggests.

Also in 1972, Heaney released *Wintering Out*, a volume that signaled both the Catholic, vestigially Gaelic presence in Northern Ireland through some of its place-lore poems and sounded a conciliatory note in poems such as "Broagh" and "The Other Side." Already, the conflict was creeping into his work with the appearance of the first of the "bog poems," "The Tollund Man." He began translating the medieval Irish epic *Buile Suibhne*, but would put it aside eventually until returning to it by 1979. Moreover, he continued to work in radio, a venue that had claimed much of his attention in the mid- to late-1960s, when he presented a number of "Schools Programmes" for BBC Northern Ireland. Now, he wrote a weekly book review for RTÈ Radio as well.

Additionally, he edited an anthology of contemporary Irish poetry whose title suggested something of his insistence on poetry's orality—*Soundings*. In April of 1973, his and Marie's last child, Catherine Ann, was born, and in October of that year he visited Denmark, where he saw the bog bodies he had read about in P. V. Glob's book *The Bog People* at a museum there. He could not help feeling, though, that his meteoric rise as a poet "happened very fast, and I knew I was being overpraised in my first three books. I wasn't as sure as other people were."[43]

After he published another poetry anthology in 1974, *Soundings 2*, 1975 saw both the publication of his prose-poem pamphlet *Stations* and his most controversial volume, *North*, which won the Duff Cooper Memorial Prize and explored the frightening, now widespread violence in Northern Ireland through ancient Scandinavian and other remote tribal atrocities. He recalled that "it wasn't until *North* was written, and had come out, that I felt I had followed a calling or done something in the name of it."[44] Despite that confirmation of his vocation as poet, by October he began teaching at Carysfort College in Dublin and in November of the next year the Heaneys had moved to a house at Sandymount, Dublin, on the Irish coast, a home they would occupy the rest of his life. He later termed his acceptance of that position a "caving-in," musing further,

> there was something terrifically enabling and freeing about the risks and exposure of living in Wicklow in that way, and you had to prove yourself... Somehow when you get onto the cushions of a salaried position, that neediness and sense of danger disappears.[45]

As his poetry garnered more awards, including the prestigious E. M. Forster Award in 1975, awarded annually by the American Academy of Arts and Letters, American universities beckoned and Heaney taught at Harvard in 1979, the year his single-best volume, *Field Work*, was published. For Heaney, *Field Work* both "moved me from the intensity of *North* to something more measured, in both formal and emotional terms" and "told me that the move into jobsville was workable... a proof that I could write poetry in my new situation" at Carysfort College.[46]

That same year, when he was beginning to plan his largest poetic undertaking to date, *Station Island*, Heaney could write confidently and optimistically about his commitment to his poetic vocation and pray for its success:

> I feel the lift I used to sense at the seaside in Portstewart, or on the coast at Dingle or Donegal. I felt that the seven years since leaving Belfast had paid

off, that perhaps steady inward effort would be possible. I felt I could trust. I have been lucky but also I think I have worked to earn this. I pray to God or whatever means the good to keep us all safe here and to sustain this effort.[47]

That prayer was answered repeatedly over the succeeding years. He would teach at Harvard again from 1984 through 1996, as the Boylston Chair of Rhetoric, after which he was named the Ralph Waldo Emerson Poet in Residence, a much less demanding post that required only six weeks in residency every two years, a position which he held until 2007. Helen Vendler, his great American champion, reveled in his presence there and he was received as something akin to a rock star. Looking back on his life at Harvard, Heaney mused, "I had begun as a . . . altar boy, scuttling in and out of the Harvard sanctuary, and ended up as a celebrant, at the middle of the liturgy." He gratefully recalled that "It's a literary community I was lucky to meet, a second living poetry environment, after the first one I'd known in Belfast."[48]

At the same time, Heaney deepened his involvement in cultural and literary life north and south of the border on his native island by joining the Field Day Theatre Company, founded by the actor Stephen Rea and the playwright Brian Friel, in 1980. That same year, he published *Selected Poems 1965–1975* and his first volume of prose, *Preoccupations: Selected Prose 1968–1978*. The prose volume demonstrated he was a sage and articulate commentator on poetry and an adept chronicler of his own life.

His new commitments on both sides of the Atlantic did not seem to slow him down. In 1983 he published under the Field Day aegis his translation of *Buile Suibhne* as *Sweeney Astray*, which would win the PEN Translation Prize in 1985, and a pamphlet poem, *An Open Letter*, drawing on the Irish pamphlet tradition established by Jonathan Swift and continued later by James Joyce with his broadside "Gas from a Burner."[49] *An Open Letter* somewhat disingenuously (because Heaney had been included in earlier British anthologies) rejected the label of "British" that Blake Morrison and Andrew Motion had given him by including him in their edition of the *Penguin Book of Contemporary British Poetry*. The 1980s saw both triumphs and great sadness; for instance, Heaney published his ambitious, Dantean volume *Station Island* in 1984 and yet his mother died that same year. His father died in 1986 and the next year, Heaney's underappreciated volume *The Haw Lantern*, which won the prestigious Whitbread Award, appeared. He referred to his father's death in October of that year as the "final 'unroofing' of the world," one which prepared him for the writing of the spare yet deeply spiritual poems of *Seeing Things* (SS 322). Heaney has often explored his love for his parents in his poetry, most memorably for his mother in "Clearances" from *The Haw Lantern*, and for his father, through a sequence of poems treating their relationship through that of Aeneas and his father Anchises in Book VI of *The Aeneid*. By the end of the decade, he had released two more volumes of prose: *The Government of the Tongue* and *The Place of Writing*.

His appointment to the Oxford Professor of Poetry post in 1989, a term that lasted five years, gave him additional opportunities to write, deliver, and publish literary criticism; many of those lectures were collected in *The Redress of Poetry: Oxford Lectures* (1995). Further consolidation of his already considerable reputation came in 1990 upon the publication of his *New Selected Poems 1966–1987* and his version of Sophocles' *Philoctetes*, *The Cure at Troy*, which Field Day toured around the island and certain passages of which both recognized the intransigence of the conflict in his native province and seemed to augur hope for an easing of that violence. It quickly became quoted by local and international politicians.

Spirit Levels: 1991–2013

Heaney published one of his best and most interesting volumes, *Seeing Things*, with its emphasis on both the concrete and spiritual things of this world and the next in 1991. Edward Mendelson proclaimed about this volume, "Having won his wrestle with politics, Heaney now wrote more and more as a visionary." Mendelson praised how *Seeing Things* "glows with breathtakingly luminous visitations to empty places and lost persons."[50] In 1993, Heaney was elected as a Foreign Honorary Member of the American Academy of Arts and Letters. And less than a year after the IRA declared its ceasefire on August 31, 1994, which was followed by the Combined Loyalist Command ceasefire on October 13, he was awarded the Nobel Prize for Literature "for works of lyrical beauty and ethical depth, which exalt everyday miracles and the living past."[51] His stirring lecture, one of the major defenses of poetry in the twentieth century, was published as *Crediting Poetry*.

A series of other books followed, including *The Spirit Level* (1996), which won both the Commonwealth Literature Award and the Whitbread Book of the Year; his translation of *Beowulf* (1999), which also was named the Whitbread Book of the Year; *Electric Light* (2000); *Finders, Keepers: Selected Prose 1971–2001* (2002), which received the Truman Capote Award for Literary Criticism; and *The Burial at Thebes* (2004), his "version" of Sophocles' *Antigone*. *District and Circle* (2006) marked a return to his home ground in County Derry and commemorated the terrorist bombings in London of 2005 and which won the T. S. Eliot Prize (2006), while *Human Chain* (2010) was awarded the 2011 Griffin Poetry Prize, the 2011 Poetry Now Award, and was named a *Boston Globe* Best Poetry Book of 2011. His translation of the Italian poet Giovanni Pascoli's lyrics, *The Last Walk*, was published posthumously in 2013.

Heaney received all the major awards for poets and writers in his time and in the last twenty years of his life was recognized with many lifetime awards. For example, he was named *Commandeur de l'Ordre des Arts et Lettres* by the French government in 1996; was awarded the David Cohen Prize for a lifetime body of work by a writer in the English language; won the Golden Wreath of Poetry for lifetime achievement in poetry at the Struga, Macedonia Poetry Festival in 2001; and claimed the Irish PEN (Poets, Essayists, and Novelists) Award in 2005 for a lifetime's contribution to Irish letters. He was also elected as a *saoi*, the highest level of *Aosdána*, the academy of artists in Ireland. The Lincoln Center, New York, hosted a three-day program devoted to his work in 2001 and he delivered the Tanner Lectures on Human Values at Cambridge the next year. In 2004, he was featured on stamps issued both in Sweden and Ireland to celebrate the four Irish Nobel Laureates in Literature—Yeats, Shaw, Beckett, and himself—and in 2014, was portrayed by himself on an Irish stamp. Two signal honors came his way in 2008 with the Royal Irish Academy's awarding of the Cunningham Medal to him, their top honor, and an unveiling by Queen Elizabeth II of a stone incised with a stanza of his poetry that marks Queen's University's centenary. In 2012, Heaney was given a lifetime achievement award by the Griffin Trust.

Seventy-one percent of Northern Ireland's inhabitants voted for the landmark Good Friday Agreement on April 10, 1998, which restored a devolved government for the province and provided the foundation for a power-sharing agreement between Catholics and Protestants. Northern Ireland's bad old days of bombings and shootings have not vanished completely and certainly periodic outbreaks of violence and ongoing segregation in schools and especially working-class neighborhoods continues to threaten the peace, but its future remains brighter than it has since the beginning of the Civil Rights movement. Invoking Yeats as a "public poet" who is "interested in the polis," Heaney implied that Yeats was exemplary for him in responding to the violence in his native province: "the whole effort of the imagining is towards inclusiveness. Prefiguring a future."[52] While affirming his allegiance to his Catholic, nationalist upbringing and that community's push for civil rights,

Heaney nonetheless held "you have to grow into an awareness of the others and attempt to find a way of imagining a whole thing" and "to open the definition and to make the domain of Irishness in Ireland—I hate to use the word pluralist, it's so prim and righteous—to make it open and available."[53] His literary and cultural work, along with that of other writers and artists, as I and other commentators have argued, helped us imagine a future province that would not be constantly riven by sectarian strife.[54]

His hectic travel schedule and generosity toward others may have helped contribute to the mild stroke he suffered in late August of 2006, after which he canceled all his speaking engagements for the next year. He remembered that "I cried. I cried, and I wanted my Daddy, funnily enough. I did. I felt babyish."[55] Heaney made a full recovery and was visited by former American President Bill Clinton while in rehabilitation (*SS* 462–3). He later went on to decline several honorary degrees because "I was either exhausted or overloaded" (463). The last years of his life saw him return imaginatively to Italy. Where earlier in his career Dante had ratified his Catholic subculture and given him the tripartite structure for *Station Island*, now Virgil's Book VI of *The Aeneid* and Pascoli's rooted nineteenth-century poems enabled him to plumb the depths of his relationship with his father and return to his home ground, respectively. Actively writing and making public appearances until his death, he remained vigorously committed to the life of the mind and academic freedom—most of all, to ensuring our belief in poetry.

"Somewhere, well out, beyond . . ."[56]
Death and After (2013–)

After *North* was published, the American poet Robert Lowell characterized it as "a new kind of political poetry by the best Irish poet since W. B. Yeats,"[57] and when Heaney died on Friday morning, August 30, 2013, from a heart condition shortly before he was to have had an operation at Blackrock Clinic outside Dublin, that tag was repeatedly trotted out, often as a headline or sub-headline for obituaries. While the comparison remains high praise, it also now serves to pigeonhole Heaney by relegating him to only Irish poetry, when in actuality, he is a world poet in a way that Yeats never was—or at least not to the same degree. It also prevents him from being compared to poets writing before 1939, when in fact such comparisons are warranted, even necessary, to thinking through Heaney's place in English and Irish literary history. For instance, influenced by the two greatest nineteenth-century poetic wordsmiths writing in English, Keats and Hopkins, Heaney has far outstripped their relatively limited but excellent output in poetry, not to mention his outstanding work in other genres never even attempted by Keats and Hopkins. Moreover, in his richer and stranger diction, facility with different forms, and superlative level of poetry over a longer period of time, Heaney's poetry surpasses that of Wordsworth, another exemplar for him. Shakespeare—leaving aside the densely poetic language of the plays—wrote superlative sonnets, while Milton wrote on a grander scale and with more majesty of language. For sheer facility of language, Heaney belongs in the same conversation with Milton and Shakespeare, although their scale and ambition make them the better poets. Yeats had a higher number of memorable and excellent poems than did Heaney, yet Yeats's poetic voice stayed so monumental that it never reached readers the way Heaney's confidential, locally inflected voice did. Another exemplar for Heaney, W. H. Auden, authored many poems that will last and enjoyed a similarly long career, although his late poetry has none of the staying power that Heaney's does. I would say instead of Heaney was "the best Irish poet since Yeats" that Yeats, Heaney, and Auden were three of the greatest lyric poets of all time writing in the English language and that it was our great fortune to have known and heard the work of one of them, Heaney, over the last fifty years.

Writing on the 75th anniversary of Yeats's death, only a few months after Heaney's passing, Terence Brown remarked:

> I cannot help thinking of Seamus Heaney when I think of Yeats's death ... Both were truly national figures who made of their deep involvement in the places they came from—whether Sligo or Bellaghy in Derry—the stuff of poetry that speaks to the world. They brought great honor on Ireland. Yeats lived through and wrote about the civil war. Heaney lived through and wrote about the Troubles. Both showed how poetry enables, helps us to comprehend and *survive*.[58]

Brown clearly invokes Auden's "In Memory of W. B. Yeats" here in his use of "survive": Auden's speaker tells us in stanza two about Yeats that "your gift survived it all"; that poetry "survives / In the valley of its saying"; and that "it survives, / A way of happening, a mouth."[59] There is no question that Heaney's own poetry and work in other genres will survive, even flourish in the future and should indeed help us "to comprehend and survive." And yet, Heaney's legacy will surely be more than his response to and thoughtfulness about the Troubles.

Heaney told Mike Murphy that "The story about you is made up quite early on and it usually doesn't change that much even if you have changed,"[60] seeming to have believed that the narrative about his work was written early and would be immutable, but like all great writers, his work will remain a site of interpretation and contention. In his recent assessment of why Heaney will remain important, the poet and critic Alan Gillis pleads, "Let him not become a heritage figure, safely reified as a token of the Troubles." Instead, Gillis points out, "He has asserted the validity of individual sensation and immediate experience in an age of disembodied corporate utilitarian anonymity ... He ... energized the pastoral in an age of ecological disgrace." Moreover, as Gillis acknowledges:

> He has been the most extraordinarily self-reflexive and meta-poetical of poets, his language almost always his subject matter, and yet he has offered unwavering and sure solidity of selfhood throughout his work, in a manner that has been anathema to many critics informed by the "linguistic turn" of continental literary theory.[61]

Another under-appreciated contribution by Heaney to poetry concerns his wide employment and re-imagining of particular forms, especially the sonnet and tercet. Such qualities and achievements suggest part of his appeal across generations and nationalities. His conviction that human beings matter and that we can still experience authenticity in a time of sameness promulgated through mass media resonates deeply, as does his commitment to the environment, especially that landscape of childhood to which we all want to revisit, if not return. And in a world where words have often become so much meaningless chatter about meaningless topics, his words still express a gravitas that steadies us when we read them.

Upon the passing of Yeats, the poet to whom Heaney has been most often compared, Auden, in his decidedly non-elegiac "In Memory of W. B. Yeats," claimed that "A few thousand will think of this day / As one thinks of a day when one did something slightly unusual,"[62] a statement that is as far as could possibly be from the worldwide sense of loss at Heaney's passing. That poem's main consolation flows from its offering poetry's survival to us as a mouth, a voice, which in turn may "Teach the free man how to praise."[63] Far from being "slightly unusual," however, the tributes that flowed after Heaney's passing were freighted with the specific details of the man's life and work and he was repeatedly praised as simultaneously a man of the people and a genius. While Auden's "elegy" for Yeats departs from elegiac conventions, the same cannot be said of the worldwide reaction, the public, collective elegy, as it were, to Heaney's death. The world stopped and many people enacted a public elegy for him by lamenting, praising, and offering consolation for the man's passing and his work. Politicians including

Bill Clinton; the Taoiseach of Ireland, Enda Kenny; along with celebrities such as Liam Neeson and Bono, the latter the lead singer of the rock group U2—all came forward to celebrate the exemplary qualities of the poet and his poetry.

Furthermore, when Heaney died, mourners did not have to try hard to make him seem like the common man as Auden attempted for Yeats in his elegy. Auden memorably stated about Yeats, "You were silly like us," trying to render normal and appealing the poet whose "Southern Californian" occultism the English poet had once denounced.[64] In contrast, hundreds of people stepped forward to offer anecdotes of Heaney's down-to-earth qualities and relaxed manner with his adoring public. Interestingly, some of them did turn to Auden's poem to elegize Heaney: Stephen Fry, for instance, observed in a direct quotation from "In Memory of W. B. Yeats" that he then spliced Heaney's passing into, "Earth receive an honoured guest [/] Seamus Heaney's put to rest."[65] Uncannily, Yeats died aged nearly seventy-four in 1939, while Heaney, born in 1939, died in 2013 at seventy-four.

Commentators contrasted the two poets' personalities in revealing ways. For instance, the Scottish writer and critic Alan Massie caught the public attitude toward this comparison when he wrote a blog after Heaney's death entitled, "Seamus Heaney Was the Greatest Irish Poet since Yeats, and a Nicer Man."[66] Yeats could be aloof, patrician, even haughty. Heaney, as the testimonials that appeared after his death attested, was a man of the people and never forgot his rural roots in County Derry. Plain-spoken yet eloquent, he wore his unofficial title as an ambassador for poetry lightly. Roy Foster, Yeats's official biographer, even noted that "Whereas Yeats's shadow was seen, by some of his younger contemporaries at least, as blotting out the sun and stunting the growth of the surrounding forest, Heaney's great presence let in the light." As Foster further observes, "Part of this was bound up in his own abundant personality. Generosity, amplitude, and sympathy characterized his dealings with people at every level, and he was the stellar best of company."[67]

If the comparisons to Yeats are much more complicated and troubled than they first appear, as I have tried to suggest here, two lines from Auden's "In Memory of W. B. Yeats"—"the words of the dead are digested in the guts of the living"[68]—seem especially apt for the discussion that broke out online about Heaney's last words, the Latin phrase, *Noli timere*, which he sent as a text message to his wife Marie minutes before he died. Writing in the widely read magazine *The Atlantic* and citing Classics professor Jennifer Ebbeler, Robinson Meyer pointed out that this phrase occurs in Jerome's fourth-century translation into Latin of Matthew 14: 27. There, Jesus reassures his disciples, who cower in a boat during a nighttime storm, by walking on the water toward them and saying, "'*Habete fiduciam ego sum nolite timere*.' Or: Be of good cheer, it's me, don't be afraid." *Nolite* is in the plural, while *noli* is singular and "makes a request of one person, like a lover, or a friend."[69] Christopher Rowse, writing in the British newspaper *The Daily Telegraph*, pointed out that "it was a brilliant stroke of Seamus Heaney to leave last words that could only be taken as a serious poetic insight." He, like Meyer, alludes to Heaney's translation of *Beowulf*, noting that "the translator, St. Jerome, cared as much for the language he was using as Heaney did in translating *Beowulf*." For Rowse, Heaney's last words captured Jerome's knowledge that "As creatures hungry for infinity yet incapable of catching it, we human beings are also afraid of being left alone in the dark."[70] And this phrase also suggests that words, and—despite Heaney's agnosticism that shades even toward atheism at times—implicitly, Jesus, as the living Word, can carry us across (an act of spiritual "translation") the gulf of our fears to safety and comfort.

But there was initial confusion about whether Heaney wrote *Nolle timere* or *Noli timere*, which led Meyer to realize that since our "Organism of language mutates" and "gets things wrong, by transcription or misunderstanding," we must perform acts of translation. Thus, "It is a translation that his poetry will eventually require. We die and the language gets away from us, in little ways, like a dropped vowel sound, a change in prepositions, a mistaken transcription. Errors in transfer make a literature."[71] Our disagreement over Heaney's last words has become a contemporary illustration of Auden's phrase, "the words of the dead are digested in the guts of the living."

Besides Heaney's very real intent to shield and give hope to his family with this lovely phrase, redolent with New Testament echoes, surely he would be happy that his last words might become a matter of interpretation for his many fans worldwide—and that these readers might derive a measure of comfort and hope from them in the process. The poet's son Mick observed that Heaney's wife and children "seized on his final words as a ... lifebuoy. It seemed to us that he had encapsulated the swirl of emotion, uncertainty and fear he was facing at the end, and articulated it in a restrained, yet inspiring way."[72]

The epitaph on Heaney's gravestone in Bellaghy, Northern Ireland is drawn from his Nobel Prize lecture *Crediting Poetry*: "WALK ON AIR AGAINST YOUR BETTER JUDGEMENT" (*CP* 11). That hope in the miraculous along with his last words in that text to his wife shortly before his death suggest his belief, over against the depredations and cruelties of history, of hope on earth and in a life beyond—

the spirit region. As he stated in his lecture to the Irish Human Rights Commission, "When a poem or literary work touches those deep chords of the individual being, something is strengthened ... An artist whose work is capable of entering the place of ultimate suffering and decision in his or her own being will bring readers to a realization of that same stratum in themselves." In such moments,

> as it begins its obscure pilgrimage through memory and conscience, the human condition will be registered at a private personal level, yet the experience will involve a sense of common human belonging. And at that moment the art and the artist become allies in the great work of "saving nations and peoples."[73]

Now and in times to come, we will turn to Seamus Heaney's work for many things—for a guide through the "Troubles," for an example of the integrity of a life well lived, for a deep engagement with the natural world, for an affirmation of language's signifying power, for the dazzling variety of poetic forms—but most of all, we will turn to him for his lasting gift that "survived it all"—hope.

Notes

1. Heaney, "The Art of Poetry: Interview with Seamus Heaney," 116.
2. The best two narrative biographies of the life remain Neil Corcoran's appendix on Heaney's life in *The Poetry of Seamus Heaney: A Critical Study*, 234–62, and Michael Parker, *Seamus Heaney: The Making of the Poet*.
3. Heaney, "Something to Write Home About," 57.
4. Qtd in Corcoran, *The Poetry of Seamus Heaney*, 235.
5. Heaney, *Seamus Heaney in Conversation with Karl Miller*, 29.
6. See Wordsworth, Book I of *The Prelude*, lines 562–4: "I held unconscious intercourse with beauty / Old as creation, drinking in a pure / Organic pleasure. . ." (*Selected Poems*, 322).
7. See "The Makings of a Music," 61–71, and the entirety of "Apt Admonishment."
8. Heaney, "Introduction," *William Wordsworth: Poems Selected by Seamus Heaney*, vii.
9. Heaney, "A Poet's Childhood," 660.
10. Heaney, "The Art of Poetry," 93.
11. Ibid.
12. Ibid., 93, 94.
13. Eliade, *The Sacred and the Profane*, 20–1.
14. Heaney, "Mossbawn," 17.
15. Eliade, *The Sacred and the Profane*, 21.
16. Qtd in Boland, "Seamus Heaney, 1939–2013."
17. Heaney, "Mossbawn," 20.

18. Heaney, "Introduction," *William Wordsworth: Poems Selected by Seamus Heaney*, ix.
19. Eliade, *The Sacred and the Profane*, 32.
20. Heaney, "An Interview with Seamus Heaney [Wachtel]," 33.
21. Corcoran, *The Poetry of Seamus Heaney*, 237.
22. Heaney, "Mossbawn," 22.
23. Heaney, "Interview with Michael Silverblatt."
24. Duffy, *The Stripping of the Altars*, 2nd edn, xiv.
25. Heaney, "Interview with Seamus Heaney" [Wylie and Kerrigan], 132–3.
26. Welch, 108.
27. Ibid.
28. For a fuller explanation of Heaney's relationship to things, see my essay, "'Deep down Things.'"
29. Ferriter, 83.
30. Rafferty, 234.
31. Heaney, "The North: Silent Awarenesses," 164.
32. Rafferty, 1.
33. Duffy, "Seamus Heaney and Catholicism," 168.
34. *Seamus Heaney: Out of the Marvelous*.
35. I discuss Heaney's Joyce as the best kind of regional exemplar in my *Seamus Heaney's Regions*, for instance on 213–18, 244–7, and 269–73. See, too, Heaney's "The Regional Forecast," 13, where he privileges Joyce as "the regional redeemer . . ."
36. *Seamus Heaney: Out of the Marvelous*.
37. Heaney, "The Poet as a Christian," 604.
38. Heaney, "The Art of Poetry," 92.
39. Ibid., 127.
40. Ricks, "Lasting Things," 900–1.
41. Heaney, "A Life of Rhyme," n.p.
42. Heaney, "The Irish Quest," n.p.
43. Heaney, "A Life of Rhyme," n.p.
44. Ibid.
45. Qtd in Corcoran, *The Poetry of Seamus Heaney*, 258.
46. Heaney, "The Art of Poetry," 99.
47. Heaney, *Station Island* Notebook.
48. Heaney, *Seamus Heaney in Conversation with Karl Miller*, 38.
49. See my discussion of the influence of Joyce's broadside on *An Open Letter* in my *Seamus Heaney's Regions*, 225–6.
50. Mendelson, "Digging Down," n.p.
51. "The Nobel Prize in Literature 1995," n.p.
52. Heaney, "The Art of Poetry," 104.
53. Ibid., 117.
54. See my *Poetry and Peace*, 167–290 and 291–9, 302–10.
55. Heaney, "Heaney Tells of His Stroke Ordeal," n.p.
56. The phrase is from Heaney's description of the ghost of Louis O'Neill in "Casualty" (*FW* 24).
57. Qtd in Corcoran, *The Poetry of Seamus Heaney*, 257.
58. Terence Brown, qtd in Lara Marlowe, "The End of Yeats: Work and Women in His Last Days in France," n.p.

59. Auden, *Selected Poems*, 89.
60. Heaney, "Seamus Heaney" [interview with Mike Murphy], 95.
61. Gillis, "Heaney's Legacy," 145.
62. Auden, *Selected Poems*, 89.
63. Ibid., 91.
64. Auden, "In Memory of W. B. Yeats," *Selected Poems*, 89. The dismissive phrase about Yeats's occultism appears in Auden's essay, "Yeats as an Example," 385.
65. Anonymous, "Heaney deserves place among the pantheon, says Dorgan," n.p.
66. Massie, n.p.
67. Roy Foster, n.p.
68. Auden, *Selected Poems*, 89.
69. Meyer, n.p.
70. Rowse, n.p.
71. Meyer, n.p.
72. Mick Heaney, n.p.
73. Heaney, "Writer and Righter," 16.

Chapter 2

Burrowing and Bogs: Early Poems, *Death of a Naturalist, Door into the Dark, Wintering Out, North*

This chapter and the fifth one pay great attention to the volumes that bookend Heaney's career—*Death of a Naturalist* and *Human Chain*—to show the arc of his poetic development, the way themes first adumbrated in the 1966 volume are carried through, re-explored, transformed, and sometimes dropped by the time of the 2010 volume. All the poetry chapters also spend more time on his best volumes—my top five, in chronological order, are *North, Field Work, Station Island, Seeing Things*, and *Human Chain*—than it does on the slighter ones, many of which nonetheless have poems I analyze that have become not only part of Heaney's canon but also of the canon of contemporary poetry in English. In my examination of individual collections, I often single out the first and last poems, the "framing" poems, since Heaney was so interested in the architecture of his books of poetry, much like Yeats, one of his exemplars. While relevant critical insights are brought to bear on the poems when necessary, my evaluation of them proceeds mainly through close reading grounded in historical and cultural contexts.

Heaney published several poems while an undergraduate at Queen's University during the period 1959 to 1961 in the student magazines *Q* and *Gorgon*. These display the strong influence of Gerard Manley Hopkins, and, to a lesser degree, Wordsworth and Dylan Thomas, on the young poet. "Reaping in Heat," for instance, published in the Autumn 1959 issue of *Q*, imagines a scene that resembles Wordsworth's "The Reaper": "slashing the drowsiness, / the mower was whetting his scythe . . ."[1] Verbs dominate as the poem opens, "Hushed / And lulled / Lay the field," and later, "Pushed / And pulled / Came the rasp of steel on stone . . ."[2] In "The Ministry of Fear," Heaney would recall about these rhymes, "I tried to write about the sycamores / And innovated a South Derry rhyme / With *hushed* and *lulled* full chimes for *pushed* and *pulled*" (N 57). Already, we see the young poet's audacity despite the unoriginality of his borrowed Romantic scene in inscribing his South

Derry speech upon the physical and poetic landscape. As the speaker goes on to state about his poetry writing during his time at St Columb's College in Derry with Seamus Deane from 1951 to 1957 in "The Ministry of Fear, "Those hobnailed boots from beyond the mountain / Were walking, by God, all over the fine / Lawns of elocution" (57–8).

And yet that temerity had not yet emerged in 1959 when Heaney published "Reaping in Heat" along with a Hopkins pastiche, "October Thought." This latter poem, published in the same issue of *Q* as "Reaping in Heat," features Hopkinsesque alliteration and assonance, along with a series of created compound words such as "mud-nest," "dust-drunk," "bog-sod," and "heaven-hue plum blue."[3] The poem falters under the weight of such linguistic arabesques, or rather, becomes *only about* such indulgences, so sensuous that meaning is lost. Here, Heaney is channeling Hopkins to such a degree that his own voice is blocked, but the poem nonetheless announces Heaney's deep interest in evocative vocabulary, a concern that would remain a hallmark of his poetry. As he pointed out later, his lecturer at Queen's, Laurence Lerner, had praised his phrase in this poem, "gorse-pricked with gold," and "while this first brush with a critical audience did not altogether confer certitude upon me, it did suggest that words I wrote might be capable of transmitting a live signal. Yet the words were more Hopkins's than mine; and yet again, while they were overdone and pastiche, they opened a seam of phonetic ore . . ."[4] Hopkins would remain an important influence, but Heaney would gradually learn to impart his own distinctive design to his poems.[5] More important for his later poetry, however, is the poem's twelve-line form, a form that Heaney would begin using heavily by 1991's *Seeing Things* and that he would return to often in subsequent volumes.

He seemed to have a firmer grasp of his own poetic in a poem published a few months later in *Gorgon*'s fourth issue in February of 1960, "Aran," a poem that anticipates a similar locale in "Lovers on Aran," "Storm on the Island," and "Synge on Aran," the latter three all collected in *Death of a Naturalist*. He recycles the image of "The dumb squat houses" in "Aran"[6] in "Storm on the Island," with its opening line, "We are prepared: we build our houses squat" (*DN* 38). Similarly, he recapitulates the "knifing wind" that "shivers" in "Aran,"[7] more effectively, in the opening lines of "Synge on Aran": "Salt off the sea whets / the blades of four winds" (39). And he simply renders the image of the "breakers" that "constantly rush / With a slow snow-smash explosion" from "Aran"[8] as "a tide / That yielded with an ebb, with a soft crash," in "Lovers on Aran" (34), with the sizzling force of the sibilants in the original lost but the "smash" sound repeated in "crash."

"Aran" presents early Heaney with an edge, determined to swap the indulgences of rhyme and Hopkinsesque rhythm and vocabulary for a heightened observation of nature's force and power where the poem's language attempts to match the harshness of the lives of Aran Islanders eking out a subsistence existence on their rocky acres.

Of these five very early poems—"Reaping in Heat," "October Thought," "Nostalgia in the Afternoon," "Aran," and "Song of My Man-Alive"—Heaney only signed his name, "Seamus J. Heaney," to "Aran." All the other poems, including the Hopkins-influenced "Nostalgia in the Afternoon" and "Song of My Man-Alive," with its definite echoes of Dylan Thomas's "Fern Hill" along with those of Hopkins, are signed "Incertus." He was thus properly "uncertain" of following too slavishly these early masters and had decided to look West for inspiration toward the Aran Islands, where, by channeling Synge, he found an early purchase on a powerful idiom that he would gradually recast into his own unique voice.

To employ theologian Alister McGrath's terms, *Death of a Naturalist* exemplifies the "disenchantment" of the world, and *Door into the Dark* dialectically demonstrates the "re-enchantment" of the world. That is, whereas Heaney discovers the dark, disturbing realities of the earth in most of *Death of a Naturalist*, in *Door into the Dark* he goes back into that darkness to discover its sacred, ramifying power. He re-enchants or is re-enchanted by his native landscape.[9] As he says in his essay, "The Sense of Place," place "was once more or less sacred. The landscape was sacramental, instinct with signs, implying a system of reality beyond the visible realities."[10] Heaney views the land as a deeper, richer reality underlying man-imposed, superficial templates such as the artificial pastoral genre that he largely rejects in *Death of a Naturalist*. Both *Door into the Dark*, with its embrace of dark images and hidden places, and the next volume, *Wintering Out*, through a recovery of a largely elided semantic landscape code, re-sacralize, re-enchant Heaney's home ground. That re-enchantment lasts largely until the bog poems proper (not "Bogland" from *Door into the Dark*), including "The Tollund Man," collected in *Wintering Out*, force their way into Heaney's consciousness and he begins, by the early 1970s, to dig deeper beneath his and other re-enchanted landscapes—Irish, Scandinavian—to discover the atavistic forces of fertility rites and ritual sacrifices that are on full, terrifying display in *North*. He then runs the risk of seeming to worship or sacralize violence itself, a temptation he largely avoids in the bog poems despite flirting with it.

Death of a Naturalist signaled Heaney's commitment to writing about his local culture of South County Derry and his desire to chart and preserve waning rural customs there such as thatching, water divining, digging turf, even fishing. As he mused a few years later after this volume's publication, "Many of the poems in that book said quite directly, 'I remember.'"[11] In so remembering and preserving his childhood culture, he was likely still drawing upon Synge's example he pays tribute to in his early poem "Aran" as an amateur anthropologist of the Aran Islands in the 1890s. *Death of a Naturalist*'s title poem, represented by a toad on the cover of the Faber and Faber edition, suggests, however, the end of a certain kind of childhood innocence in the face of nature's ominous, warlike toads, while the volume's most famous poem—indeed one of Heaney's most famous in his entire *oeuvre*—"Digging," also says goodbye to aspects of childhood such as digging potatoes and turf. And the concluding poem, "Personal Helicon," rejects the young Heaney's acting like a childish "Narcissus" (*DN* 44).

But poems displaying an awareness of the sectarianism often visited on Catholics in Ireland and Northern Ireland, respectively, such as "The Commander of the *Eliza*" and "Docker," while retained in *Poems 1965–1975*, have unfortunately not been reprinted in either his *New Selected Poems 1966–1987* or *Opened Ground: Poems 1966–1996*. These latter two volumes are much more likely to be used in both classroom settings and by regular readers since they include poetry from more volumes. Other poems such as "Poor Women in a City Church" that were not even reprinted in *Poems 1965–1975*, display a nearly reverential attitude toward the Catholicism Heaney was born into and that suffused his thinking throughout his life. The omission of such poems from these later volumes impoverishes our sense of Heaney's historical awareness of sectarianism in Ireland, practiced first by the English against the Irish and later by some Protestants against Catholics in Northern Ireland. Their absence also tends to obscure our perception of his real anger at the mistreatment Catholics experienced in the province during the 1960s, which he expressed elsewhere in his periodical essays, particularly once the violence started.[12]

Heaney's *Eleven Poems*, published for Michael Emmerson's 1965 Festival in Belfast, contained these poems: "Personal Helicon," "Mid-Term Break," "Follower," "The Diviner," "Peter Street at Bankside," "Waterfall," "Docker," "For the Commander of the *Eliza*," "Lovers on Aran," "Scaffolding," and "Death of a Naturalist," a far different and shorter gathering of his early poems than *Death of a Naturalist* would include the next year.[13] He always carefully constructed his books of poems, and by opening this first full volume with "Digging," he simultaneously declares his faithfulness to family and land and affirms his writing's independence from that agricultural tradition. By concluding it with "Personal Helicon," an inward-facing poem, he admits to some continuing degree of narcissim. One might expect these "framing" poems to be reversed (and he did begin *Eleven Poems* with "Personal Helicon"), with the poet opening the volume by noting his inwardness and desire to hear "your own call" (*DN* 44), and concluding by looking outward to the wider world, as he does in "Digging," but he subverts that expectation. The volume thus finishes with a more tentative quality that jars with the confident, declarative tone at the end of "Digging": "Between my finger and my thumb, / The squat pen rests. / I'll dig with it" (2).[14]

"Digging" opens the volume with the famous near-couplet, "Between my finger and my thumb / The squat pen rests; snug as a gun" (*DN* 1), and the air of danger conveyed by the gun simile pervades the volume, which is littered with such potentially explosive images. For instance, "Death of a Naturalist" features images of frogs sitting "Poised like mud grenades" (4), and "Trout" compares the titular fish to "a fat gun-barrel," further characterizing it with gun images, including "bull's eye," "torpedoed," "fired," "tracer- / bullet," and "volley" (26). "Dawn Shoot," a poem explicitly about hunting, also uses "bull's-eye," and features "sentry" and "rocketed" (16), along with "barrel" and "two barrels" (17). Adrian Frazier muses about this opening martial image, "As guns don't rest between a finger and a thumb, the simile is awkward, rammed into the poem. Why was the gun put in? And why did it disappear?"[15] Awkward though it may be on first inspection, the gun imagery is purposeful and accords with other such imagery in the collection, as Frazier himself notes. Heaney suggests the analogy between holding a pen and a gun (and later in the poem, a shovel) tightly to control what comes out of each—words and bullets, respectively—but moreover, the evocation of a gun implies the power of the pen and the danger associated with creative writing, not only the power to inspire, but also the power to stir up strong emotions.

Heaney later wrote evocatively about "an old, cock-hammer, double-barrelled pistol, like a dueling piece, fixed on a bracket above a door in the kitchen." It was "a completely exotic item," and after he began reading comics and adventure stories, it "linked the kitchen with highwaymen, stage-coaches, women in crinoline skirts, men in ruffs and duels at dawn in the woodlands of great estates."[16] It is impossible to know if he likens his pen in "Digging" to this particular gun, but certainly he associated guns from early in his life with adventure and excitement and he is trying to convey how he believes writing connotes such feelings as well by the opening comparison here. He mused that "Ted Hughes's poetry was a strong influence in releasing me, and the habit of explosive diction may have been caught from him. And second . . . when I set about a poem in those days, I was tensed and triggered within myself. I usually wrote at a sitting and generated a charge within me: the actual writing was an intense activity, battened down."[17]

Heaney has claimed that the primary inspiration for the opening lines was sonic, however, pointing out that "I was responding to an entirely phonetic prompt, a kind of sonic chain dictated by the inner ear. It's the connection between the 'uh' sounds in 'thumb' and 'snug' and 'gun' that are the heart of the poetic matter rather than any sociological or literary formation" (*SS* 82–3). If the "uh" sound set off this "sonic chain" of associations, then he must have happily explored the pen/gun analogy soon after. His stress on the "earscape" of the poem rather than its immediate rural landscape conveys the continuing importance of orality in his poetic register. T. S. Eliot's prose that Heaney read while at Queen's confirmed his early interest in sounds, particularly Eliot's notion of "the auditory imagination," which Eliot termed "the feeling for syllable and rhythm, penetrating far below the conscious levels of thought and feeling . . . sinking to the most primitive and forgotten . . ."[18] Certainly, Eliot's claim that sound forms the basis of poetry "confirmed a natural inclination to make myself an echo chamber for the poem's sounds."[19] "Digging" offers a glimpse of the way in which a poem presents itself to Heaney and it gives us a catalog of sounds that ring in our ears long after our reading of the poem: "a clean rasping sound" (*DN* 1); the "squelch and slap / Of soggy peat"; and "the curt cuts of an edge" (2).

Beginning with "Between," Heaney's signature preposition, "Digging" confirms him as a liminal poet, here poised between the work of the farmyard and the labor of the literary academy. He wants to affirm his father's and grandfather's hard work as diggers of potatoes and peat, respectively—and even boasts of their prowess with shovels—but simultaneously privileges the poet's vocation by evocatively writing farewell to the possibility of remaining on the farm in a series of differing stanzas that brag of his own abilities with lineation and form. Thus the poem begins with that well-known near-couplet, then follows with a triplet, a quatrain, a quintet, a two-line stanza, a quintet, a tercet, another quatrain, and a tercet. Although his métier would become the quatrain in his poems of the 1970s, here Heaney is showing off a bit and implicitly arguing that he has become already a good enough craftsman to "handle" various forms, just as the speaker boasts "the old man could handle a spade" (1).

"Digging" also shows Heaney's debt to those writers and poets who believed, like Patrick Kavanagh, that the writer's home ground was sufficient and fertile for inspiration and subject matter. Kavanagh's articulation of the difference between the "parochial" and the "provincial" was instructive at this time for Heaney and other developing writers. In "The Parish and the Universe," Kavanagh argued that

> Parochialism and provincialism are opposites. The provincial has no mind of his own; he does not trust what his eyes see until he has heard what the metropolis—toward which his eyes are turned—has to say on any subject... The parochial mentality on the other hand is never in any doubt about the social and artistic validity of his parish.[20]

Already steeped in the Catholic values of his native parish, Heaney found Kavanagh's advocacy of the local as a valid subject enabling for his early and later poetry.

On the other side of the Atlantic, the American Theodore Roethke, whose *Collected Poems* Heaney reviewed in 1968, also enabled him to trust his own poetry. He argued, "An awareness of his own poetic process, and a trust in the possibility of his poetry, that is what a poet should attempt to preserve"; and ... Roethke had "faith in his own creative instincts."[21] "Digging" manifests this poetic trust and bids farewell to Heaney's shy earlier persona of "Incertus." It simultaneously asserts confidence and declares independence. As he would write later, "I had done more than make an arrangement of words: I felt that I had let down a shaft into real life ... I didn't care who thought what about it..."[22]

While Heaney and many critics have long articulated his debt to his older Irish contemporary Kavanagh in "Digging" and other poems from *Death of a Naturalist*, this opening poem portrays the influence of a much older literary tradition—Anglo-Saxon poetry. Consider again the first stanza. Only two words are more than one syllable long—"Between" and "finger"—and the rest of them are blunt, tough monosyllables which could be found in a poem like *Beowulf*, which Heaney later translated. Moreover, the presence in this stanza and throughout the poem of medial caesuras, signified by semicolons, periods, and commas, suggest that Heaney was familiar with the Anglo-Saxon practice of breaking lines in half. Part of this familiarity may have been transmitted to him by his immersion in Hopkins's poetry, who himself was intimately familiar with Anglo-Saxon poetic features such as kennings (compound poetic words such as "whale-road" for "sea"), medial caesuras, and alliteration. Heaney indicates as much in his introduction to *Beowulf* when he points out that "without any conscious intent on my part certain lines in the first poem in my first book conformed to the requirements of Anglo-Saxon metrics."[23] The bluntness and directness of the diction in "Digging" and other poems from *Death of a Naturalist* are also indebted to the weightiness of Anglo-Saxon speech. Heaney's argument in his introduction to *Beowulf* that "what I was after first and foremost was a narrative line that sounded as if it meant business and I was prepared to sacrifice other things in pursuit of this directness of utterance," sheds retrospective light on his use of the gun in the opening stanza—to convey that his own poetry "meant business"—and on the tough, direct diction.[24] "Digging" and much of Heaney's early poetry thus derive their durability and resiliency from being anchored not only in his Kavanaghesque home ground of South County Derry but also from their grounding in the diction, lineation, and violence of the Anglo-Saxons' life-or-death world.

Finally, while "Digging" celebrates the active work of the poet's forebears, it crucially contrasts and privileges poetry's power that inheres in moments of contemplation and rest before the poem is written and his ancestors labored. Thus Heaney frames the poem with two similar images of the pen at rest, although poised for action, in the poet's hand. He would later discuss poetry's power by recourse to the famous lines from Wordsworth's 1802 Preface to *Lyrical Ballads* about poetry being the "spontaneous overflow of powerful feelings," concluding that "Wordsworth declares that what counts is the quality, intensity and breadth of the poet's concerns between the moments of writing, the gravity and purity of the mind's appetites and applications between moments of inspiration."[25] "What counts" then, the most, in "Digging," is how Heaney highlights the time "between the moments of writing" and "between moments of inspiration." Certainly, he is trying to connect his "digging" pen to the powerfully slicing implements his father and grandfather wielded, but just as important, perhaps more so, is his affirmation of poetry's power in its times of rest, when it idles and dawdles, not actively seeking or working.

"The Diviner" both affirms the traditional craft of water-dowsing and becomes another analogy for the poet's craft, which is also likened to plucking the strings of an instrument.[26] The most common image associated with the poet from the 1960s, because of the great success of "Digging," is of him as digger, as the sculpture at Bellaghy suggests,[27] but envisioning the poet as a diviner may be more appropriate to understanding his artistic search for inspiration in his early years. Heaney suggests that both divining and writing poetry depend on hovering over the right stretch of literal or metaphorical ground, respectively, until suddenly the water or the poem reveals itself to us in its quivering glory. Each of the three quatrains, arranged in roughly alternating rhymes, focuses on a moment of waiting for water to be found by the diviner. In the first stanza, Heaney signals this "hunting the pluck / Of water," by the colon following the "V" of the "forked hazel stick" held by the man (*DN* 23). Water's "pluck" gives it an agency and also connotes the playing of a stringed instrument.[28] The "nervous, but professionally // Unfussed" diviner finds the water at the beginning of the second stanza. "Unfussed," the first line of that stanza, is followed immediately by a full stop, during which his audience and the reader is forced to wait and take a breath, suspended in our anticipation. Then, "The pluck came sharp as a sting," and we and his audience exhale in relief (23), as "Spring water [is] suddenly broadcasting / Through a green hazel its secret stations" (23). These two enjambed lines signify how the water gushes toward the diviner's rod and this rushing movement is heightened by the comparison of the water to a radio that sends out its secret signals. In the original, published version of the poem, in fact, Heaney used the phrase a "green aerial" instead a "green hazel," even more strongly suggesting the likeness of the diviner's rod to an antenna.[29]

Moreover, the mysterious quality of "stations" is likely colored by his Catholic upbringing and his participation in doing the stations of the cross at St Patrick's Purgatory on Lough Derg in County Donegal and elsewhere. *Stations* would become the name of his 1975 volume of prose poems and also features in his 1984 volume *Station Island*, whose title section is based on the Lough Derg pilgrimage. Walking through the stations of the cross is a repetitive movement that nonetheless can lead to a heightened spiritual apprehension and this passage in "The Diviner" implies by extension that poets who faithfully put themselves through their paces consistently may also garner unexpected images, even poems, that are revealed to them. Heaney was very interested in the notion of the poet as a receiving station for words, images, and even whole poems. For instance, in "The Government of the Tongue," he cites approvingly Anna Swir's statement that "A poet becomes ... an antenna capturing the voices of the world, a medium expressing his own subconscious and the collective subconscious."[30] Similarly, in his essay on Sylvia Plath, he admiringly argues that "For Yeats, the poet is somebody who is spoken through," and observes of Plath that "she grew to a point where she permitted herself identification with the oracle and gave herself over as a vehicle for possession ..."[31] "The Diviner" similarly suggests that the poet, like the diviner, must give himself over to his craft, even temporarily lose himself in it, in order to receive its gifts. If so, the resulting poem will live.[32]

The third stanza of the poem builds the case for water-divining or poetry as not merely a solipsistic art, but one in which the craftsman can convey his power to an audience. The first two end-stopped lines of this quatrain feature the "bystanders" asking to try their own luck and the diviner handing over "the rod" to them (*DN* 23). Clearly, the power lies not in the rod—or the pen for the poet—but in the body of the diviner or poet who can function as a conduit for a divine power since "It [the rod] lay dead in their grasp till, nonchalantly, / He gripped expectant wrists. The hazel stirred" (23). The casual approach of the diviner to his vocation at the beginning of the poem and here belies his utmost dedication to his craft and signifies how he must become receptive to the pull of the water. Once he does so, there is another full stop in which his audience and the reader again pauses expectantly; then, as the limber green rod stirs, we are again given the excitement of water's discovery. Just as Heaney's father and grandfather in "Digging" and the blacksmith in "The Forge" from his next volume, *Door into the Dark*, are silent in their pursuit of their craft, so is the diviner, betokening his absolute devotion to it in his waiting posture. So too, the poet implies, must the writer become silent, attuned to the pluck of words and images that reveal themselves to him. If he does so successfully, not only will the poetry flow, but also, he will gain an appreciative audience as the diviner does here.

Heaney felt strongly enough about "The Diviner" to comment extensively on it in his early essay, "Feeling into Words." There, he argues that the figure of a water diviner "represents pure technique," which he has just defined as

> the discovery of ways to go out of his [the poet's] normal cognitive bounds and raid the inarticulate: a dynamic alertness that mediates between the origins of feeling in memory and experience and the formal ploys that express these in a work of art . . . it is that whole creative effort of the mind's and body's resources to bring the meaning of experience within the jurisdiction of form.[33]

The diviner, then, like the poet, must oscillate between this "dynamic alertness" to remembering past feeling and formally shaping those memories. Heaney's three quatrains that roughly rhyme *ab*1/2*ab cdcd ef*1/2*ef* order, shape, and frame the power that flows through the diviner as conduit. He argues that "The diviner resembles the poet in his function of making contact with what lies hidden, and in his ability to make palpable what was sensed or raised." As with so many other of his artist or craftsman figures whose vocation offers analogs to that of the poet, the diviner does not selfishly hoard his gift, but offers it willingly to those in need. Heaney mentions that "I am pleased that it ends with a verb, 'stirred,' the heart of the mystery; and I am glad that 'stirred' chimes with 'word,' bringing the two functions of *vates* [the Roman term for poet] into the one sound."[34] Yet while words are the proper remit of the poet, Heaney's diviner hands the bystander his wand "without a word," suggesting silence and reverence toward one's vocation, a submission to its mystery, is the proper stance of the artist. Only then can the hazel stir, can the mind move and produce images for others' sustenance and pleasure.

Another way in which Heaney's in-betweeness is manifested in *Death of a Naturalist* is through how the more ahistorical metapoetic poems about childhood and manual crafts are counterbalanced by deeply historical poems such as those about the Great Famine of 1845, "At a Potato Digging," and "For the Commander of the *Eliza*." The volume thus teeters between poems of childhood and historic poems about devastation or trauma. As the 1960s concluded and the "Troubles" in Northern Ireland thrust themselves into everyday life, Heaney turned often to specific periods of Irish and other national histories in order to gain some sort of purchase on the atrocities being committed, but in these earlier poems, he is more concerned to explore other historical wounds that had been inflicted upon the Irish psyche, none more devastating than the Great Famine.

"At a Potato Digging" offers an anti-pastoral answer to "Digging" and injects resonances of fertility rites and religious rituals into this work which Heaney would later explore much more deeply in the bog poems.[35] The tactile pleasures of digging by hand in "Digging" are absent here as "A mechanical digger wrecks the drill . . ." As the digger reveals the potato, the workers "swarm in behind" and "Fingers go dead in the cold." This newer, mechanized digging seems to dehumanize the workers, who are detached from the land in ways Heaney's father and grandfather were not in the earlier poem. These workers are compared to "crows attacking crow-black fields," and as the first section proceeds, they are portrayed as part of a timeless, quasi-religious procession: Their "hands fumble towards the black / Mother," and they are linked to "Centuries / of fear and homage to the famine god" as they "Make a seasonal altar of the sod" (*DN* 18). Heaney will reuse "altar" positively in "The Forge" from *Door into the Dark* to signify the sacred site of the blacksmith's anvil, but here the workers worship the "black / Mother" earth and seek to assuage the "famine god."

As the poem proceeds, it shifts to the perspective of the potatoes themselves in section two, then to the perspective of Irish famine victims in section three, then finally back to the current workers' perspective in section four. The potatoes are "Flint-white, purple" (18) and "white as cream" when they are split open (19). As they are "piled in pits," they are described as "live skulls, blind-eyed," a phrase that opens section three as well:

> Live skulls, blind-eyed, balanced on
> wild higgledy skeletons,
> scoured the land in 'forty-five,
> wolfed the blighted root and died. (19)

The workers in the present had previously been termed "A higgledy line" (18) and repeating that word here indicates the decrepit condition of famine victims as they scour the land for food. They are likened to the blind skulls of the potatoes themselves and that likeness signifies their dependence on the tuber, which leads to their death once the blight destroys their staple crop. Famine memorials to the victims of the Great Famine, as it is often termed, now recognize this terrible tragedy. For instance, John Behan's "Coffin Ship," Ireland's Great Famine National Monument, in County Mayo, is composed of bronze shapes that turn out to be, on closer examination, emaciated bodies (much like Heaney's "wild higgledy skeletons") that form the rigging of the famine ship, or "coffin ship," as they were often called since so many of their passengers would have died from starvation on the journey to America.[36] These victims are characterized further by mouth and more eye imagery as section three proceeds: "Mouths tightened in, eyes died hard, / faces chilled to a plucked bird" (19). They are then variously likened to birds and plants: They have "beaks of famine [that] snipped at guts" and are "grubbing, like plants, in the earth . . ." (19).

This section concludes with a horrifying portrait of the land filled with potatoes running with "pus," and hauntingly, "where potato diggers are, / you still smell the running sore." Such an image introduces a crucial motif in Heaney's work: that of the sore or, more often, the wound of history. In major poems that would follow "At a Potato Digging," particularly those from *North* in the mid-1970s, Heaney images the bog as an open wound and features victims of both ancient fertility rites and modern sectarian practices in Northern Ireland who themselves have been wounded, cut open, sometimes beheaded. The present poem concludes with the workers flopping "Down in the ditch," another sort of wound on the Irish landscape, and feasting on their lunches. Intriguingly, Cecil Woodham-Smith's classic study, *The Great Hunger*, which Heaney knew, features a photograph of an evicted Irish family taking refuge in a ditch, and the poet's use of a ditch for his laborers' repose in his contemporary poem may draw on this evocative photograph and thus suggest the similarities of current workers still dependent on the potato to their mid-nineteenth-century forebears.[37] As these workers rest, their postures and throwing away the remnants of their meal suggest further the earlier linkage of potato digging, famine, and fertility/infertility: "Then, stretched on the faithless ground, [they] spill

/ Libations of cold tea, scatter crusts" (20). Even as they seem to recognize that this offering too may be rejected by the "faithless ground," they nevertheless go through the motions of offering these libations and bread to mother earth. Such actions are habitual and immemorial, linking them to their ancestors who would appease the gods associated with the earth and harvest. Yet they have been sufficiently sundered from these forebears, in part by the introduction of the mechanical digger, such that their "offerings" are mere parodies of sincere ones from the past, and they are largely unconscious of them as rituals.

"For the Commander of the *Eliza*" extends the ship imagery that closes "At a Potato Digging" to a description of a rowboat off West Mayo during the Great Famine that is hailed by a British patrol boat, whose crew discover six starving Irishmen. "For the Commander" takes as its epigraph a passage from Woodham-Smith's work, in which a British officer discovers these skeletal figures "with emaciated faces and prominent, staring eyeballs" and reports to Sir James Dombrain, Inspector-General of the Coastguard service, who "'very inconveniently ... interfered'" (21).[38] The "Six grown men with gaping mouths and eyes / Bursting the sockets like spring onions in drills" recall the wasted figures of the starving men in "At a Potato Digging" whose skulls and eyes are likened to potatoes; here these men's eyes are compared to "spring onions," which startlingly suggests how their eyes are about to pop out of their heads. As they call in Irish for food, "'Bia, bia, / Bia'" (21), we are told "their desperation / Rose and fell like a flock of starving gulls," reminding us of the "gay flotilla of gulls" in the previous poem (20) but now the avian simile becomes ominous, even dangerous. The poem's British narrator, who has been, along with his shipmates, "kept ... right with flour and beef," knows they have "no mandate to relieve distress" because food was "available in Westport—" and is thus relieved when they refuse food to the starving men who row furiously toward him and his men. The terse language of his reaction indicts him for his unfeeling recognition of fellow human beings: "I saw they were / Violent and without hope. I hoisted / And cleared off. Less incidents the better" (21). Once this commander gets to port, he "exorcised my ship" and reported the incident to Sir James, who in turn urged "free relief" for famine victims in Westport but was reprimanded by "good Whitehall." Whitehall's reaction, which the narrator tacitly supports, is bureaucratic, stoic, and given in free indirect discourse or reported speech: "Let natives prosper by their own exertions; / Who could not swim might go ahead and sink." This report is then recalled directly and chillingly: "'The Coast Guard with their zeal and activity / Are too lavish,' were the words, I think" (22). The brevity of this utterance underscores their lack of sympathy; such scrupulous speakers who will speak so sparsely cannot even give the bare minimum of food to prevent sure starvation of their subjects whose plaintive cries in Irish testify more eloquently to their humanity than that supposedly espoused by their imperial rulers.

A series of anti-pastoral poems follow, which all show the narrator experiencing a reversal in his attitude toward the natural world from positive and ignorant to negative and more knowing. Heaney was reading Theodore Roethke's posthumous volume of poetry, *The Far Field*, by 1964, and by 1968, Heaney would note Roethke's departure from Eden, which he likely saw as paralleling and anticipating Heaney's own "fall into manhood" in these poems.[39] When Heaney writes of Roethke's departure from the "repossession of the childhood Eden" in the "greenhouse poems" of *The Lost Son* to a movement "Out of Eden," where "beyond the garden life is riotous," and "chaos replaces correspondence, consciousness thwarts communion, the light of the world fades in the shadow of death," he likely thinks of his own trajectory in *Death of a Naturalist*.[40] "Death of a Naturalist" forms a cluster of "fear poetry" with "The Barn," "An Advancement of Learning," and "Blackberry-Picking," four poems situated between the pleasing sounds and sights of Heaney's rural Northern Ireland in "Digging" and "Churning Day."

"Death of a Naturalist" firmly locates the poet again in a rural Northern Ireland landscape, with its "flax-dam" and "frogspawn" (*DN* 3) but the comforting landscape of the first stanza and the soothing sounds of the teacher's voice telling the young Heaney and the other schoolchildren about frogs mating gradually gives way to a horrifying realization on the part of the young speaker that he has stolen the frogs' babies, an early manifestation of his Wordsworthian education by fear. He said in an interview, citing Wordsworth's lines from *The Prelude*, Book I, "Fair seed-time had my soul and I grew up / Fostered alike by beauty and by fear," that "any fear I had was on the whole elemental fear. Wordsworth was afraid in the mountains, I was scared by frogs and rats . . . and frogs spawning, which went into my first poem, 'Death of a Naturalist.'"[41] In retrospect, we can see why Heaney would want this to be his title poem, for it conveys what would quickly become known as his characteristic sound and vocabulary through a series of powerful images and words. And moreover, it signals that while he was devoted to his local ground, he would not be drawn into mere pastoral celebrations of it. Instead, he would reveal its dangerous sites such as wells and bogs—and scary creatures—frogs and rats.

Notice that the characteristic poetic devices of earlier, Hopkins-influenced poems remain but have been constrained. The first line, for example, features "flax-dam festered" and the second line "heavy headed." Such alliteration does not overpower the senses as it did in the earlier, uncollected poems but enhances it; thus, the rotting flax's festering creates a sense of swollen rottenness indolent in its nature that draws the young Heaney ineluctably to itself. There is also, as in "Digging," a series of medial caesuras—on lines 2, 3, 10, 13, 15, 17, 23, 26, 29, and 30. These caesuras tend to slow down the generally longer lines than those featured in "Digging" so we too might revel in the luxurious landscape full of that rotting flax and swarming with insect life (3).

"Death of a Naturalist" also displays Heaney's proficiency with voice in a way that "Digging" does not; in this, too, it is the more accomplished poem. There is the buzzing of the "bluebottles" that "Wove a strong gauze of sound around the smell," a marvelous instance of synesthesia in line 6. The voice of Miss Walls, the children's teacher, succeeds this collective sound, a voice that attempts to meet the children on their level by discussing the sexual lives of the frogs through adverting to the children's parents: "The daddy frog was called a bullfrog, / And how he croaked, and how the mammy frog / Laid hundreds of little eggs and this was / Frogspawn." Finally, in the poem's turn from sexual innocence to vicarious experience, the "bass chorus" of the bullfrogs greets the young boy who has been taking their frogspawn to watch it be transformed into tadpoles (3). These martial frogs, "gross-bellied," were "cocked / On sods" (3–4), and "The slap and plop were obscene threats" (4). As "Some sat / Poised like mud grenades, their blunt heads farting," the boy who would later become the young man likening the pen to a gun in "Digging" flees in a brilliant trinity of active verbs: "I sickened, turned, and ran." Now the landscape has not only been revealed as dangerous, violent, but as even threatening him: "I knew / That if I dipped my hand the spawn would clutch it" (4).

In "Blackberry-Picking," the same narrator revels in the lovely blackberries he spies habitually every "Late August," but is experienced enough to know that they would quickly rot "Once off the bush ..." The poem marches along in couplets and near-couplets, lending an urgency to the children's picking of the berries. Once again, we have Heaney's characteristic love of natural images: The blackberries are described variously as "a glossy purple clot" and "big dark blobs [that] burned / Like a plate of eyes." But by the end of this simile, we realize we are also in the realm of myth and the next line and a half confirms it: "Our hands were peppered / With thorn pricks, our palms sticky as Bluebeard's." *Bluebeard* was a French folktale, most famously conveyed by French author Charles Perrault in 1659, about a nobleman with a blue beard who killed his wives and left their bodies under his castle to rot in their blood. Interestingly, whereas in the preceding poems about fear, the natural world introduces terror to the young boy in the shape of frogs and rats, here the remembrance of this fairy tale from the world of literature makes the young lad and his siblings feel like murderers of plants in the natural world. Their palms slick with the "blood" of the blackberries, they prepare to eat them after storing them in the byre, but find "A rat-grey fungus, glutting on our cache" (8). The poem thus cleverly employs and combines the festering images of the flax in "Death of a Naturalist" and the rats from "The Barn" and "An Advancement of Learning" to convey the children's horror at their spoiled feast. Just as Heaney's narrator has learned to know the rot inherent in the natural cycles of life through earlier poems, the poet has learned to teach us to closely read his poems together to gather and feast on their images that culminate in this poem.

"Blackberry-Picking" is dedicated to Heaney's creative writing teacher at Queen's University, Philip Hobsbaum, and as another poem about an educational experience, it may register Hobsbaum's star pupil's fear that without the tutelage of his master, his poems may spoil like the just-picked blackberries. But the analogy between blackberrying and poetry-making is faint, if it is there at all, unlike in "Digging" or "The Forge" from *Door into the Dark* that draw clear analogies between rural crafts and poetry.

Gail McConnell's position that the poem "draws on the Catholic theology of transubstantiation" is somewhat plausible—at least when it is confined to the first blackberry of the summer tasting "Like thickened wine" (8)—but falters when she claims that "Heaney's search for Real Presence in poetry through the blackberry, which is consumed as in the sacrament of the Eucharist," results in a theory of "Poetic productivity [that] is thus associated with sacrifice, a Christ-like act meriting reverence and gratitude. Heaney's template for the poet, then, is not only the priest but Christ himself."[42] It is hard to credit such a reading given the evidence of the poem since right after Heaney likens the first blackberry's taste to wine, a colon immediately follows that simile and then the phrase "summer's blood was in it / Leaving stains upon the tongue and lust for / Picking" (8). The blackberry is thus a natural, not a supernatural symbol in the poem, and Christ can be found nowhere in it.

Two poems that *are* saturated with Christian imagery are "Docker" and "Poor Women in a City Church." "Docker" is an angry poem and it is hard to disagree with John Wilson Foster's assessment that it is a "startling caricature not just of any docker but of a laconic Belfast docker and a Protestant . . ."[43] In *Death of a Naturalist*, this poem faces the much more reverent "Poor Women in a City Church," and implies Heaney's preference for his own Catholic community. Drawing on the architecture of east Belfast, particularly the giant cranes over the shipyards termed affectionately "Samson" and "Goliath," the poem opens with a picture of the docker drinking in isolation, a penetrating image given the historic Protestant communities' fear in Northern Ireland that they are alone and isolated. His "cap juts like a gantry's crossbeam, / Cowling plated forehead and sledgehead jaw." His lips are likened to a "vice" [sic] and the words that issue from his tight lips are figured as "Mosaic imperatives" that "bang home like rivets . . ." Heaney may be drawing upon the rumor that circulated during the building of the doomed *Titanic* in the shipyards of east Belfast that with every rivet driven into the ship's hull, the Protestant workforce cursed the Pope. Despite its cartoonish picture of the docker, the poem does give us an accurate sense of how a certain strand of Protestantism in Northern Ireland—represented by Ian Paisley's Free Presbyterian Church, for instance—has traditionally hated Catholics and used "Mosaic imperatives" to condemn them as idolaters, devil-worshippers, and worse. Some commentators have even argued that this strand of Protestantism actually founds its identity on hating Catholics and, crucially, anti-Catholicism in Northern Ireland has been not just a theological marker, but has been "used as part of the hegemonic process by which a sacred canopy is thrown around Protestants when their unity is essential to their interests."[44] Heaney's docker, then, is not just a shipyard worker but stands for a long tradition of anti-Catholicism in the North and suggests how Protestants of varying theological stripes could be united through fear and hatred of the Catholic Other. Thus we are told about him in an eerily accurate premonition of the "Troubles" that would start in a few short years, "That fist would drop a hammer on a Catholic—" and "The only Roman collar he tolerates / Smiles all round his sleek pint of porter." His unyielding dislike of Catholics is reinforced by the mechanical metal images used to describe his rigid body. The man's violent attitude in the pub is carried into his own home as the poem concludes with his family's silence "At slammed door and smoker's cough in the hall" (28).

"Poor Women in a City Church," on the other hand, nearly venerates a group of poor Catholic women praying habitually in their Catholic church, or "chapel," as it is often called in Northern Ireland. These women's reverential attitude toward God as they kneel, surrounded by burning candles, and launch "whispered calls" that "Take wing up to the Holy Name" (29), contrast the docker's attitude, who sees God as "a foreman with certain definite views / Who orders life in shifts of work and leisure" (28). The docker, who "sits, strong and blunt as a Celtic cross" (28), would never "kneel" (29) to anyone—not in church, at home, or in the pub.[45] The women finally seem to become waxen themselves as the poem concludes with a glimpse of their unwrinkled "beeswax brows," a soothing image of faith that counters the docker's angry movements and rigid brow.

While Heaney experiments with a variety of stanza forms in *Death of a Naturalist*, he writes several poems, including "The Early Purges," "Mid-Term Break," "Waterfall," "Lovers on Aran," and "Saint Francis and the Birds," in tercets, which would become his favorite form in the last thirty years of his career, in the central section of *Station Island* and in many poems from *Seeing Things* and *Human Chain* especially. These poems do not draw very heavily on Dantean *terza rima* as later Heaney tercet poems would with their slant rhymes and variations on the *aba bcb* form. The closest of these to something like true *terza rima* is "Saint Francis and the Birds," which features stanzas that resemble the *terza rima* rhyme scheme with their slant rhyme, which becomes full rhyme in the conclusion when the central concluding sound of the middle line of the last tercet, "flight," fully sets up the last, dangling line (characteristic of the end of Dante's canti in *The Divine Comedy*) that ends in "light" (40). Although "Mid-Term Break" ends in a similarly dangling last line, it chimes instead with the preceding line's "clear" and its isolation portends the loneliness of Heaney's young brother's coffin: "A four foot box, a foot for every year." This poem interestingly characterizes the poet's baby brother as "Wearing a poppy bruise on his left temple" (15), which strangely employs a flower worn predominantly by Protestants in Northern Ireland (and by others throughout Britain) to commemorate the dead of World War One. Another oddity about the poem is a biographical incongruity: Heaney's brother actually died at age three and a half, but he changes it to "four" here to match the length of his coffin.

Death of a Naturalist is dedicated to the poet's wife and a number of poems in the volume meditate on their recent marriage. Perhaps the most interesting of these is "Poem," also dedicated to Marie Heaney, in which the poet likens himself to being pregnant with a poem: "Love, I shall perfect for you the child / Who diligently potters in my brain . . ." The first quatrain imagines this child who digs with "heavy spade" and then the next two insert the speaker, perhaps as that grown child, building a wall with "a layer of sods" to keep out livestock from his garden, and then constructing a dam that would similarly be breached. The poem concludes with a quatrain that implores the poet's wife to "perfect for me this child," now likely an imagined future child of theirs, "Whose small imperfect limits would keep breaking . . ." He wants her to "arrange the world / Within our walls, within our golden ring," a lovely concluding image that holds out the marriage ring as a pure symbol of eternity that will protect them and their child in contrast to the earlier, breached walls of sod and clay (35). Heaney has never garnered sufficient critical attention for his lovely domestic poems, including "Poem," "Scaffolding," and "Honeymoon Flight" in this volume, many of which convey a quiet eroticism and delight in companionship.

Yet as important as these domestic poems are, *Death of a Naturalist* concludes with "Personal Helicon," a poem Heaney dedicated not to his wife but to his fellow Belfast Group member, Michael Longley. This poem bids farewell to childish narcissism but affirms the playful musical calling of the poet by remembering the poet's childhood gazing into wells. The alternating rhymes of the poem march these images of play along, but they are "counter-marched," as it were, by the real danger of being near wells. Children have died falling into wells or have been trapped for hours; similarly, Heaney implies, such prolonged exposure to wells is self-indulgently dangerous and leaves out the poet's audience, an inherently solipsistic maneuver. So he finally rejects staring "big-eyed Narcissus, into some spring" as "beneath all adult dignity" and instead says he "rhyme[s] / To see myself, to set the darkness echoing" (44).

Ending the volume with "Personal Helicon" accomplishes two crucial maneuvers for the poet. It suggests his future poetry will be born out of gazing inward and digging down, and it confirms his rejection of a straightforwardly pastoral mode. Dark, subterranean places would be his personal helicon or spring of inspiration for his muse (one of the two springs on the Greek Mount Helikon was the Hippocrene, considered to be a source of inspiration). Another spring associated with Mount Helikon was the site where Narcissus was inspired by his own beauty and Heaney's poem also recognizes that he could be sidetracked by the beauty of his sensuous imagination, but refuses to do so. This last phrase—"I rhyme / To see myself, to set the darkness echoing"—implies he will often portray himself searching for inspiration meta-poetically in many of his better poems, as indeed he did, which nonetheless still sounds somewhat narcissistic. The poet, however, will not look up to Mount Helikon for divine inspiration or horizontally for the Burkean sublime. He looks down into his *personal* helicon, a word that signifies two different kinds of musical instrument, an ancient early acoustical instrument and a spiraled brass wind instrument.[46] Such gazing will enable him to play an echoing, subterranean music, and indeed successive poems would sound the depths of many such dark places. The seventh-century BC pastoral poet Hesiod wrote of how he pastured his sheep on the slopes of Mount Helikon and thus Heaney's evocation yet renovation of Hesiod's Helikon in this poem also lends his aesthetic a harder edge, suggesting his poetry may well draw on rural images and sites but will not privilege the traditional encomium for nature that is the pastoral; instead, it may partake of anti-pastoral impulses in discovering the fears and dangers inherent in such landscapes as indeed it did in significant poems from this first volume.

Heaney wrote an important poem, "Antaeus," in the mid-1960s that he originally intended to publish in *Death of a Naturalist* but instead chose to open Part I of *North*. He unfortunately excludes the poem entirely from *New Selected Poems 1966–1987*. But in *Opened Ground: Selected Poems 1966–1996*, he includes "Antaeus" (dated "1966") facing "Personal Helicon." Such a placement affirms "Personal Helicon" as a privileging of gazing into subterranean depths; it also reveals the poet's fears about what might happen if he left his home ground literally or metaphorically for too long—poetic death. The ground, for Antaeus, strengthens him: "When I lie on the ground / I rise flushed as a rose in the morning," and rubbing "myself with sand // . . . operative / As an elixir." Heaney identifies strongly with Antaeus's claim that "I cannot be weaned / Off the earth's long contour, her river-veins," and that he is "cradled in the dark that wombed me." Whereas the dark earth was a mythic mother seeking appeasement in "At a Potato Digging," here it functions as a maternal figure that has birthed Antaeus and Heaney. "Antaeus" concludes with a hope and a fear, and the latter is stronger—that new heroes will come and wrestle with Antaeus, sometimes throwing him and "renew[ing] my birth"—but he vows, "let him not plan, lifting me off the earth, / My elevation, my fall."[47] To rise skyward—literally or metaphorically—would constitute a fall for this ground-dwelling hero because he would be removed from his source of strength. Even though Heaney would go on to write airier poems and even whole volumes about leaving the ground, ascending spiritually, he continued to feel that to leave his home ground constituted a real danger for his poetic inspiration and even a threat to his essential self, a belief that persists throughout his career. As he pointed out in a speech he gave on his 70th birthday that reflected upon the situation dramatized in "Antaeus," "It's no accident that when Satan wanted to tempt Christ, he took him up to the top of a high mountain." Reading the poem through this Christian intertext helps us realize how Heaney "felt . . . even back in 1966 . . . that I had better take care to remain on the near-ground level of my own life." And yet he would also strive to widen the compass of his imagination and vision since he believed he was "destined eventually to live and breathe in the imaginative air of Hercules . . ." In such an atmosphere, he would be "subject at all times to the gravities and griefs of our common human condition, but at the same time, susceptible to the lift of the heart 'when I lift up my eyes to the heavens.'"[48]

The dark that cradles Antaeus would also continue to be a source of strength and mystery for Heaney in future volumes, including his next, *Door into the Dark*. "The Forge," one of the four major poems from that volume including "The Peninsula," "Requiem for the Croppies," and "Bogland," features the volume's title in its opening line. It begins, "All I know is a door into the dark" (*DD* 7). The door into the darkness of the blacksmith's forge signifies, variously, an opening into the mysterious arena of craftsmanship, into the unconscious, and into something like the wellspring of religious experience, what Mircea Eliade terms lies at the heart of all religious culture—the Center, "a place that is sacred above all."[49] Other images of darkness occur in "The Outlaw," when Kelly's "unlicensed" bull "resumed the dark" (4, 5); "The Peninsula"— "in the dark" (9); throughout "In Gallarus Oratory," which characterizes this drystone structure on the edge of the Dingle Peninsula as "A core of old dark walled up with stone / A yard thick" (10); in the second lyric from "A Lough Neagh Sequence," entitled "Beyond Sargasso," in which "Dark / delivers him hungering / down each undulation" (27)— and in "Bogland." And many of the pregnancy poems in the volume such as "Mother," "Cana Revisited," and "Elegy for a Still-born Child" meditate on the womb's darkness. The dark, then, is not only mysterious, but also a site of fecundity—mostly biological creativity: Kelly's bull, the wombs of women, and the concluding bog in "Bogland."

Thus this volume, just like *Death of a Naturalist*, returns to the poet's childhood locales, confirming and continuing the subterranean impulses first celebrated in the earlier volume. Heaney intended the volume's title

> to gesture towards this idea of poetry as a point of entry into the buried life of the feelings or as a point of exit for it. Words themselves are doors; Janus is to a certain extent their deity, looking back to a ramification of roots and associations and forward to a clarification of sense and meaning."[50]

Often characterizing himself as having grown up in between competing cultures, languages, and histories, here Heaney holds that words both connect us to subconscious feelings—the dark—and can lead us into explications of those feelings through various doors.

"The Forge," while indubitably influenced by both Keats's sensuous music, especially in his "Ode on a Grecian Urn," and by Hopkins, particularly his poem about a blacksmith, "Felix Randal,"[51] can be read also through the originary impulse of American poet Elizabeth Bishop's autobiographical short story, "In the Village," which features a character named "Nate" making a horseshoe. While Heaney had almost certainly not read Bishop's story when he wrote his poem, he would later praise "Bishop's linguistic virtuosity which creates the delightful pure illusion of access to a pristine, prelinguistic state."[52] Similarly, his poem strives to reach such a condition by featuring a grunting blacksmith, otherwise silent, who makes his sacred music at his "altar" of an anvil that occupies the center of the forge (7). That anvil also sits suggestively in the middle of the cover of Faber and Faber's edition of the volume and its solidity, yet otherness, signal how Heaney will continue to find material anchors for his own sacred poetic music in the things and sounds of his faraway childhood. It suggests a cosmogony, just as "the construction of the Vedic fire altar reproduced the creation of the world, and the altar itself was a microcosm, an *imago mundi*," as Eliade points out.[53]

Formally, the created world of "The Forge" is a broken Petrarchan sonnet that begins regularly, *abba*, then slips into a second quatrain that contains a series of rough "c" rhymes (instead of another quatrain in *abba* rhyme), concluding with a sestet rhyming *decede* instead of the more expected *cdecde* or *cdcdcd*. Likely Heaney breaks the regular rhyme of this form to echo the content of the poem—the rough metals being broken, heated, and hammered out by the smith. This brilliant formal move also strengthens the poetry making/blacksmithing analogy at the heart of the poem, suggesting that poems must be shaped and reshaped in the forge of the mind in order to gain their proper form and ring true. Some of his most memorable poems, including "The Forge" and "Requiem for the Croppies" in this volume, are cast in sonnet forms of one sort or another. Jason David Hall has argued that "the sonnet has provided a fairly fixed point of reference throughout his career," noting further that "some of Heaney's most poignant poetry, some of his most revelatory personal and cultural commentary has been expressed in sonnet form."[54]

The end of the poem features the blacksmith, whose real-life analog was Heaney's neighbor Barney Devlin, who still occasionally worked the forge at Hillhead in his nineties, going inside to the darkness "To beat real iron out, to work the bellows" (7). This last coupling of infinitive phrases suggests that the blacksmith does real work with tough metal unlike that in modern cars (the "traffic" of line 12), and moreover, that he must work the bellows to force air into the fire and make it spring to life. Those bellows, furthermore, signify the notion of artistic inspiration and subvert the Romantic idea Heaney espouses elsewhere that inspiration visits the artist only when he is in properly receptive states; instead, the blacksmith's bellows imply that inspiration itself constitutes hard work for the craftsman and poet. As he stated in 1970, "Good writing, like good smithy work, is a compound of energy and artifice."[55] Astonishingly, Heaney left "The Forge" out of his *New Selected Poems 1966–1987*, which can only be seen as a major omission because of the place it holds in his developing poetic aesthetic. It was, however, collected and reprinted in *Opened Ground*.

Door into the Dark is not framed as strongly as *Death of a Naturalist* with its powerful opening and closing poems but nevertheless conveys a strong emphasis on epistemology. It begins musingly with "Night-Piece," a slight poem that remembers the family horses stabled on the other side of the boy Heaney's bedroom wall. But its opening line, "Must you know it again?" (1), works well to establish the volume's theme of knowledge and, in particular, its acceptance, even welcoming, of the truth that not everything is knowable. He recapitulates that verb in the first line of "The Forge"—"All I know is a door into the dark"—and many of the poems reach into the darkness of buildings like "The Forge" or "Gallarus Oratory" or into the figurative darkness of ignorance to discover and recover knowledge of hidden things, variously expressed in terms of sexuality, geography, or topography. "Bogland," the volume's concluding poem, also constitutes an area of darkness, but one raised to the level of signifying Ireland's entire occluded history, buried in the depths of boggy Irish ground, yet finally "bottomless," unknowable (42). In one of the most explicit statements he ever made about his aesthetic, written in the wake of *Door into the Dark*'s publication while working on the poems of *Wintering Out*, Heaney stated, "The dark centre, the blurred and irrational storehouse of insight and instincts, the hidden core of the self—this notion is the foundation of what viewpoint I might articulate for myself . . . It is the cloud of unknowing . . ."[56]

Knowing, or not knowing, as it may be, in this volume often comes from silent watching, as in "The Forge," or quiet doing, as in "The Peninsula," one of a number of poems in Heaney's *oeuvre* in which the narrator drives. "When you have nothing more to say, just drive / For a day all round the peninsula," the poem begins, and some of the lines, even across stanzas, such as those between quatrains one and two and two and three, are enjambed to convey the sense of flow and fluidity experienced by the narrator on his drive around the peninsula with a huge sky overhead. Heaney visited the Dingle Peninsula in western County Kerry around this time and the poem that follows "The Peninsula," "In Gallarus Oratory," depicts that drystone marvel of ancient architecture that remains out on the western edge of that land. Almost exactly halfway through "The Peninsula," Heaney brings the poem to a screeching halt, employing a full stop with the phrase "you're in the dark again." Then the narrator asks himself to "recall" a series of sights and sounds from the day's drive and as he does, he drives home, "still with nothing to say," but with a resolution. He vows to "uncode all landscapes / By this: things founded clean on their own shapes, / Water and ground in their extremity" (9). Here, he casts himself as cartographer, a code-cracker, attempting to understand the oral and written histories of landscapes through getting to their elemental essence—water and ground. He will cast aside obfuscating lenses through which to perceive the landscape—such as the pastoral mode or touristic versions of Ireland that sanitize its history—and instead seek to know the very building blocks of that terrain. Many years later, Heaney would publish another poem about a westward drive as the last poem in *The Spirit Level*, "Postscript." Both poems situate the poet in motion surrounded by the elements in order to gain epistemological insights, some that cannot even be expressed.

Written in 1966, the 50th anniversary of the Easter Rising in Dublin, "Requiem for the Croppies" imagines a central scene from Irish history—the 1798 Rebellion—from the point of view of the Irish rebel forces or Croppies, so-called because of their cropped hair, which they wore short to distinguish themselves from the English aristocracy, who often had long hair. The Rebellion grew out of the United Irishmen movement that included Anglicans, Catholics, and Presbyterian Dissenters, and was led by the former Dublin lawyer Theobald Wolf Tone, the Belfast Presbyterian Henry Joy McCracken, and others. Heaney's sonnet captures the breathlessness and excitement of this rebellion for religious equality and political reform through a succession of end-stopped lines; only two lines in the entire poem are enjambed. Just as the narrator tells us on line three that "We moved quick and sudden in our own country," so too does the poem, darting, feinting, advancing (most notably in the *volta* or turn of line 9, much the longest of all the lines), and retreating. Plural pronouns, both nominative and possessive, signal the unity of the rebelling populace as "our" and "We" are used repeatedly. This accord is shown by line 4, which portrays "The priest [who] lay behind ditches with the tramp," an unlikely pairing in normal times. The Croppies or "Croppy Boys," as they were sometimes called, are shown discovering "new tactics" daily and they employ guerrilla maneuvers such as cutting the horse reins of those arrayed against them in combat, stampeding cattle, and then retreating "through hedges where cavalry must be thrown." Vastly outnumbered by British forces and facing superior technology such as cavalry and cannon, their "fatal conclave" occurred at Vinegar Hill in County Wexford on June 21, 1798, where "Terraced thousands died, shaking scythes at cannon." Divested of uniforms or advanced weaponry in life, they are similarly denied the formal trappings of funerals when "They buried us without shroud or coffin . . ." (12).

Framed by two images of barley—line 1 ends with a description of the rebels' "greatcoats" filled with the grain—the sonnet, either a variation on the English sonnet form or a hybrid of the English and Italian forms, concludes with a powerful resurrection image of grain associated with many of these former farmers who shook scythes at British guns: "And in August the barley grew up out of the grave" (12). That last line gains a cumulative force because it chimes with "conclave" and "wave" in the alternating rhyme that precedes it.[57] Heaney noted that this powerful conclusion implies that "the seeds of violent resistance sowed in the Year of Liberty [1798] had flowered in what Yeats called 'the right rose tree' of 1916," but admitted that "I did not realize at the time that the original heraldic murderous encounter between Protestant yeoman and Catholic rebel was to be initiated again in the summer of 1969, in Belfast, two months after the book was published."[58] Despite its nationalist tinge, "Requiem for the Croppies" (its original title was the more ecumenical "Requiem for the Irish Rebels") nonetheless advances a tentative hope that the unifying spirit of 1798 might obviate sectarian tensions between Catholics and Protestants in the province.[59]

One of the longest sequences in Heaney's *oeuvre*, "A Lough Neagh Sequence," displays a remarkable knowledge of the life cycle of the eel, enabling him to reclaim the title of "naturalist" he somewhat ostentatiously divested himself of in his first volume. Additionally, this sequence gathers together the themes of the sacred, the generative, and the erotic that have been accumulating in the volume and, moreover, offers another, more oblique analogy to craftsmanship and poetry. This is the first of his major poetic sequences; others would include "A Northern Hoard" from *Wintering Out*, "Glanmore Sonnets" from *Field Work*, "Station Island" from the volume of the same name, "Clearances" from *The Haw Lantern*, "Squarings" from *Seeing Things*, "Mycenae Lookout" from *The Spirit Level*, and "Route 110" from *Human Chain*. Despite some fascinating images, it has no memorable lines and is less successful than many other sequences by Heaney.

The volume's final poem "Bogland," dedicated to Heaney's painter friend T. P. Flanagan, with whom and his wife Heaney and Marie stayed at Gortahork, County Donegal, in the fall of 1968,[60] plunges deeply into this iconic symbol of Ireland. It is the culminating symbol of darkness in the volume and its depths finally cannot be plumbed, according to the poem. He wrote of "Bogland" that "I had a tentative unrealized need to make a congruence between memory and bogland and ... our national consciousness."[61] Heaney was not only recovering and appropriating the deep bog's darkness and preservative qualities over against the flat American frontier as a site of light and fluidity, but also, he was trying out the bog to determine if it could work as the site of a confluence of Irish myth and history for a potential series of successive poems that would also enable him to make comparisons between the victims of fertility rites in ancient Jutland and the new victims of sectarian violence in Northern Ireland. The pronouns of "Bogland" are confiding, insinuating, and finally suggestive of a communal identity for the Irish: "We have no prairies"; "Our unfenced country; "Our pioneers." Whereas we might expect him to associate violence with the American West, as it stereotypically is, the poet instead links violence to the bog: "the cyclops' eye / Of a tarn"; "the sights of the sun." But the bog also is an early site of the marvelous for Heaney as he lists what treasures tumble forth from it: a skeleton of the Great Irish Elk, "An astounding crate full of air"; butter that has been submerged for many years that "Was recovered salty and white" (41). If "Digging" was an apprentice poem with Heaney tentatively then confidently declaring his intention to make the pen his vocational tool, then "Bogland" implicitly returns to that metaphor, signaling he will "excavate" the buried objects and mythologies of his home ground.

Although the poem ends by speculating that "The bogholes might be Atlantic seepage," in fact subsequent bog poems would look eastward across the Irish Sea and English Channel to Scandinavia, not America—to the ancient Danes, not recent American cowboys. Heaney's hopes for the bog as potent generator of images and ideas about Ireland in the last line—"The wet centre is bottomless" (42)—would prove true in disturbing ways with the sectarian situation in the North exploding by the time the volume appeared in 1969. At the same time, he has stated that when he wrote it, "I realized that new co-ordinates had been established. Door jambs with an open sky behind them rather than the dark" (*SS* 90).

Wintering Out, a volume nearly twice as long as *Door into the Dark*, and the first of Heaney's volumes to be split into two parts, a division that would persist for *North* and some later volumes, features a series of poems celebrating the complex, potentially unifying linguistic heritage of the province, hearkening back to Gaelic, Scottish, and Elizabethan idioms still alive on the tongues of Northern inhabitants as part of Heaney's re-enchantment of the earth. At the same time, "The Tollund Man," a picture of which adorns the Faber edition of the volume, begins an exploration of dark, atavistic forces linked to fertility rites and thus moves in the opposite direction from the linguistic poems in the volume in trying to reveal the disturbing power of violent mythologies. In its linguistic emphasis, the volume enabled Heaney to delight in exploring poetry's physiological power connected both to our bodies and the earth; yet that celebration also carries with it a linguistic agenda to recover the Irish language and aspects of Gaelic culture that it tries to hold in tension with Heaney's love of the English language and aspects of its culture. As Eugene O'Brien has argued, drawing on Heidegger's *On the Way to Language*, "Poetry is the most embodied form of language," conveying meaning "in somatic bursts of description, image, and metaphor. For Heidegger, poetry prioritizes and performs 'the physical element of language, its vocal and written character,'"[62] and numerous poems in Part I of *Wintering Out* display Heaney's delight in poetry's embodiment not just of language, but of landscape too. O'Brien suggests further, "A poem is very much a moment of Heidegerrian presencing where 'body and mouth are part of the earth's flow and growth,' and where" hearing a poem "is how 'we hear the sound of language rising like the earth.'"[63] Of all Heaney's volumes, this one cries out to be read aloud to experience this bodily and earthly movement.

The title *Wintering Out* comes from an agricultural term that conveys an ability to withstand a long winter (the phrase occurs in "Servant Boy"), but he uses it metaphorically in the volume to suggest Northern Ireland's potential ability to weather the killing season of the violence that by now had exploded across the province. As he pointed out, the title

> links up with a very resonant line of English verse that every schoolboy knows: "Now is the winter of our discontent." It is meant to gesture towards the distresses that we are all undergoing in this country at the minute. It is meant to be, I suppose, comfortless enough, but with a notion of survival in it.[64]

The conflict intrudes into his dedicatory poem for two Protestant friends, David Hammond and Michael Longley, both of whom were committed, like Heaney, to helping Catholics achieve full civil rights in the province. Part of the muted hope for survival indicated in his statement above might stem from his resonant mining of its rich dialectical and linguistic ore in poems such as "Anahorish," "Gifts of Rain," "Toome," "Broagh," "The Backward Look," "Traditions," and "A New Song," which linger on the eye and tongue and thus become part of our collective memory. But his delight in their oral registers is contraposed against the disturbing written graffito he cites in the untitled dedicatory poem: "Is there a life before death? That's chalked up / on a wall downtown" (*WO* 5). The year 1972 was the worst for violence during the "Troubles": It began with Bloody Sunday on January 30, 1972 and continued with a republican reprisal on "Bloody Friday," when the IRA exploded nineteen bombs throughout Belfast on July 21, killing nine and injuring over a hundred. In such a tense atmosphere, it must surely have been tempting to write only poems about the violence, but Heaney largely resisted that temptation during 1972 with the exception of this dedicatory poem, "The Tollund Man," and a ballad remembering the victims of Bloody Sunday, "The Road to Derry," which was not published until 1997.[65]

Wintering Out would prove to be one of Heaney's most consequential volumes for his future development both because of his reclamation of a linguistic landscape in South County Derry different from "standard" English and because it features his first bog poem with a preserved body. Neil Corcoran has claimed that *Wintering Out* was the "seminal single volume of the post-1970 period of English poetry," and as Bernard O'Donoghue has pointed out, this judgment "would command a good deal of assent."[66] Corcoran argues that *Wintering Out* and later, *North*, helped introduce "a lexicon and a register of pronunciation distinct from 'received' or standard English, and in taking etymology itself as theme and preoccupation, these volumes may also be read as paradigms of the decisive shift in cultural consciousness after the 1960s." Heaney's influence has thus led to "A great deal of the most interesting poetry of those writers who began to publish after 1970" being "written as in some sense oppositional or antagonistic to an idea of a dominant cultural or political or linguistic system."[67]

I applaud this shift in cultural consciousness and detail Heaney's contribution to it extensively in my *Seamus Heaney's Regions*, yet *Wintering Out* seems to me a lesser volume in terms of quality poems than *Door into the Dark* or even *Death of a Naturalist*. The compression of *Door into the Dark* enables a deeper exploration of various forms of knowledge and darkness than does the sprawl of the later one, whose second half is largely forgettable and diminishes the pursuit of linguistic placelore in the South Derry terrain in the volume's first half. Moreover, the signature poems in *Door* outnumber those in the later volume ("The Other Side" and "The Tollund Man") by four to two.

Perhaps more important, *Door into the Dark* offers richer and more exploratory poems such as "The Forge" and "Bogland," which are superior to the linguistically driven poems in *Wintering Out* that seem somewhat more programmatic and indicative of Heaney's increased confidence.[68] Heaney has always valued the former type of poetry; in 1968, he explicitly states

> a poet proceeds by the stepping stone of the poem . . . But the final shape and direction of his work depend on the stone that he finds, the poem that he writes and not the one he meant to write. Poems and stones, unlike concrete and journalism, do not occur pre-mixed.[69]

An important element—maybe the most crucial aspect—of his early poetic, the organic, uncertain, more tentative cast of his mind gradually slips away in *Wintering Out* to be replaced by a growing sense of certainty. Even if that surer sense of poetry stems from a seminal reclamation of non-standard dialects, Heaney's ability to dwell in ambiguity has been undercut. The exception to this tendency would be "The Other Side," which concludes with the Protestant neighbor Johnny Junkin's lovely uncertainty as he wonders when would be the best time to knock at the Heaney family's door while their nightly rosary recitation proceeds. Such a drive toward confidence and certainty on the part of the poet in the midst of violent uncertainty in the province must have given him a safe harbor, as did the move to County Wicklow in 1972. But I cannot help feeling that something is lost with the transition from the exploratory darkness of the earlier volume—what Heaney has termed the "drifty, soft-edgy aspect of those quatrain poems at the end of *Door into the Dark*" and his desire to "make the line a feeler-out rather than a foot-by-foot advance" (*SS* 113)—to the poems in *Wintering Out* that retrieve Irish cultural and linguistic remnants from the ground. That exploratory quality would return in his later poetry, perhaps supremely in *Seeing Things* and *Human Chain*, where he would investigate aspects of traditional and more unorthodox spirituality.

As the conflict grew worse, Heaney reached back toward his childhood landscape again, and a series of poems in *Wintering Out* probe particular locales whose names convey something of their history. He has called these poems "etymological daydreams of sorts, playing with the fit between place and name, responses to having been born in what John Montague called the 'primal Gaeltacht'" (*SS* 124). More interestingly, if not completely convincingly, he told Dennis O'Driscoll, citing "Anahorish," "you're right to think of their energy as phonetic rather than political . . . What happened in them was a kind of meltdown of memory-stuff and Ulster myths of belonging" (125). The telling phrase here is the last one, which implies he was determined to subvert the Protestant claim of belonging in Ulster that would exclude Catholics and Irish culture from "their" province. In the language poems of *Wintering Out*, Heaney tries to walk a fine line between recovering the "hidden Ulster, the *Uladh* of *Doire Cholmcille* rather than the Londonderry of the Plantation and the Siege" (124) while not immersing himself in that retrieval of Gaelic Ulster to the neglect of his obvious indebtedness to the English language and its literature, and, moreover, not excluding that Protestant dimension to the province.

The volume's first poem, "Fodder," quickly re-pronounces its title in Heaney's local South Derry dialect: "Or, as we said, / *fother* . . ."

It is otherwise an unremarkable poem, but does signal the poet's new receptivity to retrieving his dialect in the opening image: "I open / my arms for it / again." The closing image, too, suggests that accepting and reveling in his dialect would be a "comfort": "These long nights / I would pull hay / for comfort, anything / to bed the stall" (*WO* 13). Previously, in the poem "Follower," from *Death of a Naturalist*, Heaney had written that "My father worked with a horse-plough" (*DN* 12) and later lamented that he did not keep "wrought," the dialect word for "worked," as he did in the first version of the poem. He pointed out that wrought "carried a sense of wholehearted commitment to the task" and furthermore signaled a "solidarity with speakers of the South Derry vernacular and a readiness to stand one's linguistic ground." Because he questioned his original usage of "wrought," he "displaced" himself from the "local usage" and essentially colluded with "the official linguist censor with whom another part of you is secretly in league."[70] Perhaps this regret drove Heaney to publish the straightforwardly unashamed "Fodder" in the *Times Literary Supplement*, a review that then as now occupies a central place in English literary culture.[71] O'Donoghue contends that the poem's opening "is a kind of parenthesis . . . usually found as a textual footnote . . . the invasion of the imaginative idiom by the critical is therefore a figure for the supplantation of Standard English by local usage."[72] Such a parenthetical opening sets a precedent for later place-names in the volume, whereby Heaney assumes the mantle of amateur linguist much as he did that of amateur archaeologist in some of his locally placed 1960s poems.

A richer and more suggestive poem than "Fodder," "Anahorish," gives the name of his local school on a hill immediately: "My 'place of clear water.'" The harmonious sound of this name with its "soft gradient / of consonant, vowel-meadow," implies how salutary that place was for his attempts to recover a largely vanished Gaelic civilization and tongue, as was Broagh (*WO* 16). This poem departs from a pattern whereby, as O'Donoghue points out, by the time of "The Guttural Muse," collected in *Field Work*, Heaney had established "a contrast between hard, consonantal English and soft, vocalic Irish . . ."[73] O'Donoghue is likely thinking of poems from *Wintering Out* such as "A New Song," where the Moyola River "flood[s], with vowelling embrace, / Demesnes staked out in consonants" (33). Heaney had closed his essay on Belfast with a statement that bifurcated his poetic sources into vowels and consonants: "I think of the personal and Irish pieties as vowels, and the literary awarenesses nourished on English as consonants."[74] More interestingly and less reductively here, the hill of Anahorish (the "soft gradient") flows seamlessly into the "vowel-meadow" below;

thus a soft incline of consonants complements the innocuous qualities of the flowers/vowels. Heaney recalled how his home of Mossbawn was "bordered by the townlands of Broagh and Anahorish, townlands that are forgotten Gaelic music in the throat, *bruach* and *anach fhíor uisce*, the riverbank and the place of clear water."[75] Writing poems incorporating these townland names became his way of reinscribing the Irish language and Gaelic culture into not just poetry but also into the cultural life of Northern Ireland, whose majority-Protestant culture had tended to efface, downplay, or ignore that culture. He makes clear that Gaelic civilization's "demise was effected by soldiers and administrators like [Edmund] Spenser and [John] Davies [Queen Elizabeth's Attorney-General responsible for the Plantation of Ulster in the early 1600s], whose lifeline was bitten through when the squared-off walls of bawn and demesne dropped on the country like the jaws of a man-trap."[76] By terming Anahorish "the first hill in the world," Heaney temporarily re-experiences his childhood awe at its elevation and ascribes an Edenic air to it, re-enchanting it (16).

"Broagh," like "Anahorish," immediately tells us its meaning, beginning "Riverbank, the long rigs / ending in broad docken..." It stays almost literally on the surface of the landscape whereas the preceding poem, "Toome," plumbed its depths. And while both poems retrieve a correct pronunciation of these placenames, "Broagh" attempts to unite the divided Northern Irish populace by focusing on how the word "ended almost / suddenly, like that last / *gh* the strangers found difficult to manage" (27). Given Heaney's reclamation of Irish placenames in the volumes, it is tempting to read "strangers" as Protestants the narrator might consider interlopers to a formerly Gaelic landscape and culture. But the poem suggests that locals, both Catholic and Protestant, know how to say that "gh" and thus unite in their shared pronunciation of where they live, while "the strangers" whom we might imagine to be English visitors, even perhaps British Army soldiers who had by now been stationed in Northern Ireland since late 1969, are sundered from these locals by their inability to pronounce the word.

"Traditions" both laments the virtual disappearance of the Irish language from most parts of Northern Ireland because of the "the [English] alliterative tradition" that made Irish's "uvula" become "vestigial," and somewhat reluctantly embraces "our Elizabethan English" (31) and "the furled / consonants of lowlanders / shuttling obstinately / between bawn and mossland" (32). These last speakers, the Scots-Irish who got most of the best land in the valleys of Ulster during the Elizabethan and especially Jamesian plantations of the early to mid-1600s, are characterized by their consonants and obstinacy.

The poem concludes inclusively, however, by letting James Joyce's Leopold Bloom, the Everyman Jewish hero of his 1922 novel *Ulysses*, respond to Shakespeare's Irish character MacMorris from *Henry V*, who asks, "'What ish my nation?', 'Ireland . . . / I was born here. Ireland'" (32). Admitting the wandering Jew Bloom into Ireland, Joyce insisted on a new cosmopolitanism for a country he felt was too provincial, too nationalistic, and by drawing on Bloom's "admission" to Joyce's imagined Ireland, Heaney seems to suggest that Ireland, and even by extension Northern Ireland, are plural but unifying sites of difference characterized by varying accents, languages, dialects, and nationalities. As he has pointed out about the variety of languages written in Ireland such as Latin, Old Norse, and Norman French, "Joyce's Leopold Bloom . . . takes it for granted that a person's birth in Ireland (or indeed a translator's feel for Irish poetry) is sufficient to make Ireland his or her nation." He then further privileges "Bloom's nation—'the same people living in the same place' . . ."[77] For a volume dedicated to retrieving aspects of the Irish language and Heaney's own South Country Derry dialect, "Traditions" offers an expansive linguistic and national vista. Heaney, who stated that *Ulysses* is the one book he would take if he were abandoned on a desert island, likely wanted to manipulate poetic language in the same fabulous way Joyce did in his fiction. As he said about Joyce, "The English language is opened like an accordion or a pack of cards in the hands of a magician."[78] "Traditions" thus widens the linguistic compass of the volume considerably, yet keeps it focused on affirming non-standard English and marginalized members of society.

The earlier poems that retrieve the occluded oral Irish language encoded into the local landscape are succeeded by one of Heaney's longer and better-known poems, "The Other Side," which focuses upon the oral proclamations drawn from a rich knowledge of Scripture uttered by a Protestant neighbor to the Heaney family and his tentative attempts to be neighborly to them. If he had recovered the largely lost language of a minority people in those poems, in "The Other Side," Heaney imagines what it must be like to speak in "that tongue of chosen people," a reference to his neighbor's Presbyterian belief in predestination, the Biblical principle that God chooses believers in Christ at the beginning of time (34). This man is so steeped in Scripture that it lives on his lips and enables him to make such proclamations as "'It's poor as Lazarus, that ground,'" and to issue "each patriarchal dictum: / Lazarus, the Pharaoh, Solomon // and David and Goliath," which "rolled / magnificently" off his tongue (34, 35). John Dunlop, former Moderator of the General Assembly of the Presbyterian Church in Ireland, has described the embrace of the word of God among Presbyterians, including those in Northern Ireland, as central to their belief and worship in a way that resonates with Heaney's portrayal of his childhood neighbor. Dunlop observes that "The reading and preaching of the scriptures probably occupy between one third and one half of the service," further noting, that "Protestant emphasis upon the importance of 'the Word' affects their use of language, which is sparing in its use of ambiguity ..."[79] The type of language used by Heaney's Presbyterian neighbor, whom he has identified as Johnny Junkin elsewhere (*SS* 126), is similarly dominant yet clear and it threatens to engulf the poet's family in its verbiage "like loads of hay / too big for our small lanes ..." At other times his largely Old Testament language "faltered on a rut—" as when he declaimed, "'Your side of the house, I believe, / hardly rule by the book at all'" (*WO* 35). The judicious use of the dash indicates a theological divide between such Protestants and the Catholic Heaneys: Protestants take as their authority *sola scriptura*, "scripture alone," and Catholics rely upon scripture, the writings of the Church fathers, and church tradition. While this binary happens to be the rare one with a great deal of truth to it, the man's pointing it out suggests his belief in Protestantism's superiority to Catholicism.

Such belief is undergirded by the richness of his land contrasted with "our scraggy acres," from which he habitually will turn "away // towards his promised furrows / on the hill ..." (34, 34–5). As he views daily his fertile land and utters "his fabulous, biblical dismissal" of the Heaneys' poorer ground, and by extension their Catholic faith, he finds himself continually confirmed in his belief that he and his kind are predestined to salvation. Heaney signifies Junkin's black-and-white view of the world by concluding the poem's second section with a potentially sterile description of his brain, which "was a whitewashed kitchen / hung with texts, swept tidy / as the body o' the kirk" (35). At the same time, such language pays homage to Presbyterianism's strong support of higher education and literacy and begins admitting the presence of this "tribe" into his dream vision of the province that has largely has been comprised of Irish-influenced speakers and remnants of Gaelic culture, with the exception of the more unifying conclusion of "Broagh."

Yet, surprisingly, the poem departs from what has nearly become the poet's own "dismissal" of this man and his faith—which would constitute a mirror image of the neighbor's seeming disregard for the Heaneys and their faith—in its third section. Touchingly, the narrator recalls that "sometimes when the rosary was dragging / mournfully on in the kitchen / we would hear his step round the gable," although the man would not knock "until after the litany ..." (35). He habitually pays them a visit and will wait respectfully until they finished what would have been a nightly tradition among many Catholic families in Ireland and Northern Ireland until well into the 1980s—the family recitation of the rosary. Previously having forced what the Heaney children see as "fabulous" language on them, he now deferentially listens to what must seem to him similarly fantastic language and his deference to "the other side" offers a model for defusing tension and establishing better communication between Catholics and Protestants in the North. As the poem concludes, Heaney imagines himself standing behind the neighbor "in the dark yard, in the moan of prayers," putting himself in the man's position and seeing him tap some music with his "blackthorn / shyly, as if he were party to / lovemaking or a stranger's weeping." This poem, unlike some of the more reductive language poems earlier in the volume, ends in ambiguity and questioning, Heaney's strongest posture throughout his career. He wonders if he should "slip away" or whether he should "go up and touch his shoulder / and talk about the weather // or the price of grass-seed?" (36). By putting himself in a similar position of indecision to that his neighbor often experienced when entering the Heaneys' yard when they were reciting the rosary, Heaney manages to empathize with him and return to a poetics of uncertainty.

The "price of grass-seed" seems like a throwaway detail, but it may suggest something like grassroots conversations that could augur better cultural and religious relationships in Northern Ireland, in contrast to the "last gruel of winter seeds" eaten by the titular sacrificial victim in "The Tollund Man," who was killed in an ancient fertility rite (36, 47). Heaney brilliantly juxtaposes this potentially culturally and religiously unifying ambiguity captured in the imagined conversation about weather or grass-seed prices with the cold certainties epitomized by the "winter seeds," which led to the death of the Tollund Man and that were then resulting in the widespread atrocities of "The Troubles," a conflict plumbed as well in the sequence "A Northern Hoard," which contains multiple images of wounds, burns, and violence. "The Tollund Man," however, another tripartite poem like "The Other Side," moves not toward empathy through adapting a posture of uncertainty, but instead shows what happens when deference and ambiguity are cast aside in favor of religiously sanctioned practices that stem from unassailable convictions. The Tollund Man was found in a fetal position and that posture connects this poem of the same name as its depicted victim to those earlier ones in *Door into the Dark* about pregnant mothers, although Heaney now would employ this infantile imagery to instead suggest the limitations of such constricting ideologies that sacrifice its adherents to the wishes of the community.

Beginning with the outbreak of violence in the province again in the late 1960s, he has argued that "From that moment the problems of poetry moved from being simply a matter of achieving the satisfactory verbal icon to being a search for images and symbols adequate to our predicament." Citing Shakespeare's Sonnet 65 as a question, then Yeats's "My House" from his "Meditations in Time of Civil War" as an answer, he wondered, "The question, as ever, is 'How with this rage shall beauty hold a plea?' And my answer is, by offering 'befitting emblems of adversity.'" These emblems quickly came to include the pictures of preserved bog bodies featured in Danish archaeologist P. V. Glob's *The Bog People*, which was first translated into English in 1969.[80] Heaney stated that Glob "argues convincingly that a number of these" [bodies dating back to the early Iron Age in Jutland] likely "were ritual sacrifices to the Mother Goddess, the goddess of the ground who needed new bridegrooms each winter to bed ... in her sacred place, in the bog, to ensure the renewal and fertility of the territory in the spring." He quickly associated this sacrificial rite with "the tradition of Irish political martyrdom for that cause whose icon is Kathleen Ni Houlihan," and realized how both constituted "an archetypal pattern." Moreover, the intensely visual, "unforgettable" photographs of these bodies in Glob's book "blended in my mind with photographs of atrocities, past and present, in the long rites of Irish political and religious struggles."[81] Heaney is likely still best known for his so-called "bog poems," some of which he collected in a limited volume edition published by Ted Hughes's sister Olwyn simply entitled *Bog Poems* in 1975. He himself may have been proudest of them out of all his poetry; he told Peter Fallon that no matter what his posthumous reputation would be, "At least I have the bog poems."[82]

Out of all the bog bodies Heaney saw in Glob's book and later, in person, when he toured Danish museums in 1973, he remained most drawn to the Tollund Man. "The Tollund Man" is the first of three poems about this bog body: The other two are "Tollund" from *The Spirit Level* (1996) and "The Tollund Man in Springtime" from *Electric Light* (2001). He remembered that the Tollund Man "looked like every old country man, every great uncle at home, that I had ever seen coffined, with that kind of gentleness on the face that is partly a product of rigor mortis."[83] Beyond this personal appeal, however, such bodies as the Tollund Man and the Grauballe Man "have a double force, a riddling power: on the one hand, they invite us to reverie and daydream, while on the other hand, they can tempt the intellect to its most strenuous exertions." Heaney saw the appeal of the bog body as analogous to "the work of art," because it "asks to be contemplated ..." He believed that "it enters that realm where the religious and the aesthetic merge, because in the figure of the bog body, the atrocious and the beautiful often partake of one another's reality, coexisting inextricably in the lineaments of the transformed human features." This coalescence of beauty and atrocity is potentially redemptive. At the least, "its total adequacy as an object of contemplation balances out against its status as the remains of a mutilated or violated human being."[84] His complex position here gives the lie to a reductive and simplistic claim levied against him by Ciaran Carson when the bog poems of *North* appeared: Heaney, he charged, "seems to have moved—unwillingly perhaps—from being a writer with the gift of precision, to become the laureate of violence—a mythmaker, an anthropologist of ritual killing, an apologist for 'the situation,' in the last resort, a mystifier."[85] In Heaney's hands, the very ambiguity of the bog bodies as sites where beauty and violence uncomfortably reside together shows his proper resistance to celebrating violence, yet this ambiguity also displays his recognition of violence's appeal—especially that of religious violence.

Heaney recalled that "When I wrote this poem ["The Tollund Man"], I had a completely new sensation, one of fear. It was a vow to go on pilgrimage,"[86] and indeed the poem opens with this declared desire if not the fear, while going on to suggest how the man has become regarded as a secular saint, an impulse the poet must resist. He muses, "Some day I will go to Aarhus / To see his peat-brown head, / The mild pods of his eye-lids, / His pointed skin cap" (47). Heaney's desire to employ "beauty" to "hold a plea" with "rage" clearly informs the poem. If the Tollund Man is not beautiful, he at least occupies a position of peaceful repose, characterized in part by the "mild pods of his eye-lids," in contrast to the raging ones who killed him.

It would be almost impossible not to objectify such a remarkably well-preserved body that was fascinating in its lingering humanity and Heaney strives mightily not to do so. He even seems to strip himself nearly naked in the ambiguous and elliptical second sentence of the poem, which ostensibly depicts the Tollund Man, but seems to cast himself as the subject temporarily:

In the flat country nearby
Where they dug him out,
His last gruel of winter seeds
Caked in his stomach,

Naked except for
The cap, noose and girdle,
I will stand a long time.
Bridegroom to the goddess . . .

By delaying the main clause of the sentence until the last line of the third stanza, Heaney dislocates himself, exposes himself to us, apparently standing naked "except for / The cap, noose and girdle." The syntax and punctuation of the sentence demands multiple readings of these lines and even then, readers without the benefit of Glob's picture remain at a disadvantage. Despite the full stop between "I will stand a long time." and "Bridegroom to the goddess," the last two lines of the third stanza, Heaney further creates the illusion that he is the subject and the bridegroom to the devouring goddess—not the Tollund Man. By doing so, he not only briefly opens himself to our readerly gaze, but also, even more daringly imagines himself into a position of empathy for the condemned man who was sacrificed to appease this ravenous figure and who then became part of another, hagiographic narrative, a "saint's kept body ..." (47).

He then interrupts this ancient story from Jutland with a move into contemporary Northern Ireland and then into its recent past. He briefly imagines praying "Him to make germinate // The scattered, ambushed / Flesh of labourers, / Stockinged corpses / Laid out in the farmyards," and the "Tell-tale skin and teeth / Flecking the sleepers / Of four young brothers," who were "trailed / For miles along the lines." His desire to risk blaspheming his native Catholic faith to get "Him" (presumably the Tollund Man) to seemingly revivify these contemporary corpses from the conflict in the North and those of four young Catholic men who were killed in a sectarian attack by Protestant paramilitaries in early 1920s Ireland disturbs him and us, but is consistent with other images of imagined resurrection in his poetry, such as the sprouting barley seeds at the end of "Requiem for the Croppies" (48). He has called this section of the poem—indeed the entire poem—"a prayer" that "something would come of" the "bodies of people killed in various ... atrocities in modern Ireland, in the teens and twenties ... as well as in the more recent past ... some kind of new peace or resolution." Because "in the understanding of his Iron Age contemporaries, the sacrificed body of Tollund Man germinated into spring, so the poem wants a similar flowering to come from the violence in the present."[87]

He slips into a litany in the third section, continuing to empathize with the Tollund Man as he imagines himself driving in modern-day Denmark and reciting the names of the killing sites where bog bodies have been found: "Tollund, Grabaulle, Nebelgard ..." He thus performs a Yeatsian recitation of the locations of the bog people that may be indebted to the end of his predecessor's "Easter, 1916" when he proclaims "I write it out in a verse— / MacDonagh and McBride, / And Connally, and Pearse ..."[88] But such a song of suffering is more than simply a homage to Yeats—it also affirms what Yeats privileges as the role of the poet. Yeats does not justify the violence committed by the Easter rebels against the British ("That is Heaven's part," he says), but remembers their names in a rhyming litany that inscribes them on folk memory.[89] Similarly, Heaney does not justify the violence done to these bog bodies in ancient fertility sacrifices or that visited upon contemporary citizens of Northern Ireland during its recent conflict but does claim that the poet must remember them by memorializing the sites of their untimely deaths, inscribing a *dinnseanchas* ("place-lore") of violence. The disturbing conclusion, when he imagines himself "In the old man-killing parishes" of "Jutland," where "I will feel lost, / Unhappy and at home," shocks with its combination of knowledge and disavowal of the violence (48). He has so successfully imagined himself into this landscape, into the narratives of the Tollund Man and more recent victims of sectarian violence, that he feels simultaneously lost and grounded in that terrain, unable to speak Danish but fully recognizing in the ancient remains of the bog people the influence of the similarly intimate violence he saw around him in contemporary Northern Ireland.

Part II of *Wintering Out* features a series of poems about real and imagined women, from the bride of "Wedding Day" to the mythical woman of "Maighdean Mara," but the most resonant poem from this section is the final one, "Westering," which is subtitled "In California," and clearly draws both on the year Heaney spent in Berkeley, California, from the autumn of 1970 through August of 1971, and on John Donne's poem, "Good Friday, 1613, Riding Westward." Donne's passionate poem finally desires Christ on the cross to "Burn off my rusts, and my deformity," so that the speaker has Christ's image restored in himself and will "turn my face" toward Christ.[90] Heaney's speaker, on the other hand, recalls from the vantage point of California his drive into Donegal on Good Friday and the empty, closed towns as "congregations bent / To the studded crucifix." He imagines nails dropping "out that hour" of the cross during Jesus' greatest agony and "A loosening gravity, / Christ weighing by his hands" (80). This image of Christ's open arms echoes the open arms of the speaker in the volume's first poem, "Fodder," who welcomes a remembrance of his childhood dialect, but unlike the previous two concluding poems of the first two volumes that adumbrated the themes of the succeeding volume, "Westering" does not set up the concerns of what would become the next volume, *North*. It seems to presage a new openness in Heaney, signaled in part by his farewell to observing Catholic rituals such as the Good Friday service, and a new orientation westward toward America, but upon his return to Northern Ireland in late 1971, he turned back to exploring Catholicism in Northern Ireland, most significantly through the bog poems, and his compass turned firmly northward again as the matter of the North claimed his attention in special and terrifying ways. In retrospect, he saw that "The Tollund Man" and its depiction of intimate violence transformed into leathery beauty based on Glob's archaeological study would lay the groundwork for *North*. As he articulated, "A line was crossed with 'The Tollund Man.' The minute I wrote 'Some day I will go to Aarhus' I was in a new field of force . . ." He believed "P.V. Glob's book *The Bog People* was like opening a gate, the same as when I wrote 'Bogland'" (*SS* 157).

In 1975, the same year that *North* appeared, Heaney published a chapbook of prose poems, *Stations*, and although the two are rarely considered in conjunction with each other, they should be, since both volumes deeply consider the sectarianism underlying the violence in Northern Ireland and because some of the prose poems were to have originally been part of *North* until Heaney excised them well into the composition process.[91] *Stations*, in some ways more than *North*, sets the direction for future Heaney poems, such as *Station Island*, in its emphasizing particular sites as evocative of memory and in its staging of meetings with ghosts from his past—people whose lives are recalled so deeply they seem to emerge on the page. It also meditates more directly on the violence in Northern Ireland than does Part I of *North* and even more so than Part II of that volume does. Why did Heaney turn to the prose poem at this particular time in his career? It seems likely that the extreme violence in the North and his changing attitude toward the lyric poem may have led him to experiment with the prose poem. Jonathan Monroe argues that the genre of the prose poem reminds us "by means of its self-thematizations and its foregrounding of the relationship between form and content, of ongoing antagonistic social relations and of the sociopolitical impasses and exclusionary literary (and more broadly sociolinguistic) practices that remain to be overcome."[92] Despite his new confidence in his lyric voice articulated in the language poems of *Wintering Out*, Heaney was despairing about the conflict in Northern Ireland after his family's move to County Wicklow in 1972, and he probably turned to the prose poem as a way to symbolically stage "antagonistic social relations" through a hybrid genre divided against itself like his native province was.

Moreover, he also may have wanted to formally test his newfound confidence in the lyric since the prose poem showcases "the lyric's critique of itself as the genre where the self comes into its own voice and 'sublime' isolation becomes a privileged mode of being within literature alongside the other two primary modes, drama and novel . . ."[93] As he mused in his preface to *Stations*, when he returned to the sequence in 1974 that he had first begun during his year in California, "the sectarian dimension of that pre-reflective experience presented itself as something asking to be uttered also."[94] After his well-made poetry of the 1960s, Heaney also began reading Yeats more seriously in the early 1970s and was drawn to that great poet's lyric mode because it was "a combat zone where rhymes collide and assertions strike hard music off one another," a poetry in which "Affirmation arises out of oppositions."[95] Increasingly, Heaney would begin trying to write such poetry himself.

Jason David Hall has argued in the only book-length consideration of Heaney's prosody that his 1970s poetry "exhibited a prosodic transformation," and that this change, signaled by its "give and take between arbitrary collocations of short lines and conventional quatrains, between patterns of metrical and visual organization and between open and fixed forms," is best characterized as "contrapuntal" in the way it negotiates these tensions.[96] Hall does not address the prose poems, but they too display Heaney's contrapuntal way of thinking about poetry at the time on a grander scale—not within the lyric but between genres, a formally liminal position that sprang naturally from his penchant for straddling divisions.

Heaney reproduced a number of prose poems from *Stations* both in his *New Selected Poems 1966–1987* and in his *Opened Ground: Selected Poems, 1966–1996*. He must have come to think more highly of them over time since *Opened Ground* contains nine of them, two more than does *New Selected Poems*. By placing these prose poems before the poems chosen from *North* in both of these volumes, Heaney emphasizes their divided subgenre and his firm desire to return to exploring the sectarianism of Northern Ireland through his own life, thus preparing us for the agonizing lyrics of *North* wherein he sees the bog bodies balanced between "beauty and atrocity" and himself torn between his role as public Catholic nationalist and private poet. The prose poems, by virtue of their fraught genre, thus allow him formally to stage his own self-divisions anchored in the divided landscape of his youth. The last sentence of "England's difficulty," reproduced in both these volumes of his selected poetry as "England's Difficulty," conveys a sense of the in-between position Heaney found himself in as a child that he was now turning to as a source of strength through a specific hybrid genre. He calls himself "An adept with banter," then notes, "I crossed the lines with carefully / enunciated passwords, manned every speech with checkpoints / and reported back to nobody."[97]

North is often thought of as one of Heaney's strongest volumes of poetry, yet it was also easily his most controversial with its deeply intimate exploration of violence across cultures and tribes. It received more acclaim outside of Ireland and Northern Ireland than within the island, where it was attacked by critics from the North such as Ciaran Carson and Edna Longley, and by Dublin nationalist turned unionist Conor Cruise O'Brien. Slowly, the hostility toward it may have faded. Irish playwright Frank McGuinness is probably referencing *North* when he remarked after Heaney's death that "During the darkest days of the Northern Ireland conflict he was our conscience: a conscience that was accurate and precise in how it articulated what was happening."[98] The accuracy and the precision of the diagnosis stung consciences when applied so tellingly to the conflict in the North in poems such as "Punishment" and "Strange Fruit." Yet these and other poems in the volume also court wider cultural, historical, and literary parallels than simply to Northern Ireland and that is part of their enduring quality. In retrospect, *North* is simultaneously Heaney's most personal and local volume about his native province and the moment where he declares his intention to be thought of as a world poet by his range of references transcending Ulster and the vexed and violent situation there. It concludes what can be thought of as the first phase of his career; he himself has spoken of his first four volumes as "one book."[99]

Like *Wintering Out, North* is also divided into two parts, but it is prefaced by two poems dedicated to the poet's mother, collectively entitled "Mossbawn: Two Poems in Dedication," which is composed of "I. Sunlight," and "II. The Seed Cutters." No real hint of the horrors of the bog poems that will follow emerges here, certainly not in the first poem, which surpasses all of Heaney's previous poems about the domestic women in his life—his mother Kathleen and wife Marie. "Sunlight" catches Kathleen Heaney in a series of mundane tasks and suffuses her with a golden light. Heaney would recall and reconfigure its opening line, "There was a sunlit absence" (*N* ix), again in sonnet 8 of "Clearances," written after his mother's death and collected in *The Haw Lantern*. That sonnet imagines the space, a "bright nowhere" (*HL* 32) where a chestnut tree once stood as a site suggesting the absent presence of his mother, while this earlier poem depicts her in her busy, energetic life of chores, all of which, taken together, signify for him her "love / like a tinsmith's scoop / sunk past its gleam / in the meal-bin" (*N* x). The quiet forcefulness of this glittering image builds upon the previous light imagery conveyed by the sun on the pump and the "reddening stove" that "sent its plaque of heat / against her" (ix) as she cooks. Her love is hidden, yet so deep that it is buried in the stuff of everyday sustenance for the family and indeed forms a crucial part of that sustenance. The procession of monosyllabics in the last quatrain (all but "tinsmith's") connote Kathleen Heaney's no-nonsense approach to her domestic life and imply how much she loved her oldest boy and his siblings.

"The Seed Cutters," an ekphrastic poem, draws on Breughel's painting of men cutting potatoes, much like Auden's more famous "Musée des Beaux Arts" borrows from several of that Dutch painter's and his son's works. In its nearly perfect form as a Shakespearean sonnet rhyming *ababcdcdefe1/4fgg*, it offers an ordered world that contrasts the rapacious violence predicated upon vengeance in many of the poems that follow. The seed cutters move in an age-old ritual and "With time to kill / They are taking their time." Heaney bursts into an ode-like praise in the conclusion when he exclaims, "O calendar customs!," and one senses his continued desire for such pastoral peace (xi). Yet as we know from the anti-pastoral poems in *Death of a Naturalist*, such peace can be short-lived, and in its return to associating violence and the potato, the dominant vegetable in that first volume, particularly in the Great Famine-inflected poems "At a Potato Digging" and "For the Commander of the *Eliza*," this later poem obliquely suggests that the following poems in *North* will feature subterranean historical concerns marked by conflict and that that violence, like the actions of the seed cutters, will often be conducted ritualistically. As Daniel Tobin points out in his discussion of these two prefatory poems, they "only convey the promise of peace and protection from historical terror. They are moments of respite that stand apart amid all the tragic scene, and yet they are crucial because they set that scene in relief."[100]

If Mircea Eliade's work in the *Sacred and Profane* is centrally important to appreciating Heaney's interest in situating himself repeatedly in sacred spaces in his early life and poetry, then René Girard's thinking about religion and violence is crucial to understanding Heaney's bog poems, which form the heart of *North*. There is no evidence that Heaney read Girard as he did Eliade, but Girard's work helpfully illuminates his poetry's concern with the intertwined nature of sacrifice and bloodshed. Girard, like Nietzsche, perceives conflict as the underlying condition of society, but unlike Nietzsche in *The Birth of Tragedy* and *On the Genealogy of Morals*, Girard sees Christianity as providing solutions to that violence, not itself as a form of inwardly turned conflict by slaves who rebel against human mastery.[101] For Girard, because the sacred arises from communal violence, only a robust theory of the sacred can overcome violence. Identifying the concept of the scapegoat as central to Christianity, Girard showed how a particular victim would be killed communally, thus uniting disparate people and purging them of their violence and making the scapegoat him- or herself sacred. This locally committed bloodshed constitutes a deeply intimate act, bringing murderers and their sacrificial victims into close contact, a closeness Heaney recognizes in "Funeral Rites," when he mentions the news of "each neighbourly murder" (7).

Such a process clearly underlies poems such as "Punishment," "The Grauballe Man," "Bog Queen," and "Strange Fruit," among the bog poems in *North*. These beautiful but scarred bodies or parts of bodies act as mirrors for readers whereby we are forced to examine our own predilection for conflict, even murder. The hope in the bog poems arises from our extended contemplation of these bodies, which actually have the potential to become or at least point toward the transcendence that Girard calls for: "Only the introduction of some transcendental quality that will persuade men of the fundamental difference between sacrifice and revenge, between a judicial system and vengeance, can succeed in bypassing violence."[102] Especially in "Punishment," with its hidden theory of Christ as the ultimate scapegoat, as the gift that put an end to the need for future scapegoats, a view in accordance with Girard's argument, Heaney shows how non-Christian scapegoating perpetuated violence. And yet Girard's theory crucially leaves out the concept of beauty and thus must be supplemented by our understanding of the importance of creative abundance and beauty for Heaney—sometimes in the inspiration of the poet, seen in "North" and "Exposure," other times in the way in which the bog bodies, seen in "Punishment" and "Strange Fruit," recall Christ's beauty on the cross. Through these instances of creativity and beauty, he imagines a solution to the vengeful violence then being practiced in Northern Ireland, which itself was merely the latest iteration of a seemingly interminable process.

"Funeral Rites" offers an important context for the later bog poems with its setting in the ancient "chambers of Boyne" (N 7), site of many Neolithic passage tombs in Ireland, and in imagining the repose in death of Gunnarr Hámundarson, hero of Viking myth. In the poem's opening lines, the speaker becomes a man in part by lifting his dead Catholic forebears: "I shouldered a kind of manhood, / stepping in to lift the coffins / of dead relations." All are arranged similarly, with "their dough-white hands / shackled in rosary beads," a negative image connoting Heaney's belief about Catholicism's (or any faith's) potential restricting power. The burning candles with their wax and "hovering" fire and women (6) recall the emphasis on such Catholic markers of devotion in "Poor Women in a City Church" from *Death of a Naturalist*.

It is unclear whether the speaker realizes the irony in section two of "pin[ing] for ceremony, / customary rhythms," because these rhythms of a funeral "cortège" offer no real solace and instead indicate the ongoing nature of the problem whereby communal violence, mourning, and the sacred are intertwined in Northern Ireland and elsewhere (7). The "*purring* family cars" that "nose into line" (8) in "Funeral Rites," anticipating the similarly "respectable / *Purring* of the hearse" at Louis O'Neill's funeral in "Casualty" (*FW* 23; my emphases), are imagined as simply the latest funeral procession in a process from time immemorial. Thus "the procession drags its tail / out of the Gap of the North / as its head already enters / the megalithic doorway" (*N* 8). This serpentine image of a funeral cortège hints at the immemorial nature of evil, which is replicated in the shape of the cars.

Section three injects a crucial part of Heaney's reading of long-dead bodies—their beauty—by portraying the aftermath of the funeral procession as the speaker drives "north again / past Strang and Carling fjords" (8) and imagines "those under the hill // disposed like Gunnar / who lay beautiful / inside his burial mound . . ." (8–9). As I have argued elsewhere, Heaney's revision of this myth about Gunnarr Hámundarson, who is revenged, setting in motion a series of other violent acts, suggests that the poem "can be read as an exploration into and rejection of the utter unhealthiness of funeral customs past and present, despite their promise to placate violence."[103] Gunnarr's beauty depicted here accords with Heaney's understanding of the bog bodies, which become transformed by the passage of time (and with those bodies by the bog's preservative properties) into aesthetic objects. As Grace M. Jantzen has pointed out, "Girard has virtually nothing to say about creativity or beauty," and thus a sheerly Girardian reading of the bog poems leaves out the crucial aspect of beauty so central to Heaney's thinking about these strange bodies.[104] For Jantzen in her feminist Christian reading of violence that has rich parallels with Heaney's sense of Catholic culture and Gaelic pagan culture as feminine, conflict resolution lies not in a surrogate victim, but in "creativity, desire springing from fullness rather than premised upon a lack . . ." Since "creativity bespeaks fullness that overflows, that wants to give of its resources, express itself," Heaney looks in *North* for such creativity and beauty to fill in the absence caused by violence in some key poems, including the title poem and, less explicitly, but still resonantly, "Punishment."[105]

"North," which immediately follows "Funeral Rites," offers a tentative answer—not a solution—to the ongoing problem of northern violence, instead situating the speaker as listener to the advice of the tongue of a Viking longship, which urges him to steer clear of conflict and turn inward toward his own buried treasure of the mind to create new poems and, indirectly, new ways of imagining solutions to the conflict. Most of all, rather than offering any programmatic solution to the violence, this central poem, sometimes neglected in criticism of the volume, instead offers a return to the darkness of the inner self and its abundance as sites of creative inspiration in keeping with earlier, seminal poems such as "The Forge."

As the poem opens, the speaker finds himself back on "a long strand," where he finds "only the secular / powers of the Atlantic thundering" along with the "unmagical / invitations of Iceland, / the pathetic colonies / of Greenland" (10), and his search for inspiration seems to founder. The closed first quatrain with its full stop indicates this creative blockage, but as the speaker keeps seeking, the unenchanted language at the beginning of the second quatrain abruptly gives way to something marvelous: "[S]uddenly // those fabulous raiders, / those lying in Orkney and Dublin" speak to him and the hope offered by their voices—of peace in the future and a potential for inspiration—is given in a long second sentence that does not end until the third line of the fifth stanza. Those "fabulous raiders" are battle-scarred warriors who see through the futility of war upon war and they warn the speaker against the "thick-witted couplings and revenges, // the hatreds and behindbacks" of the tribe, whose violent words and deeds ramify for ages (10–11).

Instead of urging the speaker to wallow in deceit and bloodshed, these raiders finally quietly suggest that he "'Lie down / in the word-hoard, burrow / the coil and gleam / of your furrowed brain.'" They recommend physical inactivity and digging in the rich treasure of the speaker's mind, a variation of Heaney's long-held vow to delve into the ground of his native province. More specifically, the assonantal verbs "burrow" and the adjective "furrowed" brilliantly image his mind as a field to be plowed, a preview of the next volume, *Field Work*. Their one-line command, "'Compose in darkness'" (11), returns the dark as a fecund site of creativity to a prominence in Heaney's poetry it has not held since *Door into the Dark*. It also cleverly allows him to insert himself into a long line of Irish *filí*, or ancient poets who would lie in the darkness and memorize verse.

The poem echoes the situation Heaney found himself in once he and Marie moved to County Wicklow in August of 1972. Recalling meeting the musicians Paddy Moloney and Mick and Bianca Jagger, he remembered being a bit star-struck then knowing "that a writer had to plough a different furrow from a performer." When he took his children to the local school, he enjoyed the memory of the headmaster writing "'*file*,' i.e. poet, in the column of the rollbook where he had to enter 'Occupation of Parent.' No more of your 'lecturer' or 'teacher'" (*SS* 156). "North" thus reflects Heaney's full-time commitment to being a poet after he gave up his job as lecturer at Queen's University and his realization that to do so, he must go back into the darkness of his mind for the peace and solitude necessary for writing poetry. Once there, he became inspired again, as he began to "'trust the feel of what nubbed treasure / your hands have known.'" Finally, by closing the poem with almost three full stanzas of spoken words, he privileges orality over the written word (and implicitly over the portraits of the bog bodies he explores in the bog poems) and hearkens back to that emphasis in *Wintering Out*. He is no Pollyanna: The "fabulous raiders" even tell him that he can "'Expect aurora borealis / in the long foray / but no cascade of light'" (N 11). So he reminds himself that even if he gains access to this quiet, dark site of composition, that there will be no consistently flowing creative activity—just short bursts of inspired work.

Even if poems like "North" are the minority in the volume, contrasting the many more poems exploring sectarian and ritualized violence, they nevertheless constitute an important part of Heaney's thinking about conflict because they embrace creativity as a viable alternative to that violence, a component that has always been part of his organic aesthetic. "North" thus complements the bog poems' meditations about the bodies that issued forth from the Danish bogs that are transformed into images of both beauty and atrocity and which offer art as a meditative stay against violence. It accords with Heaney's citation from Shakespeare's Sonnet 65 when the violence in Northern Ireland began again—"How with this rage shall beauty hold a plea?"—and the way in which that sonnet ends by answering that opening question and a series of others about the ravages of time: "O! none, unless this miracle have might, / That in black ink my love may still shine bright."[106] Even though he withholds Shakespeare's answer in his couplet, Heaney nevertheless suggests through this allusion to his sonnet that the miracle of writing (and love) will last even beyond the violence, and that the "might" of writing and the emblems of adversity it creates could surpass the might of violence.

Writing's survival, even flourishing, becomes a relatively hidden but important undercurrent in the volume through the title poem. Heaney insisted in his 1989 essay "The Redress of Poetry" that while poetry has significant "power as a mode of redress . . . an agent for proclaiming and correcting injustices," poets nonetheless must uphold another "imperative, namely, to redress poetry as poetry, to set it up as its own category, an eminence established and a pressure exercised by distinctly linguistic means."[107] "North" redresses poetry as poetry and so, surprisingly, does "Punishment."

In its earlier versions, "Punishment" was more hagiographic and courted more parallels with Christ in its portrayal of the bog girl as a sacrificial victim, just as the earlier drafts of "Strange Fruit" did. Both of these poems' depictions of their particular bog bodies depend on their similarities to the beauty of the crucified Christ and thus implicitly suggest that only a consideration of Christ's beauty, created by the violence visited upon him, can offer a solution to the violence then endemic in Northern Ireland. Moreover, "Punishment" also offers a hidden narrative that privileges writing itself as capable of creating a pause in the midst of potential or actual violence.

The beauty of this bog body, misidentified as the "Windeby Girl" for many years (recent analysis shows the body to be that of an undernourished boy),[108] stems from its fragility and comparison to Catholic rosary beads and to Christ on the cross. Even though the community tried to make "her" ugly by shaving her head, the speaker aestheticizes her, likening "her nipples / to amber beads," and her ribs to "frail rigging" (N 30). Her "tar-black face was beautiful." He even finds beauty that he makes art out of in her "brain's exposed / and darkened combs," and in "your muscles' webbing / and all your numbered bones . . ." (31). The intricate structure of her brain recalls "the coil and gleam" of the speaker's "furrowed brain" in "North" (11) and suggests the speaker finds beauty within her as well. Indeed, her brain is so attractive to him that it functions briefly as a retreat for him away from the public concerns of the poem and indeed the volume as a whole.

Finally, by introducing the phrase "your numbered bones" (31), Heaney references Psalm 22, some of which Christ recited on the cross. Psalm 22 begins, "My God, my God, why hast thou forsaken me?," and that forsaken, lonely quality experienced in the glare of the public eye is thus imparted to the suffering "girl" through this intertext. That solitariness as the assembled crowd in the past gazed at Christ and, by extension, to her is heightened by the specific reference to her "numbered bones" from the first part of Psalm 22: 17: "I may tell all my bones: they look and stare upon me" (KJV). And yet Christ's loneliness as he suffered also was beautiful because of his willingness to do so for believers. Although the "Windeby Girl" was surely an unwilling victim whose sacrifice only temporarily appeased her community, nonetheless the speaker burnishes her beauty by the Psalm 22 intertext. As a deeply Catholic boy and then adolescent, Heaney appreciated Christ's crucifixion as the central drama of the Church and its beauty resonated for him. Through this deeply intertextual reference to Christ's agony on the cross, then, he realizes that the girl, "My poor scapegoat" (31) is not only pitiful but a "poor" substitute for Christ, who alone offers a solution to the cycle of violence in ancient Jutland and modern-day Northern Ireland. As Girard reminds us, "If the sacrificial victim belonged to the community . . . then his death would promote further violence instead of dispelling it."[109] Jesus' position as "Other," outside the Jewish community by virtue of his divinity, enables his efficacious sacrifice, but more important, with his sacrifice, as Moshe Halbertal points out, "The offering of the son represented a nonexchangeable gift, given without a token. As such, it announced the sole exclusive sacrifice by becoming the ultimate substitute of all substitution."[110] After the gift of Christ's sacrifice, the power of scapegoating as substitution was broken.

Rand Brandes has pointed out that the original title for "Punishment" was "Shame," which has a double connotation, not only suggesting how the contemporary republican community tried to shame local Catholic women by tarring and feathering them for consorting with British soldiers but also how that community "should feel itself for its primitive, brutal behaviour." The first title courts the similarity between the sound of Heaney's first name, "Seamus," with "Shame" and suggests his closeness to both the accused women and to his native Catholic community, and this intimacy remains, even increases, despite Brandes's claim that through the course of revisions to the original poem, Heaney increased "the distance between the poet and the poem while diminishing the accusatory tone of the working title."[111] In the earliest draft of "Shame," the vast majority of the pronouns were first-person, enabling the dead bog woman to speak directly to us: "I felt the wind on my neck / My own people shaved my head / They put a stone over me."[112] Gradually, he actually increased the use of the first-person pronoun "I" from earlier drafts, but he did so by putting himself in the woman's place and referring to the woman as "her," for instance, in the final opening lines: "I can feel the tug / of the halter at the nape / of her neck . . ." (N 30). By displacing her as eyewitness to her own murder, he thus risked her voice disappearing as he spoke for her instead, a potentially presumptuous maneuver especially for a man trying to empathize with a female victim of violence visited upon her for violating a sexual taboo. Consider also a crucial passage in an early draft: "Little adulteress, we hear / that you were flaxen haired,"[113] and its published revision: "Little adulteress, before they punished you // you were flaxen-haired . . ." (30–1). And instead of "we all might cast // the stones of silence"[114] in the earlier versions, Heaney has himself alone doing so in the final version: "I almost love you / but would have cast, I know, the stones of silence" (31). Finally, he originally ended the poem by asking, "Whose righteousness is preferable? / The groomed proconsul's // civilized contempt concern / for you and yours / or the tribe's exact and intimate revenge?"[115]

In a further revision to a typescript draft after he had entitled the poem "Punishment," he added by hand: "And a third option: / to be weighed / in the careful scale / of stylists."[116] These earlier drafts wonder whether the righteousness of "the groomed" proconsul, probably standing for the British authorities in Northern Ireland at the time, or the tribe was "preferable," but the later addition about "stylists" indicates he was beginning to think more deeply about his own "righteousness" as a "civilized" poet. He makes this concern more explicit in the now well-known final version of these last stanzas: "I who have stood dumb / ... // who would connive / in civilized outrage / yet understand the exact / and tribal, intimate revenge" (31). Now he pits himself against the "tribe" and suggests neither he nor the "groomed proconsul" nor his Catholic community is righteous. The insertion of himself into this last stanza in first-person language shows that through the revision process, he actually took on more responsibility, accusing himself of not doing enough to stop such acts as the contemporary tarring and feathering of Catholic women by supporters of the Irish Republican Army.

Another indication of Heaney's increasing emphasis on suffering and responsibility as he continued to revise the poem emerges in his excisions of deeply Christian language such as referring to the body's "headband" as "a soiled halo" and a phrase about the "the birch scourge / thrown across her settled / in the posture of a palm."[117] By gradually diminishing the hagiographic and Christian diction, he made the woman less saintly yet retained her stature as a figure of conscience and increased his own potential responsibility for her death had he been alive at the time. In this way, he borrows implicitly from the Catholic penitential tradition, "scourging" himself with the addition of personal language like the increased use of first person pronouns and the closing stanzas that portray him as hapless bystander who silently would have approved the killing. Thus he partakes more fully in her suffering, almost empathizing with her and the other women elegized in the poem. He could be accused of vicarious, even self-indulgent suffering in the final version of the poem, but that risk was apparently important for him to take.

"Punishment" finally foregrounds writing itself as a narrative stay in a time of violence through recourse to a central narrative in John's Gospel. By alternating first- and third-person point of view in the first four stanzas, Heaney suggests the inadequacy of language to portray what happened to this young woman who suffered so terribly at the hands of her 'tribe'. The key phrases in this understanding of the poem are "Little adulteress" and "the stones of silence" (N 30, 31). Coming halfway through the poem, they interject another narrative into the poem—that of the woman caught in sexual sin in Chapter Eight of John's Gospel who could become a scapegoat for the community. Girard points out that "the Gospels reveal the scapegoat mechanism everywhere, even within us."[118] Heaney's phrases here call our attention to his desire for the poem itself to function as does a crucial event in John's narrative—that of Christ writing in the sand before the woman's accusers. In "The Government of the Tongue," Heaney recalls this moment from John in the context of discussing poetry's power:

In one sense the efficacy of poetry is nil—no lyric has ever stopped a tank. In another sense, it is unlimited. It is like the writing in the sand in the face of which accusers and accused are left speechless and renewed. I am thinking of Jesus' writing as it is recorded in Chapter Eight of John's Gospel . . ."[119]

When the Pharisees suggest to Jesus that the law of Moses commands that she should be stoned for adultery, he instead stoops down and writes with his finger on the ground, ignoring them. When they keep asking him, he rises and says, "He that is without sin among you, let him first cast a stone at her," and again stoops and writes on the ground again (John 8: 7, KJV). The chastened Pharisees then leave. What he writes is not important—it is the act itself that buys Jesus time to think of a response to the Pharisees' rigidity. And that time, coupled with his leveling of blame at them, at everyone really, enables her to escape stoning and be given mercy. He tells her finally he does not condemn her and to "go, and sin no more" (John 8: 11, KJV).

Heaney further argues that Jesus' writing "is like poetry, a break with the usual life but not an absconding from it. Poetry, like the writing, is arbitrary and marks time in every possible sense of that phrase." It does not offer solutions, but "in the rift between what is going to happen and whatever we would wish to happen, poetry holds attention for a space, functions not as distraction but as pure concentration, a focus where our power to concentrate is concentrated back on ourselves."[120] Because "The Government of the Tongue" is one of the most important essays in all of Heaney's criticism, it bears special significance not just for "Punishment" but for all of Heaney's poetry. Since he sees poetry in this way as "more a threshold than a path, one constantly approached and constantly departed from, at which reader and writer undergo in their different ways the experience of being at the same time summoned and released,"[121] poetry's power lies in its enabling of a liminal space, a pause in the flow of time, whereby we can judge ourselves—not others—and potentially move forward walking in righteousness and justice. Looking back on his discussion of Jesus' writing in the sand in this essay (and implicitly on its invocation in "Punishment"), Heaney argued after the peace process had begun that in "Northern Ireland, for example," he believed that "a new language would create new possibility . . . So when I invoke Jesus writing in the sand," he argued, "it's an example of this kind of diverting newness. He does something that takes the eyes away from the obsession of the moment."[122]

Thus Heaney can call into question himself being "the artful voyeur // of your brain's exposed / and darkened combs," understandably wondering whether or not he is committing a crime of sorts in addition to the original murder of this woman in the bog by making art out of her death and indirectly out of the punishment of "your betraying sisters, / cauled in tar," then-contemporary Catholic women in Northern Ireland. He has spoken of having "Christ's challenge to the men about to attack the woman taken in adultery, a challenge that is entirely apposite in the north of Ireland to-day," in the back of his mind when he wrote the poem.[123] Even as he recognizes her as "My poor scapegoat," the poem rejects the narrative of the scapegoat necessary for the tribe to reunite and have harmony. By its focus on both Christ as the only efficacious scapegoat along with the occluded narrative from John's Gospel and Heaney's vow to "connive / in civilized outrage" (31), "Punishment," like "North," offers a hidden narrative of writing as a generative answer to violence. Art is not a solution to conflict, but it is a response that will eventually enable the conditions for human flourishing, even love.

"Strange Fruit," the only other sonnet in the volume besides "The Seed Cutters," also gathers together a series of narratives about victims past and present, but it becomes a deeply ethical poem by virtue of its dense if broken sonnet form and by giving the final gaze to the girl's head, not to us readers and viewers. The many earlier drafts of this poem featured a dense intertext of Catholic devotional narratives, including the martyred Oliver Plunkett's head that is displayed in Drogheda, Ireland. The final version restricts itself, however, to an intense examination of the bog girl's head, whose murder is linked to a story by Roman historian Diodorus Siculus; two American lynchings; and to the victims of the Celts, who often severed the heads of their enemies and who reverenced the severed head in their religion. Diodorus Siculus related a narrative about a Roman soldier who was killed by Egyptians after he accidentally killed a cat, which was the animal they reverenced most. Possibly more disturbingly, he became used to such horrific violence as he confessed in his writings, and so, Heaney suggests, have we. The late addition of the title "Strange Fruit" (the preceding version was "Teté Coupée," translated as "Severed Head") links the poem instantly to American jazz singer Billie Holiday, whose version of the anti-lynching song "Strange Fruit" visualizes the bodies of black men hanging on trees after the lynching of Thomas Shipp and Abram Smith in 1930 Indiana.[124]

The poem's compression intensifies the series of images that recall a similar procession of glimpses at the bog body in "Punishment" and attempts to show how this sacrificed girl was objectified and dismembered. Composed of fourteen lines of varying lengths, "Strange Fruit" is easily the shortest bog poem; it is also by far the most mysterious, partly because of its density. Heaney likens her head to "an exhumed gourd," and characterizes it further as wrinkled like a prune and with "prune-stones for teeth." As the sonnet proceeds, its lack of rhymes emphasizes these fragmented images of the girl's head and only in the conclusion does she regain wholeness, becoming a "terrible / Beheaded girl," who then is shown "outstaring axe / And beatification, outstaring / What had begun to feel like reverence" (*N* 32). Here, the poet rejects his own hagiographic tendency to perceive the Tollund Man as "a saint's kept body" (*WO* 47)

"Strange Fruit" stands out from the other bog poems by asking the question of whether further violence is done to a body by publicly displaying it, an ethical insight signaled when the speaker states that museum workers "made an exhibition of" it and allowed the air to begin working on "her leathery beauty" (*N* 32). However, had she been simply left in the ground to merge into it, she could have become a stereotypical trope like the one of Ireland as a woman that Heaney somewhat reductively explores in other poems from *North* like "Act of Union" and "Ocean's Love to Ireland." Moreover, by viewing her head vicariously through Heaney's poem, we are likely challenged ethically for our own voyeurism and violence more than in any other bog poem.

Section I of *North* concludes with "Hercules and Antaeus," a companion poem to "Antaeus," which opens the volume proper after the two prefatory poems dedicated to Mary Heaney. Whereas "Antaeus" affirms Heaney's affinity for the earth and its comforts, the newer poem suggests that the battle of these two mythological heroes reinscribes the intimacy and persistence of Northern conflicts past and present. Here, "Antaeus, the mould-hugger, // is weaned at last" from that ground and he now experiences "a dream of loss // and origins—the cradling dark, / the river-veins, the secret gullies / of his strength . . ." (46). Antaeus's displacement by Hercules, who "lifts his arms / in a remorseless V," may signify how triumphalist, bigoted Protestants historically marginalized Catholics in the old province of Ulster and the newer state of Northern Ireland. Once displaced, Catholics' dreams of loss become "pap for the dispossessed," a resonant phrase suggesting how they and other oppressed peoples feed on their dislocation and suppression to begin a cycle of vengeance (47). Daniel Tobin compares Antaeus to Caliban, Enkidu, and Esau, as "a figure for the culturally dispossessed," arguing further that the "symmetry" of the fight between Antaeus and Hercules "effaces differences" in Girardian terms. Once the distinctiveness of the combatants and, by extension, their communities is lost, "brutality compounds brutality until individual humanity itself is lost to a tragically self-generating process of increasing violence," an ongoing cycle of violence at the heart of culture.[125] In this way, Heaney's poem recognizes the negative potential of his own propensity—and that of his Catholic community in Northern Ireland more generally—to sustain themselves on origin myths and resentment against their very real mistreatment by the dominant, Protestant British culture. In later poems, particularly "Casualty" in *Field Work*, he would reject this culture of resentment and pledge allegiance to solitude as necessary for artistic freedom and productivity.

After the intense images and feelings evoked through the bog poems and others set in Jutland and Viking Dublin in Part I of *North*, the poems of Part II are set largely in Northern Ireland and discuss much more directly the terrible ongoing legacy of sectarianism there. An exception is the prose poem "The Unacknowledged Legislator's Dream," which draws on Shelley's phrase that "Poets are the unacknowledged legislators of the World."[126] This piece may also anticipate Heaney's poem "From the Republic of Conscience," collected in *The Haw Lantern*, which more deeply examines the poet's role in the world. Here, the poet sneaks into the Bastille and is blindfolded. Later, he meets the commandant and is imprisoned.

"Whatever You Say Say Nothing" features Heaney's most direct treatment of rhetoric in the province, both the polite type that avoids discussion of the conflict except to lament it and the sectarian type that exacerbates the situation. Despite some memorable phrases, this lengthy poem suffers from its reportorial air and wallows in the binary nature of the conflict—Catholic vs. Protestant, republican vs. loyalist. Phrases like "[F]ork-tongued on the border bit" and "Northern reticence, the tight gag of place / And times" may indicate the complex reality on the ground, but do not contribute appreciably to any sort of enlightening discourse about the conflict (52, 53). The wish that "Christ, it's near time that some small leak was sprung" in this closed conversation is appealing, but the poem itself seems to admit its incapability of doing so (53). Such an admission is understandable and certainly no one expected poets—even the great ones like Heaney—at the time to solve the conflict, but the poem's flat affect and air of defeat on this matter contrasts the more complex narrative strategies of "Punishment" and "Strange Fruit," while it also lacks the ambiguities of the 1960s poems that rest in dark and doubt about creative inspiration.

Most of Part II is composed of the six poems of "Singing School," which share a common aural emphasis. The titular phrase is drawn from Yeats's "Sailing to Byzantium," where the speaker imagines going to sixth-century Byzantium as an old man to have his body burned away so he can become pure soul imaged as a golden bird. Although these poems are written by a young Heaney (he was in his mid-30s at the time), the recourse to Yeats's great poem suggests that they will relate his education—why and how he learned to become a poet, a singer of sorts. The sequence is preceded by Heaney's quotation from Wordsworth's *The Prelude* about being "Fostered alike by beauty and by fear" that was addressed earlier in this chapter in the context of several poems from *Death of a Naturalist*. Also, more intriguingly, the second epigraph for this sequence is drawn from the moment in Yeats's *Autobiographies* when he meets a stable boy with Orange (or loyalist) sympathies and wants to die "fighting the Fenians" (qtd in *N* 56). Taken together, these two epigraphs set the autobiographical context of sectarianism for the poems that follow and suggest how beauty and fear influenced the young Heaney.

In the second lyric of "A Constable Calls," for instance, a young Heaney remembers the visit of a local constable to Mossbawn to record the crops being grown there. The man's gear and bicycle connote dread in the boy's heart. Even "the 'spud' / Of the dynamo gleaming and cocked back," reminds him of a cocked and loaded gun. After watching his father make "tillage returns" in the constable's ledger, he conflates the math being worked, his earlier dread, and his current fear of the man's gun into one brief stanza: "Arithmetic and fear. / I sat staring at the polished holster / With its buttoned flap, the braid cord / Looped into the revolver butt" (60). Heaney thus resurrects that early image of the gun in "Digging"—"the squat pen rests, / snug as a gun"— here and again links it to writing, but in a much more disturbing way. The constable's revolver is an actual weapon, however, in a way that Heaney's earlier image of the pen as figurative gun in "Digging" never becomes. The revolver "squats," as it were, in the "polished holster," deadly in its beauty. So Wordsworthian beauty is incorporated into this poem but only serves to promote and heighten fear.

An earlier draft of the poem shows how much Catholics' fear of local police Heaney injected into the published poem. He not only changed the title from the benign "Tillage Records" to "A Constable Calls," which focuses the poem on the policeman's power, not the agricultural records, but also transformed the original conclusion, "His boot pushed off / And the bicycle ticked into memory,"[127] into the final ominous image implicitly comparing the ticking of the man's bike as he cycles away with the time bomb of violence that was waiting to go off in the province: "His boot pushed off / And the bicycle ticked, ticked, ticked" (61).

This ticking sound, small but distinct, is followed by the boom of the lambeg drum in the next poem, "Orange Drums, Tyrone, 1966," a poem that recalls a prose poem about Orange drumming, "July," from *Stations*, in which the Orangemen are likened to knife wielders, termed "slashers in shirt-sleeves" who "led a chosen people through their dream," after which "The air grew dark, cloud-barred, a butcher's apron."[128] The lyric, in contrast, portrays a single drummer in an Orange parade struggling to balance the drum and play it; tellingly, "He is raised up by what he buckles under." This phrase indicates both the literal weight and support of the drum and the crushing weight of the Orangemen's tradition, which they cling to for support. The drums are "like giant tumours," presumably afflicting both the hearers and the drummers—no one is spared this cancerous bigotry. This intransigence is exemplified by the drumming of the opening phrase of a common Ulster Protestant credo: "'No Pope.'" [No priest. No surrender.] The violence foreshadowed by the ticking in the final line of "A Constable Calls" now becomes fully manifest in the beating of the lambeg drum: "The air is pounding like a stethoscope" (62).

"Exposure," the last poem in both "Singing School" and in the volume, is a pivotal one for Heaney. If the opening, prefatory poems returned us to his past childhood home of Mossbawn and recall, especially in "Sunlight," the love given him by his mother, this last one situates us firmly in his present, in wintry, rainy County Wicklow, where the poet meditates upon his vocation. He depicts himself searching for inspiration toward the beginning and in the conclusion, a desire that is expressed by his use of interstellar imagery portraying a comet, falling star, and meteorite. While he wishes, "If I could come on meteorite!", he instead "walk[s] through damp leaves" and wonders "How did I end up like this?" and weighs "My responsible *tristia*." We can see his desperation through a reversion to and reversal of an important earlier image for him. Instead of the mysterious, sacred anvil of "The Forge," we have instead "the anvil brains of some who hate me" (66). When late in the poem he admits, "I am neither internee nor informer," he successfully reoccupies his most receptive poetic position of liminality. Both words carried political charges at the time. Internees were republicans who had been interned or arrested without charge and held as potential terrorists by the British Army, while "informers" were those who would have informed on republican (or loyalist) terrorist activities to the authorities. These were extremes for Heaney since he has never advocated taking up arms to support a united Ireland and has never turned against his native Catholic community. Instead, he casts himself as "a wood-kerne // Escaped from the massacre," a reference to Irish rebels in the time of Queen Elizabeth I who hid in the forests and occasionally attacked the British. Yet while this language maintains his identification with his Catholic, nationalist upbringing, he also employs it to position himself as outside the siren calls of his community, on his own.

While he has paid too much attention to "blowing up these sparks /

For their meagre heat," perhaps a reference to focusing too much on the conflict in Northern Ireland and its origins, and regrets missing "The once-in-a-lifetime portent, / The comet's pulsing rose," he nonetheless seems to hold out hope that he might once again have a chance for that brilliant inspiration. Reading this conclusion through his desire expressed earlier in "North" to compose in the dark and watch for "aurora borealis" but not for a continual inspiration, we realize that his next volume likely will attempt to maintain this posture of poetic receptivity in order to gain moments of poetic illumination.

Looking back on this pivotal moment in his life and in the "Troubles" explored through "Exposure" in his Nobel Prize speech, Heaney recalled "listening to the rain in the trees and to the news of bombings closer to home—not only those by the Provisional IRA in Belfast but equally atrocious assaults in Dublin by loyalist paramilitaries from the North . . ." What he desired then was "not quite stability but an active escape from the quicksand of relativism, a way of crediting poetry without anxiety or apology" (*CP* 14). At this time, citing several lines from "Exposure," he felt he was "Blowing up sparks for a meagre heat. Forgetting faith, straining towards good works. Attending insufficiently to the diamond absolutes, among which must be counted the sufficiency of that which is absolutely imagined" (20). He would turn anew toward crediting poetry's power through affirming the imagination in later poems, although many of these would still be colored by the ongoing conflict in the North.

It is a commonplace in Heaney criticism to claim that his poetry changed after *North*—and as we see with the Nobel Prize speech, he himself contributed to that argument—but elsewhere he insisted that:

> A new direction is being followed already in *North*, in poems like "Hercules and Antaeus" and "Exposure." The Hercules poem, for all its mythy content, is more like what Miłosz would call "plain speech in the mother tongue." And before *North* appeared, I was already writing the first of those "Glanmore Sonnets" that would only come out five years later. (*SS* 162)

These remarks suggest that although the thrust of *North* deals with sectarianism past and present, the poet was already trying to strip away his mythologizing rhetoric from a strand of his poetry that henceforth would be barer and tauter and to imagine himself unburdened of some of that cultural and religious baggage he had inherited as a member of the Catholic minority growing up in Northern Ireland. *Field Work*'s elegies employ images of closeness and friendship with victims known to Heaney, unlike the more distant bog bodies that he could not know well in *North*. A new sense of ethical commitment to his art heightened by an awareness of a spiritual order that surrounds the poet and these victims permeates *Field Work*.

Notes

1. Heaney, "Reaping in Heat," 27.
2. Ibid.
3. Heaney, "October Thought," 27.
4. Heaney, Typescript note appended to "October Thought."
5. For the best close reading of Heaney's allusive indebtedness to Hopkins across his career, see Paulin, 349–64.
6. Heaney, "Aran," 5.
7. Ibid.
8. Ibid.
9. I am modifying the original sense of McGrath's first term here. He uses "disenchantment" to refer to the post-Enlightenment mentality adopted in the West toward seeing the earth as non-sacred, a mere resource to control or exploit, while Heaney never sees it this mechanically in *Death of a Naturalist* even though he often adopts an anti-pastoral mode. As McGrath puts it, "this erosion of a sense of wonder in the presence of nature coincides with the massive degradation and exploitation of nature through human agencies . . . What once evoked a sense of awe from appreciative and respectful human beings has now been explained away, deconstructed and desacralized" (xi). "Re-enchantment" signifies for McGrath, as for Heaney, a way of recovering the land's sacredness, "recreating" it through a renewed perception: "To re-enchant nature is to accept and cherish its divine origins and signification . . ." But McGrath, as a practicing Christian, unlike the agnostic but deeply spiritual Heaney, sees nature "as a continual reminder and symbol of a future renewed creation," heaven itself (185).
10. Heaney, "The Sense of Place," 132.
11. Heaney, "Seamus Heaney Writes . . .," 1.
12. See, for example, Heaney, "Out of London: Ulster's Troubles," "Civil rights, not civic weeks," and "Old Derry's Walls." Certainly, as Michael Parker points out, positive features of Heaney's Catholicism appear in a series of poems in his first four volumes and "Catholicism permeates both his poetic consciousness" and "its burdened and burdening vocabulary." Moreover, "The highly-charged language in which the Church's teachings were couched permeate the poet's idiolect," while his "religious metaphors and allusions . . . incarnate a potency of feeling remembered and renewed" (115).
13. Heaney, *Eleven Poems*.
14. Brandes points out that in the earlier version of *Death of a Naturalist*, entitled "Advancements of Learning," the concluding poem was "'Fisher,' a poem lacking the authority of 'Personal Helicon,' one working title of which was 'Apprenticeship'—. . . a title which offered an ending to the book that was too literary" (21).

15. Frazier, 17.
16. Heaney, "Place, Pastness, Poems," 35.
17. Heaney, "Letter to Jon Stallworthy," qtd in Stallworthy, 163.
18. Qtd in Heaney, "Learning from Eliot," 36.
19. Ibid., 37.
20. Kavanagh, 282–3.
21. Heaney, "Canticles to the Earth," 190.
22. Heaney, "Feeling into Words," 41–2.
23. Heaney, "Introduction," *Beowulf*, xxiii. He goes on to cite Hopkins explicitly in this same passage. And in "Earning a Rhyme," Heaney argued that "Hopkins's innovations . . . did . . . employ an Anglo-Saxon stress . . . they went against the grain of contemporary English verse-craft in a completely salutary way, and at the same time they went with an older English grain of collective memory and belonging" (63).
24. Heaney, "Introduction," *Beowulf*, xxix.
25. Heaney, "The Indefatigable Hoof-taps: Sylvia Plath," 170.
26. The poem was likely inspired by Heaney's viewing of water divining growing up in South County Derry but there may be a literary antecedent as well. His friend the playwright Brian Friel had already published a memorable story called "The Diviner" in the *New Yorker* on March 31, 1962 (Delaney, 244). "The Diviner" was collected in Friel's second book of short stories, *The Gold in the Sea*, published in 1966. Heaney's interest in Friel's work dates back to at least 1962, when he said he bought his first collection, *The Saucer of Larks*, "soon after it came out . . ." (*SS* 177).
27. See "Turfman Piece Marks Heaney Poem."
28. In Heaney's line, "the pluck / Of water," I hear an echo of W. H. Auden's "Look, stranger, at this island now," lines 9–11: "its tall ledges / Oppose the pluck / And knock of the tide" (*Selected Poems*, 43).
29. Heaney, "The Diviner," 5. Crowder, whose study of Heaney's revisions for *Death of a Naturalist* is invaluable, suggests that Heaney "eventually saw the concept—of spring water, located in 'stations,' broadcasting and the signal being picked up by the 'aerial' (the diviner's rod)—as too contrived" (101).
30. Heaney, "The Government of the Tongue," 107.
31. Heaney, "The Indefatigable Hoof-taps," 149.
32. Heaney mused to Jeffrey Brown about "Digging" in terms suggestive of the stirring of a poem or water in "The Diviner" that "You know, I felt—when you're beginning, you're not sure. I mean, is this a poem? Or is it just a shot at a poem? Or is it kind of a dead thing? But when it comes alive in a way to feel that's your own utterance, then I think you're in business" (n.p.).
33. Heaney, "Feeling into Words," 47.
34. Ibid., 48.
35. Parker sees in this poem "significant echoes of Patrick Kavanagh's *The Great Hunger*" (69, 69–71).
36. For an authoritative discussion of these ships, see Edward Laxton.
37. See the photograph in Woodham-Smith, "After the Eviction," located between pages 288 and 289.
38. The episode in question is described in ibid., 85. Dombrain got an officer

at the Westport depot to issue meal to the starving populace there and got the captain of the British steamship *Rhadamanthus* "to take 100 tons of meal, intended for Westport, to the Coastguard Station at the Killeries," where the six men had launched their rowboat (85).
39. Parker, 56–7. Heaney writes of Roethke's "fall into manhood" in "Canticles to the Earth," 192. I found the connection to Roethke in early Heaney on my own, but was pleased to find confirmation in Parker's study.
40. Heaney, "Canticles to the Earth," 191, 192.
41. Heaney, "An Interview with Seamus Heaney [Wachtel]," 35.
42. McConnell, 454, 455.
43. John Wilson Foster, *The Achievement of Seamus Heaney*, 9.
44. Brewer and Higgins, 14. Elsewhere, Brewer and Higgins observe, "anti-Catholicism is constitutive of the identity of those who happen to be anti-Catholic . . ." (237 n.4).
45. Foster, *The Achievement of Seamus Heaney*, 9, points out that this image of the Protestant docker as a Celtic cross is either "an unwitting incongruity or misguided stroke of ecumenism."
46. "Helicon," 2a and 2b, respectively.
47. Heaney, *Opened Ground*, 15.
48. Heaney, "Seamus Heaney's 70th Birthday Speech."
49. Eliade, *Images and Symbols*, 39.
50. Heaney, "Feeling into Words," 52.
51. For a discussion of these competing two influences on the poem and indeed on much of Heaney's early aesthetic, see my essay "The Keats and Hopkins Dialectic in Seamus Heaney's Early Poetry: 'The Forge.'"
52. Heaney, "Counting to a Hundred," 168.
53. Eliade, *Images and Symbols*, 52.
54. Hall, 84.
55. Heaney, "King of the Dark," 181.
56. Ibid.
57. For the best prosodic survey of criticism on this sonnet along with a careful explication of its sonnet form in the context of British/Irish politics, see Hall, 90–5.
58. Heaney, "Feeling into Words," 56.
59. For an analysis of the poem in this context, see my *Poetry and Peace*, 191–2.
60. For a helpful discussion of Flanagan's and Heaney's joint attraction to the bog, see Parker, 87–8.
61. Heaney, "Feeling into Words," 54.
62. Eugene O'Brien, 171, citing Heidegger, *On the Way to Language*, 98.
63. Ibid., 171, quoting Heidegger, ibid., 98, 101.
64. Qtd in Corcoran, *The Poetry of Seamus Heaney*, 28. Heaney's original quotation comes in "Mother Ireland," 790.
65. For a discussion of "The Road to Derry" in the context of the conflict, see my *Poetry and Peace*, 196–201.
66. Corcoran, *English Poetry since 1940*, 182; Bernard O'Donoghue, 55.
67. Corcoran, *English Poetry since 1940*, 196, 197.
68. After writing this sentence, I was pleased to find this argument confirmed

in Bernard O'Donoghue, whose *Seamus Heaney and the Language of Poetry* remains the best and most insightful consideration of the complexities of language in Heaney: "it is in the place-name poems in *Wintering Out* that the centrality of sound analysis . . . is most programmatic" (59–60).

69. Heaney, "Writer at Work," 13.
70. Heaney, "John Clare's Prog," 63.
71. Durkan and Brandes, 306, record that "Fodder" was published on March 17, 1972 in the *TLS*.
72. Bernard O'Donoghue, 57.
73. Ibid., 47.
74. Heaney, "Belfast," 37.
75. Ibid., 36.
76. Ibid.
77. Heaney, "Preface" to *The Penguin Book of Irish Poetry*, xliii.
78. Heaney, "Seamus Heaney," *Desert Island Discs*.
79. Dunlop, 83, 97.
80. Heaney, "Feeling into Words," 56, 57.
81. Ibid., 57, for all but the last quotation, which runs over onto 58. For a critique of Heaney's reliance on photographs and pictures' tendency to make its subjects inanimate, see my *Poetry and Peace*, 218–19.
82. Fallon, "Conversation with Richard Rankin Russell."
83. Heaney, "The North: Silent Awarenesses with Seamus Heaney," 168.
84. Heaney, "The Man and the Bog," n.p.
85. Carson, 183.
86. Heaney, "Feeling into Words," 58.
87. Heaney, "The Art of Poetry," 115.
88. Yeats, 182.
89. Ibid., 181.
90. Donne, 330, 331.
91. For a discussion of this textual history, see my *Seamus Heaney's Regions*, 193–4.
92. Monroe, 12.
93. Ibid., 27.
94. Heaney, *Stations*, 3.
95. Heaney, "The Makings of a Music," 74, 78.
96. Hall, 57, 60.
97. Heaney, *Stations*, 16.
98. Qtd in Higgins and McDonald, n.p.
99. Qtd in Corcoran, *The Poetry of Seamus Heaney*, 83. Corcoran is citing Heaney's remark that "I'm certain that up to *North*, that was one book; in a way it grows together and goes together" in Heaney, "Meeting Seamus Heaney: An Interview," 64.
100. Tobin, 108.
101. My reading of Girard's theory of outwardly directed violence as inverting Nietzsche's idea of resentment arising from the enslaved who rebels against masters and does violence to himself is indebted to Scruton's argument in "The Sacred and the Human." For another reading of Heaney's *North* through Girard's theories, see O'Neill.

102. Girard, *Violence and the Sacred*, 24.
103. Russell, *Seamus Heaney's Regions*, 147.
104. Jantzen, 29.
105. Ibid., 34, 33.
106. Shakespeare, 1373.
107. Heaney, "The Redress of Poetry," 5.
108. See my discussion of this discovery in *Poetry and Peace*, 219.
109. Girard, *Violence and the Sacred*, 269.
110. Halbertal, 37.
111. Brandes, 24.
112. Heaney, "Worksheets for 'Funeral Rites,' 'Punishment,' 'Act of Union,' 'A Constable Calls,'" 9.
113. Ibid., 11.
114. Ibid., 13.
115. Ibid.
116. Ibid.
117. Ibid., 12.
118. Girard, *The Scapegoat*, 110.
119. Heaney, "The Government of the Tongue," 107.
120. Ibid., 108.
121. Ibid.
122. Heaney, "The Art of Poetry," 114.
123. Heaney, "Broadcast of *North* Poems: 6th June 1975."
124. For a detailed discussion of the poem in terms of Catholic iconography, the Diodorus Siculus narrative, lynchings, and the song "Strange Fruit," see my *Seamus Heaney's Regions*, 169–84.
125. Tobin, 109.
126. Shelley, 508.
127. Heaney, "Worksheets for 'Funeral Rites,' 'Punishment,' 'Act of Union,' 'A Constable Calls,'" 17.
128. Heaney, *Stations*, 15.

Chapter 3

Reading the Ground and the Sky: *Field Work, Station Island, The Haw Lantern*

Heaney wrote that his four years living in Glanmore, County Wicklow, from 1972 to 1976 constituted "the first time in my adult life that I had lived continuously in the countryside, and the first time that I had lived anywhere as a full time writer, uncushioned by the routine—and salary—of a teaching position."[1] That concentrated focus on his writing led him back to reflections about his poetic vocation:

> Those four years were an important growth time when I was asking myself questions about the proper function of poets and poetry and learning a new commitment to the art. Some of the elegies and dedications to artists in *Field Work*, and a number of the more domestic pieces, could not have been written without that course in the "hedge school."[2]

The last phrase connotes something outlawed, illicit. Hedge schools were held often literally between hedges for Catholic children during the Penal Law period (starting in 1695 and not fully repealed until Catholic emancipation in 1829), after their education was outlawed by the British. Heaney thus expresses his solidarity with the Catholic minority during this dark period in the Troubles through recourse to another period when they were oppressed. And yet, for his poetry to succeed, he believed he must be independent of his tribe and thus pursued solitude with his craft concurrently. His "education" about the life of a poet was conducted in secret, as it were, at this time, removed completely from the violence in the North, and thus there is also a whiff of guilt about it.

Heaney has argued that whereas his first four volumes "wanted to be texture, to be all consonants, vowels and voicings," desiring "the sheer materiality of words," by the late 1970s, "I tried very deliberately in *Field Work* to turn from a broody, phonetically self-relishing kind of writing to something closer to my own speaking voice. And I think that from *Field Work* onwards I have been following that direction."[3]

Field Work, Heaney's best single volume, was praised critically on both sides of the Atlantic, with one commentator, Holocaust survivor Terrence Des Pres, holding up Heaney's simultaneous commitment to reality and to the life of poetry over against what he saw as largely an avoidance of reality and politics in American poetry beginning during the Vietnam War. Des Pres believed that "to judge from most recent American poetry, we stick to flowers and sidestep the rage, ignoring *what we know* or turning it to metaphor merely. We presume, against experience, that poets need not be social creatures." Heaney, he argued, gives us "a poetry that allows the spirit to face and engage, and thereby transcend, or at least stand up to, the murderous pressures of our time," such that it meets our need for "imagination regaining authority" and "spirit bearing witness to its own misfortune and struggle."[4] I cite Des Pres at such length not only because his consideration of Heaney's life and work was published in the widely read and influential *Harper's Magazine*, but also because as a Holocaust survivor, he realized the need for poetry, for literature in general, to bear witness to violence and atrocity. Heaney, by this point in his career, had become sufficiently well-known in America to be looked to by its intellectuals and artists during the Cold War as an exemplary artist.

"Oysters" and Heaney's translation from Dante's *Inferno*, "Ugolino," frame *Field Work* with two very different treatments of food yoked through violence—the pleasure of eating salty oysters with friends and Count Ugolino eating Archbishop Roger's head in hell, respectively. The oysters that Heaney and his friends eat "In the cool of thatch and crockery" (almost certainly at the famous seafood restaurant Moran's on the Weir in western Ireland) are "Alive and violated" and have been "ripped and shucked and scattered." "Oysters" is composed of quintains, signaling Heaney's move away from his preferred stanza of the quatrain in much of his 1970s poetry. His anger that "my trust could not repose / In the clear light, like poetry or freedom / Leaning in from sea" leads him to eat the "day / Deliberately, that its tang / Might quicken me all into verb, pure verb" (*FW* 11). Here he displays his newly stated desire for "plain speech" that he associated with "Hercules and Antaeus" and "Exposure" by focusing on the gustatory pleasures of his mouth and tongue. The sheer pleasure of eating oysters and his wish to be quickened into "verb" also suggest his new re-commitment to the imagination.

Field Work features "The Strand at Lough Beg," "Casualty," and "The Harvest Bow," three of Heaney's best and best-known poems and the majority of this discussion of the volume focuses on these now-canonical poems. "The Strand at Lough Beg" is a Dantesque elegy for the poet's second cousin Colum Gerard McCartney who was murdered by loyalists as he drove home from a Gaelic football match in a lonely part of County Armagh. The twenty-two-year-old McCartney was "one of two Catholics each shot by the UVF [Ulster Volunteer Force] in the back of the head at Cortamlaght, Newtownhamilton, at 11.45 p.m." on August 24, 1975, as they "were returning from the Derry versus Dublin All-Ireland semi-final GAA [Gaelic Athletic Association] match at Croke Parke in Dublin ...."[5] The killers staged a fake roadblock, pretending it was operated by the Ulster Defence Regiment, as the UVF had done July 31 of that same year when it murdered members of the Miami Showband, a popular music group. Daringly, Heaney writes McCartney's death into a Northern Irish landscape already full of place-lore about the Irish mythological figure Sweeney and which is contextualized further by an epigraph from Dante's *Purgatorio*, Canto I, lines 100–2, featuring an island, a strand, and rushes, images with which Heaney memorializes and mourns his cousin in the poem. These images are admittedly poor consolation for his cousin's sudden, shocking death. As Heaney recalled, "He was a guy—just a decent, invisible life—and suddenly he was no more."[6] His elegizing impulse for his second cousin clearly sprang from a desire simply to render his ordinary "decent, invisible life" visible and therefore to privilege it as worth living.

While it pays homage to the myth of Sweeney and to Dante's *Commedia*, "The Strand at Lough Beg" also roughly adheres to the tradition of the elegy established by John Milton in his "Lycidas" (1637). Milton established in that poem the tripartite structure of the modern elegy—lament, praise, and consolation—and Heaney's poem recreates McCartney's death in the first part through an imagining of its specific circumstances, a type of lament; places him in his home ground near Lough Beg, a sort of praise for McCartney as a rural cattle man; and finally consoles us by an image of the poet reaching McCartney immediately after his death and wiping his face clean of "blood and roadside muck" with "cold handfuls of the dew" (*FW* 18). This last instance recalls the opening of the *Purgatorio* where Virgil washes Dante's face.[7]

The opening stanza imagines McCartney's journey away from the GAA match and toward home in a long sentence that connotes his loneliness and which, after eight lines, is succeeded by a series of three speculative questions about the circumstances of his murder and then a final long sentence that masquerades as a question but turns into a evocation of consoling place. The narrator asks two questions that suggest Heaney's knowledge of the loyalists' deception from newspaper descriptions of the murder: "What blazed ahead of you? A faked roadblock?", then more imaginatively posits, "The red lamp swung, the sudden brakes and stalling / Engine, voices, heads hooded and the cold-nosed gun?" (17). Already, he tries in this third question to take back the initiative seized by his cousin's murderers in painting this picture. This two-line third question doubles the length of the first two stark questions combined and through its imaginative recreation of the possible sequence of events at the roadblock slows down and orders those events semantically while McCartney must have experienced them as a single rush, much as the two lines of this question are enjambed. Heaney as elegist thus wrests control of the narration of the murder away from the murderers and even objectifies the killers who objectified his cousin. If the poem as a whole revivifies and singularizes McCartney as a human being (not simply a representation of Catholicism, slain for his religious affiliation), rendering him whole again and showing him walking his home ground near Lough Beg, this third question intriguingly dehumanizes his murderers, reducing them to "voices, heads hooded," those who wield a "red lamp" and "the cold-nosed gun."

In another compelling way too Heaney refuses to give "ground" to McCartney's killers by dwelling on the landscape of his death—the "high, bare pilgrim's track / Where Sweeney fled before the bloodied heads." Instead, "The lowland clays and waters of Lough Beg, / Church Island's spire, its soft treeline of yew" ooze into the concluding part of the poem's first section and we realize we are back on home ground—not just for McCartney but for Heaney too. He introduces this languorous landscape of consolation with an ostensible fourth question beginning "Or in your driving mirror, tailing headlights / That pulled out suddenly and flagged you down / Where you weren't known and far from what you knew ..." (17). Those three enjambed lines may reproduce something of McCartney's rushing panic in the moment he is apprehended, but Heaney abruptly stops them and cuts off his cousin's fear with a Yeatsian, visionary colon, followed by a two-line conclusion to this stanza that features liquid sounds and long vowels in his recreation of the Lough Beg landscape. In "Mossbawn," Heaney recalls "the narrow reaches of Lough Beg," in whose center "lay Church Island, a spire rising out of its yew trees, a local mecca."[8] This site was locally renowned for Saint Patrick's having "fasted and prayed there fifteen hundred years before."[9] Reading Heaney's elegy through his recollection of Lough Beg and Church Island, we realize that he is substituting a local, known, comforting pilgrimage site for another, lesser-known, and scarier site—"the high, bare pilgrim's track" of Sweeney's flight.[10] The sounds of the concluding two lines of this section about Lough Beg and Church Island comfort with their sibilance and softness and long vowels. Interestingly, Heaney is already introducing a sonic consolation into the lonely lament section treating McCartney's death.

More than anything else, "The Strand" attempts to give comfort to the memory of McCartney, to survivors, to the poet himself, even to us as readers.

This solace flooding the long, luxuriant lines about Lough Beg at the end of the first stanza contrasts the opening lines of the poem's formal, second section of praise, showing indirectly how terrified McCartney must have been at the moment of his murder, especially if he had been frightened "to find spent cartridges / Acrid, brassy, genital, ejected," when he traipsed across the strand of Lough Beg "to fetch the cows" (17). McCartney's revulsion at the "duck shooters" who had left the masculinized shotgun shells renders him a pacifist who preferred to care for his cows. Heaney links himself to McCartney by their joint shyness and lack of decisive action in this section by arguing "For you and yours and yours and mine fought shy, / Spoke an old language of conspirators / And could not crack the whip or seize the day" (17). A further, familial connection comes then through Heaney's evocation of "Big-voiced scullions," a reference to his father's Scullion uncles who were cattle dealers. He thus contrasts their loud, weighty utterances with his and McCartney's deferential talk and movements.[11]

As the poem proceeds, it edges away from those loud voices and presumably those of the murderers who slew his cousin, becoming more deferential, even reverential as it quietly meditates upon a sacred spot for both the poet and his cousin. Heaney recalls in "Mossbawn" that although he wanted to cut a yew bough from "that silent compound on Church Island" as a child, to do so "would have been a violation too treacherous to contemplate."[12] Similarly, the poem moves to create an inviolable space wherein he can "place" McCartney beyond the reach of his killers and where Heaney can console himself by tending to his cousin's wounds. This site is an intimate one, where the poet's washing of McCartney's face tenderly and intimately is silently offered as a riposte and rebuttal of sorts to his killers who intimately yet savagely murdered him.[13]

Stephen Regan has pointed out that the poem begins with "Leaving," a "verbal participle [that] presents the dead man in the physical act of driving away from his known environment," which enacts a sort of eternal farewell. Yet this third section also seems to continue indefinitely as "Across that strand of yours the cattle graze / Up to their bellies in an early mist . . ." (18).[14] It is as if the cattle will graze forever and McCartney will live on, much like Milton's dead friend Edward King, who is envisioned as being resurrected and becoming the "Genius of the shoar" in "Lycidas."[15] Here, Heaney gives McCartney back his agency by portraying his ownership of the strand on Lough Beg where his cattle used to graze, in contrast to his killers' having taken possession of the lonely spot in County Armagh where they murdered him. Gradually, the poet steps into this scene, as the second-person pronouns that have dominated the first two parts of the poem give way to first-person plural when the poet walks with his cousin—"where we work our way through squeaking sedge"—and then to first-person singular, mixed with second-person singular signifying the consoling work of the poet. Once the narrator no longer hears his cousin's footsteps "behind me," he turns "to find you on your knees / With blood and roadside muck in your hair and eyes." Heaney here gives himself the agency he has temporarily lent to the dead McCartney and "kneel[s] in front of you in brimming grass / And gather[s] up cold handfuls of the dew / To wash you, cousin" (18). And yet this is a radically equalizing maneuver, as the living poet imagines himself kneeling in front of his kneeling dead cousin, literally on his level as he ministers to him. Just as he imagines McCartney tending his cattle forever, Heaney portrays himself as washing and caring for the body of his cousin in an ongoing present that vividly conveys his grief.

The "brimming" quality of the grass, saturated as it is with dew, signifies a sort of fullness that floods the end of the poem and reinforces the habitual, seemingly eternal life of the pastoral scene on his home ground into which Heaney has inserted McCartney. In his 1990 essay on Robert Frost, "Above the Brim," Heaney commends the American poet's poem "Birches" in language that retrospectively illuminates the hopeful, consolatory conclusion of "The Strand at Lough Beg." There, he praises "the specifically upward waft of Frost's poems, and the different ways in which he releases the feeling ... of airy vernal daring, an *overbrimming* of invention and of what he once called 'supply.'"[16] Earlier in "The Strand," Heaney lamented that McCartney was killed "far from what you knew" and then launched into his first description of Lough Beg and Church Island (17). These lines uncannily and negatively replicate the passage from Frost's essay "The Figure a Poem Makes" that Heaney then cites in "Above the Brim" to anchor his reading of Frost's "upward waft": "For me the initial delight" occurs "in the surprise of remembering something *I didn't know I knew* ... There is a glad recognition of the long lost and the rest follows. Step by step the wonder of unexpected supply keeps growing."[17] Reading back onto "The Strand" through Heaney's approving citation of Frost's submission to poetry's revelations, we see how he strips clear the killing ground in Armagh of any familiar signifiers, then gradually builds the reassuring sights and sounds of County Derry and Lough Beg/Church Island into the poem as local knowledge of a familiar place floods through and finally overbrims into the hopeful, concluding aquatic images. There is, then, a sense in which Heaney's poem itself surprises him—and us—with its "wonder of unexpected supply [that] keeps growing" until the rushes in the penultimate line "shoot green again," and the poet "plait[s] / Green scapulars to wear over your shroud" (18).

Mircea Eliade reminds us that "Every creation springs from an abundance ... Creation is accomplished by a surplus of ontological substance."[18] He is speaking in the context of myths of creation and, indeed, the conclusion of "The Strand at Lough Beg" seems to become Edenic in its overflowing, super-abundant properties. Heaney assumes the role of myth-maker here, perhaps seeking to counter the murderous story McCartney's bigoted killers likely started bragging about to their friends. By washing his cousin with dew and resituating him in his home ground through the power of his imagination, Heaney resacralizes that place and by extension, the site of the murder. Such a maneuver resembles that practiced by our archaic ancestors, who believed that "A territory can be made ours only be creating it anew, that is, by consecrating it."[19] Indeed, by dwelling so much on the cattle of the Derry landscape with which he surrounds his wounded cousin, the poet temporarily lifts McCartney into the realm of Irish myth with Cuchullain and other heroes. Lest this reading seem too far-fetched, in "Mossbawn" he recounts his reading of Irish myths by stating that "Cuchullain and Ferdia also sank deep, those images of wounds bathed on the green rushes and armour clattering in the ford."[20] McCartney seems to move comfortably in such a mythic realm that includes "The Táin Bó Cúalinge," or "The Cattle War of Cooley." As Heaney bathes his cousin's wounds with green rushes, he incorporates McCartney into this heroic Irish lineage.

In this manner, the general movement from murderous despair effected by villains to living hope characterized by heroes in "The Strand at Lough Beg" resembles Heaney's further description of Frost's brimming quality:

> It is not just the sheer happiness of composition that creates a rise of poetic levels. The opposite condition, the sheer unhappiness of the uncomposed world, is even more conducive to the art of the ascending scale. When Frost comes down hard upon the facts of hurt, he still manages to end up gaining poetic altitude.[21]

Beginning in hurt and desolation, Heaney's elegy moves into comfort and community, brimming over with watery consolation after recreating the singular figure of his pacifist second cousin, who is rendered all the more human in contrast to the dehumanizing manner of his violent killers who slew him in such an isolated spot.

"The Strand at Lough Beg" exemplifies the power of elegy in Heaney's hands and sets the tone for other moving elegies in *Field Work*, including "Casualty," another poem about a quotidian figure from Heaney's childhood world, the eel fisherman Louis O'Neill. As Helen Vendler has noted of the six elegies in this volume, "Work in the field, in this sense, arises from the obligation of survivors to celebrate those who have died: with each person, the poet has had a separate relation; in each poem, an individual must be characterized and valued."[22] Vendler implies here that in each case, Heaney had to write a particular type of elegy to convey the unique qualities of victim. Thus, shorn of the mythological trappings and long, luxuriant lines that adorn the mostly tercet-driven passages in "The Strand at Lough Beg," "Casualty," in its short, terse quatrains that are far more typical of Heaney's favorite stanza form from the 1970s, nonetheless quietly insists on O'Neill's—and by extension poetry's—worth and work.[23] During the 1970s, Heaney had been "learning to relish the poetry of Andrew Marvell and Sir Thomas Wyatt, and getting a handle on poetry of plainer speech than I had dwelt with heretofore." That poetry "led me into a new appreciation of middle Yeats, of the short three-beat line and forward-driving syntax, and that paid in, in turn, to a poem like 'Casualty' in *Field Work*."[24] The plainness of utterance and "forward-driving syntax" not only pay tribute to the plain-spoken O'Neill (and implicitly to Yeats), but also likely led to its becoming one of Heaney's most anthologized poems.

I and many other critics have focused our readings on the finally transcendent qualities of this poem, but I should point out here that its title—and Heaney was always very careful about choosing his titles—is resolutely grim, which should qualify our tendency to read this outstanding poem overly optimistically. He has said explicitly that:

> When we speak of "victims" of the troubles, we should mean what we say, and be sure that we do not simply mean casualties. Casualties, as the root of the word implies, are those killed by chance, those who happen to be picked for assassination or who happen to be on the premises when the bomb explodes. Casualty is a comfortless, neuter term, acknowledging the fact of destruction and recognizing no pattern or meaning in the destruction it refers to.[25]

So with that "comfortless, neuter term" in mind that recognizes "no pattern or meaning in the destruction it refers to," we will see how Heaney subverts the typical expectations for an elegy in English yet nonetheless inscribes hope for getting beyond tribal divisions in his moving conclusion.

"Casualty" was written five years after the Bloody Sunday murders by the British Army[26] and those thirteen who died that day are commemorated in the second section of the poem, yet the poem is framed with memories of O'Neill, whose slyness, independence, deference, hard work, and silence all exemplify positive qualities for Heaney, while the funeral for the thirteen dead functions finally as a negative symbol of constraint for the nationalist and republican community. Heaney adheres to the tripartite function of the traditional elegy, but reverses the typical order of the first two movements, beginning with an extended praise section for O'Neill, then offering up a sort of lament for both the Bloody Sunday dead and, more extensively, for the eel fisherman, as he imagines him being killed. His consolation, a memory of a boat trip he took with the dead man, departs from the traditional comfort of heaven offered in many elegies and instead privileges fluidity, solitude, and independence as qualities that enable fruitful fishing and poetry making.

The brevity of lineation in "Casualty" conveys the taciturn culture of Northern Ireland that influenced both O'Neill and Heaney to privilege silence and echoes the eel fisherman's "discreet" (*FW* 21) and non-demonstrative movements when ordering a drink at Heaney's father-in-law's pub on the shores of Lough Neagh, while implicitly contrasting the emotional gestures and rhetoric that would have understandably characterized the church services in the Bogside where the Bloody Sunday funerals were held jointly. The day itself "was a day of cold / Raw silence." While Heaney attended those funerals, he criticizes the way in which "The common funeral / Unrolled its swaddling band, / Lapping, tightening / Till we were braced and bound / Like brothers in a ring" (22). He suggests that while there was comfort in such unity, the nationalist narrative and manner of mourning were also restricting, even infantilizing. In contrast, he imagines the qualities of O'Neill's funeral, which he missed, very differently: "Those quiet walkers / And sideways talkers / Shoaling out of his lane . . ." (23).

Most of the poem, then, celebrates O'Neill's independence versus "Our tribe's complicity," which the poet attempts to free himself from as the incisive lines proceed (23). O'Neill "would not be held / At home by his own crowd / Whatever threats were phoned, / Whatever black flags waved" (22). The 49-year-old O'Neill, a father of six, broke the curfew imposed by the Irish Republican Army on the nationalist and republican communities in Northern Ireland after Bloody Sunday and, finding his regular haunts closed by their nationalist owners out of respect for the dead and fear of reprisal by the IRA if they did not close, instead went to another pub, the Imperial Bar in Stewartstown, which was Catholic-owned. While the "pub was officially closed, like other bars, in mourning for those who died on Bloody Sunday," several customers slipped in through a back door to drink. Heaney gives the impression that the IRA was behind the attack as a reprisal killing for Bloody Sunday, but experts now believe that "loyalists were behind the attack" because "the incident fits the pattern of loyalist attacks in and around Co. Tyrone" where O'Neill was killed.[27]

Heaney imagines O'Neill, never named in the poem, "as he *turned* / In that bombed offending place, / Remorse fused with terror / In his still knowable face . . ." (22–3; my emphasis).[28] Earlier, in the first section, he envisions the man watching "my tentative art" with "his *turned* back" (21; my emphasis) and thus he privileges O'Neill's observant qualities even after death and at the moment of death, respectively. O'Neill functions, then, as an epistemological exemplar, a far-seeing wisdom figure who knows others more than he is known, an extension and development of the theme of knowledge that suffuses *Door into the Dark*. Heaney's attempts to elegize him are really efforts to know him better, which he achieves finally by "placing" him on his "home ground," Lough Neagh, in the third section of the poem, much as he returns Colum McCartney to his home place of Lough Beg in order to appreciate his qualities in the previous poem.

In order to accomplish this feat, Heaney recalls the hardworking, piscine qualities of O'Neill, who was "A dole-kept breadwinner / But a natural for work," one who "drank like a fish / Nightly, naturally. . ." (21, 23). This eel fisherman loved to work, losing himself in his craft in an exemplary way for the poet, but who also, on the sly, drew his welfare check. O'Neill lived for conversation and real community— not a limited one necessitated by the sectarianism driving Northern Ireland's conflict—but an open one created by the random interactions with strangers and purposeful chatter with old friends in "warm, lit-up places," where "The blurred mesh and murmur" of conversation drifted "among glasses / In the gregarious smoke" (23). Heaney implies that such a penchant for community finally "caught" O'Neill and poignantly asks, "How culpable was he / That last night when he broke / Our tribe's complicity?" (23). Certainly, on one level, the man was responsible for his own death by violating the IRA-enacted curfew, but on another level, Heaney already seems to be absolving him by his extensive praise of his independence and desire to be free from the constraining outlook and mores of the Catholic "tribe." Shortly before he died, after giving a rare public reading of "Casualty," he contrasted political movements with their necessary "solidarity" and the creative process with its essential "solitude": "There was a question in my head . . . in those days: In a crisis in your society, do you bond or do you stand clear? Political action requires bonding and solidarity; perhaps creative action requires detachment and solitude."[29]

Thus section three, which begins with O'Neill's funeral, morphs quickly into the poet's memory of a fishing trip with him on Lough Neagh, an outing that leads into this elegy's movement toward consolation. Initially, this comfort is signaled sonically, with "the habitual / Slow consolation / Of a dawdling engine," a line that first refers to the sound of the hearse's engine at O'Neill's funeral but that then is transformed into the sound of the dead man's boat engine in the lines that follow (23). Heaney articulates this consolation not in terms of a heavenly reward for the departed, as many previous elegies in the Western tradition would have done, but by offering an analogy between fishing and poetry and finally an apologia for poetry and an explanation for the conditions where it will flourish. Making poetry is like fishing, he implies: "The line lifted, hand / Over fist" (23). Poetry emerges from the hard work of putting yourself in a receptive position, like the eel fisherman did: "To get out early, haul / Steadily off the bottom, / Dispraise the catch, and smile / As you find a rhythm / Working you . . ." (24). Notice that this activity's fluidity, signified by the "purling, turning" motion of the boat rotor or "screw" (23), renovates the static, frozen quality of "turned" twice associated with O'Neill earlier in the poem. Once the fisherman or the poet occupies such a potentially fruitful position, he then must allow the rhythm to work him, becoming insouciant, receptive to the rhythm as the words and images surface. There is the "proper haunt" of the poet: "Somewhere, well out, beyond . . ." (24). Beyond the constraining bonds of the tribe, there the poet "tasted freedom with him," and there, Heaney implies, is his own, as well as O'Neill's proper place (24). The poet also retrospectively contrasts this enabling freedom with the constricted "sad freedom" of the Tollund Man he experienced in that earlier poem as he was tortured (*WO* 48). Heaney asks Louis O'Neill's ghost, whom he calls a "Dawn-sniffing revenant, / Plodder through midnight rain," to "Question me again" (*N* 24). Was O'Neill finally culpable? The answer is a quiet but firm "no." He followed his inspiration and the poet must likewise follow his muse away "beyond" the "complicity" of the tribe to have freedom and speak independently. Although Heaney does not "murmur name upon name" of the dead as Yeats does for the rebels in "Easter, 1916," he does honor the Bloody Sunday victims while rejecting a culture that would render them martyrs for the republican cause of a united Ireland.[30]

To return to the joint consideration of elegy and the connotation of the title as a "comfortless, neuter term," we can see how in its gradual movement away from the constraining nationalist narrative toward a privileging of artistic freedom, "Casualty" changes the tripartite structure of the traditional elegy by inscribing a new pattern on the chaos in Northern Ireland in the wake of the Bloody Sunday killings. That new pattern announces itself in the short terse lines of the poem, in its trimeter, and in its announcement of a new rhythm that the poet finds "Working" himself at this time, leading him away from the violence even as he elegizes the Bloody Sunday dead and O'Neill and back toward his favorite position of solitude and detachment, from which he can question established political narratives and subgenres such as the elegy. To employ the terms Heaney utilizes in his essay on Yeats and Larkin to privilege Yeats's "The Cold Heaven," the third section of his own resonantly spiritual poem "suggests that there is an overall purpose to life; and it does so by the intrinsically poetic action of its rhymes, its rhythms, and its exultant intonation." These elements "create an energy and an order which promote the idea that there exists a much greater, circumambient energy and order within which we have our being."[31] Heaney's poetry in this new phase of his career contentedly occupies this sphere of "much greater, circumambient energy and order" despite the disorder still occurring back in his native province.

While Heaney's work in the field of elegy gives much of *Field Work* its plangent, yet consolingly commemorative air, his desire to continue playing amateur archaeologist remembering the dead or vanishing crafts of his rural County Derry upbringing colors other poems such as the sonnet sequence "Glanmore Sonnets" set both in Heaney's new home of County Wicklow in and around Glanmore Cottage and in his childhood world. Such poems, along with "The Harvest Bow," continue his life-long equation of crafts, whether plaiting harvest bows or plowing, with the careful weaving and cultivation, respectively, of poetry. "Glanmore Sonnets" movingly returns the poet to his linguistic origins in a search for inspiration and then allows him to muse upon an apologia for poetry, which he proffers in "The Harvest Bow" as promoting a tentative, frail peace.

The ten "Glanmore Sonnets," offered "For Anne Saddlemyer[,] our heartiest welcomer" (*FW* 33), strikingly situate the poet in his new home at Glanmore Cottage in Wicklow and welcome his new re-commitment to the imagination as the tragic events in his native province continued unabated by the end of the 1970s. Together, they re-envision the landscape as a new site for Heaney's art, renovating the negative images of the earth as a site of resentment and violence in poems from *North*.

For instance, the first line of the first sonnet opens "Vowels ploughed into other: opened ground" as Heaney returns to the analogy expressed in "Digging" between excavating the earth and the poetic process. He employs the medial caesura effectively to convey this re-entry into agricultural and poetic delving; therefore, the colon and the space it opens signify this newly "[re-] opened ground," a resonant phrase for his entire career and the title he chose for the thirty-year gathering of his poems. "Art" is now "a paradigm of earth new from the lathe / Of ploughs." He now introduces a woodworking tool, the lathe, to compound how effectively the ploughs open the ground they cut and thus introduces another analogy for the poet—turning wood. Now, he says, "My lea is deeply tilled," and "I am quickened . . ." (33). This latter phrase indicates the poet's anticipation of a spiritual manifestation. Heaney approvingly cites Yeats's visionary poem "The Cold Heaven," including its half-line "when the ghost begins to quicken," in his essay on Yeats and Larkin, which recalls "I am quickened" here. For Heaney, because of lines like those, Yeats's poem "conveys a strong impression of direct encounter," and "The spirit still suffers from a sense of answerability, of responsibility, to a something out there, an intuited element that is as credible as the 'rook-delighting heaven' itself."[32] After waiting for a time in this first poem, Heaney's speaker experiences something like this Yeatsian vision as the points of ellipsis in the antepenultimate line of this roughly Shakespearean sonnet give way to "My ghosts [that] come striding into their spring stations" (33). This penultimate line not only suggests the movement of the remaining nine sonnets in the sequence that introduce a series of mostly childhood memories to us, but also adumbrates the concerns of his next volume, *Station Island*, particularly the ghosts that stride into his mind as the poet returns to the penitential stations on St Patrick's Purgatory. Reading back from the ethical concern for the spirit to be answerable and responsible articulated in "Joy or Night," we see how "Glanmore Sonnets" and such poems as "The Strand at Lough Beg" and "Casualty" inaugurate a new stage in Heaney's poetry where his spiritual and ethical concerns intertwine powerfully.

The second sonnet in the sequence muses on the mystery of poetic inspiration, perceiving words as living entities: "Words entering almost the sense of touch / Ferreting themselves out of their dark hutch— . . ." After the poet recalls having "landed in the hedge-school of Glanmore" he desires having a lasting voice and seemingly has found it, since this Shakespearean sonnet (unlike the first one) ends harmoniously with the traditional concluding couplet: "Vowels ploughed into other, opened ground, / Each verse returning like the plough turned round" (34). Whereas the original appearance of this penultimate line as the first line of the preceding sonnet features a colon after "other," here Heaney replaces that colon with a comma, indicating the "gap" created by that original punctuation opened a space for him to write that has been filled and now will continue to be. Moreover, the near repetition of that earlier line extends the agriculture/poetry metaphor and makes it metapoetic. In this way, the first two sonnets of the sequence are "ploughed" into each other, signifying how a significant strand of Heaney's work tills the same ground fruitfully.

Now, after having been revivified as the Edenic etymologist he wanted to be as a child in Sonnet V, the poet recovers more voices and tongues from his past in Sonnet VII, which is directly inspired by the BBC's nightly broadcast of "The Shipping News," a favorite among households in Britain even today. In "Feeling into Words," he remembers hearing words recited by his mother, "lists of affixes and suffixes, and Latin roots, with their English meanings," and sensing that words were "bearers of history and mystery" and that they "began to invite me." He speculates further that his "sense of crafting words" may also have been "stirred by the beautiful sprung rhythms of the old BBC weather forecast: Dogger, Rockall, Malin, Shetland, Faroes, Finisterre," and that these rhythms, the recitations by his mother, and those from the Catholic catechism and the litany of the Blessed Virgin together "were bedding the ear with a kind of linguistic hardcore that could be built on some day."[33] This seventh sonnet asks us to listen with him as that "linguistic hardcore" is re-broadcast, as it were, enchanting us with the possibilities of words as mysteries. It opens, "Dogger, Rockall, Malin, Irish Sea: / Green, swift upsurges, North Atlantic flux," (*FW* 39) perhaps echoing those "ocean-deafened voices warning me" from "North" (*N* 10). These voices too invite the poet to return to his harmonious origins and listen to the rhythms that originally taught him to sing. Other voices enter from the North Atlantic to replace the official BBC accent. "Sirens of the tundra, / Of eel-road, seal-road, keel-road, whale-road": these kennings, or Anglo-Saxon poetic compounds signifying the sea, blow through the poem. As the poet spies a series of French-named trawlers sheltering in Wicklow bay, he says aloud, "'A haven,'" and as he does so, speaking that word renders it "deepening, clearing, like the sky / Elsewhere on Minches, Cromarty, The Faroes" (*FW* 39). Paradoxically, these windy voices from his past themselves become a haven for him from the winds that might buffet him and distract him from his vocation as poet.

Despite all of these newfound or reclaimed images and metaphors for poetry discovered in the "Glanmore Sonnets," the poet properly feels that while he may have found inspiration again, the medium cannot be the message, to reverse Marshall McLuhan's maxim. Therefore he asks midway through Sonnet IX, "What is my apology for poetry?" (41). Poetry and its suasive words may be mysterious, but to what end? Or rather, why?

Heaney offers his apology for poetry in "The Harvest Bow," which works as a proleptic elegy for Patrick Heaney, who would die within a few years of the writing of the poem, and to suggest how art's end may be to promote peace, even though both activities are frail and faltering and beset with danger. The elder Heaney is thus another silent artisan whose work exemplifies analogies for his son's poetry. Patrick Heaney is characterized by "the mellowed silence" and by his care and attention not only for plaiting harvest bows, but also for carrying "ashplants and cane sticks," tools of his trade as a cattle dealer, and for lapping "the spurs on a lifetime of gamecocks" (58). The poem's procession of slant- and fully rhymed couplets signifies the harmony emblematized for Heaney by the harvest bow.

By touching and "finger[ing]" the harvest bow "like braille, / Gleaning the unsaid off the palpable," Heaney awakens his tactile senses so that his hands too, seemingly forever, mimic and remember his father's hand motions as he carried those ashplants and sticks and lapped those spurs. "And if I spy," he muses, "into those golden loops / I see us walk between the railway slopes / Into an evening of long grass and midges" (58). This third stanza and the next portray father and son forever walking together, "You with a harvest bow in your lapel, // Me with the fishing rod," an eternally recurring moment of togetherness symbolized by the fragile yet intricately infinite harvest bow (58). Paul Ricœur's argument about memory illuminates this moment in Heaney's poem as "a capacity, the power of remembering (*faire-mémoire*)," but "more fundamentally, a figure of care," a position in which "we hold ourselves open to the past" and "remain concerned about it."[34] The harvest bow was made "in wheat that does not rust / But brightens as it tightens twist by twist / Into a knowable corona, / A throwaway love-knot of straw" (58). By "spy[ing] into its golden loops," the poet enters an eternal past to which he remains receptive and in which he can receive a series of images presented to him as he remembers. The more he fingers and spies into that past, the more "burnished" and "warm" (*FW* 58) it becomes, a sort of rural equivalent of the "word-hoard" that has become "nubbed" by long handling in "North" (*N* 11). More important, his love for his father is also strengthened and burnished till it becomes bright and shining, a "figure of care."[35]

The most famous line in "The Harvest Bow," "*The end of art is peace*" (*FW* 58), which begins the last stanza, is a double borrowing—from Yeats, who himself quoted Coventry Patmore's original phrase. Heaney used an epigraph from Yeats's essay, "*Samhain,* 1905," for the epigraph to *Preoccupations: Selected Prose, 1968–1978*, which he published in 1980, the year after *Field Work* appeared. The end of the quotation from Yeats gave Heaney the title for this first volume of his prose and suggests that the harvest bow stands for his devotion to his craft:

"Coventry Patmore has said, 'The end of art is peace,' and the following of art is little different from the following of religion in the intense preoccupation it demands."[36] Asserting this phrase as the "motto of this frail device" (58) surprises us at the end of the poem, which has nothing to do with war generally or the conflict in Northern Ireland specifically. Terence Brown points out the complexity of the final image because of its being likened to a snare, but he concludes, "The frail device has been left 'burnished' and 'warm' by this encounter since a malign analogy is being transformed into a benign symbol of glowing life." Brown holds that "The import of the poem overall is that conflict between a father and son is capable of resolution." Furthermore, he claims "the shared domestic space that the poem occupies ('our deal dresser') can serve as a reminder of how art can carry the marks of violence, but as a part of life it can serve as an image of peace."[37] I have written elsewhere that through the harvest bow, Heaney may perhaps perceive "a time in the future when the conflict in the province might end. This peace will be prepared for by a carefully and subtly crafted art that celebrates life in all its frailty . . ." This life may be "represented by the fragile, twisted harvest bow."[38] If so, then the pursuit of peace must similarly become an intense preoccupation, yet crucially remain subservient to art.

"The Skunk" suggests Heaney's continuing interest in erotic lyrics and displays his ongoing interaction with important poetic predecessors. Here, the poet shows his indebtedness to but finally departure from one of his exemplars, Robert Lowell, whose poem "Skunk Hour" is dedicated to another Heaney exemplar, Elizabeth Bishop.[39] While Lowell's poem features a one-time encounter with a "mother skunk with her column of kittens" who "drops her ostrich tail, / and will not scare" as she eats out of the garbage,[40] Heaney's poem begins by describing the nightly visit of a regular skunk visitor whose tail is not held down but "Up, black, striped and damasked like the chasuble / At a funeral mass . . ." By stanza three, he segues into discussing his deep and growing love for his wife, mentioning the love letters he is composing again. In the last stanza, the poem circles back to its opening image, as the speaker spies her with "Your head-down, tail-up hunt in a bottom drawer / For the black plunge-line nightdress" (48). He thus replaces a malodorous animal with his erotic vision of his wife whose white "tail" is raised as she hunts for a black "nightdress." The poem thus surprises the poet and us with this unexpected vision.

"Field Work" is one of the least powerful and evocative of Heaney's title poems. The volume's real field work has already been conducted in the major poems already discussed and this sequence of four lyrics does not advance the poet's search for inspirations in a newly rediscovered landscape or improve upon his apologia for poetry articulated in "The Harvest Bow." Its real significance for the later poetry lies in its recourse to a free-ish tercet form in lyrics one and three, a form he will use often in *Station Island*. Although there is no real rhyme scheme in those poems and certainly nothing approaching the rolling but rigid rhyme scheme of Dantean *terza rima* that runs *aba bcb cdc* and so on, each of these poems does end in a final dangling line that corresponds with such a "tail" in *terza rima*.

The last poem in *Field Work*, "Ugolino," exemplifies Heaney's penchant for concluding a volume with a poem that anticipates the aims of his next volume. "Ugolino," a translation from Dante's *Inferno*, Canti XXII and XXIII, not only continues this particular narrative that began in "An Afterwards," but adumbrates the magnificent Dantean visionary poems of *Station Island*. "An Afterwards" opens with a description of a woman who "would plunge all poets in the ninth circle / And fix them, tooth in skull, tonguing for brain" (44), a macabre, literal return to the advice offered the poet by the tongue of the Viking longship in "North" who urges him to figuratively "burrow / the coil and gleam of his furrowed brain" and ignore the "hatreds and behindbacks of / the althing" (*N* 11). In "Ugolino," the poets are the backbiters, not the solitary artists, and thus, "For backbiting in life she'd make their hell / A rabid egotistical daisy-chain." Each poet is "hasped and mounted / Like Ugolino on Archbishop Roger," the image with which the poem opens (*FW* 44).

In this latter translation, the speaker "walked the ice / And saw two soldered in a frozen hole / On top of other, one's skull capping the other's," as he is "Gnawing at him where the neck and head / Are grafted to the sweet fruit of the brain, / Like a famine victim at a loaf of bread" (61). In this passage, Heaney revises his image in "An Afterwards" of the poets gnawing at each other in their egotistical throes and instead concentrates on Count Ugolino's eating of Archbishop Roger's brain, in the process briefly courting parallels with his own "Strange Fruit" (here it is "sweet fruit"), with victims of the Great Famine in 1840s Ireland, and by drawing upon the long tradition of hunger strikes in Irish history and culture, brilliantly anticipating the Irish Republican Army's hunger strike in The Maze prison in 1981. Like those portrayed in "Strange Fruit" and the other bog poems, this weird feast is a punishment, this time for Archbishop Rogers's starvation of Ugolino and his sons, the last of whom "'Drop[ped] dead'" after several days. Count Ugolino mourns his three sons' death, recalling how he was "'blinded, / For two days I groped over them and called them'" (63). But the poem does not valorize vengeance: Ugolino seems almost as punished here as Archbishop

Roger. Just as the bog poems and "Hercules and Antaeus" reject feeding upon others who have wronged us as part of a seemingly interminable cycle, so does "Ugolino."

Instead, Heaney suggests, the job of the poet is to remember the dead, murmur their names in Yeatsian fashion, and to point toward peace with his fragile art. These dead are now added to those elegized earlier in the volume—Colum McCartney, remembered in "The Strand at Lough Beg"; Sean Armstrong, a murdered social worker who sought reconciliation between Catholics and Protestants in Northern Ireland, memorialized in "A Postcard from North Antrim"; Louis O'Neill in "Casualty"; and others, such as the composer Sean O'Riada. Neil Corcoran cannily observes that "The art of the volume" involves it holding "tensely in the same balance the song of possible reconciliation and the memorial lament. If *Field World* offers comfort, it is a comfort earned well on the other side of distress."[41] Heaney would continue to lament the dead from the conflict in the North in *Station Island*, supremely so in his series of twelve meetings with ghosts from his and Ireland's past in the titular middle section, but by that volume's conclusion, he would adopt the persona of Mad Sweeney, leaping away airily from such distresses into new songs of hope and comfort.

Heaney had visited St Patrick's Purgatory three times as a teenager in the 1950s before he wrote his long, Dantean sequence featured in *Station Island*, and he even wrote an unpublished poem about the experience in 1967 entitled "Lenten Stuff," which imagines a Lenten pilgrimage to the island. That poem memorably if somewhat flatly begins, "Now I can only find myself in one place: / Low-backed island on an inland lough. / A cold chapel takes up half the island."[42] In January of 1972, he sketched a boat on the water with waves lapping and a prospective title all in capital letters: "PENAL STATIONS."[43] He had also begun reading Dante seriously beginning in the early 1970s and was increasingly taken with revenant poems in which ghosts would appear to his speakers, as we have seen in "Casualty." Moreover, he was drawn to the notion of stations—the Stations of the Cross re-enacted by believers on St Patrick's Purgatory in Lough Derg, the poet as a receiving station for images, the stations of life. Immersing oneself habitually in particular stations or stances might lead to visionary experiences. As the body retraces familiar routes and postures, the mind and spirit are freed and rendered receptive. In "Visitant" from *Stations*, a prose poem that adumbrates Heaney's repeated meetings with ghosts in *Station Island*, the speaker recalls meeting an "awkwardly smiling foreigner," a German POW who "kept treading air, as if it were a ghost with claims on us, precipitating in the heat tremor."[44] This neglected work not only anticipates Heaney's desire to cast himself into visionary states to meet ghosts from his and Ireland's past, but also, it suggests that such specters have "claims on us" and in *Station Island*, the poet must respond to a series of such claims advanced by the spirits he meets, in the process attempting to justify his art in a time of violence.

Commentators on the poem generally neglect the sectarian connotations of the Lough Derg/Pettigo nexus, preferring instead to focus on the pilgrimage's Catholic purgation rites, but Heaney would have been aware of the area's sectarian divisions and likely found it a fitting site in which to situate his long title sequence and contemplate several atrocities in Northern Ireland. St Patrick's Purgatory is reached by boat from the village of Pettigo, which was established in the early seventeenth century as part of the English Plantation. The pilgrimage site, one of the major Catholic ones in the world, thus sits uneasily beside this Protestant village, long known as "Protestant Pettigo," on the border of Ireland and Northern Ireland. Not long after Pettigo was established around 1610, "a new, more strident and powerful Protestantism began to harass Lough Derg," as one commentator observes.[45] Pilgrims to Station Island were driven out by local Protestants, local boatmen were ordered to not take pilgrims to the island, and finally, the buildings on the islands and the penitential beds were destroyed in October of 1632. Protestants feared the annual influx of Catholics on pilgrimage to an area they were trying to Anglicize religiously and culturally and reacted accordingly. Pettigo was also a contested site in the process of the partitioning of the new Irish Free State and Northern Ireland in 1921. British forces captured the then sixty percent Protestant town from republican fighters that year and Pettigo was briefly part of the new Northern Irish state, before being returned to County Donegal since it was of no strategic importance for the British, thus becoming part of the Free State. The history of the area in and around Pettigo and Lough Derg had been conflicted for over 370 years when Heaney began writing about it and that history suggests its appropriateness as a site where he might entertain ghosts, some of whom were assassinated for sectarian reasons in recent Northern Irish history.[46]

He wrote in his essay on Dante, "What I first loved in the *Commedia* was the local intensity, the vehemence and fondness attaching to individual shades, the way personalities and values were emotionally soldered together . . ." He also enjoyed the "strong strain of what has been called personal realism in the celebration of bonds of friendship and bonds of enmity."[47] The intimacy and intensity of such encounters with specific ghosts past in Dante's great epic likely reminded him of the similar blend of these emotions that often featured in murders committed during the

Northern Irish Troubles. Although it was not his motivating factor for reading Dante, Heaney pointed out that he

> was exhilarated to read Dante in translation in the Seventies, because I recognized some of the conditions of Medieval Florence—the intensities, the factions, the personalities—as analogous to the Belfast situation. Farinata rising out of the tomb could be Paisley. The combination of personality, political fury, psychological realism. All the voices speaking, and the accusations flying, the rage and the intimacy of *The Inferno*.[48]

Moreover, he noted that Dante's *Commedia* gave his "Irish Catholic subculture ... high cultural ratification" (*SS* 472). Just as Patrick Kavanagh had ratified that subculture toward the beginning of his poetic career, now the greatest Catholic writer of all time served to endorse it even though "I was worried ... by the pastiche element, writing a poem so obviously an echo of *The Divine Comedy* ..." He believed that "one antidote to that was to make it very plain in its diction, and entirely matter-of-fact in its narrative."[49]

A series of writers had set poems on St Patrick's Purgatory, including the author of the medieval Irish epic, *Truagh Mo Thuras Go Loch Dearg* ("Vain My Journey to Lough Derg"), William Carleton, Patrick Kavanagh, Denis Devlin, and Sean O'Faolain, and thus Heaney had to not only acknowledge the literary tradition that had built up around the island and its pilgrimage but also to contribute something new to that tradition. As Peggy O'Brien points out, his poem is the first treatment of Lough Derg in literature since "Vain My Journey to Lough Derg" to "focus on the condition of the individual soul."[50] Heaney succeeds brilliantly, partly because of his chosen stanza form of unrhymed, slant rhyme, and occasionally rhyming tercets, his own modification of Dante's *terza rima*. By looking more to Dante's *Divine Comedy* than the Irish literary tradition about Lough Derg for his volume's stanza form and tripartite structure, roughly corresponding to the Italian's *Inferno*, *Purgatorio*, and *Paradiso*, Heaney lifts the site into a universal realm even as he writes about intensely local ghosts, literary and ordinary, bracketing his ghostly meetings by opening with a series of poems shot through with mythological and scriptural connotations focusing on the human soul and concluding with ethereal poems from the point of view of the flitting, tree-hopping Sweeney.

In a diary entry from September 4, 1979, Heaney wrote evocatively about his plans for his new volume:

> On Saturday in Barrie Cooke's, I began what I hope will be a large undertaking, the poem I have been thinking about set on Lough Derg—a big open form that will turn like a wheel—one of those wheels laden with water scoops that go down empty and come up full.[51]

This striking image elaborates and expands on that of the well in "Personal Helicon"; it thus represents another return to the subterranean impulses of the 1960s poetry but with a deeply spiritual cast. After some discouragement in trying to write this central sequence the previous year, he mused in his diary on December 14, 1981, "As I meet people on the island, what am I doing? Re-entering the whirlpool. Finding out what I embraced, what embraced me, so that I can divest it and be divested of it." Again employing an image connoting a downward trajectory, he mused, "The overall action is one of descending into the belly of the affections, back to the womb life of church and community, the better to know and clear it." He finally writes that he is striving "towards an ideal that is bhuddist [sic] in its paradox of attachment and detachment," noting "The freedom is spiritual" and that "Against the pull of the smothering sensuous material there must run the push of hope and search for a personal renewal and redemption. The personal freeing of the artist/self is the boon. Joyce tells this at the end."[52] Once again, and even more deliberately than he had in *North* or *Field Work*, Heaney seeks in *Station Island*, particularly its middle section, to re-enter the "smothering sensuous material" of his past and break free from those swaddling bands into a place "somewhere, well out, alone" as he felt he had at the end of "Casualty." His character James Joyce thus invites him into another such watery space of freedom and independence at the end of this long titular sequence of twelve lyrics.

Heaney dedicated *Station Island* to his good friend, playwright and short story writer Brian Friel, with whom he was by then serving on the board of directors for the Field Day Theatre Company, whose aim was to create a sort of fifth province for the island of Ireland, a salubrious artistic place that might speak truth to the impasse of the Troubles and its associated binaries. As Heaney himself put it, "We supposed our function to be analogous to the shifting possibilities represented not by synods or assemblies but by symbol . . ." Also, "we invoked the idea of the imaginary centre, the mystic fifth province which was a . . . fiction capable of the gaining the loyalty of political factions."[53] There is a sense in which the volume's famous central section itself becomes that fifth province, located near the border of Ireland and Northern Ireland, at the mythical entrance to purgatory, a place in between heaven and hell. In this space, he interrogates sectarianism in the North as well as his own poetic vocation, attempting, as Seamus Deane argued in the early 1980s about him and other poets from the North such as Derek Mahon, to "come to grips with destructive energies," and thus to "demonstrate a way of turning them towards creativity."[54] This analysis of the volume draws upon the opening and concluding sections, but focuses mainly where Heaney himself and the vast majority of criticism have—on the title section.

The first part, simply entitled "Part One," which loosely corresponds to Dante's descent into the underworld in "The Inferno," opens not with the poet "In the middle of the journey of our life / [in which] I found myself astray in a dark wood / where the straight road had been lost sight of" in his own translation from the opening Canto of *The Inferno*, but in a London Tube station on "The Underground."⁵⁵ This poem was one of two Heaney chose to represent his lifetime achievement in poetry for the David Cohen Prize and he recalled the circumstances of the poem upon receiving the prize:

> Marie and I were then on our honeymoon and as well as calling with my editor in Russell Square, we went to a Promenade concert in the Albert Hall, by the underground, of course, Marie in her white going away coat that had received a beetroot stain in the Museum Tavern the night before, both of us late and running down the corridor.

Heaney told guests he was reading it "in gratitude for all that London and the people I have known in London have given by way of literary inspiration and confirmation."⁵⁶ The London emphasis startles because of the volume's Irish setting on Lough Derg in the middle section, but its choice suggests Heaney's continuing connection to Britain and specifically to London literary life long after he left Northern Ireland for the Republic of Ireland.

He imbues "The Underground" with an added mythical dimension beyond its Dantean context in the poet's likening himself to Orpheus "—a fleet god gaining / Upon you before you turned to a reed—" and Marie to Eurydice from Ovid's *Metamorphoses*. Heaney also posits himself as Hansel "Retracing the path back" from the children's fairy story "Hansel and Gretel." As the poem concludes, he casts himself as "all attention / For your step following and damned if I look back," another reference to the Orpheus/Eurydice myth (*SI* 13). "The Underground" thus works finally as another love poem to the poet's wife Marie. We may get some additional sense of the depth of their loving relationship in Heaney's 1993 translation "Orpheus and Eurydice" when Orpheus does look back and loses Eurydice a second time: "She died again, / Bridal and doomed, but still did not complain / Against her husband—as indeed how could she / Complain about being loved so totally?"⁵⁷

"A Kite for Michael and Christopher" became one of Heaney's most winsome and personal poems because of its vivid recollection of a time with his young sons flying a kite they had made together and the way in which that kite comes to symbolize both hope and grief. He likens the kite to "the soul at anchor there," and concludes by desiring his boys to take the line in their hands before the kite falls and "feel / the strumming, rooted, long-tailed pull of grief." He wants them to "Stand in here in front of me / and take the strain" (44). Here, Heaney portrays himself as giving his sons their human birthright of suffering in the form of a child's plaything, a necessary move on a father's part as he initiates his sons into life's travails. And yet that kite still soars and points toward a soul-life beyond us.

Despite the underground, hellish Dantean context of this section, many of the poems express this desire for spiritual ascent, as in the end of "The Railway Children," in which Heaney recalls his and likely his brothers' and sisters' viewing of the "telegraph poles and the sizzling wires" from the top of a railway cutting and seeing themselves "So infinitesimally scaled // We could stream through the eye of a needle" (45). This introduction of Christ's proclamation in Matthew 19: 24—"And again I say unto you, 'It is easier for a camel to go through the eye of a needle, than for a rich man to enter into the Kingdom of God'" (KJV)—makes the railway children of Heaney's memory temporary "camels" who bulk large but who are rendered small by the vastness of the landscape and skyscape.

Heaney returns to this same passage in the concluding poetic sequence of Part One, "The King of the Ditchbacks," dedicated to the older poet John Montague, born in America, but who grew up in County Tyrone, Northern Ireland, and whose exploration of the sectarian histories of the North of Ireland in *The Rough Field* (1972) and other volumes inspired the younger poet. As the speaker takes on a sort of headdress of fishnet stuck through with "leafy twigs" (57) and becomes "King of the ditchbacks," an outlaw roaming the margins of a "pigeon wood," he sees himself as "top-knotted, masked in sheaves," a harvest figure, and as "a rich young man // leaving everything he had / for a migrant solitude" (58). Now "stripped" of the weighing objects and burdens he has taken up in his past and in this first section, the poet-speaker is prepared to undergo the "migrant solitude" of a pilgrimage on Station Island, the purgatorial setting of Part Two.

"Station Island," running around thirty-five published pages, is divided into twelve parts in which the poet meets ghosts and attempts to discern from these encounters his vocation. It employs quintets, tercets, and a variety of other stanza lengths, but its turn in seminal poems to the tercet suggests not only how Heaney pays homage to Dante's great *Divine Comedy*, but also how at the level of form he was working out his new poetic that would be more attuned than ever to spiritual concerns.

By roughly following the Stations of the Cross with some significant departures (he meets William Carleton while he is parked beside a road and James Joyce as he disembarks from the ferry at the parking lot after the pilgrimage), Heaney humbles himself, becoming receptive to the visions about which he writes. He suggested in an essay published in 1984, the same year as this volume, that "The poet is stretched between politics and transcendence and is often displaced from a confidence in a single position by his disposition to be affected by all positions, negatively rather than positively capable."[58] Here, he draws upon Romantic poet John Keats's term "negative capability," which Keats defined as the state "when man is capable of being in uncertainties, Mysteries, doubts, without any irritable reaching after facts and reason."[59] Stuart M. Sperry has pointed out that Keats's formulation of this concept is not an "ultimate declaration," but a process by which "it qualifies itself in the uncertainty it affirms, a kind of irony of which Keats himself was to become increasingly conscious."[60] For Heaney, who had memorized Keats's "To Autumn" in his teenage years and who formerly had gone by the pen name of "Incertus," such an ironically indeterminate concept must have been very attractive to him in his forties as he attempted to come to terms with a host of factors assailing him—particularly the continuing conflict in Northern Ireland and the question of his poetic vocation. He thus likely reveled in this Keatsian uncertainty while deathly certainties reigned on the ground in the North even while realizing the fleeting nature of this indeterminate position. Neil Corcoran argues that "At the centre of this pilgrimage ... there is not presence but absence, figured frequently as a 'space,'" but the situation is more complex than Corcoran allows.[61] This process of, first, undergoing something like Keats's negative capability, whereby Heaney allowed his self to be virtually taken over by a series of personalities, and second, the subsequent process of then emptying himself out, enables the poet himself to become that space. Thus divested of his former preoccupations by the end of the sequence, he may then embark upon new poetic endeavors.

In the first section of "Station Island," Heaney encounters the ghost of his childhood neighbor Simon Sweeney, thus introducing the Sweeney name rhyming with his own surname that he will revisit and adopt as a persona in Part Three of the volume. In the myth about "Mad Sweeney," that figure is angered by ringing bells, and this section opens with "A hurry of bell-notes" to herald Simon Sweeney's appearance. He holds a bowsaw "stiffly up like a lyre," a classical Greek and national Irish symbol that additionally suggests his status as a poetic figure of sorts akin to the ancient Irish *filí* or bards. This Sweeney, like his mythical namesake, is also an outlaw whose presence indicates Heaney's continuing desire to break free from the constraints of his Catholic "tribe" in the volume. The poet calls him "'an old Sabbath-breaker'" but remains fascinated by this "'mystery man,'" more so, the poet suggests, than the rituals of Catholicism (61). Thus the young Heaney with his "'First Communion'" face watches the man who clearly has not attended church that day "'cutting timber,'" working on a Sunday, a violation of the commandment to rest on the Sabbath. After the bells ring out again, Heaney sees "a crowd of shawled women" going through the corn (62), and together they "conjured" a "field" that was "full / of half-remembered faces," behind whom the poet follows as "a fasted pilgrim, / light-headed, leaving home / to face into my station." Simon Sweeney urges him to "'Stay clear of all processions!'", but the poet seems "drugged" by "the murmur of the crowd" and their tramping feet as he processes into the first station of the cross, ignoring Sweeney's advice (63).

In Section II, the first section of the sequence rendered in unrhyming and some slant-rhymed tercets, another sort of outlaw, the Protestant convert William Carleton, appears to Heaney. The poet read Carleton's autobiography and suggested when *Station Island* appeared that Carleton's growing up

> in sectarian Tyrone with [Protestant] yeomen and [Catholic] Ribbonmen and all the constraints upon the emerging self that were there, and all the aspirations ... still stands in some way for the experience of people in ... 20th-Century Ulster.[62]

Carleton, who grew up Catholic and then converted to Protestantism, became vehemently anti-Catholic but he rejects bigotry toward both Catholics and Protestants, telling the poet that he recalls "'hard-mouthed Ribbonmen and Orange bigots'" who "'made me into the old fork-tongued turncoat / who mucked the byre of their politics'" (65). In "Whatever You Say Say Nothing," the poet had condemned himself and the liberal Catholic populace of Northern Ireland for being "fork-tongued on the border bit: / The liberal papist note sounds hollow // When amplified and mixed in with the bangs / That shake all hearts and windows day and night" (N 52). Caught between a desire to reject violence while understanding the resort to it by members of their repressed tribe, such Catholics speak with forked tongues according to Heaney, and here, so does Carleton in his turn away from Catholicism and embrace of Protestantism. Heaney recalls his own exposure to Ribbonmen growing up in southern County Derry, but rejects them as sectarian, stating that they "'played hymns to Mary'" and were only "'a frail procession'" (*SI* 65) whose "'Obedient strains ... tuned me first

/ and not that harp of unforgiving iron // the Fenians strung'" (65–6). His rejection of violent Irish nationalism through the country's symbol of the harp recalls Simon Sweeney's lyre-like bowsaw and positions himself as outside that bellicose tradition. He appeals to Carleton's similar upbringing undergoing "'this Lough Derg station, / flax-pullings, dances, summer crossroads chat'" and experiencing "'always, Orange drums.'" But Carleton finally rejects both Heaney's identification with the natural world and his spiritual aspirations, telling him that "'We are earthworms of the earth, and all that / has gone through us is what will be our trace'" (66). While Carleton may symbolize the problems and possibilities of the Northern Irish experience in the twentieth century, he is ultimately too limited in his view of human life and would sunder it both from the beauty and majesty of the natural world and from transcendent, non-sectarian spirituality for Heaney.

Sections III through VI do not feature well-known writers like Carleton, but instead give us encounters with an aunt, a missionary priest, two former schoolmasters and Patrick Kavanagh, and an early crush from Heaney's youth, respectively. As Section III begins, the poet returns to his pilgrimage and hears rosary beads clicking and smells candle wax burning. He recalls an object of his Aunt Agnes, a sister of his father who died of tuberculosis in the 1920s, "A seaside trinket" that is a "toy grotto with seedling mussel shells / and cockles glued in patterns over it . . ." (67).[63] This "house of gold / . . . housed the snowdrop weather of her death / long ago" and he would keep it in the family's sideboard. As both a *memento mori* and a Catholic venerational object, the toy grotto reminds the young boy not just of his aunt's mortality in the midst of the litany but also of his own. It "was a white bird trapped inside of me / beating scared wings" when the family recited the litany together (67). As he kneels down to perform the station in the present, he thinks of "walking round / and round a space utterly empty, / utterly a source" (68), which anticipates a space of loss he will write about in a verbatim phrase from the last sonnet from "Clearances" concerning the death of his mother in *The Haw Lantern* through musing upon the absence of a chestnut tree.

Section IV continues a motif of decomposition first begun with Carleton's words to Heaney about his having "'learned to read in the reek of flax / and smelled hanged bodies rotting on their gibbets'" (65), along with his concluding words about their being "'earthworms'" (66), and continued at the end of Section III with the "bad carcass and scrags of hair / of our dog that had disappeared weeks before" (68). Here, Heaney employs again the only occasionally loosely rhyming tercets that he did in Section II to convey his encounter with the shade of Terry

Keenan, a young priest he had known as a boy who died as a missionary in a Brazilian rainforest where "'Everything wasted. / I rotted like a pear. I sweated masses . . .'" (69). Keenan, like Simon Sweeney and Carleton, is puzzled that Heaney is on the pilgrimage and even says "'all this you were clear of you walked into / over again. And the god has, as they say, withdrawn.'" This ghost recalls the brevity and lack of influence his vocation had in the rainforest, musing, "'On that abandoned // mission compound, my vocation / is a steam off drenched creepers'" (70). Through Keenan, the poet seems to be saying goodbye to his childhood faith and questioning his own vocation. And yet, as one commentator has pointed out, Keenan's speculation in the conclusion that Heaney has come to say "goodbye" to his faith is sheer conjecture on his part; moreover, Heaney has been about to utter a renunciation when he meets the priest, which could signify his "beginning a renewal of his faith . . . a starting point or point of departure from which the Christian, turning his or her back on one path, begins a spiritual journey on another path."[64] At the least, Heaney here employs the dead priest's specter to contemplate his own formerly strong Catholic faith and poetic vocation.

Section V highlights this question of the poet's vocation by featuring three shades whose work comes ever closer to Heaney's vocation—Barney Murphy, Heaney's schoolmaster at Anahorish School; another teacher who likely is Michael McLaverty, who taught Heaney at St Joseph's College of Education in Belfast and was the subject of "Fosterage" in the "Singing School" sequence of *North* (N 66); and "a third fosterer," Patrick Kavanagh, the poet whose reclamation of the local in his poems like "The Great Hunger" exemplified Heaney's own desire to write of his native ground and culture. After the earnest utterances of Murphy and McLaverty, Kavanagh's teasing is unexpected but funny. As he wryly points out, "'Sure I might have known / once I had made the pad, you'd be after me / sooner or later. Forty-two years on / and you've got no farther!'" (73). Kavanagh refers here to his own poetic sequence set on Station Island from 1942, "Lough Derg," and his suggestion mirrors that voiced earlier by Carleton and Keenan—that Heaney is simply repeating what others have practiced before him—whether Catholicism or writing and has not gone beyond their vision and work. Despite Heaney's grand plans for this volume, the charge stings and may have some truth to it, as he seems to admit by ventriloquizing Kavanagh.

Section VI opens with the poet wondering about an early female crush from the poet's youth, who is described as "Freckle-face, fox-head, pod of the broom, / Catkin-pixie, little fern-swish . . ." (75). This former play companion recalls Dante's meeting of his lifelong love Beatrice when she was eight and he was twelve. Henry Hart points out that this little girl is also "a vegetation goddess in modern dress," who can be likened as well to the "legendary garrulous wife of ass-eared Midas," and "embodies characteristics of the Virgin Mary as well as the poet's wife . . ."[65] The rapid succession of these female figures, reminiscent of an Expressionist drama such as August Strindberg's *A Dream Play* (1901), proves not bewildering but comforting to Heaney, who concludes this section with two visions.

The first sees his wife Marie transformed into Demeter, the goddess of agriculture: "Until that night I saw her honey-skinned / Shoulder-blades and the wheatlands of her back . . ." He concludes with another natural image, from Canto II of Dante's *Inferno*, where the poet is renewed by flowers rejuvenated by Lucy's radiance: "*So I revived in my own wilting powers / And my heart flushed, like somebody set free. / Translated, given, under the oak tree*" (76). Revivified and returned to himself, Heaney roots himself in the etymological image at the heart of his home county, Derry, which comes from the Irish *Doire*, signifying "oak grove."

Firmly back in the present, the poet confronts one of the most troubling ghosts in his poetry—that of William Strathearn, a Catholic murdered in his general store in Ahoghill, County Antrim, on April 19, 1977 by two loyalist paramilitary members, supported by two members of the Royal Ulster Constabulary, the latter two later being convicted of the killing.[66] Strathearn's innocence, his matter-of-fact idiom, and acceptance of his murder unsettles the poet despite this shade's reassurances. As Strathearn appears, "His brow / was blown open above the eye and blood / had dried on his neck and cheek." He tries to put Heaney at his ease, murmuring, "'Easy now,'" and telling him, "'it's only me. You've seen men as raw / after a football match . . .'" (77). The man was a football player, described by Heaney later as "still that same / rangy midfielder in a blue jersey / and starched pants," but the reference to wounded men after a football match quickly brings to mind Colum McCartney, who was killed coming home from a Gaelic football match. McCartney's shade, who Heaney will meet in the next section, thus hovers uneasily in the background of this section. Strathearn's "athlete's cleanliness" that is "shining off him" contrasts his "ravaged // forehead and the blood" and his calm demeanor (79). After he recounts the story of his murder by the two men who lied that they needed medicine for a sick child to get him to unlock his front door, Heaney ruefully tells him that the men were caught and jailed.

As this "perfect, clean, unthinkable victim" stands smiling at him, the poet "surprised myself" by asking forgiveness: "'Forgive the way I have lived indifferent— / forgive my timid circumspect involvement.'" But Strathearn's ghost simply responds, "'Forgive / my eye,'" and muses, "'all that's above my head,'" before "he trembled like a heatwave and faded" (80). Strathearn thus simultaneously seems to dismiss his own ability to forgive by invoking a common phrase—"my eye"—while asking for the poet's forgiveness for his horrible appearance. The procession of tercets in this section and its conclusion with a dangling last line recalls Dantean *terza rima*, although Heaney purposely varies the rhymes.[67]

After breaking back into a succession of lengthy stanzas with long lines in Section VIII where he meets the shade of Tom Delaney, an archaeologist friend who had worked at the Ulster Museum in Belfast, Heaney guiltily meets the accusatory ghost of Colum McCartney in the second half of that section. Both these spirits, like many who have preceded them, died in their prime: Delaney was thirty-two and McCartney only twenty-two. Heaney's cousin reappears to him as "a bleeding, pale-faced boy, plastered in mud," who accuses him of not getting back home fast enough when "'your own flesh and blood / was carted to Bellaghy from the Fews.'" The poet had been with other poets in Jerpoint on the Sunday McCartney was murdered and his cousin accuses him too of seeking his own comfort and not being sufficiently upset: "'They showed more agitation at the news / than you did'" (82). McCartney answers Heaney's defense in which he deploys an emotional first-person series of images—"'I kept seeing a gray stretch of Lough Beg / and the strand empty at daybreak. / I felt like the bottom of a dried-up lake'"—with two end-stopped rhyming lines: "'You saw that, and you wrote that— not the fact. / You confused evasion and artistic tact.'" The succession of monosyllables in this first line of the couplet thunder down upon the poet's head, while the mixture of monosyllables and polysyllables in the second line signify the confusion his cousin accuses him of experiencing. McCartney continues on, arguing that he "'directly'" accuses "'The Protestant who shot me through the head,'" but also "'indirectly'" accuses Heaney "'who now atone perhaps upon this bed / for the way you whitewashed ugliness and drew / the lovely blinds of the *Purgatorio* / and saccharined my death with morning dew'" (83).

Clearly still suffering guilt from writing "The Strand at Lough Beg" with its cleansing image of wiping his cousin's brow with morning dew, compounded now by our memory of the cleanly attired athlete William Strathearn in the previous section, Heaney has McCartney castigate him for using Dante to saccharine his murder, ostensibly employing literature rather than dealing directly with the brutal reality of his cousin's murder. Considering this passage along with the phrases in the previous section about the clean-living and neatly attired William Strathearn, perhaps the poet is also suggesting that he is not so much sugar-coating his cousin's murder and that of Strathearn but returning them to what they were in life—able-bodied men of vigor and power. The lesson here overall, though, seems to be that he should become a more openly political poet, but Heaney will reject this possibility by the end of Section XII in ventriloquizing James Joyce's command to not follow the lead of those who would constantly rebel against colonial power and instead be his own man.

In Section IX, however, the poet powerfully allows the Irish Republican Army hunger striker Francis Hughes, who died in February of 1981, along with Bobby Sands and eight others, to speak. By withholding his own response to Hughes, who was from his home district of Bellaghy, until the end of this section, Heaney thus allows a republican voice to proclaim its belligerent place as a central part of the conflict in Northern Ireland and retreats to a posture of relative silence, neither condoning Hughes's violence nor affirming the implacable British attitude toward Irish nationalists and republicans under Prime Minister Margaret Thatcher. While he rejected the violence republicans committed for the sake of an independent Ireland, Heaney argued that "during the hunger strike, some form of terrible sacred drama was being enacted," noting that "It was a moment for poetry to strike through social and political concerns, and to say that this was an *awesome* sacrifice. I regret that somehow I didn't make an intervention. I certainly felt the stress, but it ended up in silence."[68] In this section, his retrospective "intervention" in the controversy, he places Hughes in the context of Irish hunger throughout history, courting a parallel with the Great Famine, which he first explored in "At a Potato Digging" and "For the Commander of the *Eliza*," from *Death of a Naturalist*.

Heaney has recalled being at a college dinner in Oxford, a quintessentially English and Protestant event, while Hughes's very Irish and Catholic funeral wake was occurring back in Bellaghy, pointing out that "for some it was necessarily a domestic rite of mourning, whilst for others it was inevitably a show of political solidarity"[69] that captured "a classic moment of conflicting recognitions, self-division, inner quarrel, a moment of dumbness and inadequacy ... the classic bind of all Northern Ireland's constitutional nationalists." As constitutional nationalists, Heaney and others felt a "conflict between on the one hand their commitments to cultural and political ideals which are fundamentally Ireland-centred ... and on the other hand their disavowal of support for the violent means of the Irish Republican Army ..."[70] His sense of entrapment, feeling marginalized as a constitutional nationalist who rejects IRA violence, thus colors this anguished portrayal of Francis Hughes.

Whereas Heaney had previously disavowed dwelling on violence in "North" by following the advice of the longship's tongue to "'burrow the coil and gleam / of your furrowed brain'" (*N* 11), as Section IX opens, Hughes describes his own brain and stomach as dessicated and empty: "'My brain dried like spread turf, my stomach / Shrank to a cinder and tightened and cracked'" (*SI* 84). Rather than the black, moist, "good turf" Heaney's grandfather dug long ago on Toner's Bog he recalled in "Digging" (*DN* 2), the poet offers instead an image of dried turf. And we surely cannot help thinking here of Ugolino and his sons' starvation, explored in "Ugolino," just as the following line, "Often I was dogs on my own track" (*SI* 84), recalls the dogs hunting Sweeney who "fled before the bloodied heads, / Goat-beards and dogs' eyes in a demon pack" (*FW* 17) to whom Colum McCartney is likened in "The Strand at Lough Beg." After Hughes speaks thirteen and a half lines, his spirit disappears as Heaney muses how "This voice from blight / And hunger died through the black dorm" where he rests in the present on Station Island (*SI* 84). The poet's mention of "blight" immediately evokes the specter of the potato blight that causes the Great Famine in Ireland and yokes Hughes's cause briefly to that national calamity.

After recreating Hughes's funeral mass and "the [IRA] firing party's / Volley in the yard," Heaney muses, "Unquiet soul, they should have buried you / In the bog where you threw your first grenade . . ." (84). He captures his ambivalent attitude toward Hughes by his prose description of the republican hunger strikers' deaths: "And those who so totally chose the role of victim in order to expose the total intransigence of those in power had no recourse when the government refused to relent but to follow the fatal logic of their choice."[71]

The poet then dreams of being adrift on a "mucky, glittering flood" where a "Strange polyp," his "softly awash and blanching self-disgust," floats, leading him to cry out, "'I repent / My unweaned life that kept me competent / To sleepwalk with connivance and mistrust.'" Somehow in this phantasmagoric dream, "like a pistil growing from the polyp, / A lighted candle rose and steadied up / Until the whole bright-masted thing" (85) gets back on course and his self-disgust floats away, until it returns in the fourth and last section.

Staring at his face in the mirror, Heaney speaks aloud for the first time in this section: "'I hate how quick I was to know my place. / I hate where I was born, hate everything / That made me biddable and unforthcoming'" (85). This self-hatred surely stems from some regret that he did not resist British oppression like Hughes did, that he had "sleepwalked with connivance and mistrust," a phrase that returns us to his similar outrage in "Punishment" that led him to proclaim he would "connive / in civilized outrage..." (*N* 31). And yet this self-flagellation about whether or not to become more outspoken about the violence in Northern Ireland, rehearsed supremely in *An Open Letter* (1982), has to stop he realizes, and thus he moves into an affirmation of his core identity in terms of rock and water, concluding with a mysterious image of "the tribe whose dances never fail / For they keep dancing till they sight the deer" (*SI* 86). This possible reworking of Yeats's final picture of the inextricability of the dancer and the dance in "Among Schoolchildren"[72] suggests instead of dwelling on the scorched-earth policies of the factions caught up in the Northern Irish conflict, Heaney must learn a different sort of hunger through another kind of hunt: the desire to embrace and revel in joy through focusing on art itself, losing himself in its rhythms.

The tenth section of "Station Island" recalls both a family mug that was transformed into a "loving cup" for traveling actors and the resurfacing of an otter "with Ronan's psalter / miraculously unharmed," an episode from *Sweeney Astray* (87), thus together confirming "The dazzle of the impossible [that] suddenly / blazed across the threshold" (88). The shining realm of the impossible gleams ever brighter as the volume proceeds and, indeed, Heaney's diction itself and his lineation becomes lighter and happier.

Section XI, Heaney's translation of Juan de la Cruz's (St John on the Cross's) poem *Cantar del alma que se huelga de conoscer a Dios por fe* (122), also concerns the possibility of the beyond, here figured as an "eternal fountain, hidden away" (89), "So pellucid it never can be muddied, / and I know that all light radiates from it / although it is the night." In approving terms Heaney borrows from the conclusion of "Bogland," he goes on to claim, "I know no sounding-line can find its bottom, / nobody ford or plumb its deepest fathom / although it is the night" (90). Such lines constitute a desire to return to the bottomless pool of the poet's imagination glimpsed in "Bogland," now reconfigured as a living, overspilling fountain whose ascetic vision proclaimed by de la Cruz Heaney re-appropriates here for his aesthetic purposes. Concluding that "I am repining for this living fountain. / Within this bread of life I see it plain / although it is the night" (91), Heaney seeks, not new life in Christ, the fountain of living water or the bread of life He is often characterized as in the New Testament, but a new life in his art, free from restraining, constricting discourses still operating in Northern Ireland and to which he feels he was too long enslaved.

Thus, James Joyce, the exemplar of freedom and artistic independence, appears to the poet in the twelfth and last section, advising him to go out on his own and make new art. This section has become the most discussed passage in all of "Station Island" and one of the most well-analyzed passages in all of Heaney's poetry. He felt it was crucial to conclude his middle part of the volume not with someone from the North of Ireland like William Carleton, who converted to Protestantism, and not with a member of the artistic aristocracy like the Protestant-born William Butler Yeats, but with the Catholic-born Joyce. While disavowing Catholicism, Joyce used it as the foundation for much of his artistic philosophy, just as Heaney has done in much of his poetry and as he has just rehearsed in Section XI. Heaney wrote in a 1982 review of Joyce's poetry employing aquatic terms that anticipate similar language in this last section: "The great poetry of the opening chapter of *Ulysses* ... amplifies and rhapsodizes the world with an unlooked-for accuracy and transport. It gives the spirit freedom to range in an element that is as linguistic as it is airy and watery ..."[73] Heaney sought this independence throughout "Station Island" through his immersion in Keatsian negative capability whereby his personality has been supplanted temporarily by a series of revenants, whom he now dismisses from his sight to focus on Joyce and his advice.

Perhaps exhausted from his pilgrimage, Heaney sees himself in the opening of this section as "Like a convalescent," needing help and therefore he grasps Joyce's "fish-cold and bony" hand, the latter phrase beginning the aquatic imagery to follow, and is guided by him into the car park. Joyce, who "seemed blind," now becomes his guide as the poet relies now on him, not Dante's Virgil, who led the Italian poet in his *Divine Comedy*. The quality of Joyce's voice seems as important as the advice he will soon proffer; it is "eddying with the vowels of all rivers," a nod to his last strange work, *Finnegans Wake*, particularly a character from that book, Anna Livia Plurabelle, who represents the spirit of the Liffey River in Dublin. And yet that mellifluous voice also is "cunning, narcotic, mimic, definite / as a steel nib's downstroke, quick and clean" (92), an evocative combination representing Heaney's attempt to limn Joyce's polyglot sound that ranges across languages and creates new ones in the process.

Joyce tells him that his "'obligation / is not discharged by any common rite'" (92), arguing that "'What you must do must be done on your own // so get back in harness. The main thing is to write / for the joy of it'" (92–3). Whereas he disavows Heaney's pilgrimage as a "'common rite,'" Joyce urges the poet to go on an artistic pilgrimage that will be hard work (symbolized by the "'harness'") but should stem from joy. The tercet lines here break into near-*terza rima*, with the last word of the middle line of these two stanzas setting the rhyme for the next and the last word of the first and third framing lines chiming closely, a process that continues into the next stanza. Urging him to "'Cultivate a work-lust,'" Joyce admits that the pilgrimage has been effective in rendering Heaney an empty vessel ready to fly away: "'You are fasted now, light-headed, dangerous. / Take off from here.'" In a procession of simple verbs, he tells him to "'Let go, let fly, forget. / You've listened long enough. Now strike your note.'" Rather than dwell in silence as he has for much of his poetry and in this middle part of *Station Island*, Heaney now wants to sound his voice and speak out—but on his own terms, not those set by Colum McCartney, Francis Hughes, or, finally, even by Joyce himself. The poet's immediate response to Joyce's advice suggests he is stepping out in artistic freedom, however: "It was as if I had stepped free into space / alone with nothing that I had not known / already" (93).

But after he quotes a passage in Stephen Dedalus's diary at the end of Joyce's novel *A Portrait of the Artist as a Young Man* concerning Dedalus's realization that "tundish" is a real English word even though his English dean had earlier rejected it, Joyce jeers at him and urges him to follow an independent course. He harangues Heaney, telling him "'The English language / belongs to us,'" and that he should not follow the politics of nationalist resentment or embrace Catholicism: "'That subject people stuff is a cod's game, / infantile, like your peasant pilgrimage.'" Instead, he again urges the poet to strike out on his own, saying, "'Keep at a tangent,'" and "'swim // out on your own and fill the element / with signatures on your own frequency, / echo soundings, searches, probes, allurements, // elver-gleams in the dark of the whole sea'" (93–4). Both Joyce's insistence on the solitude necessary for artistic freedom and the image of baby eels recalls the similar position Heaney privileges at the end of "Casualty" when he remembers his long-ago fishing trip for eels with Louis O'Neill. The seeming embrace of solitude also poetically confirms Heaney's affirmation of T. S. Eliot's "auditory imagination" in his essay, "Learning from Eliot": "What one learns ultimately from Eliot is that the activity of poetry is solitary . . ."[74] Finally, the association of the poet with a receiving station also corresponds with positive language from Heaney's essay "The Government of the Tongue," where he praises the Polish poet Anna Swir and quotes her statement that "A poet becomes . . . an antenna capturing the voices of the world, a medium expressing his own subconscious and the collective subconscious."[75]

Having become this sort of antenna through undergoing something like Keats's negative capability, then emptying out those voices, Heaney seems poised to take Joyce's advice and become a figure of the solitary artist, but his quotation from Stephen Dedalus earlier in the poem, approving though it is, also signals that Heaney realizes Joyce's ironic treatment of Stephen at the end of that novel as he feels he must leave faith, country, and even family and friends behind to achieve artistic stature. Stephen's quest to become a writer has failed at the beginning of Joyce's next novel, *Ulysses*, whereas Joyce himself had lifelong relationships with his wife and friends that he treasured. Therefore, although Heaney ostensibly seeks to follow Joyce's advice, he will not choose solitariness and certainly not solipsism, but will remain firmly ensconced in his own community of family and friends. The upward trajectory of Joyce's advice, however, does suggest that Heaney has now committed to writing a new kind of similarly soaring poetry, and the last section of the volume, "Sweeney Redivivus," exemplifies that new style and content in its ethereal nature and occasional employment of the buoyant tercet form that had appeared in some of the poems from "Station Island."

"Sweeney Redivivus" consists of a series of twenty mostly short lyrics that limn potential directions for Heaney's future poetry as he imagines himself taking on the persona of "Mad Sweeney," who was cursed by St Ronan after he hurled a spear at him and then doomed to flit among the trees in his native Ulster the rest of his life. Heaney had finished his translation of *Buile Suibhne*, which he titled *Sweeney Astray*, in 1983 (its original title is *The Frenzy of Sweeney*) while still working on *Station Island*. Henry Hart argues that Heaney's Sweeney is "fundamentally a self-portrait of Heaney: the artist adored by an audience that he mistrusts, who studies and documents the military maneuvers in his Northern homeland from the safe distance of a Southern wood . . ." This figure "mocks the pretensions of politicians and identifies with those creatures . . . who can fly above such things, and who relishes the solitude of the hermit-artist and his ability to scrutinize everything, including his life and art, with 'scrupulous meanness.'"[76] And yet there are marked differences between the poet and Sweeney, especially in the calculated, fine details Heaney draws that contrast his calculated, soaring "flight" with Sweeney's ragged, spur-of-the-moment flights, along with the differences between Heaney's faith in art and Sweeney's "faith," an admixture of curiosity and perseverance in living. Both, however, delight in their newfound solitude and in the new creations they have become, which identities enable them to soar beyond old divisions.

Heaney signals these differences between himself and his new hero with his opening poem in this section, "The First Gloss," and the title poem. In the first of these, he tells himself, echoing the pen/shovel simile in "Digging," to grip "the shaft of the pen" and step out in an artistic faith he will "Subscribe to . . ." (97). Sweeney's faith is harder to locate. He is partly driven by curiosity and partly by the will to survive in a hard country that is hostile to him. In "Sweeney Redivivus," this emphasis on writing continues, as Sweeney comes to himself and sees "the hedges thin as penwork" and the "hard paths and sharp-ridged houses," all of which could come from a pen-and-ink sketch. Yet clearly Heaney shares with Sweeney his enjoyment of being alive, his having become strange and fantastical, even to himself in his new, airy identity. The last three lines signal this incredulity: "And there I was, incredible to myself, / among people far too eager to believe me / and my story, even if it happened to be true" (98).

An image of a ball of twine unwinding runs through this title poem and the next, which implies Sweeney's and Heaney's new freedom. He signifies this independence with this image of looseness and liberation that slackens the terseness and tautness inherent in the tone of many encounters the poet had with ghosts in "Station Island." Sweeney opens "Sweeney Redivivus" by musing that his head is "like a ball of wet twine / dense with soakage, but beginning / to unwind" (98), while the next poem, "Unwinding," is framed with images of this unraveling. The twine's unwinding seems to betoken a journey into the past that would lead to new knowledge in the future. "Unwinding" concludes, "So the twine unwinds and loosely widens / backward through areas that forwarded / understandings of all I would undertake" (99).

In "The First Flight," Sweeney reflects back on "a time when the times / were also in spasm—" and how he was viewed as "a feeder off battlefields" (102) so that he "mastered new rungs of the air / to survey out of reach / their bonfires on hills," likely a reference to pagan fires where druids murmured spells for good battle weather. He recalls "the people of art," probably druids, "diverting their rhythmical chants // to fend off the onslaught of winds," but he "would welcome" these winds "and climb / at the top of my bent" (103). Learning to fly and flit, relying on the capricious winds was Sweeney's new art, and Heaney implies here that he must similarly learn how to soar in his future poetry.

"Unwinding," "The First Flight," "Drifting Off," "The Cleric," "The Hermit," and "*In Illo Tempore*" are all in tercets, but with none of the slant and full rhyme seen in the tercet-driven poems of "Station Island," a move that suggests despite his growing affection for the tercet and occasional forays toward *terza rima*, Heaney wanted to keep his verse options open and thus veers away in these poems from what he might have viewed as the constrictions of rhyme, associated with the claims exerted upon him by those ghosts. Free from their voices and from the chiming of rhyme, he proceeds airily with no rhyme, tentatively feeling his way forward like Sweeney must have done in the early days of his curse when he stepped from treetop to treetop.

The volume concludes with a nod to the American Jack Kerouac's famous travel novel, *On The Road*, with an image of the poet driving to open the poem of the same name. Kerouac's novel exemplifies the subgenre known as the *roman á clef*, a thinly disguised work of fiction, and its intertextual presence solidifies Heaney's autobiographical identification with Sweeney throughout this third part of *Station Island*. Here, he presents another image of vacant space, "the empty round / of the steering wheel," but this image, unlike the earlier images of empty space throughout "Station Island," signifies how Heaney has acquired a new poetic identity and now is able to manipulate a vehicle's steering wheel to move through space and mark it as his own, to make it into a place of habitation. Despite affirming his life in the particular place of his house on Sandymount Strand in the previous poem, here he desires to make "all roads one," to inhabit every place on earth and do so in a way that leads to spiritual exaltation.

Thus, he now identifies with the "rich young man // leaving everything he had for a migrant solitude" from "The King of the Ditchbacks" in Part I and begins interspersing lines from the passage in Matthew 19: 16–22 (KJV), where the rich young ruler asks Christ what must he do to be saved. Heaney quotes Christ's famous reply that disappointed the young man and led him to reject His teaching, "*Sell all you have / and give to the poor*" from Matthew 19: 21 (119–20), and follows with a vision of heavenly treasure, although not what Christ was promising—eternal life. As soon as he quotes Christ's admonition to give to the poor, Heaney imagines himself doing so in a brilliant act of negation that he does not represent in words, simply saying,

> I was up and away
> like a human soul
> that plumes from the mouth
> in undulant, tenor
> black-letter latin. (120)

Yet just as quickly, he seems to re-assume the guise of Sweeney, calling himself "one for sorrow, / Noah's dove, / a panicked shadow" (120), and the rest of the poem follows him as he flits from place to place again, always on the road until he at last stumbles upon "a drinking deer" incised into the rock of a cliff cave that waits with "strained / expectant muzzle / and a nostril flared // at dried-up source" (121).

This passage also briefly revisits Scripture, specifically Psalm 42: 1 (KJV)—"As the hart panteth after the water brooks so panteth my soul after thee, O God"—yet this cave drawing of a deer thirsting for water departs from the Psalmist's expectation of spiritual dryness being quenched.[77] Instead, Heaney concludes, he "would meditate / that stone-faced vigil" until the miraculous occurs and "the long dumb-founded / spirit broke cover / to raise a dust / in the font of exhaustion" (121). Such imagery reminds us of the "eternal fountain" in Section IX of "Station Island," which translates the St John of the Cross poem along with the rain showers that accompany James Joyce in Section XII. Both of these aquatic appearances announce a new faith for the poet, not a return to Catholicism, but in a revivified art. This third springing forth of water from a dry and dusty place nearly overwhelms us with its unexpectedness and life-giving force. Confirmed in his new identity, embracing a newfound faith in his considerable art, Heaney would produce in *The Haw Lantern* (1987) a confidently spiritual set of poems that enter new realms of the marvelous.

If *The Haw Lantern* seems a slighter volume compared to Heaney's preceding work, it is, but only insofar as the previous three volumes—*North*, *Field Work*, and *Station Island*—are three of the best collections in his career, matched only by the power and meditative quality of *Seeing Things* and the wintry yet still lightsome *Human Chain*. Heaney himself, resorting to the boat analogy that would run throughout the later *Seeing Things*, called *The Haw Lantern* "a light craft . . . [that] tacks and veers along, but I think of it as a recovery book—recovery of writing 'for the joy of it,' as instructed in 'Station Island' by the old artificer himself" (SS 291). *The Haw Lantern* contains some of his best sonnets (the sequence "Clearances") and a number of fine poems, but sandwiched as it is between the Dantesque *Station Island* and the Dantesque and Virgilian *Seeing Things*, its aims seem—and are—smaller. Any poet would rightly be proud of the volume, but one senses that Heaney is preparing for something on a larger scale, as indeed he was. Peter Filkins admits that "the book veers decidedly away from the epic-making of Heaney's last collection, *Station Island*," but argues that he gives us the "pared down purity of a successful . . . poet reassessing his art mid-career, chiseling away at any existent dross so that his own style does not overcome him."[78] Certainly the style of *The Haw Lantern* is restrained yet nonetheless evocative. For instance, the turn toward the tercet registered so movingly and eloquently in *Station Island* continues here in poems such as "From the Frontier of Writing," most of "Parable Island," "From the Republic of Conscience," and "The Disappearing Island," to name only some of the tercet poems. Similarly, the pared-down sonnets of "Clearances," a title that bespeaks Heaney's efforts to attend to aching absences such as that of his mother, are similarly terse and constrained. If Heaney is journeying "on the road" by the conclusion of *Station Island*, *The Haw Lantern* visits some seminal sites both real and imagined in these poems, perhaps none more fascinating than the fantastical poem "The Mud Vision," one of many autobiographical ones.

The mid- to late-1980s was a tumultuous, emotional time for the poet because his mother Margaret died in October of 1984 and his father Patrick passed in October of 1986. Their deaths released Heaney emotionally and spiritually, as he has stated, although only the loss of his mother is reflected in *The Haw Lantern* since it was finished by the time his father died. Soon after he had begun dreaming of and formulating a new vision for his poetry signaled in "Sweeney Redivivus," he started mourning the loss of his parents. Helen Vendler argues that "These deaths caused a tear in the fabric of Heaney's verse, reflecting the way in which an inalterable emptiness had replaced the reality that had been his since birth."[79]

That rich and brimming emptiness the poet explores so well in *Station Island* and now in *The Haw Lantern* draws upon Heaney's reading of Mircea Eliade's "book on sacred and profane space" (*The Sacred and the Profane*), which he recalled he discovered "in the early eighties" (*SS* 309). Reading "Sweeney Redivivus" and the journeys that follow in *The Haw Lantern* through Eliade reveals a deeply spiritual dimension to Heaney's new poetic quest as he repeatedly dislocates himself from hearth and home. "If possessing a house implies having assumed a stable situation in the world," Eliade insists, "those who have renounced their houses, the pilgrims and ascetics, proclaim by their 'walking,' by their constant movement, their desire to leave the world, their refusal of any worldly situation." Whether Heaney walks or drives on his new roads, he exemplifies this want to become otherworldly and find "the supreme truth," or the "Hidden God, the *Deus absconditus*."[80] While it is tempting to read this poetic/spiritual quest as Christian, we must recall the poet's conception of *Station Island* cited above as striving "towards an ideal that is bhuddist [*sic*] in its paradox of attachment and detachment," and realize how he is also drawing on this Buddhist tradition. If the poet has been "reborn" by the end of *Station Island*, he has like Buddhists, died to "profane existence," as Eliade explains, "in order to be reborn to another mode of being, that represented liberation" (Hinduism also holds this belief). Dying to "the profane human condition—that is, to slavery and ignorance—in order to be reborn to the freedom, bliss, and nonconditionality of *nirvāna*" summarizes well the condition Heaney wants to occupy at the start of *The Haw Lantern*.[81] But as we will see, he can never fully slip the bonds of attachment to material things and life—so deeply is he grounded in the incarnational tradition proclaimed by Irish Catholicism. Thus, even the visits to other worlds or dream visions he experiences in this volume often feature concrete things with a stubborn persistence or even numinous qualities.

For Heaney, whose new volume would so thoroughly explore boundaries, "Eliade's book gave" him an awareness of how the "desacralizing of space" was accelerating with his generation and "he helped you to see the accidentals of your autobiography and environment as symptomatic of spiritual changes in your world" (*SS* 309). Many of the poems under consideration here attempt to re-sacralize long-ago or future spaces—partly to fend off this rampant process of de-sacralization, but also to recover or create sites for the poet to dwell in afresh and himself become recharged, re-energized, even potentially re-sacralized as a holistic body and soul.

"Alphabets," the opening poem in *The Haw Lantern*, traces the educational arc of the poet's life and takes as its animating and originary symbol the letter "O," which signifies, variously, the *omphalos* of his home life back in County Derry; the increasingly widening world outside that parish; the poet's aspirations to writing; his time as a teacher, drawing on exemplars such as Shakespeare, some of whose plays were staged in the wooden "O" of the Globe Theatre in London; the lost world of his childhood; and finally the entire orbit of his life. It exemplifies with special force Eliade's contention that "It is his familiar everyday life that is transfigured in the experience of religious man; he finds a cipher everywhere."[82]

The first section begins with the young Heaney learning about animals through his father's making shadows on the wall: "He understands / He will understand more when he goes to school." At Anahorish School, already elegized in "Anahorish" from *Wintering Out* but unnamed here, he continues to learn through borrowing from animal shapes such as the "swan's neck and swan's back / [that] Make the 2 he can see now as well as say." As this section ends and "Smells of inkwells rise," the boy spies "A globe in the window [that] tilts like a coloured O" (*HL* 1).

Section two focuses upon the rarified languages such as Latin the older schoolboy Heaney learns where "he was fostered next in a stricter school / Named for the patron saint of the oak wood," St Columb's College in Derry City. There he also learns "new calligraphy" whose letters "were trees," with "capitals . . . orchards in full bloom, / The lines of script like briars coiled in ditches." There too he dreams of becoming a poet, imagining himself "the scribe / Who drove a team of quills on his white field" (2).

"The globe has spun" again as section three starts and now Heaney the young teacher "stands in a wooden O. / He alludes to Shakespeare. He alludes to Graves" (2). As he recalls harvest at home with its grain and potatoes, he realizes they and that world have become a cipher, an "O" of loss—"All gone, with the omega that kept // Watch above each door, the good luck horse-shoe." He finally likens himself to an astronaut looking back on earth who sees "The risen, aqueous, singular, lucent O / Like a magnified and buoyant ovum—" and is enchanted by its unique life. Concluding with one more image of an "O" offered beside this startling interstellar one, the poet recalls "my own wide pre-reflective stare / All agog at the plasterer on his ladder" who writes the family name "With his trowel point, letter by strange letter" (3). The entire poem resonantly and reverently charts the growth of the poet's life through his apprenticeship to wondrous signs and letters and by its conclusion, we are similarly enchanted, mouths agape, as we, like the poet, are ready for him to dream new "Os," new worlds into being as he does in the following pages.

"Terminus," the very next poem, suggests how Heaney's particular cast of mind that values being in-between was formed and gave him a rich way of envisioning the present and future worlds he would create. Another three-section poem, its unrhymed two-liners contrast the relative lushness of the alternately slant- and fully-rhyming quatrains in "Alphabets." But these stanzas perfectly convey how the poet continually found himself between opposites, ranging from "An acorn and rusted bolt," an "engine shunting / And a trotting horse" (4). Thus, he confidently proclaims at the beginning of the third section, "Two buckets were easier carried than one. / I grew up in between" (5). "Terminus" remains perhaps the fullest short encapsulation of this crucial liminal cast of Heaney's mind that has enabled him to write so thoughtfully and well about opposing cultures and to continue to draw on the wealth of resources he has acquired from English and Irish linguistic, cultural, and literary traditions.

The strange thirteen-line poem "The Haw Lantern" interrupts this trajectory of Heaney's emphasis on liminality in a series of poems throughout the volume. It is an almost-sonnet turned upside down, with five lines, then a break preceding the last eight lines, nearly reversing the traditional octave/sestet structure of the Petrarchan sonnet minus one line.[83] In this topsy-turvy formal world, fruit blossoms at the wrong time. Thus the poem opens, "The wintry haw is burning out of season" (7), and as it continues, the haw lantern, or crabapple as it is more commonly known, takes on a life of its own.

Occasionally, "it takes the roaming shape of Diogenes / with his lantern, seeking one just man," and "you flinch," seemingly gazed at by this resurrected god with "its pecked-at ripeness that scans you, then moves on" (7). Diogenes was the best-known of the Cynic philosophers and a wisdom figure whose appearance here deepens the mythical air of the volume, even if its "presiding genius" is Hermes, the god associated with "trial or testing" who "stands over the volume's several poems of ethical scrutiny or inspection," according to Neil Corcoran.[84] Diogenes valued "direct verbal interaction over the written account" to discern truth, and "the life he lived is as much his philosophical work as any texts he may have composed."[85] Because of these characteristics, he was likely attractive to Heaney as a model interlocutor in this poem, someone who could directly confront others on ethical issues, including those associated with the conflict in Northern Ireland, upon which the poet himself had occasionally taken a silent stance.

The setting of "The Haw Lantern" is resolutely grounded as well, however, and it recalls that of "Servant Boy," with a sense here too of a people's persistence in hard weather, whether the actual cold winter or the season of conflict the inhabitants of Northern Ireland have endured. The haw is "a small light for small people," which wants them to "keep / the wick of self-respect from dying out ..." (7). Heaney suggested that the poem "discovered a bedrock disappointment; it couldn't not admit the stuntedness and small-mindedness that prevailed in Northern Ireland, but at the same time it allowed for a flicker of light" (SS 290). His lingering disappointment in the ongoing violence and atmosphere of distrust and recrimination can be seen in the rapidity of the poem's close and Diogenes' ongoing search for one just man. After the speaker flinches at Diogenes' gaze, the Greek philosopher moves on, leading Vendler to conclude, "By the end you have failed the test; the haw-lantern has moved on, and the one just man is still unfound."[86]

Like "The Haw Lantern," "From the Frontier of Writing" also focuses upon an unyielding gaze as part of an ethical situation, while dwelling on borders and liminality, as did "Terminus," examining two encounters the narrator has with British soldiers at roadblocks. This open space the narrator visits twice is the opposite of the rich, full, round spaces symbolized by the letter "O" he recalls in "Alphabets." Instead of being a brimming source of inspirational power, this space is surrounded by a "tightness and a nilness . . . / when the car stops in the road . . ." Interestingly, the conflation of the gun and writing that first appeared in "Digging" reappears here when the narrator, likely Heaney himself, spies soldiers in the distance "eyeing with intent / down cradled guns that hold you under cover" before he "drive[s] on to the frontier of writing / where it happens again." Released from the first interrogation by "a rifle [that] motions" him on, the speaker is now himself a sort of negative "O"—"a little emptier, a little spent / as always by that quiver in the self, / subjugated, yes, and obedient" (HL 6). Here, the poet employs his real and imagined experiences at such British Army roadblocks, long a feature of life in Northern Ireland for Catholics especially, and recalled in such earlier poems as "The Ministry of Fear" in *North*, to demonstrate how such subjugations deprived the Catholic populace of confidence and depersonalized them, temporarily emptying them of their personalities, a pernicious version of Keats's negative capability. One of the last poems in the volume, "From the Canton of Expectation," also delineates the history of Heaney's experience as a Catholic growing up in the province, gathering at benign nationalist celebrations that he remembers being conducted by the Catholic society of Ribbonmen in section two of "Station Island," being "confirmed" through such meetings, then turning "for home and the usual harassment / by militiamen on overtime at roadblocks" (46). Back in "From the Frontier of Writing," while at that frontier, the first experience of being interrogated repeats itself and the poet finds himself again in the sights of a "marksman," but the conclusion of the poem is suffused with relief and freedom that contrasts the tenseness and "nilness" stemming from the two incidents (6).

Is the "frontier of writing" symbolically also the border between Northern Ireland and Ireland? Heaney discusses partition in his 1993 lecture given at Oxford when he was Professor of Poetry, entitled "Frontiers of Writing." He notes the long history of Irish political leaders, writers, and places that are "invoked under two different systems of naming" and points out that "one of its unignorable causes is the border in Ireland, a frontier which has entered the imagination definitively, north and south, and which continues to divide Britain's Ireland from Ireland's Ireland." He further argues that "whether the north and the south are to be regarded as monolithic or pluralist entities the fact of the border, of partition, of two Irelands on one island, remains the salient fact."[87] The border divides farms, watercourses, and other geographic areas willy-nilly, and for inhabitants living along it its existence is not only a daily annoyance, but sometimes a danger, especially during the Troubles when army patrols such as the ones evoked here, or other patrols operated by loyalist or republican paramilitary units, stopped cars and interrogated owners about their religious and political identities.

While "From the Frontier of Writing" and "From the Republic of Conscience" traverse national and imaginative borders, the lovely "Clearances," dedicated "in memoriam M. K. H., 1911–1984" (in memory of Margaret Kathleen Heaney), explores the relationship between son and mother in some of his most moving lyrics. The prefatory lyric recalls Margaret Heaney as one of her son's first teachers, drawing on the advice she got from her uncle about splitting blocks of coal. Even the biggest one would split easily "*If you got the grain and hammer angled right.*" This advice became an early analogy for the budding poet between hammering coal and making poetry. He asks her in conclusion, "*Teach me now to listen, / To strike it rich behind the linear black*" (24). The eight sonnets that follow exemplify the riches Heaney has gleaned from his childhood experiences with his mother. The two most moving of these are sonnets two and three, which link the shining comforts of his mother's kitchen duties to her entrance to heaven and her deathbed, respectively.

Margaret Heaney's kitchen was a site of polish and respectability: "Polished linoleum shone there. Brass taps shone." The place settings and the food were all "present and correct" and Heaney and his brothers and sisters would often hear his mother's advice, represented here in a series of "Don't" commands. This hybrid sonnet that is broken into an octave and a sestet structurally akin to a Petrarchan sonnet opens with an *ab*1/4*ba* rhyme (roughly adhering to that form's *abba* opening), which is then followed by a couplet and then a near couplet in the second half of the octave (departing completely from the expected second *abba* rhyme in the Petrarchan sonnet). In the last six lines that run something like *efeg*1/4*fg* (breaking the normal rhyme of the Petrarchan sestet), Heaney's mother enters heaven. It too gleams like her kitchen, with her father "rising from his place" with a "clean bald head" to welcome her home. And then "they sit down in the shining room together." Margaret Heaney has come home to God and her earthly father, "bewildered" but at home in this shining heaven (26).

Sonnet 3 again resembles a Petrarchan sonnet with its division into eight and six lines, but it too departs from the expected rhyme, then interestingly concludes with a full couplet, a maneuver borrowed from the Shakespearean sonnet that harmonizes sound and content. Here, the memory is a singular one, contrasted with the habitual sights and sounds of the poet's mother in Sonnet 2. Once when the rest of the family was at Mass, Heaney peeled potatoes with his mother. As the vegetables fall "one by one / Like solder weeping off the soldering iron: / [They are] Cold comforts set between us, things to share / Gleaming in a bucket of clean water." Again here the purity and cleanliness of the domestic space beckon to the poet, preserving with clarity his relationship as the eldest child with his mother. In the sestet, he experiences a flashback to this scene of peeling potatoes with her while the priest offers up prayers for her as she dies. Heaney peacefully recalls, "Her breath in mine, our fluent dipping knives— / Never closer the whole rest of our lives" (27), and in that moment, the memory of that domestic task offers him more comfort than the priest can.

The seventh sonnet offers a glimpse into Heaney's parents' relationship and particularly into his father's taciturnity, even toward her, and his great love for her that he finally verbalizes to the great delight of their children as she lies dying. While Heaney and his mother were always close when he was at home, epitomized by his comment about their "*Sons and Lovers* phase" (30) in the previous sonnet, the children did not often see displays of affection from their father toward their mother according to Sonnet 7. Thus, "In the last minutes he said more to her / Almost than in all their life together," and promises her that she'll be in "New Row" soon, an idiomatic location in heaven also mentioned in the second sonnet. The children are thrilled when he calls her "good and girl," but this jubilation is quickly replaced by a realization that that her death has created a space that was "emptied / Into us to keep, it penetrated / Clearances that suddenly stood open. / High cries were felled and a pure change happened" (31). They have a charge to keep this space open, to keep Margaret Heaney's name and memory alive, and the eighth and last sonnet offers Heaney's first response in doing so.

Formally, the eighth sonnet is one of his most distinctive ones, opening *abab*, then running *cdcd*, adhering perfectly to the rhyme scheme of the Shakespearean sonnet, but then departing in the last six lines from this alternating rhyme scheme to conclude with two sets of triplets—*eee* and *fff*. Thinking about the subject of his mother's death through this strange form enables us to understand that the regular Shakespearean form of the first eight lines of the sonnet approximates the expected rhythms of Margaret Heaney's and her family's life, while the last six break that rhythm in an unexpected but delightful way. The last two triplets establish a pleasing sonic and visual space, suggesting that the site opened by her death has its own music and life that goes on forever.

The poem opens with Heaney thinking of "walking round and round a space / Utterly empty," symbolizing where the family's chestnut tree had died—perfectly recapitulating the same phrase from the third lyric of "Station Island" about the poet's dead Aunt Agnes. The repetition startles, making us link Margaret Heaney's death with Agnes's; the spaces created by their deaths are heightened by the absence formed by the death of the chestnut tree. With Heaney's memory of the tree being cut down, the sonnet sequence turns full circle, back to the sequence's opening nine-line poem about splitting coal. Splitting coal and felling trees well require a sharp tool and accurate knowledge of the surface's grain. Just as that tree was felled long ago, in the present, "High cries were felled" in the last line of the seventh sonnet. The "pure change" promised in that previous poem is glimpsed here, as the space where the chestnut tree formerly dwelt now comes to stand for the space representing Margaret Heaney's life: "Its heft and hush become a bright nowhere, / A soul ramifying and forever / Silent, beyond silence listened for" (32). What seems like a gleaming nihilism in the antepenultimate line quickly becomes a silent soul in the last two lines that branches out indefinitely, one more arboreal comparison between the chestnut tree and Heaney's mother, but which also promises her ongoing life in the memory of the extended and growing Heaney children, grandchildren, and eventually great-grandchildren. Heaney even pointed out in language redolent of these last lines that when "the family began to branch up and out and over her, she got great reward and pride from them" (*SS* 311). Sheltered in their love that grows over the sacred location that used to contain her, Margaret Heaney is rendered here extending her loving influence into the lives of her descendants indefinitely and they themselves become vessels that are re-sacralized, in Eliade's terms, by dwelling upon her life.

Because of this stunning exploration of such spaces in this sonnet sequence, Vendler memorably terms *The Haw Lantern* "Heaney's first book of the virtual," praising how a poet who is "so immediately responsive towards the tactile and the palpable" can shift and "direct his view towards the invisible, the virtual," thus "admit[ting] into representation those 'clearances' representing things that have been felled."[88]

Nowhere does Heaney better display his talent as a "virtual" poet in this sense than in "The Mud Vision," the most striking poem in the volume and one which conveys both a sense of the miraculous still available to the Catholic populace in his childhood and adolescent years, and the loss that now pervades that community since the faith has declined. It strikingly exemplifies what Heaney had learned from reading Eliade about the desacralization of space.

"The Mud Vision" draws implicitly on the supposed appearance in the late 1950s of the Virgin Mary to a woman in Ardboe, County Tyrone, "on the shores of Lough Neagh," along with an earlier experience, about "a lighting effect [that] occurred that was sudden, brilliant, and unforgettable" during a "local dramatic society's production of a play that told the story of another apparition of the Virgin, this time to the three children at Fatima . . ."[89] But instead of explicitly articulating those experiences, Heaney writes instead of a "rose window of mud" that appeared in the Irish Midlands (*HL* 48), perhaps to disguise the historical context. He borrows the mud vision from

> the shape that the artist Richard Long created on a wall of the Guinness Hop Stores during the Rose exhibition in 1984. Long dipped his hand in mud hundreds if not thousands of times to make a flower face of mudprints, and, in the free-ranging way of the imagination, my memory of it surfaced and coalesced with those other earlier occasions of wonder.

Heaney believes that the poem is "embedded in memories of life in an older Ireland, but it also gestures towards an Ireland that is still coming into being."[90] The poem opens by picturing just this conflation of tradition with modernity, juxtaposing "Statues with exposed hearts and barbed-wire crowns" with "The dozing bellies of jets," "punks with aerosol sprays," and "Our first native models and the last of the mummers . . ." (48).

After "the gossamer wheel, concentric with its own hub / Of nebulous dirt, sullied yet lucent," appears, everything becomes colored by its presence, and "some / Took to wearing a smudge on their foreheads / To be prepared for whatever" (48). Here, Heaney is clearly drawing on the Christian tradition (especially common in Catholic and high-Church Protestant denominations) of wearing on their foreheads crosses made of ashes on Ash Wednesday to start the Lenten season. Everyone begins to watch, wait, and wonder for other such manifestations as the mud vision and they are described as "A generation who had seen a sign!" (49).

When the mud vision of "Original clay, transfigured and spinning" (48) finally disappears, the believers allow outsiders—"experts / [who] Began their *post factum* jabber"—to take their joy and sense of being privileged to have seen a unique vision away from them and "Just like that, we forgot that the vision was ours, / Our one chance to know the incomparable / And dive to a future." All they can say at the end is that "we survived," but they lost "our chance to be mud-men," and instead became "convinced and estranged," figuring "in our own eyes for the eyes of the world" (49).

Using language borrowed in part from Eliade, Heaney argues that the people in the poem "have entered the world of media-speak and postmodernity. They've been displaced from a culture not unlike that of de Valera's Ireland—frugal, nativist, and inward looking, but still tuned to a supernatural dimension; and they find themselves in a universe that is global, desacralized, consumerist, and devoid of any real sense of place or pastness" (*SS* 288). Although by this point in his life, Heaney was no longer a believer, he nonetheless mourns this inability to be enchanted, whether by religious visions or by the suasive properties of words in a poem. He believes in a sacred role for the poet, having stated that "poetry has a binding force, a religious claim upon the poet . . . I also assume that the poet still has in some sense a tribal role . . ."[91] The populace in the poem, of Ireland until fairly recently, retained this capacity and it set them apart from most of the disbelieving modern world, especially in the West. Once their ability "to be mud-men" slipped from their fingers, they were rendered more homogeneous, growing indistinguishable from other rationalist peoples. Heaney placed himself in this generation of the Irish, noting that "The desacralizing of space is something that my generation experienced in all kinds of ways: faith decaying and the *turas*—the turn around the holy well or the Stations of the Cross—losing its supernatural dimension . . ." (*SS* 309). The poem thus shows the arc of his own career from the early, "muddy" poems like "Digging" and the bog poems to the more spiritual ones of the 1980s that are nevertheless still grounded, literally and metaphorically, in the mud and bogs of Heaney's childhood and earlier Catholic faith.[92]

At the end of the penultimate poem in the volume, "The Disappearing Island," Heaney gives us one last vision—that experienced by a group of islanders who unknowingly camp one night on a whale that finally breaks "beneath us like a wave." They realize that the land only "seemed to hold firm" when "we embraced it *in extremis*," likely a symbolic suggestion that our faith allows us to maintain a real grip on a material life that may prove illusory (*HL* 50). Eliade points out that "One of the paradigmatic images of creation is the island that suddenly manifests itself in the midst of the waves," and the islanders seem themselves "born" when they spy and land on the "island."[93] When the whale dives below the surface, they then experience a sort of baptism, dying to their old selves and being reborn. The speaker concludes by declaiming, "All I believe that happened there was vision" (50), and indeed, Heaney has called this poem "a form of *aisling*, a vision poem about Ireland, even though it is an *aisling* inflected with irony . . ." (*SS* 289). He was slowly learning that "much of what we accepted as natural in our feelings and attitude was a cultural construction, yet I was slow to begin the deconstruction" (289). Moreover, as Heaney had discovered from reading Eliade, the waters "disintegrate, abolish forms, 'wash away sins'; they are at once purifying and regenerating. Their destiny is to precede the Creation and to reabsorb it . . ."[94] "The Disappearing Island" therefore may represent Heaney's attempt to signify a persistent, underlying myth that precedes and supersedes our cultural constructions—something we can rest safely in despite the desacralizing impulses and trajectory of the postmodern world.[95]

Thus, the last poem in the volume, "The Riddle," addresses the question of epistemology directly, asking how we can "sift the sense of things from what's imagined // And work out what was happening in that story / Of the man who carried water in a riddle." Heaney seems happy enough here to leave the question up in the air, concluding by offering another question rather than an answer: "Was it culpable ignorance, or was it rather / A *via negativa* through drops and let-downs"? (*HL* 51). Vendler points out that this poem "changes the Hades-myth of the daughters of Niobe, who carried water in a sieve, into the poet's punishment—to carry water in the never-ending riddle of value."⁹⁶ She further observes that Heaney employs two terms from his childhood Catholic faith, "culpable ignorance" and the "*via negativa*" to us as a way of also himself interrogating his own values at the time. Culpable ignorance "is the sin of those to whom the gospel has been preached but who provide only the stony ground on which the seed cannot take root" and the poet suspects he may be in this state himself, but by using negative theology, defining God by what He is not, "one adheres to piety by rejecting the false rather than by ascertaining the true."⁹⁷ One suspects that she is right in arguing that Heaney felt he might "be of more use to his fellow-men" in admitting his doubts "than he would by rallying them too sanguinely to singly conceived causes,"⁹⁸ yet as we have seen in "The Mud Vision," he nonetheless yearns for that sense of the miraculous. These admissions about metaphysical doubts would continue in *Seeing Things*, even as that volume opened us and the poet himself to a world of the marvelous he had never given us so fully before.

Notes

1. Heaney, "Seamus Heaney Writes . . .," 1.
2. Ibid.
3. Heaney, "The Art of Poetry," 106, 105–6.
4. Des Pres, 74.
5. McKittrick et al., 565.
6. Qtd in de Bréadun, 13.
7. Dante, *Purgatory*, 76: "I . . . held up to him my face begrimed with tears; / And so he brought my native hue once more / To light, washed clean of hell's disfiguring smears."
8. Heaney, "Mossbawn," 19.
9. Ibid.
10. In the original published version of the poem, however, Heaney had not yet added the line about Sweeney ("The Strand at Lough Beg," 34–5).
11. In his introduction to his translation of *Beowulf*, Heaney references the line, "big-voiced scullions," noting that "when the men of the family spoke, the words they uttered came across with a weighty distinctness, phonetic units as separate and defined as delph platters on a dress shelf" ("Introduction" [*Beowulf*], xxvi).
12. Heaney, "Mossbawn," 19.
13. Regan, 19, cites a 1991 interview [Heaney, Interview with Melvyn Bragg] in which he observes that McCartney's death is "mitigated by the gentleness of the landscape he comes from and his being reunited with that benign landscape."
14. Ibid., 17. Actually, McCartney was driving away from Dublin toward his

home environment where Heaney quickly imagines him in his prime.
15. Milton, 164.
16. Heaney, "Above the Brim," 74; my emphasis. I am grateful to my graduate student Elizabeth Fredericks for suggesting that Heaney is drawing upon his sense of Frost's "brimming" here, though the development of the argument is my own.
17. Qtd in ibid., 75; my emphasis.
18. Eliade, *The Sacred and the Profane*, 97.
19. Ibid., 32.
20. Heaney, "Mossbawn," 23.
21. Heaney, "Above the Brim," 75.
22. Vendler, 60.
23. For an explanation of how "The Strand at Lough Beg" is written mostly in disguised or "hidden" tercets after its opening four lines, see my *Seamus Heaney's Regions*, 251.
24. Heaney, "The Poet's Perspective," n.p.
25. Heaney, "Unidentified Fragments."
26. Durkan and Brandes note that "Casualty" appeared in the *New Yorker* on April 2, 1979.
27. McKittrick et al., *Lost Lives*, 150.
28. Whereas the girl's head at the end of "Strange Fruit" is given agency in the final lines with Heaney's portrayal of her as "outstaring axe / And beatification, outstaring / What had begun to feel like reverence (N 32), here, O'Neill is rendered helpless by being depicted as having a "cornered outfaced stare" that is "*Blinding in the flash*" (FW 23; my emphasis). Heaney's "Blinding in the flash" phrase likely is drawn from a contemporary newspaper account of the explosion that is cited in McKittrick et al.: the bar's owner told the inquest that "the front wall started coming down around us, and there was a *blinding flash*" (150; my emphasis).
29. Heaney, "Reading at Baylor University."
30. See Yeats, 181.
31. Heaney, "Joy or Night: Last Things in the Poetry of W. B. Yeats and Philip Larkin," 149.
32. Ibid., 148–9.
33. Heaney, "Feeling into Words," 45.
34. Ricœur, 505.
35. For much the best close reading of "The Harvest Bow," which he terms "something very like an exemplary Heaney poem, all the more so for the fact that its complex implications are not to be completely unfolded" (87), see Peter McDonald, "Heaney's Implications."
36. Heaney, *Preoccupations*, 7.
37. Terence Brown, 311.
38. Russell, *Poetry and Peace*, 250.
39. While Michael Cavanagh acknowledges Heaney's great respect for Lowell, including how he represented "poetry so confident of its right to speak in an ungoverned tongue that it need not defend itself" (111), he argues convincingly that *Field Work* opposes what Heaney saw as the "ferocious and confrontational nature of *Life Studies*" in its "conspicuously tender" and "intimate" poems, which differ from Lowell's only seemingly tender poems

since he "writes about his loved ones" there "as if from behind a pane of glass" (120). See Cavanagh, 137–44, for a helpful analysis of how Heaney's "The Skunk" does not "simply borrow from or allude to 'Skunk Hour'; it is an answer to that poem, a rival vision of things, a place where Heaney ... enacts his independence" from Lowell (137–8).

40. Lowell, 192.
41. Corcoran, *The Poetry of Seamus Heaney*, 109.
42. Heaney, "Lenten Stuff."
43. Heaney, "PENAL STATIONS" Sketch.
44. Heaney, *Stations*, 17.
45. Cunningham, 56.
46. A rejected poem with a sectarian context for the "Station Island" sequence was originally entitled "III" and was to follow "II" where Heaney meets William Carleton. "III" portrays the poet being stopped and interrogated by British troops as he nears Lough Derg. As he stops, he feels the situation "has all the pure calm of nightmare, / like standing throat deep in a pool, your head / a severed head on a pane of water," a return to the severed head image of "Strange Fruit" (Heaney "III").
47. Heaney, "Envies and Identifications: Dante and the Modern Poet," 18.
48. Heaney, *Seamus Heaney in Conversation in Karl Miller*, 34.
49. Ibid., 34–5.
50. Peggy O'Brien, 157.
51. Heaney, *Station Island* Notebook.
52. Ibid.
53. Heaney, ["Talk on Field Day"].
54. Deane, 48.
55. Heaney, "Canto I," 3.
56. Qtd in Flood, "Seamus Heaney Chooses."
57. Heaney, "Orpheus and Eurydice," 18.
58. Heaney, *Place and Displacement*, 8.
59. Keats, *Selected Letters*, 60.
60. Sperry, 62.
61. Corcoran, *The Poetry of Seamus Heaney*, 121.
62. Qtd in de Bréadun, 13.
63. Corcoran, *The Poetry of Seamus Heaney*, 117, identifies the girl as Heaney's Aunt Agnes.
64. Molino, 156.
65. Hart, *Seamus Heaney: Poet of Contrary Progressions*, 171.
66. John Weir, a former member of the Royal Ulster Constabulary and driver of the getaway car for the Strathearn murder, confessed his role in this killing and detailed the activities of the murderers in "The Troubles I've Seen." For the official narrative about this murder, see the entry on Strathearn in McKittrick et al., 716–18.
67. For a thorough analysis of Heaney's variations on *terza rima* in this section, see my *Seamus Heaney Regions*, 263–5, 269. I argue that he uses para-rhyme in Section VII to achieve "a chiming of the first and third lines in each tercet throughout, although he does not use the rhyme of his initial second line to begin the rhyme of his second stanza as normal *terza rima* would do" (265).

68. Heaney, *In Conversation with Karl Miller*, 23.
69. Heaney, "Frontiers of Writing," 187.
70. Ibid., 188.
71. Ibid., 187.
72. See Yeats's concluding couplet to that poem, "O body swayed to music, O brightening glance, / How can we know the dancer from the dance?" (217).
73. Heaney, "Joyce's Poetry," 423.
74. Heaney, "Learning from Eliot," 40.
75. Qtd in Heaney, "The Government of the Tongue," 93.
76. Hart, *Seamus Heaney: Poet of Contrary Progressions*, 138–9.
77. Heaney knew the passage well, as would anyone raised in the Christian faith, and he even quotes most of it in the sixth sonnet from "Clearances": "As the hind longs for the water, so my soul . . ." (*HL* 30).
78. Filkins, 184.
79. Vendler, 111.
80. Eliade, *The Sacred and the Profane*, 183–4, 184.
81. Ibid., 199.
82. Ibid., 183.
83. I thought of this construction of the poem on my own, but was pleased to find it confirmed by Vendler, who calls the first "modest five lines . . . an almost-sestet to introduce the more consequential octave that follows . . ." (117–18).
84. Corcoran, *The Poetry of Seamus Heaney*, 135.
85. Piering, n.p.
86. Vendler, 118.
87. Heaney, "Frontiers of Writing," 188, 189.
88. Vendler, 113.
89. Heaney, "The Home Place: The Mud Vision," n.p.
90. Ibid.
91. Heaney, "Current Unstated Assumptions about Poetry," 650.
92. Heaney "updated" his explanation of the poem's populace in his reading of it shortly before he died, suggesting they are "Alienated from what has been brought upon them . . . rather like the Irish population in the wake of the Celtic Tiger, listening, bewildered, to experts. Economists. Regulators. Apologisers. Apologists" ("The Home Place: The Mud Vision," n.p.).
93. Eliade, *The Sacred and the Profane*, 130.
94. Ibid., 131.
95. Following ibid., the poem seems to assert that "every construction or fabrication has the cosmogony as paradigmatic model. The creation of the world becomes the archetype of every creative human gesture, whatever its plane of reference may be" (45).
96. Vendler, 119.
97. Ibid., 121.
98. Ibid., 122.

Chapter 4

Radiance: *Seeing Things, The Spirit Level, Electric Light*

Heaney published his *New Selected Poems 1966–1987* in 1990 after turning fifty in 1989. The volume gathers his selections from his first seven volumes, but he also made sure to include seven prose poems from *Stations* and five sections from his translation, *Sweeney Astray*. Including those prose poems and translations suggests how he viewed that work in other genres as complementing his poetry from the same period. Moreover, the prose poems and the sections from *Sweeney* suggest a poet more formally adventuresome than admirers of Heaney the lyric poet may realize, maybe even than he presents: after all, the volume's title promises poetry only.

He opened what may be thought of now as the penultimate stage of his career with the publication of *Seeing Things* in 1991, a rich and strange volume featuring spiritual insights but also meditations on common objects. The volume's title likely draws on the determination of one of his favorite poets, Wordsworth, to "see into the life of things." Heaney similarly sought to appreciate not only the life of objects freighted with emotional memories for him, but also to see visions normally beyond our ken.[1] The phrase, "You're just seeing things," has become pejorative, but here he invites us to apprehend with him things we normally might not and consider them a welcome part of our consciousness.

He chose to frame the volume with his own translations from Book VI of Virgil's *Aeneid* and Canto III of Dante's *Inferno*, lyrics he entitled "The Golden Bough" and "The Crossing," respectively. These poems together signify crossings into the underworld, both a recapitulation of the opening strategy of *Station Island* and a poignant meditation on the poet's relationship with his father. Heaney has often proclaimed his fondness for Book VI of Virgil's epic and after the death of his father, he became even more enamored of it. Neil Corcoran believes that despite his secularism as a mature poet, Heaney's continued attraction to an afterlife is figured most powerfully in his later work by allusions to and evocations of Virgil, and especially of the descent into the underworld in Book VI of the *Aeneid* . . . In such places, the *Aeneid* seems to constitute a kind of displaced Catholicism, supplying a supportive mythology for a poet whose secularism continued to require such a thing.[2]

This undergirding belief system, buttressed also by the poet's continuing interest in Dante, seemed to anchor Heaney sufficiently in the last three decades of his career and enable him to remain attuned to the capacity of humans to love beyond the bounds of this world.

In lines 98–148 from the *Aeneid* he translates as "The Golden Bough," his clear love for his father emerges in line 110: "I pray for one look, one face-to-face meeting with my dear father" (*ST* 3). The language here is both more Christian and intimate than that given in a leading translation of the *Aeneid* by Robert Fitzgerald, who translates the line spoken by Aeneas as "may I have leave / To go to my dear father's side and see him."[3] Heaney's prayerful line sets up the motif of seeing in the volume—and especially seeing beyond this mortal world. It specifically resonates with one of the last lines from section three of the volume's title poem, when he recalls his father's near-drowning after a horse reared up and tumbled a cart and sprayer into the river. When Patrick Heaney returns to the family home, "his ghosthood immanent," the poet recalls, "That afternoon / I saw him face to face . . ." (20), a line that echoes the wished-for "face-to-face meeting" from "The Golden Bough." Other echoes of the Anchises/Aeneas relationship abound in the volume: "Man and Boy" concludes with Heaney's recreation of his father's running to tell the news of his own father's death, then imagines Patrick Heaney about to "piggyback me / At a great height, light-headed and thin-boned, / Like a witless elder rescued from the fire" (17). This dream sequence neatly reverses the situation in Book II of the *Aeneid* when Aeneas carries his father Anchises away from Troy.

Aeneas must grasp the golden bough and pluck it; if he is favored by fate, it will break loose and he can then descend into the underworld to see his father again. By situating this translation at the beginning of the volume, Heaney implies the subsequent poems will test whether he will be favored as a poet to conjure up poetic images of and meetings with his father—and, by extension, whether he will be able to naturally grasp his vocation again. He noted that much of his poetry takes its cues from the English Romantic poets, then mused that it was

> something that should come forth naturally "as the leaves to the trees," as Keats says, something that comes through the quotidian patterns of your life. Poetry doesn't quite have to do with industry or intention. It is related

more to the unconscious and to your lifeline or your destiny line . . . I always believed in poetry as a grace . . ."[4]

Poetry thus is Heaney's golden bough and his translation concludes with the Sibyl of Cumae stating to Aeneas that his ability to take hold of the bough is ordained already by fate:

> "Take hold of it boldly and duly. If fate has called you,
> The bough will come away easily, of its own accord.
> Otherwise, no matter how much strength you muster,
> you never will
> Manage to quell it or cut it down with the toughest of blades." (5)

Seeing Things represents Heaney's firm attempt to "take hold" of poetry "boldly and duly" and to write a poetry simultaneously more concrete and more spiritual than any he had ever done so before. The volume steps out in the faith that the gift of poetry will continue to present itself to him.[5]

Aeneas desires to see his father once more "Among these shadowy marshes where Acheron comes / flooding through" (3), and *Seeing Things* as a whole is replete with poems that employ images of boats, floating, and water. Heaney had long been drawn to water—to the local rivers and streams and bogs surrounding him as a child; to Lough Neagh, the largest lake in Britain and Ireland; to Lough Derg where "Station Island" is set. Now, he turns to the aquatic to render his quotidian subject matter dream-like and sometimes ghostly. When he wrote in 1997 that "Somehow, the landscape of the poem needs to undergo the kind of flooding that will make it a reservoir, make it newly available as a breathable and lucid element," he could easily have been describing his poetic agenda in *Seeing Things*.[6] Therefore he submerged his formerly solidly anchored poetry with memories of the ordinary and fantastic and transformed that poetry into something lighter and airier, "breathable and lucid."

The title sequence exemplifies Heaney's gradual move toward the marvelous and away from the murderous in his work. "Seeing Things" demonstrates how he links watery content to tripled phrases and a tripartite structure to enable meditation in that volume. In the first section, a remembered boat trip from the island of Inishbofin to the mainland anticipates Heaney's translation of the crossing with the ferryman Charon from Dante's *Inferno* that concludes the volume. The anchorage of the first two end-stopped lines and the procession of solid nouns quickly give way to an uncomfortable buoyancy for the speaker. The poem begins with a set tableau: "Inishbofin on a Sunday morning. / Sunlight, turfsmoke, seagulls, boatslip, diesel" (18). The phrase "Sunday morning" and these sensuous images recall Wallace Stevens's great contemplative poem, "Sunday Morning," but Heaney domesticates his images yet makes them dangerous, whereas Stevens's "late / Coffee and oranges in a sunny chair, / And the green freedom of a cockatoo"[7] symbolize an exotic, relaxed insouciance. The risky boat trip that follows becomes an act of faith, much as sending the boat of poetry out upon the waters of the world does.[8]

When the boat lurches, the speaker admits, "I panicked at the shiftiness and heft / Of the craft itself," observing further, "What guaranteed us—/ That quick response and buoyancy and swim—/ Kept me in agony." He sets off the heart of the poem here with the intermediate punctuation of the dash, with the opening and closing phrases framing the crucial third phrase, which itself highlights a triple set of nouns—"response," "buoyancy," "swim." As this first lyric concludes, he imagines looking "from another boat / Sailing through air, far up, and could see / How riskily we fared into the morning, / And loved in vain our bare, bowed, numbered heads" (18). Learning to trust the boat's movement across the sea enables him to have this visionary prayer of sorts for himself and the other occupants, whose "bare, bowed, numbered heads" recall the Biblical passage about each hair on our heads being numbered. In Luke 12: 7 (KJV), Christ proclaims, "But even the very hairs of your head are all numbered. Fear not therefore: ye are of more value than many sparrows." Heaney's allusion to this passage from Luke's Gospel enables him to urge us not to be afraid on our own risky journeys wherever they might be, a clear exhortation that resonates with the message of the graffito on the present study's cover. He thus suggests that once a literal or imaginative journey is launched, we take on risks and are alone in the craft we step onto, trusting in its buoyancy for our safety. Finally this first part of the poem, and indeed the volume as a whole, exemplifies his contention in *Crediting Poetry* that poetic form both anchors the poem and us in everyday reality yet releases us into the spirit realm.[9]

The following two sections of "Seeing Things" also employ aquatic imagery to intimate how art is an act of faith that can convey us into the unknown if we surrender ourselves to it fully. In the second section, the speaker thus gazes at an image of John the Baptist baptizing Jesus "On the façade of a cathedral." Yet as he stares at the "Lines / Hard and thin and sinuous" that "represent / The flowing river," this artwork grows stranger and he imagines the peripheral aquatic life not represented there:

Down between the lines
Little antic fish are all go. Nothing else.

> And yet in that utter visibility
> The stone's alive with what's invisible:
> Waterweed, stirred sand-grains hurrying off,
> The shadowy, unshadowed stream itself. (19)

These lines amply suggest Heaney's growing conviction to render the invisible visible through his own poetry that leads us into imagined worlds that are just as real as the ostensible focus of the artwork.

By adapting a fairy-tale opening—"Once upon a time my undrowned father / Walked into our yard"—the third section revives the poet's dead father and memorializes him through retrieving a family narrative in the oracular tradition. It returns, too, to the image portrayed in the closing line of the first section—the passengers' "bare, bowed, numbered heads"—when the speaker recalls seeing his father's bare head after he survives a near-drowning: "scatter-eyed / And daunted, strange without his hat, / His step unguided, his ghosthood immanent" (20). Stripped of his farming equipment, which "went over into a deep / Whirlpool, hoofs, chains, shafts, cartwheels, barrel / And tackle, all tumbling off the world, / And the hat already merrily swept along / The quieter reaches," the miraculously surviving father anticipates his own "ghosthood" many years later. Indeed, the fairy-tale opening and this fantastical incident are now given additional narrative authority and heft with the introduction of another scriptural passage. The speaker implies he was given a premonition of how it might be to know his father in the afterlife, echoing the prayer of Aeneas to see his father again in Heaney's volume-opening translation, when he notes that "That afternoon / I saw him face to face," which echoes the passage from 1 Corinthians 13: 12 (KJV), "For now we see through a glass, darkly; but then face to face: now I know in part; but then shall I know even as also I am known." Taken in its Pauline context, this allusion indicates how once upon a time, Heaney the child no longer "spake as a child" and "understood as a child," and "thought as a child," but briefly "put away childish things" (1 Corinthians 13: 11, KJV). He had something like full foreknowledge of the afterlife, rendered through a fairy-tale ending: "there was nothing between us there / That might not still be happily ever after" (20). "Seeing Things" thus offers us a collection of invisible but no less real happenings—the unseen lift of a boat and, by extrapolation, the poem; the hidden, imagined aquatic life in the cathedral's stone façade; the unglimpsed near-drowning of Patrick Heaney—and renders them vividly visible in this trinitarian, visionary poem.

Other poems in the volume, however, deeply ponder the life of things rather than dwelling on narratives. Childhood marks a particularly intense engagement with things and some commentators believe this attachment to things stems from their otherness, while another argues they help "extend the self into the world, the living and changing being into more lasting forms."[10] "The Pitchfork," for instance, treats this object as an extension of the self, finally ascribing a nearly eternal quality to it as it sails "Evenly, imperturbably through space, / Its prongs starlit and absolutely soundless . . ." Just as the pitchfork "felt like a javelin, accurate and light" (25), so too does the titular subject as it is swung in "A Basket of Chestnuts": "The lightness of the thing seems to diminish / The actual weight of what's being hoisted in it" (26). Perhaps the supreme example of the first half of the volume's attention to the weightiness of things and airiness of them when hoisted and put into motion occurs in "Wheels within Wheels," as the speaker remembers spinning the back wheel of a bicycle and making the spokes disappear. When he recalls that the "pedal treads / Worked very palpably at first against you / And then began to sweep your hand ahead / Into a new momentum—", we sense that this was one of the first times the young Heaney was able to briefly escape the weightiness of things, almost of gravity itself, "as if belief / Caught up and spun the objects of belief / In an orbit coterminous with longing" (48). After that initial wheel rusts, the young boy finally recaptures some of its accelerating power when visiting a circus where cowgirls whirled lariats around their heads and became "*Perpetuum mobile*. Sheer pirouette," surrounded by other whirling figures and objects, wheels within wheels (49).

In the quatrain-driven "The Biretta," objects shift shapes multiple times: Heaney muses upon the priest's traditional three-peaked hat, "the triple-finned black serge, / A shipshape pillbox . . .", which he finally turns "upside down and it is a boat— / A paper boat, or the one that wafts into the first lines of the *Purgatorio* / As poetry lifts its eyes and clears its throat" (28, 29). He has observed recently that when he was an altar boy, he was "always fascinated by the materiality and the weight of" the priest's biretta and that "as a child, I tended to be frightened of priests with birettas on their heads" (*SS* 327). Yet he quickly adds that

> there was something trim and shipshape, almost airborne, about the feel of the thing . . . there was a momentary temptation to launch it into the sanctuary like a paper dart or a little black-winged stealth bomber. In the end I let that impulse stand for poetry's impulse to outstrip the given, and turned it instead into the boat of imagination that Dante launches in the opening lines of the *Purgatorio* . . . (327)

The biretta, then, has at least a dual function for Heaney, signifying both the material and the frightening world and also the airiness and possibility of the world beyond the material toward which poetry can point us.

By extrapolation, it symbolizes both his somewhat constraining former doctrinal Catholicism and the heaviness of his earlier poetry and the way in which he has turned to Catholicism and its ethereal promises in his airier, more recent poetry.

Heaney goes on to muse in "The Biretta" that the hat can also be transformed by the imagination into "that small boat out of the Bronze Age / Where the oars are needles and the worked gold frail / As the intact half of a hatched-out shell, / Refined beyond the dross into sheer image" (*ST* 29). Here Heaney references the golden boat, part of a cache of precious objects discovered at Broighter, County Derry, which is pictured on the American edition of *Seeing Things* and which Dennis O'Driscoll terms "part of Heaney's ancestral inheritance as a Derryman . . ."[11] Yet by the next stanza, the poet admits that "it's as likely to be the one / In Matthew Lawless's painting *The Sick Call*, / Where . . . it's all / Solid, pathetic and Irish Victorian" (29). Here, Heaney seems to admit how the crashing weight of everyday reality that befalls us through sickness or other calamities can act as a drag upon the imagination. But he confessed that his reading of the biretta in the Lawless painting here is actually fairly sympathetic:

> It's an unspectacular, very sympathetic study, nicely successful in conveying the priest as somebody halfway between a man of sorrows and a man of service. And the hat is so ordinary, so unstylish, it seems like an objective correlative of all that. It's certainly the opposite of what the hard-edged tricorn biretta stood for: the hard line, the pulpit bark, the articulated and decided authority of *unam sanctam catholicam et apostolicam Ecclesiam*. (*SS* 327)

Thus Heaney's portrayal of the biretta in Lawless's painting symbolizes the imagination in its representation of the priest's sympathy for his parishioner that he is rowing to see, over against the traditional ecclesiastical authority of the Catholic Church. The biretta is heavy yet light, hard yet sympathetic. His ability to transform it in so many ways betokens the nimbleness of his imagination and his desire to show how things can take on a life of their own for different perceivers.

In *Seeing Things*, he consistently elevates, levitates, and raises the clayey things of his childhood to new heights as he does supremely well in "The Settle Bed." A functional thing like the settle bed that is "Trunk-hasped, cart-heavy, painted an ignorant brown. / And pew-strait, bin-deep, standing four-square as an ark" (*ST* 30) and has an "un-get-roundable weight" is thus re-imagined later in the poem as part of an airy procession, "a dower of settle beds tumbled from heaven" (31). Thus, "whatever is given // Can always be reimagined, however four-square, / Plank-thick, hull-stupid and out of its time / It happens to be" (31). If heavy, material things can be made airy and lightsome, so can the poet's state of mind and his poetry. By extension, the poem implies, so can the weighty matter of sectarianism in Northern Ireland.[12]

This motif of heavy objects made light continues in the "The Skylight," the seventh lyric of the sonnet sequence "Glanmore Revisited," where Heaney explores the narrative articulated in Mark 2: 1–12 about the paralytic being lowered to Jesus by his friends and healed. The heavy weight of the friend and his subsequent healing and ability to walk parallel both the poet's sense of release when his wife had a skylight inserted into his study at Glanmore Cottage and a given poem's ability to be released and take on a life of its own. Heaney had originally opposed putting a skylight in his Glanmore Cottage study but his wife had it done while he was away on a trip. He had "liked it low and closed, / Its claustrophobic, nest-up-in-the-roof / Effect." The length of the octave in this hybrid sonnet with a rhyme scheme that fits neither that of the Petrarchan nor that of the Shakespearean sonnet after an *abab* opening reminiscent of the Shakespearean sonnet signifies Heaney's opposition to having such an opening cut in his nest-like study. Likewise, the relative terseness of the succeeding sestet reinforces his shock upon seeing the skylight: "extravagant / Sky entered and held surprise wide open." Thus for a time, "I felt like an inhabitant / Of that house where the man sick of the palsy / Was lowered through the roof, had his sins forgiven, / Was healed, took up his bed and walked away" (39). The cumulative heaviness of the sick man's body, his illness, and his sins constitute a weight (represented by the "heavy" octave) that connotes Heaney too felt a significant burden lifted from him and his poetry once this skylight was opened. It symbolized his ability to look skyward—literally and metaphorically—and away from the killing grounds of Northern Ireland. "The Skylight" signifies a new commitment to poetry's buoyancy and potential—to its ability to open spiritual windows beyond ourselves. Moreover, in language redolent of this poem, Heaney has argued that a poem "must be all of a piece, must grow its own legs, arise, take up its bed, and walk. Ideally it will have that element of surprised arrival."[13] The surprise of the skylight likely also suggests the surprise of the just-arrived poem that has grown and risen to walk forth from the poet's mind.

In "Fostering," the concluding poem of Part I of *Seeing Things*, Heaney rehearses his turn toward (really return to) spiritual matters, employing the Shakespearean sonnet form to structure his meditation on how he finally moved from the relative constraint of his earthy, watery childhood landscape to the airscape of the marvelous. Here, although he does not employ tercets, the use of the sonnet enables him to make a formal farewell of sorts to his previously favored quatrain. The relative solidity of the octave—two quatrains married, as it were—enables Heaney to formally signify the opening "heavy greenness—"of the picture the young boy spies at school (52). The "in-placeness" of the windmills and millhouses lead him to reflect upon his own flooded, muddy landscape of South Derry: "My silting hope. My lowlands of the mind." This medial full caesura may signify that he felt how brooding upon that scene stopped up the flowing river of his creativity to some degree, and that "Heaviness of being. And poetry / Sluggish in the doldrums of what happens," carries over into the sestet, which traditionally makes a turn in thought at this point from the subject first mooted in the octave. If poetry is likened to a ship, as indeed it is throughout this volume, here Heaney sees his own poetry as a burdened ship constrained by daily events, a "doldrums" that prevents any inspiration from filling its sails. That his sluggishness of the ordinary floods into, as it were, the opening lines of the sestet suggests even more strongly its constraining power upon his imagination and led to "Me waiting until I was nearly fifty / To credit marvels." As the poem finally moves into the concluding couplet, a "lift-off" occurs: "So long for air to brighten, / Time to be dazzled and the heart to lighten" (52). This last, buoyant verb leads us into the long sequence of Part II, "Squarings," with its visions of the afterlife and the extraordinary. Heaney's procession of three infinitives in the last line and a half of "Fosterling" charges the atmosphere of the midpoint of *Seeing Things* with a heady anticipation of the future poems that promise to deliver on this grammatical potential.

"Squarings" is itself broken into four smaller divisions—"Lightenings," "Settings," "Crossings," and "Squarings"—with twelve twelve-line lyrics in each of those four sections for a total of forty-eight poems. Each lyric is simply assigned a number and the numbers continue throughout the entire "Squarings" sequence so that it ends with "xlviii," or "48." This numbering strategy enables the poet to focus our attention on the content of the lyrics as a sort of set of numbered "snapshots" he offers us, none more important than the other. Heaney originally had not planned such a sequence, but after writing the second lyric as a kind of diptych to the first one, and then a third lyric to form a triptych, the word "squaring" "offered a way ahead" and "suggested that I might try to do twelve of these twelve-liners, and since that didn't seem impossible, I decided to try it."[14] A devotee of the sonnet, Heaney had been experimenting with forms that approached that fourteen-line form since early in his career, as his Hopkins pastiche from 1959, "October Thought," demonstrates. After Heaney's close friend Ted Hughes read the "Squarings" sequence (what Heaney first called "The Quartet" in perhaps a nod to Eliot's late masterpiece, "The Four Quartets"), he declared in a letter to Heaney, "I like the way the form avoids the closure of the sonnet—less ceremonious, more open on every side—yet suggests a formal music, a chosen measure, just as compact."[15] Given his growing penchant for the unrhymed or pararhymed tercet and his affection for the quatrain in his 1970s poetry, the evolution of the twelve-liner—four groups of tercets—seems an organic formal evolution for Heaney, a sort of hybrid form that nods to his predilection for quatrains in its overall number of four stanzas and that gestures to his fondess for the tercet as the final formal stanzaic unit of his career. The twelve-liner, then, helped keep him formally anchored yet responsive to fluid promptings that could not be contained or corralled by form.

Yeats became the governing poetic spirit over the entire "Squarings" sequence and that poet's commitment to being a visionary attuned to spiritual realities beyond the material world bulked large for Heaney at this time. At the same time, the bleak realism of another exemplar, Philip Larkin, begins the sequence and prevents its full spiritual liftoff, particularly in its opening lyric. Heaney had been working on annotating a selection of Yeats's poetry for the *Field Day Anthology of Irish Writing* in the Reading Room of the National Library in Dublin one August afternoon in 1988 when, he tells us, the first poem of the "Squarings" sequence arrived, a surprise in the sense that "The Skylight" implies poetry always is:

> There was a definite sense of release, of a pressure lifted, a light let in, and I'm sure that had something to do with the given-ness of the lines. A great sense too of the dimensions of Yeats's achievement, the boldness of his imagining, the extravagance of his concerns with life after death, with the adventures of the soul when it leaves the body, with its "shiftings," as he calls it one place.[16]

This first poem concerns the afterlife and imagines its contours in an unblinking chronicle that if it does not resonate with and reflect the resurrection of the body promised in Heaney's Catholicism, nonetheless offers a picture of the soul wandering free in another country.

This opening lyric of "Lightenings" begins with a half line, "Shifting brilliancies," which employs Yeats's occult term for the soul leaving the body (55). It may also echo the advice of the longship's tongue in "North" to the poet to "'Expect aurora borealis / in the long foray / but no cascade of light'" (N 11). Heaney had originally considered calling the poem "Shiftings," and in an earlier draft had rendered the initial half line as "Brilliant tourbillons."[17] "Tourbillon," a French word, means a whirlwind or a skyrocket that ascends in a spiral flight,[18] and combining the two meanings of the word renders a double image of spiraling light and wind. Perhaps Heaney felt finally that such a picture of the escaping soul was too dramatic and settled instead for the Yeatsian "Shifting brilliancies," a quieter but nonetheless evocative phrase that leaves us surprisingly ill-prepared for the fairly bleak world we encounter in succeeding lines.

There, in the "winter light / In a doorway," we spy "A beggar shivering in silhouette," a representation of the soul awaiting judgment in the afterlife. This minimalist environment, a "Bare wallstead and a cold hearth rained into—" seems a let down after the opening half-line, a sort of Beckettian bleakscape where there is "Nothing magnificent, nothing unknown. / A gazing out from far away, alone" (55).[19] This "commanded journey" and the gritty knowledge of nothingness recall Philip Larkin's horrifying poem about the afterlife, "Aubade," along with the opening poem proper of *Seeing Things*, "The Journey Back," in which "Larkin's shade" quotes Dante's *Inferno*, Canto I, and then states that his own travel toward the afterlife "'felt more like the forewarned journey back / Into the heartland of the ordinary'" (9). Like Larkin's speaker in "Aubade," Heaney's speaker believes there is only "old truth dawning: there is no next-time-round. / Unroofed scope. Knowledge-freshening wind" (55). Now, the previously transformative power of the skylight in the poem of that name and the positive feeling of surprise there and in "Fosterling" are replaced, brought down to earth, as it were, by the thudding plainness of these lines and their stark vision. Even the ever-new surprise of poetry's arrival in the mind seems lessened here, laid bare, despite Heaney's protestation that the lyric is "still susceptible to the numinous" (*SS* 319). It is a vision from which "Squarings" never fully recovers, despite a procession of succeeding poems that credit the power of the marvelous, even the miraculous. If Yeats's spirit governs the sequence, Larkin's appeal to the ordinary, even his tendency toward nihilism, offers a counterbalance to such rapturous delights.

This lyric crystallizes Heaney's argument about Yeats's and Larkin's competing visions in his 1990 essay, "Joy or Night: Last Things in the Poetry of W. B. Yeats and Philip Larkin." Heaney states there that as Larkin got older, "his vision got arrested into a fixed stare at the inexorability of his own physical extinction. Human wisdom ... seemed ... a matter of operating within the mortal limits, and of quelling any false hope of transcending or outfacing the inevitable." Citing Yeats's "The Cold Heaven" whose life-affirming spirit he will later offer as a counter to Larkin's hopeless "Aubade," Heaney then claims that "Yeats's poem still conveys a strong impression of direct encounter" in which "The spirit still suffers from a sense of answerability, of responsibility to a something out there, an intuited element that is as credible as the 'rook-delighting heaven' itself."[20] But there seems nothing of Yeats's "exultant intonation" in Heaney's first lyric in "Lightenings," and while it may be intended to manifest "the idea that there exists a much greater, circumambient energy and order within which we have our being," as he perceived in the rhymes, rhythms, and joyful intonation of Yeats's astonishing poem, thematically and formally, it is an altogether quieter, more lonely affair.[21] Even the relative brevity of this lyric contrasts the much fuller lineation of Yeats's poem. Yet the poems that follow embrace both the sensuous materiality of human existence along with the energy of poetry itself as a respite from this bleak vision of the afterlife and, taken together, finally offer a sort of counter-spirituality to it.

If Heaney's pared-down, bare imagining of the afterlife begins the sequence, in subsequent poems he revels more fully than ever in some ways about this material life, which is occasionally shot through with amazing moments of splendor and the fantastic. Thus, in the very next lyric, "ii," he responds to the "Unroofed scope" of the bare afterlife he has just imagined in a series of imperative lines that return him to the concreteness of his Glanmore Cottage and to the bedrock of sensation itself, into which he drives himself and the poem. He has even stated that the second lyric is "a kind of antiphonal response . . . to the line with which the first poem ended . . ."[22] Line one thus opens as a reversal of unroofing revealed in the last lines of "i": "Roof it again. Batten down. Dig in." After his exposure to the insensate world in the previous lyric, he craves physicality experienced through his senses: "Drink out of tin. Know the scullery cold . . ." He therefore anchors himself back in the cottage's materiality, taking "squarings from the recessed gable pane," and vows to "Sink every impulse like a bolt. Secure / The bastion of sensation. Do not waver / Into language. Do not waver in it" (*ST* 56). At first, even language seems a wavering from the bedrock of sensation here, but then the last line suggests that sufficiently material language can secure us and give us respite from those forces that would dislodge us otherwise.

Thus secured in that familiar rural world of flagstone and hearth, iron and tin, he presents us several pictures of images that together lay the foundation for the entire forty-eight-poem sequence in clay and sky and most of all, for the life of poetry itself. For if Heaney finally rejects the Christian world of the afterlife, and seemingly Yeats's light-riddled soul on the roadside in what he believes is knowledge of the nothingness beyond this world, he nonetheless affirms poetry and poetic knowledge and thus, indirectly perhaps, the existence of the soul.

Heaney had been reading the Catholic thinker Jacques Maritain's 1953 study, *Creative Intuition in Art and Poetry*, during the time he composed the entire "Squarings" sequence and Maritain's thinking about this subject deeply confirmed his own conception of poetry, first shaped by the English Romantic poets. Heaney cites Maritain's last chapter, "The Three Epiphanies of Creative Intuition," in his uncollected essay, "Sixth Sense, Seventh Heaven," wherein he meditates upon Wordsworth's famous articulation of poetry in the 1802 Preface for Wordsworth's and Coleridge's *Lyrical Ballads* as "emotion . . . recollected in tranquility."[23] He outlines Maritain's account of the poetic process as beginning with the "Poetic Sense of Inner Melody," continuing with a coalescence into "Action and Theme," which together result in "the actual writing, what he chooses to call Number or Harmonic Expansion." Both Maritain and himself, he claims, are most interested in this second stage and Heaney positively cites Maritain's affirmation of "creative emotion," which gives life to action and theme.[24] Maritain's theory of poetry is Aristotelian and Thomistic, and even though Heaney does not finally share Maritain's Catholic faith and belief that art gestures toward and is in some ways analogous to that faith, he nonetheless believes that poetry itself is a site of super-abundant activity, a teeming site of life where words collide and are charged with peculiar energies that summon poet and reader alike. Poetry's living power constitutes the subject of the subsequent forty-seven lyrics that follow the bleak lyric "i" and while their verbal felicities cannot compensate for what he thinks is his sure knowledge of the nothingness inherent in the afterlife, they nonetheless offer rich explorations of poetry's power to enchant us and transport us to other worlds.

Lyric "iii," for instance, situates the poet in an analogous way to a schoolboy preparing to shoot marbles, beginning with the question, "Squarings?", and then offering a definition: "squarings / Were all those anglings, aimings, feints, and squints / You were allowed before you'd shoot . . ." (57). The introduction of squarings in the game of marbles strikes a note of spontaneity to counter the rigid pictures of a bleak afterlife and utterly material world in lyrics "i" and "ii", respectively. Moreover, this improvisational posture suggests that this lyric and the ones that follow throughout the entire larger "Squarings" sequence will traffic not so much in certainties, but in possibilities grounded in this world and open to those beyond it. Indeed, "iii" ends with just this suggestion, musing upon "that space / Marked with three round holes and a drawn line. / You squinted out from a skylight of the world" (57).

Lyric "v" returns to these three holes for marbles that the poet's uncle "thumbed in the concrete road" in the 1920s before emigrating to

Australia, and it confirms Heaney's embrace of a jazz-like, spontaneous spirit in "Squarings," undergirded and inspired by the twelve-line form. As he sees those holes in his mind's eye, he posits that they are "Three stops to play / The music of the arbitrary on," and urges himself to "Improvise. Make free / Like old hay in its flimsy afterlife // High on a windblown hedge" (59). This notion of the poet recalls Heaney's statement that T. S. Eliot's deeply nuanced "auditory imagination" "confirmed a natural inclination to make myself an echo chamber for the poem's sounds."[25] It also resonates with his adoption of the airy, flitting Sweeney persona in the last third of *Station Island*.

And yet we sense that these poems not only confirm Heaney's growing desire to become more lightsome in his poetry, but also to do so through the venue of form. When the twelve-line form first came to him, "It seemed solid as an iron bar," and then he "began to treat it as a different kind of *barre*, a stimulus to repeating the exercise . . . The form operated for me as a generator of poetry" (*SS* 321). The twelve-line form offered him considerable technical opportunities. Composed of four tercets, his favorite stanza form for the last part of his career, it allows for four quick "snapshots" of an object or a situation that form a composite picture.

Moreover, as "v" demonstrates, within those lines, he could illustrate the content by manipulation of the lineation. The first three-and-a-half lines are enjambed, conveying the rush of memory the poet experiences in recalling those long-ago marble holes. Then there is a medial caesura in the middle of line four, an endstop, succeeded by "Three stops to play / The music of the arbitrary on." The formal pause, that is, enables us to sense the poet beginning to play his music on the holes or "stops" of the poem itself. He then gives us two-and-a-half lines that are enjambed, running across the tercet divisions, as the first set of enjambed lines do. These later lines conclude with a full stop, followed by a series of shorter stops and then two concluding enjambed lines:

> The empty bottle. Improvise. Make free
> Like old hay in its flimsy afterlife
>
> High on a windblown hedge. Ocarina earth.
> Three listening posts up on some hard-baked tier
> Above the resonating amphorae. (*ST* 59)

This procession of longer lines interspersed with shorter, more staccato words and partial lines demonstrate the type of music Heaney wants to blow throughout the rest of "Squarings" as he improvises lines to capture the essence of fleeting memories from his past and other, imagined situations.

The most memorable and best-known of all the lyrics in the forty-eight-poem sequence is "viii," which treats the appearance of a ghost ship at the monastic settlement of Clonmacnoise in Ireland. It opens with a plausible source, "The annals say:", but what follows is so fantastic that it is difficult to credit. But the poem's willingness to assay the marvelous credits poetry itself, in Heaney's terms from his Nobel Prize address, and it seeks to lead us back into a belief in poetry's capacity to awaken us to wonders beyond our ken, if not faith. The ship that "appeared above them [the praying monks] in the air" materializes out of thin air and catches its anchor on the "altar rails" and stops. The monastery is another world to the crewman who climbs down to try to free the anchor rope and, similarly, the monks regard him and his ship as Other. When the abbot informs his monks that "'This man can't bear our life here and will drown,'" they help free the ship: "So / They did, the freed ship sailed, and the man climbed back / Out of the marvelous as he had known it" (62). From the perspective of each community the other is the marvelous, the wondrous. This momentary two-way traffic between earthly life, represented by orthodox Catholic Ireland, and the life of the Yeatsian imagination suggests how impoverished each life is without interaction with the other, yet at the same time, how dangerous immersion in another world can be for those not used to it. The poem thus not only seeks to awaken us to the possibilities the imagination can generate, but also serves as a warning about what can happen when imagination and reality collide. Heaney noted how he realized that both this lyric and English metaphysical poet George Herbert's "The Pulley" are "about the way consciousness can be alive to two different and contradictory dimensions of reality and still find a way of negotiating between them . . ."[26] For Heaney, both poems are about the "frontier of writing" that his later poetry, beginning with *The Haw Lantern*, has addressed. Thus he concludes his essay, "Frontiers of Writing," stating unequivocally, "within our individual selves we can reconcile two orders of knowledge which we might call the practical and the poetic . . . each form of knowledge redresses the other and . . . the frontier between them is there for the crossing," then cites his lyric about the ghostly ship at Clonmacnoise again.[27] This twelve-liner encapsulates Heaney's latest development of his long-standing interest in liminality and is perhaps the clearest poetic articulation of his desire to be lodged in this world yet attuned to the marvelous possibilities beyond the five senses but discernible through his poetic sixth sense. As he suggested elsewhere, "when a poem manages to get up on its own legs" and move, "a sixth sense of possibility grows into a gleeful seventh heaven of reward."[28]

These first twelve poems of "Squarings," which Heaney entitles

"Lightenings," conclude with a meditation on the word "lightening" that demonstrates how, despite Heaney's own loss of his Catholic faith, he nonetheless remains open to that Christian "heaven of reward." After defining "lightening" as "alleviation, / Illumination," he settles on a meaning he seems to prefer: "A phenomenal instant when the spirit flares / With pure exhilaration before death—", lines that themselves suggest that flaring and then the spirit's passage with the judiciously placed dash. He then imagines the "good thief in us harking to the promise!" As this thief hangs on the right side of Christ, he seems to briefly contemplate something like the nihilistic afterlife Heaney envisions in lyric "i," "Scanning empty space . . ." But the poem concludes after giving us a series of lunar images of his aching body with the promise of Christ's words to him: *"This day thou shalt be with Me in Paradise"* (66). At least rhetorically, Heaney therefore credits the possibility of the Christian heaven for believers, a complement to the heaven of the marvelous world from which his ghost ship sailed in lyric "viii."

Such paradises fade from view for a time in the next section, "Settings," in favor of quiet visions from the poet's childhood. In "xiii," for instance, he ponders "Hazel stealth. A trickle in the culvert," and revisits his family kitchen at Mossbawn: "Chairs on all fours. A platerack braced and laden. / The fossil poetry of hob and slate." Re-entering this scene "as the adult of solitude," he recalls "the definite / Presence you sensed withdrawing first time round" (67). Whether this phrase signifies the *deus absconditus* or the remembrance of a parent's death is unclear; Heaney has set the stage for a series of quiet lyrics or "settings," whereby he re-adopts his favorite posture of listening and observing. Thus, in "xv," he remembers "Stable straw, Rembrandt-gleam and burnish // Where my father bends to a tea-chest packed with salt," with "his right hand foraging // For the unbleeding, vivid-fleshed bacon . . ." Here, the poet casts himself as a childlike Joseph from the Book of Genesis, who "owned the piled grain of Egypt," standing "in the door, unseen and blazed upon" (69).

Two of the last poems of "Settings," "xxi" and "xxii," ponder the soul again by recourse to Catholic teaching and Yeats's poetry, respectively. In "xxi," Heaney recalls firing a .22 rifle and hitting a handkerchief square "sixty yards away." Firing the gun gave him "A whole new quickened sense of what *rifle* meant," and immediately he reverts to prelapsarian language from the beginning of Genesis: "And then again as it was in the beginning / I saw the soul like a white cloth snatched away"; he believes that firing "that shot" was a "sin" that he commits "against eternal life— / Another phrase dilating in new light" (75). To his credit, the non-believing Heaney again makes room for the language of faith and he cleverly employs a dash again—here to signify the bullet's flight through the air.

One of the most intriguing poems in the entire larger "Squarings" sequence, "xxii," explicitly explores the state and habitation of the soul through recourse to Yeats's poetry and settles upon form as the proper dwelling for both poetry and the soul. This lyric was originally entitled "Small Fantasia for W.B.," and the poem explores possible dwelling states for the soul by investigating different aspects of Yeats's thought—both the poet's gritty desire to embrace our earthly desires, foul though they may be, and the haughty, elitist mask that the poet could don. Thus Heaney seems to answer his own question, "Where does spirit live?", by answering with a question, "On dungy sticks / In a jackdaw's nest up in the old stone tower // Or a marble bust commanding the parterre?" Along with drawing upon Yeats's desire to "lie down in the foul rag and bone shop of the heart" in "The Circus Animals' Desertion," the first part of this answering question explicitly recalls part six of the sequence "Meditations in Time of Civil War," "The Stare's Nest by My Window," where Yeats asks honeybees four times to "Come build in the empty house of the stare" or starling.[29] The old stone tower certainly references Yeats's Norman tower, Thoor Ballylee. The two locations where the soul might "roost at last" appear to be either in the fragility of the "jackdaw's nest" on the flat, exposed roof of Thoor Ballylee, which recalls Heaney's sense of being "unroofed" in the 1980s by his parents' deaths, or the marble, monumental places suggested by Yeats's marble bust. In the end the poet settles for neither fragility nor seeming stony permanence but affirms instead poetic form, asking "How habitable is perfected form?", and further, "What's the use of a held note or held line / That cannot be assailed for reassurance?" (76).[30] In its final form, this lyric ends "(Set questions for the ghost of W.B.)," which weakens the original last line, "That cannot be assailed for reassurance?," and simply renders it as one of a series of questions in the poem rather than the most important question of them all. Keeping the original last line also paradoxically calls form's permanence into question to some degree even as it privileges it.[31] The question's rhetorical force affirms both form's dynamism and its autonomy. As Denis Donoghue has articulated, "Form transfigures what otherwise merely exists, and by that transfiguration it maintains the validity of freedom. It is not creation from nothing, but a further creation from the otherwise created. Form is content as imagined . . ."[32] Heaney finally places his faith not in the scaffolding of the Catholic church nor in the fragile nest of the jackdaw nor in marble monumentality, but in the poem's form. Its habitability stems from its generative, creative properties, which in turn create a kind of eternal ongoingness every time the poem is read or recited.

In his Nobel Prize address, Heaney argues that lyric poetry can achieve an "adequacy" from "the resolution and independence which the entirely realized poem sponsors," an adequacy that stems "as much" from "the energy released by linguistic fission and fusion, with the buoyancy generated by cadence and tone and rhyme and stanza, as it has to do with the poem's concerns or the poet's truthfulness." He continues: "In fact, in lyric poetry, truthfulness becomes recognizable as a ring of truth within the medium itself" (*CP* 28). The independent lives of poems guarantee their movement and energy, and they are adequate to their encounter with the world outside themselves because of their realization as created worlds with integrity.

Through the force of the poem's form, through its created freedom and rolling energy, Heaney can cross the frontier of writing between reality and the realm of the imagination, a frontier he treads repeatedly in the third section of the overall "Squarings" sequence, "Crossings," nowhere more than in "xxxiv," which begins with a quotation from Yeats and ends with a vision of a "Vietnam-bound soldier" on a bus in California. The Yeats passage, "*To those who see spirits, human skin / For a long time afterwards appears most coarse,*" is a near-paraphrase of a passage in a letter from that poet to Dorothy Wellesley (*SS* 88). When identifying this quotation from Yeats, Heaney remembered the soldier memorialized in the poem, noting "he looked doomed and there was a pallor on his brow . . . it gave him that ghost-who-walks look. I'll never forget it. A crossing, for sure. The airport bus as death coach" (324). The youthful lad "could have been one of the newly dead come back, // Unsurprisable but still disappointed," with "His shaving cuts, his otherworldly brow" (*ST* 88). Haunted by this appearance of the soldier, "The face I see that all falls short of since" (88), Heaney elegizes him through re-animating some of what were likely his last moments in America through the force of the poem's form. The longer lineation in the first three tercets, particularly the poem's longest line, "He could have been one of the newly dead come back," now subsides in the last tercet, which features the shortest lineation in the poem and thus may symbolize the soldier's short life.

"Crossings" concludes with "xxxvi," a lyrical tribute to Heaney's early friendship with his fellow Northern Irish poet Michael Longley, with whom he once went on a civil rights march in Newry. That "crossing," their traversing "through a valley," becomes both biblical (recalling "through the valley of the shadow of death" in the Lord's Prayer) and Dantesque, when the poet recalls "We were like herded shades who had to cross // And did cross" to the car they arrived in. Once Heaney and Longley sit in the car, it "gave when we got in / Like Charon's boat under the faring poets" (90), a prefiguring of the last poem in *Seeing Things*, "The Crossing."

By the time Heaney writes the last twelve lyrics, which share the title of "Squarings" with the larger forty-eight-poem sequence, he appears sufficiently "squared up" to his task of firmly situating himself (and us too, by extension) in the form of the poem and offers a series of solid "seats" that signify form's durability. The 39th lyric thus pictures someone sitting "in the basalt throne / Of the 'wishing chair' at Giant's Causeway," where "The small of your back made very solid sense" (93). Lyric "xl" returns the poet to the "earth house" of his childhood cottage at Mossbawn, its "clay floor" and "Ground of being," where "I inherited / A stack of singular, cold memory-weights / To load me, hand and foot, in the scale of things" (94).

But gradually such solidity fades away in the final poems of the sequence, just as in "xliii," the hare's "prints stop, just like that, in snow. / End of the line. Smooth drifts. Where did she go?" (97). The sense of departure ghosts these last poems, and in "xliv" Heaney ponders the fate of those who have passed away. Have they really, he wonders, *"All gone into the world of light?"* He seems to favor a mysterious nihilism instead, more tempered than his barren images of the afterlife with which the entire "Squarings" sequence starts back in lyric "i." So "All gone" becomes analogous to the moment when "the rod butt loses touch and the tip drools" after a fish is lost (98). The last and forty-eighth lyric epitomizes his newfound belief in imaginative truth. He muses that "Seventh heaven may be / The whole truth of a sixth sense come to pass," and this lyric intuits "how things once in the offing, once they're sensed, / Convert to things foreknown . . ." He pictures himself as driving once again, this time at dawn, "when light breaks over me / The way it did on the road beyond Coleraine" up near the northern coast of Northern Ireland. There, he believes, "Out in mid-channel between the painted poles, / That day I'll be in step with what escaped me" (102). Hovering in this liminal, aquatic space, he hopes to eventually receive the fleeting thing—the "Seventh heaven"—that he has tried to attain in his poems but that often eludes him like that hopping hare.

The Spirit Level, Heaney's first volume after winning the Nobel Prize in 1995 and dedicated to Helen Vendler, continues his exploration of this seventh heaven. It won both the Commonwealth Literature Award and the Whitbread Book of the Year. This title signifies a carpenter's tool with a bubble or "spirit" that must be balanced in the middle for a line or wall to be straight, but it also courts connotations with spirituality. Now "squared" up to his subjects after *Seeing Things*, Heaney furthers his exploration of the spirit world, yet always grounds these forays in the incarnational—the things of this world. The bees on the Faber and Faber cover suggest the sweetness of poetry in a time of continuing suffering worldwide and recalls the poet's evocation of Yeats's honeybees in "Meditations in Time of Civil War" that he desires to build in the stare's empty nest. Heaney references these bees explicitly in his Nobel Prize speech, observing the poem's combination of being "tough-minded" and "tender-minded":

> It satisfies the contradictory needs which consciousness experiences at times of extreme crisis, the need on the one hand for a truth-telling that will be hard and retributive, and on the other hand, the need not to harden the mind to a point where it denies its own yearnings for sweetness and trust. (CP 26–7)

Similarly, these poems both tell the truth and allow sweetness and light to flood in, keeping our consciousness alive both to continuing suffering and the possibility of its alleviation.

"The Rain Stick" and "Postscript" frame *The Spirit Level* and these two poems traffic in the marvelous dimension of the otherworldly that Heaney kept exploring as the 1990s proceeded. While "The Rain Stick" urges us to listen, even to music we have often heard before, "Postscript" implores us to see afresh. The former poem starts with "Upend" and the latter concludes with "open," together suggesting how the poet wants to upend our expectations as readers, as thinkers, as human beings, and by so doing, to open us to the possibility of music and visions beyond our normal ken (*SL* 1, 70).

"The Rain Stick" is written in Heaney's now common loose tercet form and seems even more unmoored from the *aba bcb* rhyme scheme of *terza rima* than previous poems. And yet the enjambment of a series of lines echoes the onrushing power of the *terza rima* rhyme scheme and highlights the falling "water" sound that the rainstick makes when "played" or upended. For instance, the first two and a half lines are enjambed to signify the hidden music of both *terza rima* and the rain stick itself: "Upend the rain stick and what happens next / Is a music that you never would have known / To listen for . . ." By the second tercet, speaker and rain stick fuse as Heaney returns to his theory of the poet being an echo chamber for the sounds of his poetry: "You stand there like a pipe / Being played by water, you shake it again lightly . . ." Paradoxically, the dry seeds of the original cactus falling sound like liquid—"subtle little wets," "glitter-drizzle, almost-breaths of air." At the end of the poem, the poet again invokes Christ's parable in Matthew 19: 24 of its being easier for a camel to enter the eye of a needle than for a rich man to enter heaven:

"You are like a rich man entering heaven / Through the ear of a raindrop. Listen now again" (1). Interestingly, in Heaney's refiguring of the parable, the listener becomes "rich" by hearing the music of the rain stick and can thus enter a heaven of delight through "the ear of a raindrop," the sound made by the stick. He implies that we too may be enriched by attending closely to this and the poems that follow.

Another unrhymed tercet poem, "St Kevin and the Blackbird," has become one of Heaney's paradigmatic poems of carefulness and forgetting. If the listener's body becomes a conduit of music in "The Rain Stick," in the latter poem, the saint's body is transformed into a prayer as he shelters a blackbird nesting on its eggs in his outstretched hand. The poem's paratactic opening—"And then there was St Kevin and the Blackbird"—suggests its narrative follows a series of other such stories that the speaker might have just told and imparts a conversational feel. St Kevin's duty to the supernatural world leads him to kneel in the posture of a cross and this position in turn enables him to take on a new responsibility to the natural world. Because "the cell is narrow," he must hold "One turned-up palm" out "the window, stiff / As a crossbeam . . ." As the saint "feels the warm eggs, the small breast, the tucked / Neat head and claws," he finds "himself linked / Into the network of eternal life," a phrase that subtly implies his commitment to the natural life cycle even as he kneels in prayer (20).

After a section break following the first four tercets, the tone changes from a reverential, even somber one connoting Kevin's agony in maintaining this posture "for weeks" so that the eggs can hatch to another paratactic rhetorical maneuver introducing a lighter tone, one which nonetheless works well to show how this saint becomes so self-forgetful in his single-minded care for the bird that he forgets it and everything else, becoming a silent receptacle for God's will. Thus, "And since the whole thing's imagined anyhow, / Imagine being Kevin." Heaney wonders whether Kevin is "Self-forgetful or in agony all the time," pondering in a series of successive questions his pain, his connection to the "shut-eyed blank of underearth," and whether he has a "distance in his head?" As he stays kneeling in the shape of the cross, praying, he is "Alone and mirrored clear in love's deep river," and seems to become Heaney's exemplar of sacrificial love. If God never forgets even the sparrow and Kevin cares so deeply for this blackbird and her eggs, God must care even more for us, we might conclude. But the poem sidesteps such a conclusion and instead moves into a tripartite clause Heaney offers to convey Kevin's deep journey out of himself and toward Another as he prays, "'To labour and not to seek reward . . .'" (20). This prayer "his body makes entirely / For he has forgotten self, forgotten bird, / And on the riverbank forgotten the river's name" (21). The repetition of "forgotten" followed by three different nouns drums home Kevin's habitual praying and waiting. Even though the eggs are never portrayed as hatching, the poem nonetheless implies the hope that words can be incarnated and literally shape our posture, our attitude. If this process is entered into unselfishly, as in Kevin's case, words can lead us out of ourselves and into attention and care for the Other—whether animals or other human beings. Such a stance exemplifies the Christian concept of *kenosis* or self-emptying, a habit that practiced enough, as Douglas E. Christie argues, enables us to live in "This emptiness, this dark place, this desert—utterly desolate and seemingly bereft of hope . . ." Such a no-space finally "becomes a kind of home, a place in which to dwell and apprehend the mystery of the world."[33] Heaney's St Kevin occupies this type of home in which he can feel the pain and suffering of the blackbird, its slowly hatching eggs, and by extension, the travails of the entire world. The poet himself became a sort of St Kevin in this regard, agonizing often over whether he had done the right thing by putting himself in the place of others and often empathizing with them.

In language resonant of this poem expressed in *Crediting Poetry*, Heaney recalls being "bowed to the desk like some monk bowed over his prie-dieu, some dutiful contemplative" trying "to bear his portion of the weight of the world . . . constrained by his obedience to his rule to repeat the effort and the posture" (*CP* 19–20). But finally, he relates, "I straightened up. I began a few years ago to try to make space in my reckoning and imagining for the marvelous as well as for the murderous." And so he then tells the story of St Kevin and the blackbird, arguing that St Kevin's bowed posture exemplifies his own renewed attention to the life of the imagination in poetry. He sees the saint as occupying "the intersection of natural process and the glimpsed ideal, at one and the same time a signpost and a reminder" (20). For Heaney, Kevin's carefulness and forgetfulness manifest "that order of poetry where we can at last grow up to that which we stored up as we grew," a cryptic remark that suggests Kevin as an exemplar for sustained attention to poetry over a lifetime. Heaney values this story not only for these reasons, however, but also because its "trustworthiness and its travel-worthiness have to do with its local setting" (21). St Kevin and his narrative could spring from almost any local culture and, if sufficiently grounded, could express the life of that culture and how careful observation of it might provide a base for a poetry poised between "natural process and the glimpsed ideal," the liminal state that the saint and increasingly Heaney seemed to occupy.

The very next poem in the volume, "The Flight Path," remains one of Heaney's more ambitious sequences, linking as it does various flights with his rise as a poet but finally privileging the quiet ascent of a figurative, hopeful dove. Its middle sections, however, are marred by the reportorial sections four and five, which are flat and relatively unimaginative. It begins with the poet's memory of his father's folding a piece of paper into a boat. While the young boy watched, "A dove rose in my breast / Every time my father's hands came clean / With a paper boat between them, ark in air . . ." Drawing on the Biblical story of Noah's ark in the book of Genesis, Heaney suggests how every time the paper boat was launched, he would hope that it would last, but instead, even as hope represented by the dove would rise within him, "a part of me . . . sank because it knew / The whole thing would go soggy once you launched it" (*SL* 22). It is difficult not to equate the repeated launch of such fragile paper arks with the venture of poetry, particularly since Heaney had spent so much of *Seeing Things* linking various boats with poetry and closes *Crediting Poetry* with his analogy likening poetic form to "both the ship and the anchor" (*CP* 29). Much of the rest of the poem meditates implicitly and sometimes more explicitly upon how poetry can take off and sail or fly in particular conditions.

The next two sections look up rather than down, "Into those *full-starred heavens that winter sees*," a quotation from Thomas Hardy's "Afterwards." Section two features the speaker standing in Wicklow, almost certainly at Glanmore Cottage, "under the flight path / Of a late jet out of Dublin," which creates "a wake through starlight" (*SL* 22). Heaney then imagines all those who stay behind when such planes take flight, putting himself in their place. Section three recalls a series of flights to America, including those to Manhattan, California, and Cambridge, Massachusetts, where the poet taught for many years at Harvard. These highly end-stopped lines, also featuring many medial and other caesuras, contrast the many enjambed, flowing lines of the first two sections. The punctuation thus renders the many flights of this third section and the poet's memory of them as a series of short bursts, staccato entries into America and re-entries back into Ireland. Glanmore is repeatedly evoked toward the end of this section as the safe haven Heaney had always felt it to be, and he hammers home that message in such repetitive lines as "So to Glanmore. Glanmore. Glanmore. Glanmore. / At bay, at one, at work, at risk and sure" (23). Even if these iterations do not make for great poetry, they seem necessary "rivets" that the poet must bang home in the midst of a long sequence so concerned with departures and arrivals, and they hearken back to lyric "ii" in "Squarings" where the poet revels in the concreteness of Glanmore Cottage, which, especially after he and his wife bought it from Ann Saddlemyer in the late 1980s, became even more "a silence bunker, a listening post, a holding, in every sense of that word. It holds meaning and things, and even adds meaning" (*SS* 325).

Sections four and five concern two incidents Heaney had on the way to and within Northern Ireland, respectively, the first a run-in with the notorious Sinn Fein Director of Publicity Danny Morrison who said at the 1981 *Ard Fheis* (political party conference), "Who here really believes that we can win the war through the ballot box? But will anyone here object if with a ballot paper in this hand and an Armalite in this hand we take power in Ireland?"[34] As the exhilarated poet rides the train from Dublin to Belfast "One bright May morning, nineteen-seventy-nine," Morrison enters his compartment "As if he were some *film noir* border guard—" and the poet quickly flashes back to a dream he had "When he'd flagged me down at the side of a mountain road" and told him to drive a van, presumably laden with explosives to Pettigo, the border village that serves as launching point for trips to Station Island (*SL* 24). Morrison sits down across from Heaney and asks, "'When, for fuck's sake, are you going to write / Something for us?'" The shocked poet replies, "'If I do write something, / Whatever it is, I'll be writing for myself'" (25). Again, while this portion of the poem clearly does not rise to the level of Heaney's greatest poetry, it must have seemed necessary for him to write at the time. He has recalled making "the speaker a bit more aggressive than he was at the time," but "faithfully" rendering "the presumption of entitlement on his part . . ." (*SS* 257). Heaney "simply rebelled at being commanded." And despite having "toyed with the idea of dedicating the Ugolino translation [from *Field Work*] to the prisoners [Republicans on "the dirty protest" in the H-blocks]," he mused that "our friend's intervention put paid to any such gesture. After that, I wouldn't give and wasn't so much free to refuse as unfree to accept" (258). And yet the poet follows his recreation of this encounter with ten lines about the dirty protests with a line beginning, "The gaol walls all those months were smeared with shite," and concluding with three lines from "Ugolino," so even if he did not dedicate "Ugolino" to the dirty protestors, he nonetheless recalls that poem years later here in a sort of tribute to them that is qualified by remembering one of them, Kieran Nugent, as having "red eyes . . . / Like something out of Dante's scurfy hell . . ." (*SL* 25). Nugent was the first IRA prisoner to refuse to wear prison-issued clothes and instead wore the blanket, becoming the first "blanket-man" and thus initiating the first of a series of protests—the blanket and dirty protests, followed by the devastating hunger strikes.[35]

Section five captures another memory from Heaney's past—this time at a roadblock when he tells a startled policeman that he came "from 'far away' . . ." "And now," he muses, "it is—both where I have been living / And where I left—a distance still to go . . ." (25). This shortest section of the poem is followed by the second-shortest and last, which opens with lines suggesting the poet wants to maintain the element of surprise in both his flights and in his poetry: "Out of the blue then, the sheer exaltation / Of remembering climbing zig-zag up warm steps / To the hermit's eyrie above Rocamadour." As he sees a lizard that seems like a lunar vehicle, he salutes him, and the poem concludes, "And somewhere the dove rose. And kept on rising" (26). This section, featuring his solitary, pilgrim-like ascent, and the opening section about his father's paper boats are the strongest parts of the poem, and together they indicate that that the fragile business of poetry is best conducted alone, without the pressure of other travelers, both welcome and unwelcome (like Danny Morrison). Only then, the poet implies, can his hope—troped by the dove that nearly frames the poem—of future poems visiting him "Out of the blue" have a chance of coming true.

A much more daring and artistically successful poem, the five-part "Mycenae Lookout," visits the land- and seascapes of Aeschylus' *Agamemnon*, a world Heaney would explore more fully in his version of Sophocles' *Philoctetes*, *The Cure at Troy*. Perhaps because the subject matter was more distant and foreign to him than his childhood and the matter of Northern Ireland explored in "The Flight Path," here the lines reflect his sure and rich sense of vocabulary and rhyme. For instance, the opening section, "The Watchman's War," drives along in full and near-couplets, a rarely used rhyme scheme for the poet. His keen-eyed observer of the war tells us "I'd dream of blood in bright webs in a ford, / Of bodies raining down like tattered meat / On top of me asleep— and me the lookout / The queen's command had posted and forgotten . . ." He unforgettably likens his tongue to "the dropped gangplank of a cattle truck, / Trampled and rattled, running piss and muck, / All swimmy-trembly as the lick of fire . . ." (29). The pounding monosyllables, interspersed with the by-now classic Heaney ear for onomatopoeic phrases such as "tattered meat," the percussive "piss and muck," and the Anglo-Saxon coinage of "swimmy-trembly" represent Heaney at the top of his form. We apprehend the horrors of war directly through the watchman's indelible language here and later in this section, when he recalls waiting ten years for the war to recommence, staring at the horizon, "the raw wound of that dawn / Igniting and erupting bearing down / Like lava on a fleeing population . . ." (30).

These long lines, redolent both of dawn's redness and of blood-gore, are immediately succeeded by the clipped tercets of section two,

"Cassandra," which relate that prophetess's story. While the watchman observes, we are told in the opening of this section about Cassandra, the daughter of King Priam and Queen Hecuba of Troy, "No such thing / as innocent / bystanding" (30). Cassandra seems to epitomize the spoils of war with "Her soiled vest, / her little breasts, / her clipped, devast- // ated, scabbed punk head ..." (30–1). Her condition elliptically recalls that of the young Windeby "girl" in "Punishment" with her shorn head and slender body. In Aeschylus' version of the story, Cassandra agrees to have sex with the god Apollo in exchange for the gift of prophecy, but when she changes her mind and refuses to sleep with him, he curses her by never allowing others to believe her. Despite warning the Trojans that Paris's abduction of Helen would start the Trojan War, foretelling the Greeks hiding in the wooden horse, and the eventual downfall of Troy, Cassandra was not believed by her people and considered mad. In Heaney's rendition, she is seen as "the char-eyed // famine gawk— / she looked / camp-fucked // and simple" (31). After the fall of Troy, Cassandra was raped by Ajax in Athena's temple and because the Greeks did not punish him, Athena sank most of their fleet as they sailed home from Troy.

Later, King Agamemnon took Cassandra as his whore and his wife Clytemnestra, who had started an affair with Aegisthus while he was away fighting, murdered both Agamemnon and Cassandra. Her murder is told in language as shocking as any Heaney has ever employed, made all the more so by its directness, simplicity, and masculine rhymes:

Little rent
cunt of their guilt:

in she went
to the knife,
to the killer wife ... (32)

The abruptness of her death startles, notably when she says finally, "'the light's // blanked out'" (33).

Helen Vendler terms "Mycenae Lookout" "the emotional centerpiece of *The Spirit Level*," in part because "It speaks from the impotent position of the ordinary citizen caught in the crossfire of civil atrocity, and it predicts the endemic resurgence of violence in culture, as well as representing culture's reiterated attempts to cleanse itself of that violence."[36] The watchman certainly feels that impotence and we feel it with him, as, for instance, in section three, "His Dawn Vision," when he awakens and "felt the beating of the huge time-wound / We lived inside." As he looks down on his civilization, he spies, "Small crowds of people watching as a man / Jumped a fresh earth-wall and another ran / Amorously, it seemed, to strike him down" (34). The timeless, brutal language here recalls the bleak futuristic vision of Auden's "The Shield of Achilles," in which "A crowd of ordinary decent folk / Watched from without and neither moved nor spoke / As three pale figures were led forth and bound / To three posts driven upright in the ground."[37] Heaney suggests, as did Auden before him, that we will be always be inhumane and murderous to each other, and, almost as bad, that most of us will watch that inhumanity and not lift a finger to help. Again, the situation of "Punishment" echoes in the background here, particularly the line in which Heaney accuses himself that he has "stood dumb . . . " (*N* 31).

The fifth and concluding section, "His Reverie of Water," cannot finally wash clean the rampant butchery and deceit of the preceding events narrated in the poem, but its vision of "fresh water" in the form of "A filled bath, still unentered / and unstained," (*SL* 36) and later, the water gushing from "iron pumps" is compelling, all the more so when the poem clearly enters the realm of contemporary Northern Ireland and its hope for healing after the 1994 ceasefires, a period explored more fully in a later poem, "Tollund." When the watchman describes the "set of timber steps" that lead "up / and down from the Acropolis // to the well itself," a staircase where "defenders" and "invaders" would meet, "the ladder of the future / and the past, besieger and besieged," suddenly we are no longer just in ancient Greece. These loaded terms signify how nationalists and republicans in Northern Ireland saw themselves as "defenders" of Ireland against the "invaders," or the descendants of Protestant settlers who had been planted there in the early 1600s. Conversely, some Protestants would still see themselves as "defenders" of the North from those they would consider "invaders," the Irish. Both communities see themselves as "besieged" by a threatening force—the other "tribe." This dialectic of hatred and conflict, troped as "the treadmill of assault // turned waterwheel," seems interminable until Heaney flashes back to that long-ago water pump, his personal Greek *omphalos*, at Mossbawn that he describes in the gorgeous conclusion.[38] He employs a paratactic maneuver to link these last three stanzas to the preceding ones: "And then this ladder of our own that ran / deep into a well-shaft being sunk . . ." That local ladder is connected with a seemingly primal, pure source of water that is so rejuvenating the workers come back up to the surface "like discharged soldiers testing the safe ground, // finders, keepers, seers of fresh water / in the bountiful round mouths of iron pumps / and gushing taps" (37). The well-diggers blend here with the "discharged soldiers," Greek and Trojan, of the Trojan War, with the republicans and loyalists of the Troubles in Northern Ireland, until all are rendered "finders, keepers, seers of fresh water," new Cassandra figures able to peer into the future and glimpse a bountiful future free from killing.

"Tollund," the second poem Heaney would write about the Tollund Man and his burial site, qualifies this gushing optimism about the end of seemingly interminable wars at the end of "Mycenae Lookout," but does so in such a quietly confident and realistic way that we accept it as a matter of course. The six quatrains feature envelope rhymes that run roughly *abba cddc*, etc. This rhyme scheme in a longer poem resembles the sixteen-line sonnets of George Meredith's sequence, *Modern Love* (1862), but outstrips even that form by being twenty-four lines. Some of the quatrains have perfect rhymes, such as two, three, and five, and others, such as one, four, and six, feature quarter and half rhymes. This lack of full rhyming contributes to the poem's realistic tone and thus qualifies the tentative hope about the stoppage of killings. Dated "September 1994," the poem was written in the wake of the IRA ceasefire of August 31, 1994 and before the Combined Loyalist ceasefire on October 13 that year.

Shortly after the IRA had announced their ceasefire, Heaney returned to Denmark, which enabled him to once again write indirectly about the conflict in Northern Ireland as he had in the bog poems of the early- to mid-1970s. This time, instead of visiting the Tollund Man in the museum as he did on his visit to Jutland in 1973, he experienced the actual site where the man's preserved body had been discovered in the 1950s. While the landscape of this part of rural Denmark and by extrapolation the terrain of Northern Ireland in 1994 look familiar—"The low ground, the swart water, the thick grass / Hallucinatory and familiar," modernity has crept in. There is a "satellite // Dish in the paddock," and ancient markers such as a standing stone have been "resituated and landscaped, / With tourist signs in *futhark* runic script / In Danish and in English. Things had moved on." Partly because the literal landscape of this part of Denmark and the figurative landscape of Northern Ireland have changed, they have been rendered familiar yet strange to the speaker and his companion: He calls it "user-friendly outback / Where we stood footloose, at home beyond the tribe, // More scouts than strangers . . ." As we reconnoiter this new territory—charged with the language of new technology ("user-friendly")—and the open frontier of something like the Australian outback through the purposefully plain style Heaney employs, which is largely stripped of his characteristic otherness and wondrous air, we are reassured by the perspicuity of the language and its simplicity. Thus, even though the speaker calls himself and his companion "ghosts who'd walked abroad," specters who have had "to make a new beginning," they are familiar, comfortable shades revisiting an old haunt (69).

As they—and by extension the province of Northern Ireland—now try to "make a go of it, alive and sinning," they are all "Ourselves again, free-willed again, not bad" (69). Heaney has spoken of his time at Tollund in the wake of the IRA ceasefire as "like a world restored, the world of the second chance, and that's why there's an echo of that Shakespearean line, 'Richard's himself again,' in the last stanza" (*SS* 351). "Ourselves again" also plays on the English translation of the formerly IRA-linked Sinn Fein motto, "Ourselves alone," which connotes the siege mentality of many nationalists and republicans in Northern Ireland: Heaney has even pointed out that "I liked the complicating echo of the words 'Sinn Fein' in the phrase 'ourselves again'" (351). Moreover, the lack of rhyme between "ghosts who'd walked abroad" and "Ourselves again, free-willed again, not bad" suggests that just as the North has begun to slip out of old patterns, so has the poem diverted from the regular rhyme scheme in three of its preceding stanzas, even as it retains the chiming "beginning" and "sinning," which may signify a continuity of old customs, patterns, even, perhaps, violence. Certainly, the ceasefires did not hold and were eventually broken, but nevertheless that cessation betokened both a breakthrough and the public's exhaustion with the violence. As Heaney has articulated, even in the wake of the IRA's bombing of London's Canary Wharf in 1996, "I couldn't see things being rolled back to their pre-ceasefire state. Too many adjustments, small but significant, had been made, not just in the public arena but at the core of most people's consciousness." He felt that "The collective resolution had firmed up—again, not optimistically, just more or less obstinately" (351). The repetition of "Ourselves again, free-willed again" thus could imply a return to inner freedom and an escape from the seemingly pre-determined life that reigned for so long in Northern Ireland with its fixed cycles of violence and repressive sectarianism. Heaney does not ascribe saintly status to himself or others who made that time of terror more bearable, more understandable, and may even have helped usher in its demise, so he simply says they were "not bad." Too often during the Troubles, deathly certainties of religious and political affiliation flourished, so the downbeat, realistic tone evoked by "not bad" seems a fitting counterbalance to that divisive mindset.

"Tollund" finally implies that a condition of free will and choice are not just the ideal human condition but the normal state for human beings in the North or anywhere—and that the "Troubles" were a long diversion from that path. Its realistic, steady language—"Things had moved on"—signifies Heaney's hope that the religious and political intractability of life in the province might continue to improve through the labor of fellow human beings attuned to their joint spirituality. As he articulated the situation in an essay written shortly after the 1994 IRA ceasefire, "The cessation of violence is an opportunity to open a space . . . where hope can grow." Citing Czech dissident Václav Havel's definition of hope, he holds that hope is "a state of the soul rather than a response to the evidence. It is not the expectation that things will turn out successfully but the conviction that something is worth working for . . ." He argues that "Its deepest roots are in the transcendental, beyond the horizon."[39]

The last poem in *The Spirit Level*, "Postscript," employs a paratactic opening about a coastal drive in County Clare, thus making it seem linked to the preceding poems, but its concluding image spies the future from a deeply emotional liminal state expressed through a medial geographic position. This sixteen-line poem with occasional faint slant rhymes ("stones" and "swans," and "white" and "it") urges the reader to "make the time to drive out west" along "the Flaggy Shore" in "September or October, when the wind / And the light are working off each other . . ." At that time of year with that combination of wind and light, the driver will find herself between an ocean that "is wild / With foam and glitter" and "The surface of a slate-grey lake [that] is lit / By the earthed lightning of a flock of swans . . ." It is difficult not to think of Yeats here—both his "The Wild Swans at Coole" and the crucial passage from the third stanza of "Easter, 1916," where

> The horse that comes from the road
> The rider, the birds that range
> From cloud to tumbling cloud,
> Minute by minute they change;
> A shadow of cloud on the stream
> Changes minute by minute . . .[40]

Two collocations of Yeatsian triple flux obtain here—a galloping horse, flying birds, and tumbling clouds, succeeded by "A shadow of cloud on the stream"—and this moment in Heaney's poem portrays multiple images of flux as well: the wind, light, and "foam and glitter" of the ocean, the birds' lighting on the lake surface like "earthed lightning." As the speaker woefully laments, "Useless to think you'll park and capture it / More thoroughly." In fact, the only way to provide even an approximation of such flutterings, ripplings, and flux is to drive, to put oneself into motion as well. In so doing, "You are neither here nor there, / A hurry through which known and strange things pass / As big soft buffetings come at the car sideways / And catch the heart off guard and blow it open" (70). Here, Heaney heightens his favorite poetic posture—silent and listening, in-between—by adding movement. This mobile position enables not only an apprehension of the life outside the automobile but also of "strange things." His heart, its guard down, is blown "open," not by a piercing bullet but by a stream of images and things known and unknown. "Postscript" responds in some ways to Heaney's early poem from *Door into the Dark*, "The Peninsula," discussed in my first chapter, about his drive into western Kerry to see the Blasket Islands and Gallarus Oratory. But "Postscript" is the stronger poem because it multiplies images of motion so well and successfully catches the poet up into these. In so doing, it conveys a sense of not only a poet on the move, but also of a poetry that continued to stay open to movements of the spirit and heart as he aged.

In 1998, only two years after the publication of *The Spirit Level*, Heaney released *Opened Ground: Poems, 1966–1996*, a volume coming so soon on the heels of the *Selected Poems* that it is worth briefly asking why Heaney would release essentially another *Selected Poems* only nine years later. Part of the reason stems from his increased recognition after he won the Nobel Prize (the volume ends with *Crediting Poetry*, after all) and his likely desire to gather thirty years' worth of poems in the wake of that award. Intriguingly, he seeks here to give a different shape to his career than in the previous *Selected*, featuring more selections from each volume of poetry he had published, placing "Antaeus" in a separate space between *Death of a Naturalist* and *Door into the Dark*, containing even more prose poems from *Stations* (nine now), jettisoning all but one passage from *Sweeney Astray* ("Sweeney in Flight") but now including a translation from the Middle English, "The Names of the Hare" (1981), and featuring occasional poems like "Villanelle for an Anniversary," his poem for Harvard's 400th anniversary, and "A Transgression" (1994), along with a passage from *The Cure at Troy*, which he entitles "Voices from Lemnos." Cutting the extra Sweeney passages and including the other new additions enables Heaney to cast himself more powerfully as a world author, a translator from more traditions than just the Irish—Middle English, Greek—while also demonstrating his increasingly public bent with his occasional poems and Nobel Prize speech.

Heaney has recalled that after having written "Electric Light," there was no doubt in his mind that it would become the title poem of his 2001 volume. This phrase connotes not only the arrival of electricity in his grandmother's house when he was a boy, but it is also "associated in my mind with a beautiful line from the Mass for the Dead—'*Et lux perpetua luceat eis*' / 'And let perpetual light shine upon them' . . ."[41] After settling on the title, he realized that light unified the entire volume—"that there was light all over the place, from the shine on the weir in the very first poem to the 'reprieving light' of my father's smile in the penultimate line of the penultimate poem in the book."[42] Heaney's penchant for the elegy, evidenced since *North*, continues in this volume with elegies for Ted Hughes, Joseph Brodsky, and the poet's father and grandmother—"On His Work in the English Tongue," "Audenesque," "Seeing the Sick," and the title poem, respectively. There are also a series of eclogues that work well along with the lovely "Sonnets from Hellas." On the other hand, poems such as "Known World," "The Real Names," and "The Bookcase" are mostly composed of scraps of remembered conversation and constitute some of Heaney's weakest in the volume (and in his *oeuvre*) and their inclusion makes *Electric Light* uneven in quality. Although the elegies and eclogues are superb, with the elegies in particular showing Heaney to be one of the very best postwar elegists, one cannot dismiss Robert Potts's assessment in what was a widely read review of the volume in *The Guardian* newspaper that "there is perhaps a too-easy reliance, born of facility, on now-traditional symbols, whether Heaney's own or from what Larkin called 'the myth-kitty.'"[43] Heaney's continuing interest in Virgil and superb reworking of some of that classical poet's eclogues do show him breaking new ground in his always allusive poetry, as does his turn back toward the medial caesura common in Anglo-Saxon poetry (a practice influenced by his recent translation of *Beowulf*), particularly in some of the better poems in the second half of the volume such as "On His Work in the English Tongue" and "Seeing the Sick." I tend to agree with one of Heaney's best critics, John Wilson Foster, who argues that "Heaney is at his best, his heartbreaking best, when writing in memory of the personally known dead" in this volume.[44] Certainly he covers familiar (home) ground again and the objects here such as the loose box and the bookcase in the poems of those names are not presented in the attractive and mysterious way they are in, say, *Seeing Things*, while the "conversational" poems I list above seem particularly flat. Still, any poet would be proud of the best (often elegiac) moments in this uneven volume.

The volume is framed by two poems that emphasize light and illumination—"At Toomebridge" and "Electric Light." The former poem introduces the flood motif that pervades many of the poems that follow. The water that spills over the weir from Lough Neagh falls "shining to the continuous / Present of the Bann." The checkpoint, presumably erected by the British Army during the Troubles, was there, and it was also the site where "the rebel boy was hanged in '98." Yet in the midst of recalling such strife and violence, the poet nonetheless knows this spot was also "Where negative ions in the open air / Are poetry to me" just as the "slime and silver of the fattened eel" used to be (*EL* 3). "At

Toomebridge" thus seemingly says farewell to Heaney's muddy, earthy medium and announces a return to that local landscape whereby he might glean new inspiration through the other elements—air, light, and water. The more ambitious "Electric Light" turns inward to the treasures of both the poet's grandmother's domestic interior, which was the first in the area to have electric light, and to her "puckered pearl" thumb-nail, an object that perdures "in the Derry ground" (80, 81).

"Out of the Bag," one of the longest poems in the volume and written in unrhymed tercets, ponders the role of the family physician, Dr Kerlin, a sort of Merlin figure for the Heaney children, who delivered them all. It is classic Heaney in its rich vocabulary, ranging from the "trap-sprung mouth / Unsnibbed and gaping wide" of the doctor's bag that the children believed they arrived in, to the doctor's eyes, "Hyperborean, beyond-the-north-wind blue . . ." (6, 7). The visitations by Dr Kerlin are interleaved with the poet's memories of visiting the temple of Asclepius and of assisting as the thurifer at Lourdes in 1956. One way this happens is through the connection made between Kerlin's "soapy big hygienic hands" and the grown poet's desire at the Greek temple to "be visited in the very eve of the day / By Hygeia, his daughter, her name still clarifying / The haven of light she was, the undarkening door" (8, 9). The cleanliness of the doctor's hands and that symbolized by Hygeia lead toward physical and psychic health, respectively. The visits to Lourdes and Greece mix together with Dr Kerlin's many visits to the Heaney house in a sort of phantasmagoria resulting in a series of miraculous births—of Heaney babies, including the poet, and of the birth of his consciousness as a poet. That "birth" is symbolized by the "undarkening door," a phrase that looks back toward the opening line of "The Forge"—"All I know is a door into the dark" (*DD* 7)—and recalls the trajectory of his future poetry, represented in Heaney's confession to his friend the writer Brian Friel after publishing *North* that "I no longer wanted a door into the dark—I want a door into the light."[45] Stepping back into the daylight of his biological birth and his later desire to write about literal and figurative light after dwelling for so long on Northern darkness, the poet proceeds in the next poem, "Bann Valley Eclogue," to meditate indirectly upon the birth of a new Northern Ireland, inspired by Virgil's eclogues.

Virgil was a consistent figure in Heaney's imaginative life since he first read the *Aeneid*, particularly Book VI, as we saw in our discussion of *Seeing Things*, and when David Ferry's translation of the *Eclogues* with a parallel Latin text was published in 2000, he recalled "for a while I was captivated entirely" (*SS* 389). As he grew older he even made implicit comparisons between Virgil and himself, as he does in an essay about Ted Hughes that opens with a full-throated affirmation of Virgil as a northern poet whose origins anticipated Hughes's and Heaney's own. "Once upon a time," he muses, "there was a poet, born in the north of his native country, a boy completely at home on the land and in the landscape, familiar with the fields and rivers of his district, living at eye level with the wild life and the domestic life."[46] Thus he links Virgil, the Northern England-born Hughes, along with himself—each as poets who lived close to the land and were similarly knowledgeable about "the fields and rivers of his district." "District" becomes the key word here, Heaney's "tell," as it were. He often employs "district" to refer to his local landscape and parish of Bellaghy and the title of *District and Circle* would pay homage to that original district.

"Bann Valley Eclogue" features a dialogue between the poet and Virgil about a "child that's due" (*EL* 11) and the future state of Heaney's native province. He knew the origins of the pastoral intimately and even pointed out in an essay treating Virgilian eclogues and contemporary pastoral poetry that the mode "usually involves a self-consciously literary performance, so it becomes vulnerable to accusations of artificiality." Furthermore, he observed that the pastoral runs the risk of seeming "an upholstered convention rather than a first-time discovery."[47] Despite these reservations, here and elsewhere in the volume, he daringly turns to the pastoral mode, particularly the subgenre of the conversational eclogue as practiced by Virgil, in order to signal the possibility of new births—both in Northern Ireland and in his own poetry.

After an epigraph from Virgil's Eclogue IV, which is, as Stephen Harrison points out, a millennial monologue poem that alludes "to myths of religious cycles of renewal in connection with the end of civil war," the poem opens with an impassioned prayer to the "Bann Valley Muses" to "give us a song worth singing, / Something that rises like the curtain in / Those words *And it came to pass* or *In the beginning*" (11).[48] These snatches of Scripture about the Christ child's birth from Luke 2 and from the opening of the Book of Genesis, respectively, rhetorically instantiate a new beginning in these twinned births, biological and political. The narrator even asks, "Maybe, heavens, sing / Better times for her and her generation" (11). Heaney was not only born in the Bann Valley, but also that river marks a traditional divide between the western, heavily Catholic part of Northern Ireland and the eastern, historically Protestant eastern part of the province, although in recent decades, the city of Belfast that dominates eastern Ulster has become home to many more Catholics. The poem thus employs the imaginary "Muses" of this traditionally divisive river and valley to, if not heal the sectarian rift, at least give him the words by which he might begin imagining what the future province might be. Heaney read the poem on *RTÉ* 1, the state Irish television channel, on December 31, 2000, and that occasion contextualizes the poem's (and the poet's) hopes for a brighter future in Northern Ireland, especially in the wake of the Good Friday Agreement of April 10, 1998, in which Catholics and Protestants agreed on a power-sharing government.[49] Turning back to such an ancient mode as the eclogue may seem anachronistic at such a moment, but Heaney believed that "What keeps a literary kind valuable is its ability to measure up to the challenges offered by new historical circumstances, and pastoral has been confronted with this challenge from very early on." He points out further that in Virgil's first eclogue, he is "actually testing the genre he inherited from Theocritus and proving that it is fit for life in his own deadly Roman times."[50] In a similar fashion, Heaney here employs the pastoral mode of the Virgilian eclogue not only to prove its fitness for life in his own "deadly" Northern Irish (and globalized) times, but also to reinvigorate it and show how a subgenre dedicated to reasoned discussion could augur, model, and even contribute to peace in his own province.

Virgil first responds to the poet in "Bann Valley Eclogue" by offering him some Latin words that might aid this process: "*Carmen, ordo, nascitur, saeculum, gens,*" literally translated as "song or poetry," "order," "is born," "lifetime" or "generation," and "nation." The listing of two nouns, followed by the present tense indicative verb *nascitur*, followed in turn by two more nouns, does not make much of a Latin sentence, but the meaning is clear enough by Virgil's continuing statement: "Poetry, order, the times, / The nation, wrong and renewal, then an infant birth / And a flooding away of all the old miasma" (11). The birth of poetry, order, a generation, a nation—all separate, distinctive events, signified by each word being set off in commas—these "births" are now succeeded and supplanted by "an infant birth," echoing the phrase from Luke 2 in the first stanza and a sort of Biblical flood like that which covered the earth in Genesis that purged it from all ungodliness and sin.

Those renewing waters of life that draw on crucial narratives from the New and Old Testaments, respectively, are secularized and applied to the birth of a new time in the life of Northern Ireland in the second stanza of Virgil's response. As he points out, "Whatever stains you, you rubbed it into yourselves," but after this laying of blame upon the shoulders of the entire populace, Heaney inserts a medial caesura in this stanza's third line, followed by a contrasting conjunction to suggest a new emergence of a different order in the province:

> But when the waters break
> Bann's stream will overflow, the old markings
> Will avail no more to keep east bank from west.
> The valley will be washed like the new baby. (11)

Now he refigures the Bann as a unifying flood, not as a dividing river separating Catholic from Protestant. Heaney wrote elsewhere about "all boundaries" being "necessary evils," but also held that "the truly desirable condition is the feeling of being unbounded, of being king of infinite space."[51]

As the eclogue continues after the poet responds to Virgil by citing the evidence of a recent "noon-eclipse" as a "millennial chill" gathers, Virgil replies more optimistically, "Eclipses won't be for this child," and offers a sort of prayer, "Let her never hear close gunfire or explosions." And the poet concludes by recalling scenes from his childhood on "St Patrick's mornings" spent collecting shamrocks for his mother, then speaks directly to the coming child, perhaps both a Heaney grandchild and the new province, the latter washed clean of sectarianism, both of which he hopes will be born in the new millennium. He muses, "Child on the way, it won't be long until / you land among us," and expectantly observes, "Your pram waits in the corner. / Cows are let out. They're sluicing the milk-house floor" (12). This image of triple abundance and fertility—the child, the milk cows, and indirectly the newly cleansed province, free of its accumulated dung—arrives not with a bang or a whimper to borrow from T. S. Eliot's "The Hollow Men," but in quotidian fashion, couched in straightforward language. So too, Heaney implies, might the new Northern Irish state be birthed—by directly addressing past wrongs in straightforward language.

One of the most moving poems in the volume, one which continues this language of being washed clean, occurs in the fourth lyric, "The Augean Stables," from "Sonnets from Hellas," which deals both with one of Hercules' famous labors and with the aftermath of the murder of a man from near Heaney's birthplace after the 1994 ceasefires. This loose Petrarchan sonnet opens with the poet remarking that his "favourite bas-relief" depicts the goddess "Athene showing / Heracles where to broach the river bank" and the result of that hero's redirection of the Alpheus river—the washing clean of the "deep dung strata / Of King Augeas's reeking yard and stables." After the octave concludes following the "packed floors deluging like gutters . . .," the sestet shifts into the present, as Heaney and his wife find themselves in "Olympia, down among green willows," in "The lustral wash and run of river shallows" upon hearing of the murder of Sean Brown on May 7, 1997. The shift from the relatively regular Petrarchan rhyming of the first quatrain in the octave *ab1/4ba* to the sestet's irregular rhyme of *e1/2efghi* sonically signifies how Brown's murder shattered the fragile harmony of the peace process in Northern Ireland. Moreover, the way in which the more exalted language of the middle of the poem—lines 7–10—gives way to the ordinary language of the last four lines makes this potentially transcendent poem thud back to earth as the poet and his wife "imagined / Hose-water smashing hard back off the asphalt / In the car park where his athlete's blood ran cold" (41).

Elegizing Brown, who helped run the Bellaghy Gaelic Athletic Association club, by remembering him in Olympia casts him as a sort of epic Greek athlete, just as the rushing water from the hosepipe in Bellaghy and the Greek river water running near "green willows" recalls the poet's washing of his cousin Colum McCartney's bloodied face with "cold handfuls of the dew" and the plaiting of "Green scapulars to wear over your shroud" in "The Strand at Lough Beg" (*FW* 18). This washing of the athletic Brown's blood off the asphalt also associates him with another murder victim from the Troubles Heaney elegized in "Station Island": the former football midfielder William Strathearn, who is portrayed as "always" having "an athlete's cleanliness / shining off him ...," and characterized as "the perfect, clean, unthinkable victim" (*SI* 79, 80). In this composite portrait of Sean Brown as a contemporary Olympian figure that builds upon two other victims of the Troubles Heaney elegized, he rejects the "heroic" qualities supporters of paramilitary groups would give them and shows them to be the thugs and killers they were.

Heaney wrote a letter to the *Irish News*, a nationalist-leaning newspaper, in which he recalled Brown's having presided over an event in January of 1996 to celebrate Heaney's having won the Nobel Prize. He clearly saw Brown as a figure of unity for Protestant and Catholic alike in the community, recalling the attendance of members of those communities. Furthermore, he noted that he saw that ceremony as "like a purification, a release from what the Greeks called the miasma, the stain of spilled blood," concluding that "It is a terrible irony that the man who organised such an event should die at the hands of a sectarian killer."[52] Brown's death qualifies the optimism of "Bann Valley Eclogue," particularly the hope expressed by Virgil that there will be a "flooding away of all the old miasma" (*EL* 11), the same Greek term Heaney employs in his letter.

If Sean Brown's death looms over those poems and qualifies their relative optimism, the example of two other Olympian figures to Heaney—W. B. Yeats, whose situation Heaney likens to his own in

"Glanmore Eclogue," and J. M. Synge—bulks large for him in that Wicklow-centered eclogue. Certainly, Heaney's comparison of himself to Yeats was long since warranted: Heaney had gradually become the type of public poet for the entire island of Ireland that no one had been since Yeats and had done so in a much less patrician manner than had Yeats. The homage to Synge, figured as Virgil's herdsman Meliboeus, however, is more sustained that Heaney's analogy of himself to Yeats and finally more substantial. We might recall Heaney's early poetic renderings of his "Syngescape" in "Synge on Aran" and "Lovers on Aran" in *Death of a Naturalist*. Now, in full possession of Glanmore Cottage in County Wicklow near Synge territory, Heaney can more confidently explore and claim for himself Synge's persistent theme of loneliness and transform that loneliness into the solitude he always needed for poetic inspiration. He thus demonstrates his point from his essay on Virgilian eclogues that "literariness as such is not an abdication from the truth," and that literature's "diversions are not to be taken as deceptions but as roads less travelled by where the country we thought we knew is seen again in a new and revealing light."[53] "Glanmore Eclogue" allows Heaney to playfully insert himself into the tradition of the Irish Literary Renaissance's founders—Lady Gregory, Yeats, and Synge—while also assaying a fresh appreciation of the Wicklow countryside around Glanmore Cottage and his own poetic career in a somewhat new guise by the conclusion of the poem—not as the bird-like Sweeney, the mask he had adopted in the early- to mid-1980s, but as a lark-like singer of simple seasonal songs from the Irish language.

The character "Myles" (perhaps a nod to the Irish satirist and novelist Brian Nolan, better known as Flann O'Brien, also known by his pen name Myles naGopaleen) pens "Glanmore Eclogue" by pointing out to "Poet" his many advantages: "A house and ground. And your own bay tree as well / And time to yourself. You've landed on your feet. / If you can't write now, when will you ever write?" The poet replies simply, "A woman changed my life. Call her Augusta / Because we arrived in August . . ." (35). Thus Heaney transfigures the Synge scholar Ann Saddlemyer, who finally had sold him Glanmore Cottage in the 1980s, into a type of Lady Augusta Gregory figure and himself as a Yeats figure. Yeats summered at Gregory's home, Coole Park, for twenty years, from 1897 to 1917, crucial times in his development as a poet, and Heaney implies by the comparison that Saddlemyer's loan of, then sale of, the cottage to him and his wife Marie was similarly foundational to his own poetic trajectory.

Heaney, whose career became gradually more peripatetic as the years wore on, the accolades piled up, and his commitments to teaching and reading abroad increased, seems especially drawn to the character Meliboeus, standing for John Synge, as the poem proceeds. After the civil war in Rome between Julius Caesar's assassins and his avengers such as Marc Antony ended with Antony and his supporters victorious around 42 BC, land around Italy was seized and redistributed with Meliboeus forced off of his land.[54] Synge, who wandered to France after graduation from Trinity College, Dublin, then around County Wicklow and the Aran Islands in his short life, devoted much of his drama to writing about tramps and itinerants and by the time he wrote this poem, Heaney must have felt similarly well- or better traveled and steeped in the loneliness that Synge often employed as his theme. Thus he features Saddlemyer, the world's leading Synge expert, who "knows the big glen inside out, and everything / Meliboeus ever wrote about it, / All the tramps he met tramping the roads," as the all-knowing landowner and scholar (35). Feeling homed and grounded in Glanmore Cottage, his retreat, refuge, and writing studio for many years, he can nonetheless affirm with Synge as Meliboeus who "Was never happier than when he was on the road / With people on their uppers. Loneliness / Was his passport through the world," that "His spirit lives for me in things like that." These things include "Midge-angels / On the face of water, the first drop before thunder, / A stranger on a wild night, *out in the rain falling*" (36). Heaney similarly feels ecstatic when recognizing the extraordinary, even miraculous in the quotidian.

As an indication of how he has gradually changed from the shy young poet with the pen name "Incertus" early in his career to a man and writer who transformed himself through his imaginative work, Heaney slyly likens himself to Synge's Christy Mahon, who underwent a similar process in *The Playboy of the Western World* (1907) when he states, "Meliboeus would have called me 'Mr Honey'" (36). Thus changed, the mature poet concludes this eclogue by translating a "summer song" from the Irish, the language Synge knew so well. Replete with birdsong and a series of active verbs that seem to impart agency to flora such as heather and bog-cotton, along with deer and the sea, this song of four quatrains celebrates not only the Irish language and Synge's role in promoting it through his inimitable Irish-inflected plays written in English, but also the bounty of summer in contemporary Wicklow and the harvest of words Heaney was given over the years in this place because of Saddlemyer's generosity. He likely is the lark of the last stanza, "A little nippy chirpy fellow" who "Hits the highest note there is . . ." This harmonious natural world and the abundance of poetry and song seem to last forever as signified in the last line of the song and the poem itself: "Summer, shimmer, perfect days" (37). This is a song the poet never would have allowed himself to sing in the older, darker days of Northern Ireland, when it was beset with civil strife; but now, with "peace being talked up" (36) and the rise of the so-called Celtic Tiger economy in Ireland, he allows himself the luxury of recollection in tranquility and sounds a series of grateful notes to Synge and Saddlemyer for gifting him such an artistic example and site of inspiration, respectively.

Heaney's interest in Virgil not only led him to write the eclogues from *Electric Light* but also helped him in mourning the death of his dear friend Ted Hughes, whom he came to see as a sort of modern-day Virgil figure. Four poems from the latter, shorter half of the volume stand out, headed by Heaney's poetic tribute to Hughes: "On His Work in the English Tongue," followed by "Audenesque," "Seeing the Sick," and the title poem. The first two are the more memorable and striking, though there are moments of quiet power in the latter two. More literary antecedents run through these poems, including Wilfred Owen, Miłosz, Auden, Yeats, and Hopkins, all of whom had been important to Heaney for decades at this point.

Heaney was shocked at the death of Hughes on October 28, 1998 and delivered the funeral eulogy in Westminster Abbey a few days later, noting at the time that "No death in my lifetime has hurt poets or poetry more than the death of Ted Hughes. And no death outside my immediate family has left me feeling more bereft."[55] I have argued elsewhere for Hughes's great importance, along with that of Kavanagh, Frost, and Hopkins, as exemplary writers of the region for Heaney.[56] Coming on the heels of the Good Friday Agreement a few months earlier, Hughes's passing qualifies some of Heaney's Easter optimism about that political breakthrough. Thus he opens "On His Work in the English Tongue" with a telling two and a quarter lines shot through with a profound sense that the Northern Irish Troubles' legacy would take many years to work through, along with a broadside against contemporary literary theories such as postmodernism and postcolonial theory, whose titles suggest an artificial completeness insufficient for understanding complex processes such as conflict and literature: "Post-this, post-that, post-the-other, yet in the end / Not past a thing. Not understanding or telling / Or forgiveness" (61). The poem affirms Hughes's poetry and its debt to the Anglo-Saxon language and culture even as it suggests that it finally lifted clear of the earth to soar among the spirit world. Hughes was Virgilian not just in his humble northern background, but for his serious reception of his "poetic calling, the spiritual dimensions within which he conceived of it and the responsibility which he felt to it and for it."[57] Heaney always voiced his strongest praise for those poets who, like himself, felt the weightiness of their vocation and "On His Work" affirms that combined gravitas and spirituality in Hughes, whose early poetry led the younger Heaney to feel "like one come out of an upper room / To fret no more and walk abroad confirmed" (61).

Both Hughes's ear and his appreciation for our soul-life evidently affirmed Heaney's own acoustic, as he indicates in stanza two with his comparison of reading a Hughes poem then likening it to a local bridge he would stand under as a boy. Under "the single span and bull's eye of the one / Over the railway lines at Anahorish— / So intimate in there," he was closely connected to the "cranial-acoustic of the stone / With its arch-ear to the ground, a listening post / Open to the light, to the limen world / Of soul on its lonely path . . ." (61). Grounded in this elemental acoustic world, the young Heaney was similarly attuned to the light-filled spirit world outside that bridge, which clearly functions as a sort of subconscious for him.

The rest of the poem offers an apologia for Hughes's affirmation of passive suffering in his poetry and of his regional English voice and vocabulary by recourse to the *Beowulf* poet, Wilfred Owen, and Czesław Miłosz. Heaney opens stanza three by rejecting Yeats's famous refusal to include Owen in his 1936 edited collection, *The Oxford Book of Modern Verse*, on the grounds that the English poet indulged in too much emotion when he wrote of the horrors of World War One: "Passive suffering: who said it was disallowed / As a theme for poetry?" He then links Hughes to the *Beowulf* poet, whose great epic he had just finished translating and which is dedicated to Hughes, whom he saw continuing that anonymous poet's exploration of passive suffering through a rich and strange vocabulary that was essentially Anglo-Saxon in origin. Thus, he introduces the narrative of King Hrethel's son's accidental killing of his older brother, who "snaps the grief-trap shut / On Hrethel himself," and follows that incident with a dash, then a new stanza with a paratactic opening as he moves to Hughes: "And the poet draws from his word-hoard a weird tale / Of a life and a love balked, which I reword here / Remembering earth-tremors once on Dartmoor . . ." Employing the Anglo-Saxon kenning for "sorrow" as "grief-trap" and "word-hoard" for "vocabulary" demonstrates Hughes's facility with words like the *Beowulf* poet displayed, just as the tale of Hrethel's son and Hughes's "tale / Of a life and a love balked" (a reference, perhaps, to Hughes's ill-fated marriage to Sylvia Plath?) connects the king and the English poet in their joint familial suffering (62). Heaney argued that Hughes's voice "is in rebellion against a certain kind of demeaned, mannerly voice" and that "Hughes's great cry and call and bawl is that English language and English poetry is longer and deeper and rougher than that."[58] Quoting from lines 4 and 9 of Wilfred Owen's "Strange Meeting" and combining them in the last line of this stanza—"*To sullen halls where encumbered sleepers groaned*" (62)—allows Heaney to place Hughes on a continuum of poets writing in English from the *Beowulf* poet through Owen and beyond and implicitly rebuffs Yeats again on the issue of passive suffering.[59]

After a long near-reproduction of a passage from *Beowulf* (lines 2444–65) on this kind of sorrow in stanza four that he refashions to show the universality of suffering and to connect Hrethel and Hughes, Heaney concludes with a fifth stanza drawing on Miłosz's poetry to privilege Hughes's attention to the soul and to affirm poetry's role in promoting things of the spirit.[60] This stanza too is indebted to the conventions of Anglo-Saxon poetry. Each line contains a medial caesura, common to that poetry, which was often broken into half lines to aid memorization for oral recitation. These weighty, solemn lines echo the strength of the stony bridge in the second stanza and suggest that even though the soul cannot be seen, it nonetheless exists and has an ineffable heft. If, as this stanza has it, "Soul has its scruples. Things not to be said, / Things for keeping . . . / . . . Things for the aye of God / And for poetry," then certainly Miłosz's contention that the soul is "'A dividend from ourselves,' a tribute paid / By what we have been true to. A thing allowed" (63), captures the unspeakable nature of the soul, able to be expressed only to God and through poetry. Interestingly, Heaney uses the word "things" repeatedly here to convey mysteries of the soul and by so doing, "things" them into being, as it were, with this sufficiently vague yet weighty word.

In *Stepping Stones*, Heaney compares Hughes to Hopkins's blacksmith Felix Randal, noting that "I think of a 'bright and battering sandal' that has more power than pitch, more effulgence than finish, and generally more mana" (*SS* 339), and Heaney implicitly links Hughes through "On His Work in the English Tongue" to the penultimate poem in the volume about Heaney's dying father, "Seeing the Sick," through Hopkins's "Felix Randal." In the comparison between Hughes and Hopkins, he is quoting the last half line of Hopkins's poem, "his bright and battering sandal!"[61] Heaney also likens Patrick Heaney to Felix Randal in "Seeing the Sick" when he opens that poem by musing, "Anointed and all, my father did remind me / Of Hopkins's Felix Randal" (*EL* 79). The opening half-line is taken nearly verbatim from the start of Hopkins's sixth line, "Being anointed and all."[62] Later, the speaker notes that he had "None of your fettled and bright battering sandal" that Randal had in his prime, drawing on the conclusion of Hopkins's poem. Thus he now qualifies the analogy to Felix

Randal and states instead of being characterized by that brightness Patrick Heaney instead was clothed in "Cowdung coloured tweed and ox-blood leather," apparel befitting his salt-of-the-earth mentality and origins. Our vicarious knowing of Patrick Heaney's vigor and power in his prime, compounded by that of the brawny Randal, adds pathos to the portrait of the dying man, grown "'wee in his clothes'— / Spectral, a relict—. . ." Much like the connection to rural nature that Heaney admired in Hughes, the poet lovingly recalls his father's precision as a cattleman: "The assessor's eye, the tally-keeper's head / For what beasts were on what land in what year . . .," but then quickly muses, "But then that went as well. And all precaution" (79).

Three of the lines in this final stanza feature medial caesuras, which connect Patrick Heaney and Hughes to the *Beowulf* poet and Anglo-Saxon culture. Heaney's father, like his Scullion uncles, spoke with weightiness and was a man of few words. When he was dying, he seemed to have "thrown off" the "unbelonging, moorland part of him / That was Northumbrian," and yet by describing that part of him in such detail, Heaney reaffirms his father's northernness in an English context that links him to Hughes and the *Beowulf* poet. Thus in the dead center of the poem, he renders him as "Ghost-drover from the start. Brandisher of keel" (79). Spectral cow-driver that he has now become, Patrick Heaney seems to linger from beyond the grave in all his weightiness, although grown smaller.

An earlier but less compelling elegy in *Electric Light*, "Audenesque," praises another figure from the north—Heaney's dear friend the Russian poet Joseph Brodsky.[63] Intriguingly, Heaney wrote "Audenesque" on the anniversary of Yeats's death, "(Double-crossed and death-marched date, / January twenty-eight)," and pays light-hearted tribute to the Russian poet by mimicking the concluding trochaic tetrameter couplets of the third section of Auden's "In Memory of W.B. Yeats" throughout: "Joseph, yes, you know the beat. / Wystan Auden's metric feet . . ." (64). Where Auden's poem, however, finally lauds poetry itself, not so much Yeats the man or his poetry, and shows how poetry becomes independent of the poet after his death, Heaney's poem stays focused on elegizing Brodsky and shows how inimitable the Russian poet was. Auden's poem works in many ways as a subversion of the tripartite conventions of the elegy. It really does not personally lament the passing of the man in any extended fashion, merely letting machines register that fact: "O all the instruments agree / The day of his death was a dark cold day."[64] It certainly does not praise Yeats, and it offers no heavenly consolation as traditional elegies like Milton's "Lycidas" do, even though it works as a wonderful meditation on the role of poetry and especially on how its reception by readers might eventually lead to hearts freed from hatred and flowing fountains of something like Auden's vaunted belief in Agape love.[65]

Heaney's "Audenesque" Hibernicizes the frozen world (New York City) from which Auden wrote his "elegy" and thus gestures towards Brodsky's polar Russia: "Dublin Airport locked in frost, / *Rigor mortis* in your breast" (64). He does not express the hope of warmth and community that Auden does in his conclusion, instead dwelling at length on Brodsky's icy death: "Ice of Archangelic strength, / Ice of this hard two-faced month, / Ice like Dante's in deep hell / Makes your heart a frozen well" (65).

Instead of, like Auden, focusing on our reception of poetry and our potential transformation of it into a unifying force—possibilities that elsewhere in his poetry he often celebrates—Heaney spends the majority of the remaining poem remembering Brodsky's zest for life and irreverence, as in the quatrain where he remembers "Politically incorrect / Jokes involving sex and sect, / Everything against the grain, / Drinking, smoking like a train" (65). This larger-than-life friend and poet whose "Nose in air, foot to the floor, / Revving English like a car / You hijacked when you robbed its bank," now has been silenced and for a moment, even Heaney's trust in language seems to falter when he muses, "Even your peremptory trust / In words alone here bites the dust" (66).

Yet in the final stanza, he finally ushers Brodsky into a community of dead poets using language of drawn from the Eucharist: "Dust-cakes, still—see *Gilgamesh*— / Feed the dead. So be their guest. / Do again what Auden said / Good poets do: bite, break their bread" (66). Here he slyly recapitulates Auden's insistence in "In Memory of W. B. Yeats" that "The words of a dead man / Are modified in the guts of the living," but suggests instead by our "feeding" upon the words of a great dead poet like Brodsky and reshaping him in our own image to a degree, we might be breaking bread with the dead.[66] "Audenesque" not only elegizes Brodsky, then, but also affirms finally with Auden that while "poetry makes nothing happen: it survives /. . . / . . . / . . . it survives, / A way of happening, a mouth."[67] Brodsky's poetry enabled poetry's survival, just as Auden's did before him, and now Heaney's will as well.

"Electric Light" thuds back to earth a bit after Heaney's elegies for Hughes and Brodsky, but it too, like they do more implicitly, affirms poetry as a good by dwelling upon how the quotidian can become marvelous. Lingering behind this poem is Patrick Heaney's smile in "Seeing the Sick," the previous poem, which is described as "a summer half-door opening out / And opening in. A repriving light" (79). That light heightens the surprise and delight of the poet who remembers in this last poem of the volume "the first house where I saw electric light," which is itself colored by the memory of his grandmother's "smashed thumb-nail" that was "puckered pearl, // Rucked quartz, a littered Cumae" (80). This last line blends the "rucked" bed of his grandmother's thumbnail with his perception of her in retrospect as a "littered Cumae," a modern-day incarnation of the priestess or sibyl that prophesied at the Greek colony of Cumae near Naples, Italy. This allusion links her and this last poem to the earlier Virgilian eclogues since Virgil relates the narrative of the Cumaean sibyl in Book VI of *The Aeneid*. While pointing out that the poem does not state explicitly that this woman is his grandmother, Heaney has noted that "there are clues to show that she is ancient, archetypal and central to the family."[68]

Heaney's grandmother's importance as a sibyl lies not so much in her prophesies (the original Sibyl was Aeneas' guide to the underworld when he sought his father Anchises and Virgil's fourth Eclogue has her prophesying a Messianic figure), but in her way of speaking, which was an early model for his regionally grounded poetry. When he remembers her asking him urgently that night he stayed with her and wept out of loneliness and homesickness, "'What ails you, child, // What ails you, for God's sake?'", he connects her dialect to the water outside the Sibyl's cave here: "Urgent, sibilant / *Ails*, far off and old. Scaresome cavern waters / Lapping a boatslip." In the next stanza, her "Ails" leads out to the wider world, to the water slapping the ferry in Belfast Lough on the narrator's way back from England: "Lisp and relapse. Eddy of sybilline English" that he hears "As ferries churned and turned down Belfast Lough . . ." (80). That rhythm, crucially, leads him into "The very 'there-you-are-and-where-are-you?' // Of poetry itself" (80–1). Heaney remarked that this middle section is "meant to suggest a journey into poetic vocation" in connecting his grandmother's strange verb and "historical and literary England," itself symbolized by Chaucer's Southwark and Shakespeare's Globe Theatre.[69] And that has made all the difference. From his experience as a young child afraid in his grandmother's house, staring at her pearly thumbnail and hearing her "sibylline" lisp, Heaney learned to credit everyday marvels and hear poetry in them. When he remembers that "A touch of the little pip would work the magic" that would turn on the electric light, just as he got to work the dial on the wireless or radio that enabled him to search "at will the stations of the world" (81), he was experiencing magical-seeming technologies that led him into literal and metaphysical illuminations, lights and sounds that would inspire him to become a poet dedicated to the quotidian mysteries of his local and wider world.

Notes

1. The passage occurs in line 49 of Wordsworth's "Lines Composed a Few Miles above Tintern Abbey," *Selected Poems*, 67.
2. Corcoran, "Seamus Heaney Obituary," n.p.
3. Virgil, 163. In Heaney and Hass, Heaney has also noted that Robert Fitzgerald "had been a father figure in my life at Harvard," and that "when Robert died, there was a memorial reading held for him. And I thought, 'Book Six.' I thought of the bit where Aeneas meets his father in the underworld . . ." (16). Thus "The Golden Bough" memorializes both Patrick Heaney and Fitzgerald, double father figures for the poet.
4. Heaney, "Seamus Heaney," *Reading the Future: Irish Writers in Conversation with Mike Murphy*, 87.
5. He must have been confirmed in his chosen analogy of himself as an artistic Aeneas picking the golden bough by Ted Hughes's response to the "Squarings" sequence that equates the poems to ripe fruit: "They are brimful of a ripe, easy beauty. As you close your hand round each one, it comes away clean & whole—perfect moment for picking" ("To Seamus Heaney," 564).
6. Heaney, "Seamus Heaney," *Metre* 3 (1997): 15.
7. Stevens, 66.
8. Heaney has many "Sunday morning" poems, including some of his most significant later work, such as "Tollund" from *The Spirit Level*.
9. In discussing Yeats's "Meditations in Time of Civil War," Heaney lauds "the sheer in-placeness of the whole poem as a given form within the language," arguing that "Poetic form is both the ship and the anchor. It is at once a buoyancy and a holding, allowing for the simultaneous gratification of whatever is centrifugal and centripetal in mind and body" (*CP* 52, 53). Thus, Yeats's poem "does what the necessary poetry always does, which is to touch the base of our sympathetic nature while taking in at the same time the unsympathetic reality of the world to which that nature is constantly exposed" (*CP* 29).
10. Martens points out that Bachelard argues for this view of otherness emanating from childhood things in his *La Terre et les Rêveries du Repos* (43); she takes the opposite view that things extend the child's sense of self (44).
11. O'Driscoll, 146.
12. In this regard, see my analysis of "The Settle Bed" in my *Seamus Heaney's Regions*, 374–7.
13. Heaney, "Sixth Sense, Seventh Heaven," 117.
14. Ibid., 123, 124.
15. Hughes, "To Seamus Heaney," 564, 564–5.
16. Heaney, "Sixth Sense, Seventh Heaven," 119.
17. Ibid., 121.
18. "Tourbillon."
19. This description of the afterlife uncannily echoes some remarks Heaney wrote on November 16, 1980, when he was despairing over writing "Station Island": "Very exhausted and despondent . . . But feel the need . . . to linger in the broken bare site of [the] Lough Derg poem. It is like a build-

ing site, abandoned in November. Cold. Mucky. Puddled ... Hopeless ... But hope still there, even as you shiver at the barefaced, broken nothingness of it all" (*Station Island* Notebook, 98).

20. Heaney, "Joy or Night: Last Things in the Poetry of W. B. Yeats and Philip Larkin," 147, 148.
21. Ibid., 149.
22. Heaney, "Sixth Sense, Seventh Heaven," 123.
23. Qtd in ibid., 115.
24. Ibid., 116, 116–17.
25. Heaney, "Learning from Eliot," 37.
26. Heaney, "Introduction," *The Redress of Poetry*, xiii.
27. Heaney, "Frontiers of Writing," 203.
28. Heaney, "Sixth Sense, Seventh Heaven," 115.
29. Yeats, 348, 204. The "dungy sticks" where the spirit might live also recall the Bishop's response to Jane in Yeats's "Crazy Jane Talks with the Bishop": "'But love has pitched his mansion in / The place of excrement ...'" (ibid., 259–60).
30. Heaney may be slyly returning here to "Casualty" and linking fishing with the questioning ghost of Louis O'Neill, "The line lifted, hand / over fist" (*FW* 23) to the questions he has for Yeats and the "held line."
31. See Heaney, "Small Fantasia for W. B.," 76.
32. Donoghue, 13.
33. Christie, 274.
34. Qtd in Brendan O'Brien, *The Long War*, 127.
35. Morrison has a disturbing tribute to Nugent, "In the Simplicity of His Defiance—Kieran Nugent," celebrating his violent career that Morrison published after his death.
36. Vendler, 156–7.
37. Auden, *Selected Poems*, 207.
38. See his prose poem, "Sinking the shaft," which first explores this installation of the Heaney family water pump (*Stations*, 8).
39. Heaney, "Cessation—1994," 50.
40. Yeats, 181.
41. Heaney, "*Lux Perpetua*," 9.
42. Ibid.
43. Potts, n.p.
44. Foster, "Seamus Heaney: *Electric Light*," 120.
45. Heaney, "Interview with Seamus Heaney" [Randall], 20.
46. Heaney, "Suffering and Decision," 221.
47. Heaney, "Eclogues *in Extremis*," 1.
48. Harrison, 122.
49. Ibid., points out Heaney's reading of the poem at that time.
50. Heaney, "Eclogues *in Extremis*," 2.
51. Heaney, "Something to Write Home About," 51.
52. Heaney, "Letter to the *Irish News*," qtd in McKittrick, 1408.
53. Heaney, "Eclogues *in Extremis*," 4.
54. Heaney shows his familiarity with this issue of the evictions of Meliboeus and others from the opening Virgilian eclogues in "Eclogues *in Extremis*," 3–4.

55. Heaney, "Funeral Eulogy for Ted Hughes," n.p.
56. Russell, *Seamus Heaney's Regions*, 9–12 and 126–8. For an appreciation of the long relationship between Hughes and Heaney, see Hart, "Seamus Heaney and Ted Hughes: A Complex Friendship."
57. Heaney, "Suffering and Decision," 224.
58. Heaney, "Meeting Seamus Heaney," 73–4.
59. See Owen, 125, for the text of "Strange Meeting" that includes these lines.
60. See Meg Tyler on Heaney's changes to his own translation to universalize Hrethel's suffering and apply it to Hughes here (152–4). Tyler argues convincingly that with his opening and closing changes to this passage that link Hughes and Hrethel, Heaney "makes a gesture of companionship and comfort" (154).
61. Hopkins, 87.
62. Ibid., 86.
63. I cannot agree with David Wheatley, "Seamus Heaney, *New Selected Poems 1966–1987* and *New Selected Poems 1988–2013*," who in reviewing Heaney's *New Selected Poems 1988–2013*, is pleased by the omission of the "statuesque" elegy for Hughes and claims, "(Much more successful is the sprightly elegy for Joseph Brodsky, 'Audenesque')" (n.p.).
64. Auden, *Selected Poems*, 88.
65. The relevant lines here are "And the seas of pity lie / Locked and frozen in each eye," which express an emotional and intellectual frozenness that thaws by the time of Auden's last stanza: "In the deserts of the heart / Let the healing fountain start, / In the prison of his days / Teach the free man how to praise" (ibid., 90, 91).
66. Ibid., 89.
67. Ibid.
68. Heaney, "*Lux Perpetua*," 9.
69. Ibid.

Chapter 5

Return: *District and Circle, Human Chain,* and Late Uncollected Poetry

Winner of the most prestigious prize for poetry in the United Kingdom, the T. S. Eliot Prize, along with the *Irish Times* "Poetry Now" Award, *District and Circle* both returns Heaney to his home district of Bellaghy in Northern Ireland and signifies his continued commitment to representing the suffering of others globally by incorporating the titles of two of London's Underground lines in the wake of the bombings there in July, 2005. The title poem bespeaks his continuing interest in underground, subterranean spaces evinced from the beginning of his poetry by dwelling in the London Underground and interacting with actual and ghostly denizens there. It intimates the local type of community that Heaney increasingly portrays in his later poetry—that of the living and the dead, a circle, a community he would himself join far too soon. Other poems circle back to Heaney's rural childhood celebrating intriguing objects such as the turnip-snedder and the harrow-pin and recalling incidents from World War Two in Northern Ireland, while still others elegize recent atrocities such as his September 11th poem, "Anything Can Happen." Finally, "The Tollund Man in Springtime" and the last poem in the volume, "The Blackbird of Glanmore," hint at revivified energies in Heaney's verse, a new sprightliness and movement to it seen in the confidence and surety of the various forms on display throughout the volume. In his review of *District and Circle*, Peter McDonald, who criticized what he called "a preponderance of dutiful and unsurprising verse" in *Electric Light*, praised the volume and noted it "shows . . . how genuinely new poetry can escape from the clutch even of the poet's own reputation, to become original, moving, and necessary all over again."[1]

The opening poem, "The Turnip-Snedder," anchors us vicariously in the vast mass of that ancient machine that was operated "In an age of bare hands / and cast iron" (*DC* 3), while the concluding poem, "The Blackbird of Glanmore," enables the poet to look back on his brother's early death at nearly four and himself in the present, preparing himself for the bird's "ready talkback," presumably adopting a songlike posture in a give-and-take manner. Both poems feature a solid stance epitomized by the snedder's weight and the poet's being "absolute" for the blackbird (78). Much of *District and Circle* renders love powerfully and potentially permanently, an impulse articulated at the end of "The Aerodrome." Dwelling in love and community steadies the poet for the ground-shifting realities occurring around him such as the September 11th terrorist attacks and those in London nearly four years later.

"The Aerodrome," set at the Toome Aerodrome built during Heaney's childhood in World War Two, turns on a young boy's waiting with a woman by the perimeter as they watch a pilot calling and expresses the boy's fear that she might "rise and go" with him rather than stay with the child (11).² Instead, she squeezes his hand, leading him to realize, "If self is a location, so is love: / Bearings taken, markings, cardinal points, / Options, obstinacies, dug heels, and distance, / Here and there and now and then, a stance" (12). Borrowing from the straight lines of "Markings" and drawing on the language of marbles from lyrics "iii" and "v" in "Squarings"—all from *Seeing Things*—Heaney redeploys that idiom here and extends it to create a discourse of love characterized by its definiteness and trustworthiness.

In contrast, "Anything Can Happen," subtitled "after Horace, Odes, I, 34," dwells not on love and its ability to anchor us but on hatred and how it unsettles us. It returns us to the formal terrain of Heaney's 1970s poems driven by quatrains, but this poem's seeming structural solidity crumbles in concert with the toppling Twin Towers of the World Trade Center as it proceeds. "Anything Can Happen" was first written as a pamphlet poem with a short accompanying essay for Amnesty International, a group Heaney had long supported and for which he had written "From the Republic of Conscience," collected in *The Haw Lantern*. It gives voice to the uneasiness that crept into many Americans' lives after radical Muslims slammed two airliners into the Twin Towers in New York City, were forced by passengers to crash a third plane into a Pennsylvania field, and rammed a fourth plane into the Pentagon in Washington, DC. In so doing, it troubles Heaney's move away from the murderous killing grounds of Northern Ireland featured in earlier poems toward the marvelous and skyward epitomized in later poems such as "viii" from "Squarings" about the ghost ship of Clonmacnoise because this atrocity comes out of "a clear blue sky" (13). The simplicity of utterance and the spare diction emphasize the poem's truth-telling impulse to register what happened that September morning and to lament not only the terrorists' victims but also, more indirectly, to mourn for a world lost, a simpler time without the fear of terror in the skies.

While "Anything Can Happen" is clearly a poem about the September 11th attacks, part of its appeal and staying power stems from the fluidity and non-specificity in its title as well as its mythic context. If "Anything Can Happen" as the title and the poem itself collectively tell us three times, who are we to argue with this rhetoric? This refrain not only suggests how those vicious attacks came out of nowhere but implies that in their wake, anything can happen anywhere at any time to anyone in the newly shaken post-9/11 world. Moreover, Heaney's recourses to Jupiter's galloping his thunder cart and horses and to "Stropped-beak Fortune / [that] Swoops," mythologizes the attacks, making them seem timeless and more ominously, inevitable (13).

When the poem concludes, its last quatrain seems broken open, exposed, akin to the new world order after that fateful September day. Two of these lines, like many of those that precede them, return to the alliteration and medial caesuras Heaney had long ago discovered in the Anglo-Saxon poets. Thus "Ground gives. The heaven's weight / Lifts up off Atlas like a kettle-lid." The repetition of the "g" sound, coupled with an absence of articles in this terse half-line, imparts an air of mystery that is quickly succeeded by the onrushing enjambment of the "heaven's weight" that falls off of Atlas's shoulders. Now, suddenly, a new, revisionary mythological intertext—Atlas as unable to hold up the sky—works in the opposite direction of the earlier mythical intertexts in the poem—Jupiter, Fortune—suggesting that the surety and firmness that inheres in the Atlas narrative now has collapsed. The unthinkable has happened: the Twin Towers topple; Atlas drops the heavens. And thus, in the last two lines of the poem, "Capstones shift, nothing resettles right. / Telluric ash and fire-spores boil away" (13). This second use of a medial caesura echoes the fracturing of the earth, which then is abruptly cut off by the line's being endstopped. Then the last line returns to the image of the heaven being like a kettle-lid, now envisioning the earth as a sort of kettle where "ash and fire-spores boil away."[3]

"Anything Can Happen" risks trying to capture such a heart-wrenching and sorrowful atrocity in a mere sixteen lines and, in its use of myth, disturbingly intimates that these terrorist attacks were fated, inevitable. But they were not, even if their perpetrators became as gods and martyrs to their supporters. Another attack was thwarted when passengers forced the hijackers to run a plane aimed at the Capitol into the Pennsylvania ground instead, heroically sacrificing themselves, and thus the poem's title might also imply their heroism and free will.

Turning to unrhymed tercets in "Helmet," Heaney continues his use of alliteration and medial caesuras, but by employing a varying lineation and heavy use of enjambment with only two fully end-stopped lines, writes a fluid, life-affirming counter-narrative drawing on the language of his recent translation of *Beowulf* that contrasts the deadly inevitability and unsettling of "Anything Can Happen." If the earlier poem traffics in abstractions and impersonality—the terrorists are only called "Those overlooked" (13)—"Helmet" abounds in intimate details and individuality by focusing on the human elements of Boston firefighter Bobby Breen that were literally imprinted on his helmet. These include his name rendered "in scarlet letters," the "tinctures of sweat and hair oil / In the withered sponge and shock-absorbing webs / Beneath the crown—", and the "Leather-trimmed, steel-ridged, hand-tooled, hand-sewn" "crest" of the helmet (14). Startlingly, Heaney here revisits a word from "Anything Can Happen," the "crest" of one of the Twin Towers that was torn off by "Stropped-beak Fortune" and set down "bleeding" on the other tower (13). Instead of the "bleeding" architectural top of the Twin Tower, likened implicitly to the crest of a bird ripped off by a stronger avian predator, he presents us—just as Breen long before the September 11th attacks gave the poet his helmet—the red crest of a real hero's helmet, a man who saved lives, not took them. The intricately fashioned, hand-worked crest and its signifying of heroism thus contrasts the impersonal, precise, and murderous tower-toppling of the September 11th hijackers. But finally, Heaney employs this hard and hand-tooled helmet, his "fire-thane's shield, / His shoulder-awning"—a couple of kennings that hearken back to the *Beowulf* poet's penchant for such devices—to signify how even many of the brave firemen fighting the fires that broke out in Manhattan that September morning collapsed and died. The enjambment of the last three-and-a-half lines powerfully brings home the terror that was visited upon those brave men who rushed into the Twin Towers while survivors ran past them in the burning and rubble-strewn stairwells: "while shattering glass // And rubble-bolts out of a burning roof / Hailed down on every hatchet man and hose man there / Till the hard-reared shield-wall broke" (14).

"Rilke: After the Fire," which appears shortly after "Helmet" and "Anything Can Happen" and which forms a triptych about destruction with them, reinforces those poems' projection of a new absence in the world, but also tentatively posits that those gifted ones who remember a created and beautiful space before it is destroyed can render it whole again for their hearers and readers. If Heaney had written earlier of the bright, ramifying absence of the long-departed chestnut tree in his childhood backyard to signify the loss of his mother in the last sonnet of "Clearances," here he invokes another kind of emptiness, a flat and dull one, to suggest how all had changed with the terrorist attacks on American soil. In this later version of Rilke's poem, even "Early autumn morning hesitated, / Shying at newness, an emptiness behind / Scorched linden trees still crowding in around / The moorland house, now just one more wallstead ..." (16). One cannot help but think here of the vacant space, the "footprint" where the Twin Towers stood, but with "wallstead," Heaney revisits another of his own poems, the first lyric in the "Lightenings" sequence from *Seeing Things*, which pictures the afterlife as a "Bare wallstead and a cold hearth rained into—" (*ST* 55). Something of that imagined space's emptiness and dreariness is conveyed by his re-introduction of "wallstead" here, rendering this new absence null and void.

But with the appearance of "the son of the place" and his narration that takes "great pains // To make them realize what had stood so," the poet introduces a note of hope into the newly desolate reality occasioned by the World Trade Center attacks and by extension into any atrocity if life-affirming stories are iterated. The task is difficult, for those who lived before such cataclysmic events must work to fill that empty space which, "now that it was gone, it all seemed / Far stranger: more fantastical than Pharaoh." For those living in the new reality of aching absence, the storyteller, the poet, the one who remembers how it used to be, is himself rendered strange, just as the son of the place is in "Rilke: After the Fire": "And he was changed: a foreigner among them" (16).

Subsequent poems such as the long sequence "District and Circle" and "To George Seferis in the Underworld" probe underground spaces—the London Underground or subway and something like the mythological underworld. "District and Circle" never explicitly mentions the London terrorist attacks of July 7, 2005, but coming in the wake of the triptych of September 11th poems and given its title, it silently mourns the absence of those 52 murdered victims who were killed by four homicide-bombers, radicalized Muslims, who set off bombs on the Piccadilly and Circle Underground lines and later bombed a London bus. In contrast to the mythical dimensions of his 9/11 poems, this "7/7" (as the London attack is commonly called) poem instead explores ordinariness of encounters on the Tube whose extensive lines run under London for miles in manifold directions. The five lyrics of thirteen, fourteen, thirteen, fourteen, and then twelve lines suggest a sonnet sequence of sorts and recall Kevin Young's conception of the structure of John Berryman's *Dream Songs* (long influential for Heaney, particularly for "Station Island"): "just as the *Dream Songs* sets up what feels like a form, it proceeds to dismantle it; the dismantling is integral to the form."[4] Similarly, as "District and Circle" proceeds and the Heaney figure is gradually brought into a sort of community with various crowds in the Underground, the sonnet form gradually disintegrates into a broken twelve-liner that concludes the sequence. The underground setting enables Heaney to undergo another series of dream meetings with nameless figures in contrast to his uneasily intimate meetings with ghosts from his past in *Station Island*. He originally had written two sonnets, then added three more sonnet variations after the attacks because "a poem called 'District and Circle' was going to have to bear additional scrutiny . . . Not particularly to do with the atrocity, more an attempt to convey the actual experience of an ordinary journey by Tube, which almost always has something oneiric about it" (*SS* 410). Heaney's sequence enables him to explore young and older versions of himself, echoing what Young has remarked about *Dream Songs*: "the poems are not a song of 'myself' but a song of multiple selves."[5]

The narrator in the sequence is a double figure for the poet—both his earlier self that he remembered "when I first journeyed on a London tube train; somebody who was much less at home, more anxious and 'out of it' than I would come to be later on," and the contemporary self who exhibits "awareness of the potential of a journey nowadays on a London tube train" and a realization of "all such journeys underground, into the earth, into the dark" (410). One recalls how Eliot's narrator "assumed a double part" when speaking to the "familiar compound ghost" in "Little Gidding," another poem influential for Heaney.[6]

The opening of "District and Circle" returns the poet full-circle, so to speak, not just to his long-ago lonely riding of the London Underground, but also implicitly to his home ground, particularly to his breakthrough poem "Digging," where he offers his underground art as a complement to the digging done by his father and grandfather. When he "trigger[s] and untrigger[s] a hot coin / Held at the ready" in "District and Circle" (*DC* 17) he echoes the potential violence registered in the opening simile of "Digging": "Between my finger and my thumb, / the squat pen rests, / snug as a gun" (*DN* 1). It is almost as if he will fire the coin at the Irish busker he always encounters in the corridor of the Underground, just as he affirms the power of the pen as a weapon early in "Digging." But while it seems to be sufficient to liken his pen to his forebears' spade in that early poem, here it seems to be enough to "trigger and untrigger" the coin and to recognize the other man as Irish too; the busker then gives him "passage" down the corridor.

Just as the poet experienced a momentary community with the ghostly interlocutors he meets in "Station Island," in "District and Circle" he enjoys a temporary community with living but seemingly ghostly crowds that surround him on a series of Tube journeys, what he calls in an anticipation of the title of his last volume of original poetry, "a human chain" in the third near-sonnet. A line from Eliot's

"The Waste Land"—"A crowd flowed over London Bridge, so many, / I had not thought death had undone so many"—likely provides the initial part of Heaney's image of "A crowd half straggle-ravelled and half strung / Like a human chain, the pushy newcomers / Jostling and purling underneath the vault" (*DC* 19).[7] But a line from Heaney's good friend Joseph Brodsky's poem, "Verses on the Death of T. S. Eliot," may have more directly inspired Heaney's likening the crowd to a dispersed chain: "He latched his door on the thin chain of years."[8] The "purling" of the "newcomers" recalls the phrase Heaney employed to convey Louis O'Neill's boat motor churning through Lough Neagh on that long-ago trip recalled in "Casualty": "The screw purling, turning / Indolent fathoms white" (*FW* 24). That sound helped entrance Heaney into a vision about the hard work of poetry, which must be conducted in solitude, "Somewhere, well out, beyond . . ." (24). Here, however, the poet is thankful that "I re-entered the safety of numbers" (*DC* 19) as the noisy crowd turns and purls amid the chaos, carrying him along to the doors of the Underground train.

The last two lyrics conclude the journey of the poet underground as he finally boards the Tube train "across the gap" and is whisked away, "Spot-rooted, buoyed, aloof . . ." (20). This buoyant train recalls the sofa "train" Heaney and his siblings ride in "A Sofa in the Forties," which seems to have "achieved // Flotation" (*SL* 7). As he moves deeper underground in the last lyric, "crowd-swept, strap-hanging, / My lofted arm a-swivel like a flail," he sees "My father's glazed face in my own waning / And craning . . ." Grown older and more confident than the earlier, forlorn self portrayed earlier in the sequence, the poet-narrator realizes with a shock how much he resembles his father, another "self" of sorts for him. As he habitually "hurtled forward" through the Underground on a series of visits to London, the motion leads him into contemplation, "Reflecting in a window mirror-backed / By blasted weeping rock-walls. Flicker-lit" (*DC* 21). Those "blasted weeping rock-walls" may simply be the normal state of the subterranean terrain surrounding the trains, but it is hard in the wake of the July 7, 2005 terrorist attacks on London not to see them as blasted by bombs, weeping not water but tears in a pathetic fallacy.

The circular journeys of the universalized Underground give way to the local news of the district in the poems following "District and Circle," many of which feature the bright, clean edges of words and implements. It is almost as if Heaney re-employed "the curt cuts of an edge" in "Digging" and excavated a series of words and tools to burnish in these poems (*DN* 2). In "To George Seferis in the Underworld," the poem immediately following "District and Circle," Heaney continues his ghostly conversation with denizens of the underworld, in this case with the Greek Nobel Laureate who translated Eliot's "The Waste Land" into Greek in 1936, believed in using demotic language in his work, and exemplified a commitment to local culture for Heaney, just as Eliot did. Heaney muses in this poem's conclusion that he wants "a chance to test the edge / of *seggans*, dialect blade / hoar and harder and more hand-to-hand / than what is common usage nowadays: / sedge—marshmallow, rubber-dagger stuff" (*DC* 23). Such a recovery of *seggans* as a dialect word (recalling his heavy usage of such words in *Wintering Out* and elsewhere in his poetry) and its signifying power becomes a crucial maneuver in this volume since it suggests that Heaney believes that words have gradually lost their rhetorical power to evoke a particular thing or even person. Instead, he privileges the Roman conception of *verba* ("words") as *res* ("things") in many instances from his later poetry; words have a heft and power to them as they always have had in his work, but now the things themselves, which often are used to pierce or cut, have become coincident with the word that signifies them.

And moreover, the poems that feature these objects themselves become instances of *res*; Heaney even has stated that a poem is "the *made* thing."[9] He believed that art as a thing is sufficient unto itself and thus is healthy and sound, noting that

> The virtue of poetry and art in general resides in the fact that it is first and foremost a whole *thing*, a hale *thing*, a *thing* formally and feelingly sound, right within itself, a *thing* to which the ultimate response—if not always the immediate response—is "yes."[10]

Elsewhere, he affirms this stance, arguing that the word "poetry" is "a noun aspiring . . . to the condition of verb—a noun because *as a work of art it must retain a definite thinginess*, but verb-like nevertheless, because it represents an act of mind and an act of making."[11] Hopkins's insistence that his poems about natural objects "instress" or capture the "inscape," or distinctive individual identity of the thing or person, exemplifies this sense of the poem as *res* and *verba* for Heaney.[12]

Heaney's interest in things, their inner lives, and the emotional pressures they exert upon us likely also arises in part from his deep interest in the Romantic poets, especially Wordsworth, who argued in his and Coleridge's "Preface" to *The Lyrical Ballads* that poetry should make the ordinary extraordinary.[13] He actually cites this passage from the "Preface" in his introduction to the selection of Wordsworth's poems he edited: "a common incident is viewed under a certain 'colouring of imagination'; ordinary things are presented . . . in an unusual way . . ." They are "made interesting by the poet's capacity to trace in them, 'truly though not ostentatiously, the primary laws of our nature.'"[14] His approval of this poetic strategy in Wordsworth suggests he has similarly traced "the primary laws of our nature" through seeing into the life of things. In "Wordsworth's Skates," he hears "the whet and scud of steel on placid ice," and sees something imperishable about the Romantic poet's skates, "Not the bootless runners lying toppled / In dust ... / Their bindings perished, // But the reel of them on frozen Windermere / As he flashed from the clutch of earth along its curve / And left it scored" (*DC* 24). Such lines recall the lovely language of Book I of *The Prelude* when Wordsworth recalls himself and his boyhood companions, "shod with steel," hissing "along the polished ice in games / Confederate."[15] More important, Heaney celebrates the perduring, memory-evoking qualities of the steel in Wordsworth's skates that enabled him to score the surface of frozen Lake Windermere. Such things have a literal cutting edge, implying the continuing importance of words that are sharp, that can slice into a subject and get a grip on it.

Returning to the subject of spades he first raised in "Digging," Heaney imagines Séamus MacGearailt making a "side-arm" for Eoghan Rua Ó Súilleabháin in his translation from Ó Súilleabháin's eighteenth-century poem "Poet to Blacksmith." The shovel as a gun—here a "side-arm"—continues to appeal to Heaney, even though he drops this image by line two, calling the implement a "suitable tool for digging and grubbing the ground, / Lightsome and pleasant to lean on or cut with or lift ..." (27). The airiness of the imagined spade recalls that of the pitchfork in the poem of that same name in *Seeing Things*, which is "accurate and light" and has a "springiness" to it (*ST* 25). He wants "The thing to have purchase and spring and be fit for the strain" (*DC* 27), echoing the last line of his "A Kite for Michael and Christopher": "You were born fit for it. / Stand in here in front of me / and take the strain" (*SI* 44; my emphases). The spade finally stands here as an analog for poetry, much as Heaney's blacksmith's anvil and the work done upon it function in "The Forge." He wants a "well shaped" poetry himself and, "best thing of all, the ring of it, sweet as a bell" (*DC* 27). Such a poetry, like "the saw's greased teeth" in Heaney's elegy for Czesław Miłosz, "Out of This World" (49), can cut into its subject matter and excavate truths from the poet's subconscious.

Two of the best poems in the latter half of the volume suggest that after Heaney's meditations on the terrorist attacks in New York and London and then his turn toward things that epitomize his re-embrace of hard-edged words, he wanted to reimagine a figure from his earlier poetry—the Tollund Man—and return to a bird-like figure, not Sweeney but a blackbird this time, which would enable him to begin singing a new, sprightly music. These "above-ground" poems of resurrection are anticipated in the second lyric from "District and Circle" when the poet descending to the "underworld" of the Tube laments

>   ... the light
> Of all-overing, long since mysterious day,
> Parks at lunchtime where the sunners lay
> On body-heated mown grass regardless,
> A resurrection scene minutes before
> The resurrection ... (18)

The light, the sunbathers, the mown grass, the repetition of "resurrection"—all coalesce here to evoke a vision of new life springing into being, which Heaney celebrates supremely in his Tollund Man sequence and "The Blackbird of Glanmore."

"The Tollund Man in Springtime," another sonnet sequence, forms a triptych with Heaney's earlier poems "The Tollund Man" (*Wintering Out*) and "Tollund" (*The Spirit Level*). Together, the three chart the evolution of the conflict in Northern Ireland and its aftermath and also show how Heaney's poetry evolved. If "The Tollund Man" meditated upon the trans-cultural, trans-temporal dimension of violence in ancient Jutland and contemporary Northern Ireland and "Tollund" upon the possibility of peace in the province, then "The Tollund Man in Springtime"—much longer than the first two with its six sonnets—explores the imagined future life of this figure and, by extension, the life of Northern Ireland and poetry itself.

The sequence starts with the Tollund Man's reawakening "to revel in the spirit / They strengthened when they chose to put me down / For their own good." Somehow, his revivification is spurred by the energy associated with his sacrifice as a scapegoat. Now, he is "an absorbed face / Coming and going, neither god nor ghost," and has passed "into your virtual city" and is "Unregistered by scans, screens, hidden eyes ..." (*DC* 53). While the Tollund Man is not employed as a Christian symbol or as having died as the result of a Christian sacrifice, his death and new life nevertheless emit a kind of resurrection energy that suggest how, late in his career, Heaney still privileged image, word, symbol, and myth over the linearity, surety, rationality, and near-worship of science that many moderns embrace. More important, he remained convinced that our refusal to remain open to the enduring presence of myth and spirituality in our lives would make our culture flattened and dull. Scans and screens, despite our daily dependence on them, can only register certain superficial realities.

Mircea Eliade, whose work Heaney drew upon earlier in his career, argued that "it is the presence of the images and symbols that keeps the cultures 'open': starting from no matter what culture ... the 'limit-situations' of man are fully revealed, owing to the symbols that sustain those cultures." He believed, as did Heaney, that "If we neglect this unique spiritual foundation of the various cultural styles, the philosophy of culture will be condemned to remain no more than a morphological and historical study, without any validity for the human condition as such."[16] Heaney's newly revived Tollund Man escapes our world's attempt to scan or register him; he stays "off the grid" as those do today who seek a simpler life. The Tollund Man "keeps the cultures 'open,'" and his presence in this volume suggests the residual, abiding presence of mythic and spiritual realities in our lives and how they still offer us entry to a transcendent plane of being above and beyond this world. Moreover, he finally represents poetry itself, which Heaney argued we need "because it is a source of images which have an inner inevitability and a sure claim on our understanding as a source of possible meanings." As he put it, "the image—the poem, the work of literature—is a way of holding our own against the inchoate and the insubstantial."[17] Perhaps that urge to hold "our own" suggests why each sonnet in this sequence, if not following established rhyme schemes for the form, nonetheless is fully fourteen lines, complete and whole.

At first, the sequence re-tells the Genesis story as the second lyric portrays the Tollund Man, "so long unrisen," remembers being disinterred. Once

> ... a spade-plate slid and soughed and plied
> At my buried ear, and the levered sod
> Got lifted up; then once I felt the air
> I was like turned turf in the breath of God,
> Bog-bodied on the sixth day, brown and bare,
> And on the last, all told, unatrophied. (54)

This process is the airiest type of digging, so different in kind from that spade-work imaged in "Digging" so long ago. Bodied back into existence by the archaeologist's spade, the Tollund Man is "like turned turf in the breath of God," made like Adam and Eve "on the sixth day." Remarkably he is "unatrophied," just as the picture of him in P. V. Glob's *The Bog People* demonstrates.

But the poem teases as it proceeds, returning in its third lyric to that time "Between when I was buried and unburied. / Between what happened and was meant to be." Then, for hundreds of years, he was "Disembodied.", and the full stops here and in the lines just cited indicate how time stopped for him then (55). By the very next sonnet, however, which opens with a quotation from Miłosz and a Molly

Bloom-like affirmation, "'The soul exceeds its circumstances.' Yes.", the Tollund Man escapes from his "display-case" through verbalizing himself back into being, telling his various body parts to be like nature. Thus, he "Told my webbed wrists to be like silver birches, / My old uncallused hands to be young sward, / The spade-cut skin to heal, and got restored / By telling myself this" (56). The Genesis reference disappears and he accomplishes his restoration, this creation, this resurrection through narrative, speaking himself into new life, an implicit argument for how poetry can subtly revivify us. Just as Miłosz, the silent presence behind this poem, "developed a fierce conviction about the holy force of his art, how poetry was called upon to combat death and nothingness,"[18] Heaney himself believed that poetry "is a way of coming at the things that happen in time a second time ... in an active, searching, renovating way." Within "the extra time of the poem we are released for a moment from the world of necessity, the world of morality, the world of politics, the world indeed of religion."[19] Thus the freedom of the Tollund Man implies how poetry can release us from our besetting obligations, even our beliefs, into a liberating space. Halfway through this fourth sonnet, the man realizes, "Late as it was, / The early bird still sang, the meadow hay / Still buttercupped and daisied, sky was new." It is an eternal summer morning even though it is late in mankind's history and the birdsong, flowered hay, and new sky, shorn even of the definite article here, together betoken poetry's release of us into a strange new world, where even though we might smell, like the Tollund Man, "exhaust fumes, silage reek," we can still look skyward, at and beyond "transatlantic flights stacked in the blue" (56).

Just as the Tollund Man in the last three sonnets is in the world but not of it, as Christians are often encouraged to be, so poetry can allow us to live in the world but not be conformed to it. In the fifth sonnet, the Tollund Man remembers learning from "Cattle out in rain, their knowledgeable / Solid standing and readiness to wait," while he waited, entombed in Jutland peat. Now in the present, revived and on the move, he finds "whatever it was I knew / Came back to me. Newfound contrariness." Thus, in a variation on a solitary posture often returned to by Heaney, perhaps supremely so at the end of "Casualty," he "stood off," in "check-out lines, at cash-points, in those queues / Of wired, far-faced smilers," a "Bulrush, head in air, far from its lough" (57). Heaney conveys his solitude again by removing reassuring articles—not "a bulrush," but instead, "Bulrush"; not "my head in air," but simply, "head in air."

In the last sonnet, the Tollund Man could be dismayed when the "bunch of Tollund rushes—roots and all—" he carried with him everywhere finally turns to dust, but he refuses to be contained even when this literal ground of his being crumbles. Instead, in an image rife with meaning for Heaney, "As a man would, cutting turf, / I straightened, spat on my hands, felt benefit, / And spirited myself into the street" (58). By drawing upon the literal dust of his past sustenance and using it to mix with his own spit on work-hardened hands, he can liberate himself from that past to a large degree and re-imagine his future. So too, Heaney implies, he might do himself. These last lines recall the moment recalled in *Crediting Poetry*, when he, like his newly revived Tollund Man here, "straightened up" and "began . . . to try to make space in my reckoning and imagining for the marvelous as well as for the murderous" (*CP* 20). But the conclusion of "The Tollund Man in Springtime" does more than just rehearse Heaney's move from the "murderous to the marvelous" he began making in the late 1970s. It also signifies his desire to move beyond even the celestial reach of his later poetry and into something else, perhaps reborn as a poet, revivified like his bog man is here.

He signals that desired new poetic life in "The Blackbird of Glanmore," the volume's concluding poem that begins by viewing the blackbird as an ill omen like that one of his neighbors remembered being nearby in the days leading up to the poet's young brother's death long ago. But he quickly rejects this superstition, instead perhaps remembering the birdsong ringing out around the Tollund Man in his new life of springtime, stating, "Hedge-hop, I am absolute / For you, your ready talkback, / Your each stand-offish comeback," and praising the bird's ongoingness: "Your picky, nervy goldbeak— / On the grass when I arrive, // In the ivy when I leave" (*DC* 78). These pared-down lines and the alliterative string of adjectives themselves suggest that in his next volume and beyond, Heaney would be singing new songs in vibrant forms, as indeed he does in *Human Chain*.

The opening poem of *Human Chain*, "'Had I Not Been Awake,'" suggests his continuing connection to the natural world and its ability to inspire him to airy flights of the imagination. In this sense, the poem and subsequent ones in this magnificent volume exemplify the ongoing truth of John Wilson Foster's contention in 1995 that "chiefly through his adoption since *Sweeney Astray* and *Station Island* of the tree as a major site and symbol, Heaney has attempted to seam smoothly his two poetics. One gains the air only through the agency of the rooted."[20] The cover of the American edition of *Human Chain* gives credence to Foster's formulation, featuring a wall covered with branching, interconnected vines on which the bottom two-thirds are green, the color of Earth, and the top third blue, the color of sky. The opening lines of the poem convey the poet's excitement at "A wind that rose and whirled until the roof / Pattered with quick leaves off the sycamore // And got me up, the whole of me a-patter, / Alive and ticking like an electric fence" (*HC* 3). The sycamore's pattering leaves make the poet's heart go "a-patter," electrifying him. This "courier blast" begins the volume with a clarion call to readers that Heaney stands ready as ever to admit the extraordinary into his poetry, and the poems that follow make good on that promise (3).

Neil Corcoran noted that while the volume has no elegies for poets—something he takes Heaney to task for in his volumes after *Field Work*—it "nevertheless constitutes one of this poet's most perfect elegiac utterances. In a newly chastened and simplified language and form, a swift transparency of means, the book breathes a pure elegiac serene ..."[21] And Roy Foster, in his reminiscence of the poet after his death, notes the volume's "almost daunting economy of line" along with its "whispering sense of elegy—not just because many of the poems were dedicated to the dead, but also because they looped back to his earliest images of pen nibs, farm routines, animal life, the rituals of neighborhood, and love. This sense of an ending was perhaps a sign of poetic prescience."[22] The volume achieves this elegiac tenor through what we might term its "proleptic self-elegies" in the wake of the poet's stroke, its elegies for recently departed friends, such as the musician David Hammond, and through its elegies for the poet's father.

Human Chain is intertwined with another tercet-heavy volume, *Seeing Things*, through complementary poems such as "In the Attic" and "The Settle Bed" and "Miracle" and "The Skylight," respectively, and other poems from *Human Chain* make clear that Heaney's search to remember and burnish the memory of his father, which drives many of the more poignant poems in the earlier volume, continues here through his imaginative autobiographical revision of Aeneas' search for his father in the Underground from Book VI of Virgil's *The Aeneid*.[23] Heaney had signaled his long interest in Virgil—he observed he was part of the last generation of schoolboys who knew passages from the *Aeneid* by heart, particularly Book VI, which is the ur-text for *Human Chain*—many years before in the concluding section of his "The Strand at Lough Beg," where he imagines himself washing his murdered cousin's face with dew, much as Virgil washes Dante's face early in the *Purgatorio*. Also, as we have seen, he turned to versions of Virgilian eclogues in several memorable lyrics from *Electric Light*. But in order to write his deepest, most profound poetry about his relationship with his father, he turned again to Aeneas' search in the Underworld for his father Anchises, a translation of which opens *Seeing Things*, as we have seen in the previous chapter.

In Robert Fitzgerald's translation, Aeneas tells the Sibyl of Cumae of his earnest longing to see his father shortly after meeting her: "One thing I pray for: / since it is here they say one finds the gate / Of the king of under world, the shadowy marsh / That wells from Acheron, may I have leave / To go to my dear father's side and see him."[24] Later in that book, after meeting his father in Elysium, Aeneas tries to embrace his shade three times, but each time, he slips through his grasp:

"But let me have your hand, let me embrace you,
Do not draw back."
                           At this his tears brimmed over
And down his cheeks. And there he tried three times
To throw his arms around his father's neck,
Three times the shade untouched slipped through his hands,
Weightless as wind and fugitive as dream.[25]

In section "iv" of the sequence "Album," the second poem in *Human Chain*, Heaney recalls the first time he wanted to embrace his father, remembering how it does not happen then but does the second two times, when his father is incapacitated by drink and age, respectively. He regrets not embracing him "on the riverbank / That summer before college, him in his prime," but is glad he did during his next chance, when a drunk Patrick Heaney "needed help / To do up trouser buttons" at "New Ferry" (6). Memorably, "the third // Was on the landing during his last week, / Helping him to the bathroom, my right arm / Taking the webby weight of his underarm" (6). Thus Heaney revisits and revises Aeneas' failed three embraces of the shade of his father Anchises by gratefully recalling the two times he did embrace his father while he was living. One of Patrick Heaney's grandsons achieved the third embrace, "rush[ing] him in the armchair / With a snatch raid on his neck, // Proving him thus vulnerable to delight ..." (7). Such moments adapted and transmuted from Virgil prove the truth of Stephen Heiny's claim that in the poet's treatment of Virgil in *Human Chain*, "Heaney omits any hint of the epic manner. He keeps so far from the grandeur of epic that he never risks the self-ridicule that comparison with the epic would entail."[26]

"Album" thus resurrects Patrick Heaney, in the process enacting a conversation with an early poem of Heaney's from *Death of a Naturalist*, "Ancestral Photograph." Instead of the actual snapshot of Patrick Heaney's cattle-dealing uncle portrayed there along with Patrick Heaney himself, who "sadden[ed] when the [cattle] fairs were stopped," cut off from this vital aspect of his family heritage (*DN* 14), "Album" offers a retrospective of five "pictures," as it were, across its five tercet-driven sections. The first three sections portray the poet's relationship with his parents. The first recalls him as a boy standing with his parents "on airy Sundays / Shin-deep in hilltop bluebells, looking out / at Magherafelt's four spires in the distance." The lack of demonstrativeness in their love for each other—but its real depth, all the same—is shown by his recalling the definition of love as "steady gazing / Not at each other but in the same direction" (*HC* 4). Section "ii" remembers his trip to Derry City with his parents when he started St Columb's College at twelve, particularly how he looked back at them upon their departure and saw them "all the more together / For having had to turn and walk away, as close / In the leaving (or closer) as in the getting." Section "iii" doubles back to his parents' wedding meal, when they celebrated first becoming a married couple, imagining a seaside meal in winter where the poet hovers, an uneasy guest, "Uninvited, ineluctable" (5). Heaney thus portrays his father repeatedly as part of a deeply knit couple with his mother in the first three sections, then his own relationship with his father when they were on their own in section "iv," and finally Patrick Heaney's relationship with his grandson in section "v." In each "snapshot," Patrick Heaney is never alone but pictured with a loved one, suggesting how he was always bound into his close family community.

But after following "Album" with another pen poem, "The Conway Stewart," about the lovely fountain pen his parents gave him when they left him in Derry for school that long-ago day in 1951, the poet sunders his father and mother in an even more moving poem, "Uncoupled." This meditation, offered in two twelve-lined sections, the first treating Margaret Heaney and the second Patrick Heaney, renders his parents in timeless motion doing habitual tasks the poet always associated with them. The separately numbered sections as well as the white space separating them create the effect of their "uncoupling." Both sections are composed of a single sentence beginning with "Who is this," which is slowly unrolled by the unrhymed tercets. Margaret and Patrick Heaney, even though separated in death and in the poem's sections, are united through the ash imagery Heaney deploys. "Who is this coming to the ash-pit / Walking tall," he asks about his mother, and he shows her carrying the family "firebox, weighty, full to the brim / With whitish dust and flakes still sparking hot . . ." "[W]hile she proceeds / Unwavering, keeping her burden horizontal still," she disappears around "the henhouse" (19) and Heaney's father appears, "Working his way towards me through the pen, / His ashplant in one hand // Lifted and pointing . . ." (9–10). She carries the ashes; he, Joyce-like, holds an ashplant. Margaret Heaney walks away from her audience (Patrick Heaney and son?), while Patrick Heaney works "his way towards me through the pen" (9), speaking indistinguishably, "calling to where I'm perched / On top of a shaky gate, // Waving and calling something I cannot hear ..." (10). In both situations, the loss is immeasurable despite the temporary solace of imagining each parent back in her and his familiar environments, respectively. When Patrick Heaney's eyes "leave mine and I know / The pain of loss before I know the term" (10), that averted gaze feels like a permanent withdrawal and indeed stands for his lasting departure from earth.

After another poem about the poet's father, "The Butts," which describes both the contents of his father's old suits and the family's taking care of him in his last days, Heaney turns to his own stroke during 2006 in several poems, "Chanson D'Aventure," "Miracle," and "Human Chain." This triptych of stroke poems meditates on both the intimate particulars of his stroke and its aftermath while also casting it in the context of gratitude for the human chain of friends, wife, and wider community, who not only helped carry him to the ambulance the night of his stroke, but also, were with him during his time of recovery—particularly his wife Marie. The epigraph to "Chanson D'Aventure," "Love's mysteries in souls do grow, / But yet the body is his book," is taken directly from John Donne's "The Ecstasy," while later lines in the poem proper borrow from Donne's poem as well. This epigraph suggests that the poet's body becomes his longest-running creation, as it were, and it imparts a concrete, physical context to this and the other stroke poems that balances their counter-tendency toward the spiritual and even transcendent, particularly in "Miracle." Taken together, these seemingly opposed trajectories become Donnean in their unity of body and soul, a unity Heaney clearly privileged through his relationship with his wife. The first two sections of "Chanson" attempt to convey the poet's deep closeness to his wife; thus, the epigraph could just as easily have been another line from Donne's poem, "we two, one another's best."[27]

Heaney's title, which promises a rollicking song of adventure, may artificially seem to attempt to put an optimistic gloss on the subject of the poet's paralysis and then recovery, but in fact the stroke itself does engender an adventure for Heaney—from the ambulance ride, during which he and his wife are able to revisit and deepen their long relationship, to his recovery through physical therapy in the third section. The procession of active verbs that begin the poem impart just this air of adventure: "Strapped on, wheeled out, forklifted, locked / In position for the drive, / Bone-shaken, bumped at speed" (13). And yet Heaney himself, surrounded by all this flurry of action, is unable to move and likely signifies his fear of his own impending absence if he is to die, not appearing until after the nurse and his wife do—toward the end of line 5 as "me flat on my back—", a supine posture tellingly conveyed by his employment of the dash. When he recalls in the second line of stanza three that "Our eyebeams threaded laser-fast" (13) he draws on the seventh and eighth lines of "The Ecstasy"—"Our eye-beams twisted, and did thread / Our eyes, upon one double string"—but more important, he signifies how their darting eyes convey the only action besides that of the speeding ambulance and are conjoined to show their unity, love, and fear of what may happen.[28]

Section two meditates upon that fear of their separation, shown by their temptation to "have quoted Donne / On love on hold, body and soul apart," in the last lines of stanza four, section one, by beginning with a line drawing on Keats's "To a Nightingale": "Apart: the very word is like a bell" (13). It repeats Keats's line verbatim, save for his opening "Forlorn," which is followed by a colon like Heaney's "Apart."[29] Then, Heaney offers a moving series of closely linked sonic and tactile images—the bell pulled by "the sexton Malachy Boyle outrolled / *In illo tempore* in Bellaghy" (13), the one Heaney "tolled in Derry" at St Columb's College, and his hand in the present that "lay flop-heavy as a bellpull" (14).[30] The weight of that paralyzed hand contrasts the lively "gaze" of husband and wife that is "ecstatic and bisected" (the "ecstatic" recalling Donne's "The Ecstasy") and the motion of the ambulance that "careered at speech through Dungloe . . ." (14).

Gaze and hand are united powerfully again throughout the third section, in which the poet likens himself to "The charioteer at Delphi [who] holds his own," despite having lost "His six horses and chariot . . . / His left hand [is] lopped // From a wrist protruding like an open spout, / Bronze reins astream in his right, his gaze ahead / Empty as the space where the team should be . . ." Heaney privileges this famous statuary because of its defiance and optimism—in his depiction, the charioteer seemingly expects his team of horses to return so he continues holding the reins. Moreover, "His eyes-front, straight-backed posture like my own / Doing physio in the corridor" (14), suggests that the poet approves not just of his attitude signified by his posture but finds in that posture a literally exemplary one for himself as he learns to walk again after his stroke. But another example finally intrudes into the poem, one first advanced in his early poem "Follower," collected in *Death of a Naturalist*, where Heaney recalls how "I stumbled in" the "hob-nailed wake" of his father, remembering, "I wanted to grow up and plough, / To close one eye, stiffen my arm." Instead, "I was a nuisance, tripping, falling, / Yapping always" (*DN* 12). In the present, he draws inspiration not just from the Delphi charioteer, but from moments when he did not fall and was enabled to plow a straight and steady course when assisted by his daddy: "As if once more I'd found myself in step // Between two shafts, another's hand on mine, / Each slither of the share, each stone it hit / Registered like a pulse in the timbered grips" (*HC* 14–15). "Another's hand on mine" recapitulates the poem's earlier image of Marie Heaney holding her husband's "dead" hand in hers. "Chanson D'Aventure" memorably intimates the presence of a human chain of hand-holders for Heaney throughout the arc of his life, from his father's helping hand on his as he wielded the plow as a boy to his wife's hand on his as they shot toward the hospital, to, presumably, the hand of the physical therapist on the recovering poet's hand.

His gratefulness for his father's help in plowing when he is a boy that motivates him as an older man to learn to walk again thus forms another link in the human chain of father and son troped by the frequent references to Virgil's Aeneas and Anchises elsewhere in the volume. The preceding poem, "The Butts," had, after all, concluded with a reversal of the father helping the son by drawing upon the poet's memories of taking his elderly father's "lightness," placing his hands "well in beneath / Each meagre armpit / To lift and sponge him" (12). This scene may be ghosted by Philip Sidney's remark in "The Defense of Poesy": "Who readeth Aeneas carrying old Anchises on his back that wisheth not it were his fortune to perform so excellent an act?"[31] Moreover, by figuratively taking the hand of these three literary exemplars, Virgil, Donne, and Keats, whose work had often sustained him before, Heaney binds himself to their evocative poetry, showing in the process how we are sustained by both those known to us personally and unknown, past and present.

The next two "stroke poems" make clear the importance of this human chain, featuring moments of crisis including the poet's own stroke and humanitarian situations. In "Miracle," he revisits the narrative from Mark's Gospel, 1: 1–12 (first explored in "The Skylight" from *Seeing Things*) in which Jesus heals a palsied man because of the faith expressed by the man's friends in lowering him down through a roof to Christ. Heaney and his wife, along with two other couples, had been staying at the playwright Brian Friel's house in Donegal when he was felled by the stroke and "Miracle" focuses on their "faith" in physically getting him out of the house to the waiting ambulance. Thus the poem, which begins *in medias res*, privileges "Not the one who takes up his bed and walks / But the ones who have known him all along / And carry him in—". Again, as in "Chanson D'Aventure," Heaney emphasizes bodily physicality, which gradually shades into the hope of miraculous healing: "Their shoulders numb, the ache and stoop deeplocked / In their backs, the stretcher handles / Slippery with sweat." Once he is "made tiltable / And raised to the tiled roof, then lowered for healing," they can finally relax as "they stand and wait // For the burn of the paid-out ropes to cool, / Their slight lightheadedness and incredulity / To pass, those ones who had known him all along." Their lightheadedness and incredulity stems from not just their amazement at what has taken place, but also likely from their having participated in what they hope is the beginning of a miraculous healing. The title signifies not only this hope, but also the miracle of friends, conveyed by the repetition of the phrase in the second and twelfth lines—"ones who have known him all along"—who would care for the poet so much that they would form this human chain to pass him on toward healing (16).

"Human Chain" itself does not directly discuss the poet's stroke but rather, through referencing his own childhood lifting of bags of grain, attempts to empathize with the exertion of "bags of meal passed hand to hand / In close-up by the aid workers, and soldiers / Firing over the mob . . ." By so empathizing, he recalls how he would give the grain sack "the heave—" (another judicious use of the dash that here signifies the sack's flight through the air) and then experience "The eye-to-eye, one-two, one-two upswing / On to the trailer, then the stoop and drag and drain / Of the next lift." He thus implicitly likens his own paralyzed body that was lifted by friends and ambulance personnel to those long-ago grain sacks he swung and the "bags of meal" he sees "passed hand to hand" to help the starving in the present. In each case, he registers the intimate eye contact, "The eye-to-eye," which was necessary for the proper passage of the grain and which returns us to his "laser-fast" gaze into his wife's "eyebeams" in the ambulance in "Chanson." Despite his profound gratefulness at the human chain that he sees extended in the humanitarian aid sequence at the beginning of this title poem, he closes it by offering his realization that once the burden of grain sacks or the human body is released, it is "A letting go which will not come again. / Or it will, once. And for all," a marvelous series of three short sentences that progressively contract and signify death, the ultimate "letting go" (17). "Human Chain" is a prescient poem for a man who would die three years after this volume was published.

And yet other poems in the volume such as "A Herbal" more optimistically reincorporate the poet into his home ground and into his human chain of family and friends. One of the longest poems in the volume, "A Herbal," after Guillevic's "*Herbier de Bretagne*," locates the poet firmly back in his home place in a series of deftly sketched short lines. In the poem's antepenultimate section, Heaney affirms,

> If you know a bit
> About the universe

> It's because you've taken it in
> Like that,
>
> Looked as hard
> As you look into yourself,
>
> Into the rat hole,
> Through the vetch and dock
> That mantled it. (43)

There are echoes here of "Personal Helicon," the concluding poem in *Death of a Naturalist*. But the childish narcissism rejected at the end of that poem by the adult poet is now redeveloped, redeployed, reworked. Moreover, while the adult poet then "rhyme[s] / To see myself, to set the darkness echoing" (*DN* 44), a maneuver that still smacks of narcissim, here the poet privileges looking into the wider world equally as "hard / As you look into yourself"—and that wider world contains the squalid and disgusting, "the rat hole," just as it does the quotidian and earthly, "the vetch and dock."

Assuming his now long-held liminal position in the last two sections of "A Herbal," the poet shows how seeming dislocation can actually ground and comfort, allowing the boy and now the man to occupy a dialectical space that stood him in good stead his whole life. First, he situates himself between a series of plants and flowers:

> Between heather and marigold,
> Between sphagnum and buttercup,
> Between dandelion and broom,
> Between forget-me-not and honeysuckle . . . (*HC* 43)

The reiteration of "Between" places him thoroughly in the landscape around his childhood home of Mossbawn, and then it quickly gives way to glimpses of a wider world:

> As between clear blue and cloud,
> Between haystack and sunset sky,
> Between oak tree and slated roof,
>
> I had my existence. I was there.
> Me in place and the place in me. (44)

It matters not one whit that that landscape has been irredeemably changed, as Heaney has admitted to Dennis O'Driscoll: "if you see the place now, it's completely different, looks like a small industrial estate . . . that old sense of tillage and season and foliage has disappeared. Once trees and hedges and ditches and thatch get stripped, you're in a very different world. You're deserting the ground for the grid" (*SS* 24). For as Edward Casey argues, "place outlasts much that vanishes, including many of the events that happen in its midst and the dwellings built on it."³² Heaney's conception of Mossbawn as a lasting place has a similar perduring quality to that which Casey delineates here. As the poet recalls about his home place, merely iterating the associated spots in that district "turns them into what Wordsworth once called a prospect of the mind. They lie deep, like some script indelibly written into the nervous system."³³ Casey anticipates Heaney's lament for the superficial replacement of the "ground" with the "grid," believing that "Beneath chronometry and cartography alike there is a primordial topography—a *chorography*, a 'tracing of place'—at one with the most intimate layers of our psychical lives."³⁴

Through his memory, through the looking glass of this and other poems, Heaney recovers that "primordial topography," that long-lost world: he re-enters it and affirms how it molded and still molds him. When he concludes "A Herbal" by asking

> Where can it be found again,
> An elsewhere world, beyond
>
> Maps and atlases,
> Where all is woven into
>
> And of itself, like a nest
> Of crosshatched grass blades? (44)

this seeming lament has already been answered by the carefully constructed world of the poem, "Where all is woven into // And of itself," an intricate design evoked by Heaney's own "crosshatched," woven words. Tasting this poem like the herbal of its title enables us to enter that world and become temporarily part of it as well.

Heaney continues exploring the most important world in the volume by returning to Book VI of the *Aeneid* in the following poem, "Canopy." Early in Book VI, Aeneas finds "The golden leafage, rustling in light wind," and "at once briskly took hold of it / And, though it clung, greedily broke it off . . ."³⁵ Now he can gain access to the Underworld by presenting this limb to the Sibyl and later Charon. The speaker in Heaney's poem stares at the "young green" on the trees in Harvard Yard (45) and listens to their whispering and singing, concluding by musing,

> If a twig had been broken off there
> It would have curled itself like a finger
> Around the fingers that broke it
> And then refused to let go
>
> As if it were mistletoe
> Taking tightening hold.

Or so I thought as the fairy
Lights in the boughs came on. (46)

The comparison of the twig to mistletoe borrows from Virgil's description of the magical golden bough that Aeneas must pick: "Where glitter of gold filtered between green boughs. / Like mistletoe that in the woods in winter / Thrives with yellowish berries and new leaves—..."[36] Heaney's "book-bough," Virgil's Book VI of the *Aeneid*, glimpsed in "The Canopy" and plucked at the beginning of "Route 110," enables his flight into the air, in John Wilson Foster's formulation with which I began this discussion of the volume.[37]

The best place poems in *Human Chain* function similarly to "A Herbal" and "A Canopy," giving us the consolation of their words to evoke lost worlds. Heaney pointed out that the early poetry of Virgil "could not have been written without his memories of that first life in the unfashionable, non-literary world of his childhood," and indeed, despite Heaney's steeping of himself in English, Irish, and world literature, the same is true for him.[38] For instance, in "The Riverbank Field," posing himself a translation question from Book VI of the *Aeneid*, "Ask me to translate what Loeb gives as / 'In a retired vale . . . a sequestered grove,'" he vows to "confound the Lethe in Moyola // By coming through Back Park down from Grove Hill / Across Long Rigs on to the riverbank—. . ." (47).[39] This determination to overcome the memory loss that occurs with age and which is expressed most poignantly in "In the Attic" from this volume allows him to revisit the site of a memorable early place-lore poem, "Broagh," from *Wintering Out*, and as he does so, to put his own Northern Ireland gloss on Virgil. "'[T]hose peaceful homes' / Of Upper Broagh" are surrounded by "Moths then on evening water / . . . not bees in sunlight, // Midge veils instead of lily beds . . ." (47).[40] Whereas he emphasized in "Broagh" the potentially unifying dialect of this section of his native province, here he privileges the quotidian insects and flora of the area. But he reveals that "the willow leaves / Elysian-silvered" and the grass, the latter conducive to "passing spirit-troops," were the same for him as they were for Virgil (47). He concludes this section by translating more lines from Virgil's *Aeneid*, Book VI, which serves as a sort of invocation to the muse for inspiration to begin the following central poem of the volume, "Route 110." Thus he proclaims,

"'All these presences
Once they have rolled time's wheel a thousand years
Are summoned here to drink the river water

So that memories of this underworld are shed . . .'" (48)[41]

With the Lethe now "confound[ed]," and the conduits of memory wide open, the poet now begins "Route 110" with Heaney's memory of buying a used copy of Book VI of the *Aeneid* and touring through the old Smithfield Market in Belfast on Saturdays, filled with pet shop rabbits and canaries and a jumble of objects including "racks of suits and overcoats that swayed / When one was tugged from its overcrowded frame / Like their owners' shades close-packed on Charon's barge" (50). This brief return at the end of section two to Dante's *Inferno*, Canto III, explored more negatively by Heaney at the end of *Seeing Things* in "The Crossing," is dissipated quickly by the quotidian bus driver winding his handle at the beginning of section three to unroll the destination names on the Route 110 bus running to "Cookstown via Toome and Magherafelt" (51). These passengers on this earthly conveyance "Flocked to the kerb like agitated rooks / Around a rookery, all go // But undecided" (50), a greatly pared-down but imagistic recapitulation and transformation of Virgil's lines in Book VI about the souls waiting to board Charon's barge, who are variously likened to autumn leaves and migrating birds: "Here a whole crowd came streaming to the banks ... [they are likened to] migrating birds from the open sea / That darken heaven when the cold season comes / And drives them overseas to sunlit lands."[42]

Heaney continues this avian imagery when he even renders himself as a dark bird in the fourth section, recalling "The standard-issue railway guard's long coat," which is "coal-black, sharp-cuffed as slate," that he would wear to cause "dismay" "by doorstep night arrivals, / A creature of cold blasts and flap-winged rain" (51). But he then lightens this darker bird imagery by recalling, "come finer weather, up and away / To Italy, in a wedding guest's bargain suit / Of finest weave, loose-fitting, summery, gray / As Venus' doves ..." (51). These doves recall the two doves from his mother that lead Aeneas to the golden bough in Book VI,[43] and their association with that glittering wood illuminates Heaney's memory in section five, which is then burnished by a remembrance of a gleaming object from childhood. Section five opens by asking "Venus' doves?", then quickly replaces them with the non-mythological birds of childhood: "Why not McNicholls' pigeons / Out of their pigeon holes but homing still?" Those homing birds lead him into his memory of the votive jampot filled with oats featuring "each individual grain / Wrapped in a second husk of glittering foil" from chocolate bars that "old Mrs. Nick, as she was to us," placed "'To give the wee altar a bit of shine'" (52).

In turn, Heaney's memory of walking home one night, his path illuminated by that borrowed jampot and its shiny oats, is succeeded by four sections associating various lights with wakes and roadblocks. Sections "vi" and "vii" discuss the young Heaney's first participation in a wake—the one held for Michael Mulholland. The Irish wake has traditionally included both mourning and fun—Joyce famously called it a *"funferal"* in *Finnegans Wake*.[44] Wakes have featured prominently in Irish literature, including in John Synge's 1903 drama *The Shadow of the Glen*, which Declan Kiberd has termed a "mock-wake."[45] While Synge, steeped in the Gaelic traditions of the wake he experienced on the Aran Islands off the west coast of Ireland, transformed those aspects of it into parody, Heaney writes seriously and respectfully of Mulholland's wake as an educational cultural and religious experience. As he sits up with others, he is mystified to see "the family [who] rose // Like strangers to themselves and us." Transformed by their grief, the Mulholland family is not even granted the comfort of a body (much like Synge's women are not given the body of Michael in his *Riders to the Sea* [1904]): "A wake / Without the corpse of their own dear ill-advised / Sonbrother swimmer, lost in the Bristol Channel." As Heaney and others "kept conversation going / Around the waiting trestles" for "three nights," he would have learned how to listen, contribute conversation, and observe decorum. After the coffin is put in place on the fourth night, the seventh section opens with the transformation of "The corpse house" into "a house of hospitalities / Right through the small hours," replete with a card game, cigarettes, biscuits, and tea, even as past deaths are remembered orally, thus ensuring that Mulholland's passing is gathered into this long song of suffering: "The antiphonal recital of known events / And others rare, clandestine, undertoned" (53). Resorting to educational language, Heaney recalls himself as an "Apt pupil in their night school..." (54).

Section "viii" recalls another informal educational rite of passage, the young Heaney's dates he would go on as a teenager while his mother watched at the window his driving away in a car whose "brakelights flicker-flushing at the corner" were "Like red lamps swung by RUC patrols / In the small hours on pre-Troubles roads..." (54). These red warning lamps thus signal both his mother's fear at his potential sexual experiences and the monitory lights held by the Royal Ulster Constabulary out on patrol in the 1950s as they reveled in their nearly unchallenged power, which enabled them to hassle Catholics, a practice Heaney recalled in "The Ministry of Fear," the first section of "A Singing School" from *North*: "policemen / Swung their crimson flashlamps..." (*N* 58).

In the ninth section of "Route 110," Heaney links the body-less long-ago wake of Michael Mulholland with that of "Mr. Lavery, blown up in his own pub / As he bore the primed device" of a bomb that exploded and killed him during the early days of the Troubles by asking "And what in the end was there left to bury" of him? John F. Lavery was killed on December 21, 1971 after he removed an IRA bomb from his pub on the Lisburn Road in Belfast, a sacrificial act that saved many lives. Heaney compounds Mullholland's and Mr Lavery's bodily absences by recalling his fisherman friend he had elegized in *Field Work*: "Or of Louis O'Neill / In the wrong place the Wednesday they buried // Thirteen who'd been shot in Derry?" Intriguingly, by again not listing the names of the Bloody Sunday dead, a practice he began in "Casualty"—a refusal to chant a litany as Yeats had done for the male leaders of the Easter Rising in "Easter, 1916"—Heaney risks eliding their particular lives, abstracting them into simply "Thirteen who'd been shot in Derry?"[46] He does go on to remember "bodies / Unglorified, accounted for and bagged / Behind the grief cordons," which he contrasts with those soldiers from the British Army, whose bodies were placed "In war graves with full honours," and with those members of paramilitary groups, whose graves are annually "Fired over on anniversaries / By units drilled and spruce and unreconciled" (*HC* 55). The private grief of those "unglorified" victims of the Troubles thus becomes just as valuable in these lines as the public, commemorated grief of those who mourn their more famous dead.

To contrast these relatively unremembered deaths and destroyed bodies, Heaney begins the last section of the poem by drawing upon another episode from Book VI of the *Aeneid*, lines 855–63, when "Virgil's happy shades in pure blanched raiment / Contend on their green meadows . . ." (55). The hopeful, vernal colors of white and green set the happy tone for these last three sections, contrasting the red and black colors of blood and grief in the previous three. Comparing these playful games to "a sports day in Bellaghy," the poet recalls "Slim Whitman's wavering tenor amplified / Above sparking dodgems, flying chair-o-planes," a series of ethereal images, which are succeeded by the grounded image of "teams of grown men stripped for action / Going hell for leather . . . / Leaving stud-scrapes on the pitch and on each other" (56).

The hustle and bustle of those unrhymed tercets—all drive and verve—are now followed by two quiet sections taking waiting as their subject—waiting for an otter and waiting with shades on the bank. By the third stanza of section eleven, somehow "the solid ground / Of the riverbank field" becomes a site of ambiguity and spirituality, "as if we had commingled // Among shades and shadows stirring on the brink / And stood there waiting, watching, / Needy and ever needier for translation" (56–7). This commingling draws upon the communion of the saints, *communio sanctorum*, the Christian belief in the unity of believers living and dead, formulated in the Apostle's Creed and articulated by Saint Paul in 1 Corinthians 12. At the same time, since the entire lyric sequence draws on Virgil's *Aeneid*, Book VI, a pagan sense of this communion, or to draw again on the volume's title, this "human chain," persists as well. As the unnamed people stand waiting, they are "Needy and ever needier for translation," this last word a nod surely to Heaney's own translations and ruminations on Virgil, but also to his growing desire himself to cross over, or literally be "carried across" to the other side of this world.

In that state of expectation and communion, closer to death than to life, life suddenly erupts in stanza xii with a paratactic phrase: "And now the age of births." After he moots the pending arrival of the mother and child from the "nursing home," he brings "a thank-offering for one / Whose long wait on the shaded bank has ended, / . . . my bunch of stalks and silvered heads . . ." This gift retrieves the foil-wrapped oats the poet recalls Mrs McNicholls preparing for the church altar in stanza v, but the "silvered heads" also must refer to the hair of the gathered grandparents and other older relatives waiting for this baby's coming. This rush of silvery light "Like tapers that won't dim," scatters the gloom of stanza xi, and its glow is made strong "As her earthlight breaks and we gather round / Talking baby talk" (57).

"Route 110" is classic Heaney—a poem full of motion that nonetheless signifies his continued grounding in the south Derry landscape of his youth. One of his many "road" poems, it traverses his native province yet glimpses personages from other provinces—the realms of the dead and the newborn—that beckon to him. It shows how he indeed "confound[s] the Lethe in Moyola" and travels back in time yet remains sufficiently in the present that he can look forward to his eventual death, his "translation" into another substance surrounded by shades who have gone before him, but also welcome new members to his family. It is both a *summa* of his career and life and a road-map forward. Coming home, even in memory, he suggests, might involve, soon enough, leaving the home of earth.

Two poems later, in "Loughanure," dedicated to the painter Colin Middleton, he ponders the realm of the afterlife, musing upon Middleton's painting of the same name, asking "So this is what an afterlife can come to? / A cloud-boil of grey weather on the wall / Like murky crystal, a remembered stare—" (59). This image recalls the bleak "winter light / In a doorway," and the "Bare wallstead and a cold hearth rained into—" of lyric "i" in "Lightenings," the first sequence in "Squarings" (*ST* 55). It pales beside the earlier visions of the afterlife offered by past masters:

"This for an answer to Alighieri / And Plato's Er?" (*HC* 60). Heaney senses there might be something more, desires it, and thus wonders in section iii, reverting to the language of his childhood and adolescent Catholicism, "And did I seek the Kingdom? Will the Kingdom / Come?", musing, "The idea of it there, / Behind its scrim since font and fontanel, // Breaks like light or water . . ." (60). Although he quickly deflates the eruption of eternal life in a Christian context with a story of Middleton bending over and looking between his legs "Like an arse-kisser's in some vision of the damned," the possibility of everlasting life gleams on in the poem, suffusing his recounting of a Gaelic story with a paradise inside a "fairy hill" where the character Caoilte was "led to a crystal chair on the hill floor / While a girl with golden ringlets harped and sang . . ." (61). The notion of translation, introduced toward the end of "Route 110," persists in this fourth section and in the last one as Heaney recalls he did not have enough Irish while studying the language in Rannafast, County Donegal, in 1953 to hear and understand this story. If he had, "Language and longing might have made a leap / Up through that cloud-swabbed air, [where] the horizon lightened / And the far 'Lake of the Yew Tree' gleamed" (61). "Loughanure," finally another "road" poem for Heaney, concludes with him as a grown man, driving fast through that long-ago landscape near Mount Errigal in Donegal, "unhomesick, unbelieving," but still "trying / To remember the Greek word signifying / A world restored completely . . ." (62). Simply entertaining the possibility of that restored childhood world he returns to in the last two stanzas might suggest his continued openness to the restoration of the world as a whole through a providential act, perhaps at Christ's Second Coming, although he explicitly does not invoke this eschatology.

Continuing this theme of translation, a cluster of poems centrally concerned with writing, "*Colum Cille Cecinit*," "Hermit Songs," and "'Lick the Pencil,'" leads the volume toward its conclusion and indicate Heaney's long-running tendency to write poems about the act of writing itself, beginning with his breakthrough poem "Digging." The first translation in "*Colum Cille Cecinit*," "*Is Scíth Mo Chrob Ón Scríbainn*," aligns the poet with the ancient Irish scribes and suggests the freshness and vitality of their verse through his use of vibrant colors. To wit, the first stanza runs, "My hand is cramped from penwork. / My quill has a tapered point. / Its bird-mouth issues a blue-dark / Beetle-sparkle of ink." The direct connection of hand and writing convinces, as does the lovely comparison of the quill's open end to a "bird-mouth." The "scribe-speaker" articulates the specificity of the writing act as well through his penchant for alliteration: "bird-mouth," "blue-dark," and "Beetle-sparkle" (69). By stanza two, Heaney can compare this ancient scribe to Joyce, whose opening word in *Finnegans Wake* is "riverrun":[47] "Riverrun on the vellum / Of ink from green-skinned holly." The fresh-cut holly emphasizes the sparkling blue-dark ink, which overruns the page and enables the scribe's "small runny pen" that "keeps going / Through books, through thick and thin," an image of the persistence of writing through Irish history, linking anonymous scribe, Joyce, and Heaney (69).

The following poem sequence, "Hermit Songs," dedicated to Helen Vendler, returns to the notion of poetry as song mooted in "Chanson D'Aventure," but playfully traffics in the tools of the trade, pen and ink, paper and erasers, rather than the "adventure" of Heaney's stroke. He returns here to a position that has always been attractive to him despite his gregarious personality—that of the hermit, ensconced in a hidden space, able to write with no interruptions. While at Glanmore Cottage and in his Dublin study he occupied such a space, but here he uses the desire of becoming a hermit as a chance to offer a retrospective on how he approached writing with a variety of physical implements starting as a schoolchild. Thus he meditates upon homemade materials for book covers, "cut-offs of black calico, / Remnants of old blackout blinds," along with "Brown parcel paper, if need be. / Newsprint, even" (71), "Bread and pencils" (72), "Rubbings out with balls of bread-pith," "Penshafts sheafed in black tin—was it?—", and "nibs in packets by the gross, / Powdered ink, bunched cedar pencils, / Jotters, exercise books, rulers / Stacked like grave goods on the shelves" (73). By section six, Irish mythology combines with writing implements to produce a wondrous dream. After musing upon how Cuchulain flung needles up in the air for the entertainment of the embroidery women that quickly formed "a glittering reeling chain—", he likens that chain of needles to "a gross of nibs / [that] Spills off the shelf, airlifts and links / Into a giddy gilt corona," reminiscent of "The Mud Vision" in *Seeing Things* (75). He also remembers going to the running stream at Anahorish "for water / To turn ink powder into ink—", a silent, lonely errand he undertakes as a boy "hermit" of sorts (76). As the poem ends, he recalls writing "In steady-handedness maintained / In books against its vanishing" (77). That desire to be remembered through his writing is given added poignancy in the penultimate poem of the book, "In the Attic," when he ruefully admits that "I age and blank on names," and that "the memorable bottoms out / Into the irretrievable . . ." (83, 84). These books he catalogs to preserve memory at the end of "Hermit Songs" include the medieval Books of Lismore, Kells, Armagh, and Lecan that he tropes in conclusion as "The cured hides. The much tried pens" (77). He thus links himself again to these ancient Irish scribes as he did in "*Is Scíth*

Mo Chrob Ón Scríbainn," and hopes his own work will be as indelible as theirs.

"'The Door Was Open and the House Was Dark,'" the poem following "'Lick the Pencil,'" presumably a title given to a former schoolteacher whose death is memorably evoked through recourse to a passage from Colmcille in its conclusion, elegizes Heaney's longtime musician friend David Hammond. A thirteen-liner, this poem flirts with the sonnet length of fourteen lines, but memorably falls incomplete, its shorter lineation suggesting, perhaps, that Hammond's life was incomplete when he passed away. The silence that greets the speaker upon calling, presumably, Hammond's name through the open door grows "Backwards and down and out into the street / Where as I'd entered (I remember now) // The streetlamps too were out." At first, he becomes afraid, then realizes this silence simply signifies the absence of his jovial old friend, who often enlivened parties at Heaney's house and those of others. Upon this apprehension, he resolves to chart Hammond's new absence as "Only withdrawal, a not unwelcoming / Emptiness, as in a midnight hangar // On an overgrown airfield in late summer" (81). This tercet-driven poem's last dangling line recalls similar lines at the end of Dante's canti in *The Divine Comedy*, and the fuller sense of *terza rima* that obtains across several stanzas' rhyming patterns, unlike the unrhymed tercets of many other poems in the volume, further elegizes Hammond in its harmonious music.

Human Chain concludes with Heaney's translation of Giovanni Pascoli's poem "*L'Aquilone*" as "A Kite for Aibhín," which both welcomes Heaney's granddaughter named in the title and serves as his farewell to us. Perhaps inspired by the Romantic notion of the wind as signifying poetic inspiration, "A Kite" begins with a memory of air: "Air from another life and time and place, / Pale blue heavenly air is supporting / A white wing beating high against the breeze . . ." The juxtaposition of the "white wing" against the "Pale blue heavenly air" visually stirs and intrigues us about its identity and then, by line 4, the surprise is revealed—not a bird but a kite—"And yes, it is a kite!" (85). One cannot help thinking here of the appearance of the terrorist-controlled airplanes on September 11, figured in "Anything Can Happen" as Jupiter and "his thunder cart and his horses" that rage "Across a clear blue sky" (*DC* 13). Heaney now supplants that earlier image of horror appearing out of "a clear blue sky," making even the sky itself "heavenly" and the kite a symbol of freedom and joy. In the present, the poet "take[s] my stand again, halt[s] opposite / Anahorish Hill to scan the blue, / Back in that field to launch our long-tailed comet" (*HC* 85).

Re-entering his childhood in this way, he pictures the kite as having near-agency through a series of action verbs introduced paratactically to suggest this image's ongoingness: "And now it hovers, tugs, veers, dives askew, / Lifts itself, goes with the wind until / It rises to loud cheers from us below." Perhaps the kite is asked to do too much—or to be too much—in these last two tercets, which are followed by a single resonant line. Both "a thin-stemmed flower" and "a windfall"—how can it be both opened flower and fallen fruit?—it "Rises," seemingly forever, and the speaker's hand remains open, "like a spindle / Unspooling . . ." But what carries the poem to its triumphant, soaring finale is precisely the narrator's seeming loss of control—of the kite string, even, he suggests, of his images—that he revels in. Heightening this lack of restraint, the last two tercets are fully enjambed, creating the sensation that the poem, like the kite, soars, and its long lines enhance this effect. The open, loose hand and the speaker's resolute posture portrayed through his "planted feet" create a position of both receptivity and rootedness (85). The poem itself thus seems both buoyed and anchored like the poet, just as Heaney suggests form should be: "Poetic form is both the ship and the anchor. It is at once a buoyancy and a holding, allowing for the simultaneous gratification of whatever is centrifugal and centripetal in mind and body" (*CP* 29). Back on Anahorish Hill, having survived his 2006 stroke with his faculties intact, the poet stands firm, dreaming of the future troped by the soaring kite that stands both for his grand-daughter's life, just now taking off, and his own life, nearing its end.

Transformed from mere object by virtue of its flight and Heaney's imagination, the kite sails above us, suggesting both the intimacy we can have with things and their ultimate beyondness. It also suggests the animated quality of poetry as it hovers near us yet eludes us sometimes. Finally, it achieves what Heaney speaks of in "Place, Pastness, Poems" as "a kind of moral force" because the kite is yet another thing "seasoned by human contact." Such things "insist upon human solidarity and suggest obligations to the generations who have been silenced, drawing us into some covenant with them."[48] Heaney's poem looks back to his earlier "A Kite for Michael and Christopher" and the suggestion there that their holding of the kite string will equip them for the strain of suffering in their own lives (*SI* 44) and forward to the joy he hopes his granddaughter Aibhín will have in her own life that will be lived mostly without him. After "string breaks and—separate, elate— // The kite takes off, itself alone, a windfall," this tail end of the poem, a dangling line of modified Dantean *terza rima*, becomes identified with the kite's tail (*HC* 85). Thus the poem seems to pull off a magic trick, nearly slipping the bounds of the page and floating away, much as "the phantom / *Verus* has slipped from 'very'" at the end of "Album" when the poet recalls his three attempts to embrace his father through Aeneas' three attempted embraces of Anchises (7). The rolling enjambment of the preceding lines in "A Kite" halts abruptly with Heaney's judicious use of the dashes that set up "separate, elate," while the eye-rhyme of "separate" and "elate" offer a seeming sonic harmony that is then dashed joyously by the last line, which has nothing to rhyme with and is "itself alone."

These last two lines convey the ecstasy Heaney imagines in his own passing and soaring beyond this world, complete and utterly fulfilled in the true realization of himself, while the phrase from the last line, "itself alone," also twits Sinn Fein, whose motto is "Ourselves alone," and echoes yet modifies a phrase from the end of "Tollund," "Ourselves again" (*DC* 69). Finally occupying the position of solitude free from the sectarian constraints of his native province, Heaney sees himself as both flying away from such attitudes and falling, a ripe fruit ready to be harvested by another's hand. Though a few uncollected poems would follow, along with a suite of other translations from Pascoli, "A Kite for Aibhín" clearly says goodbye to his family and his reading public. It fulfills both Heaney's description of the "resolution and independence which the entirely realized poem sponsors" (*CP* 28) and his own sense of the arc of his life, having moved from the uncertainty signified by his early pseudonym "Incertus" to the firm moral and artistic stance coupled with the freedom suggested by the kite flier and the kite itself, respectively.

I close this discussion of Heaney's poetry by looking briefly at a few of his lovely late poems—"Banks of a Canal," "In a Field," "In Time," and "The Latecomers"—that indicate continuities and new directions in his work. They display Heaney's continuing stylistic evolution toward a more pared-down, almost epigrammatic style, one driven by clusters of active, imperative verbs and more nouns shorn of their articles, exemplified by "In Time" and "The Latecomers." They also suggest his continuing penchant for the tercet: Both "The Latecomers" and another late poem with which I began this study, "On the Gift of a Fountain Pen," are composed in tercets, with occasional reversions to full *terza rima*.

Heaney's "Banks of a Canal" shows his continuing connection to the land and the imagining of the world beyond ours. He has commented that the lyrics of early Patrick Kavanagh, written when that poet was still living in County Monaghan before his move to Dublin in 1939, feature "matter-of-fact landscapes, literally presented, but contemplated from such a point of view and with such intensity that they become 'a prospect of the mind.'"[49] And yet the poem's title evokes Kavanagh's celebrated Canal Bank sonnets, written during his self-imposed exile to Dublin in the 1950s, poems in which, Heaney argues, accepting Kavanagh's own claim that he had "a poetic rebirth in these surroundings," centered upon the Grand Canal and Baggot Street Bridge.[50]

"Banks of a Canal," with its purposely missing initial definite article, attempts such a Kavanaghesque rebirth, yet the painter in question is French and his subject Italian; the poem was inspired by a painting done by the artist Gustave Caillebotte, "Banks of a Canal, near Naples, *c*.1872," and submitted by Heaney for an anthology of literature inspired by paintings in Dublin's National Gallery. The poem itself reverses the trajectory of Caillebotte's painting, in which the broad canal flows in the foreground and curves away to a pinpoint in the distance, where we can see buildings, clouds, and sky. Heaney instead opens with the specific word "canal" and discovers a world within it, then zooms back to the specific characteristics of the canal as an entity in itself: "Say 'canal' and there's that final vowel / Towing silence with it, slowing time / To a walking pace, a path, a whitewashed gleam of dwellings at the skyline."[51] The "-al" of "canal" works like a boat to tow silence with, to usher in quiet, which in turn slows time down so that we may see slowly and revealingly with shut mouths and open eyes. This notion of retarded time unites these later poems. Consider the in-between, prepositional title and the situation of granddaddy and daughter dancing in "In Time" and the poet's injunction to "Make time" in "The Latecomers."[52] Once silent, we can hear the water speak, "'My place here is in dream, / In quiet good standing. Like a sleeping stream, / Come rain or sullen shine I'm peaceable.'"[53] The water is sufficient to and in itself, its peaceableness outlasting the vagaries of weather and time.[54]

The confidence of the poem's last lines, "*I know* that clay, the damp and dirt of it, / The coolth along the bank, the grassy zest / Of verges, the path not narrow but still straight / Where soul could mind itself or stray beyond"[55] recalls the opening line of Heaney's poem "The Forge," "*All I know* is a door into the dark" (*DD* 7), which itself echoes the urn's closing remarks about truth and beauty being sufficient knowledge in Keats's "Ode on a Grecian Urn."[56] Presumably stilled and silenced himself as he contemplated Caillebotte's painting of a country canal near what even in the later nineteenth century would have been the sprawl of Naples, Heaney now seems reborn from his deep identification with the canal, whose wetness, dirt, and cool temperature remind him of his home ground, the boggy landscape around Mossbawn in Northern Ireland. In his essay on the Italian poet Giovanni Pascoli, Heaney makes explicit the connection between the rural part of Northern Ireland where he grew up and the Italy of Pascoli's and Caillebotte's day:

> [M]uch of Pascoli's home ground is also familiar ground to me—in an anthropological sort of way. Many of the scenes in [his collection] *L'Ultima Passegiata* [*The Last Walk*], evoking rural life in late 19th century Italy, were still there to be witnessed in mid-20th century Ireland.57

The walking pace that leads us along "Banks of a Canal" therefore seems as much indebted to Pascoli as to Caillebotte and Kavanagh. Hovering faintly in the background too is what Heaney has elsewhere identified as the literally pedestrian pace of Wordsworth's blank verse, driven by his walking "up and down the gravel path, the crunch and scuffle of the gravel working like a metre or a metronome . . . aided by the automatic, monotonous turns and returns of the walk, the length of the path acting like the length of the line."58

The poem makes a final homage in its form—to another Italian poet, Petrarch—because it takes the form of a Petrarchan sonnet with two quatrains rhyming roughly *ab*1/4*ba*, followed by a sestet rhyming *cde*1/2*d*1/2*e*1/2*c*. Heaney thus constrains his subject, which threatens to widen to include the world, or at least Western Europe, through recourse to the tight shape of this Italian sonnet form, which itself largely breaks down in the sestet, which in a regular Italian sonnet would rhyme either *cdcdcd* or *cdecde*. Breaking and scattering the rhymes established in the first three lines of the sestet into near rhymes that do not follow the usual pattern suggests not only Heaney's artful knowledge and redeployment of the form, but also how that broken music opens a place for the wandering of the poet and the soul. By recasting the Biblical injunction, "strait is the gate, and narrow is the way, that leadeth unto life, and few there be that find it" (Matthew 7: 14 KJV), Heaney implies the path to poetry is "not narrow but still straight" or easily seen (for the canal in question is certainly curved!), can allow the soul to "mind itself or stray beyond," a guide in time of need, but at other times, a boundary that can be transcended.

Heaney has long been interested in the World War One poets, particularly Wilfred Owen and his deeply humane empathy for others, even those we consider enemies, but he also has praised other soldier-poets such as Francis Ledwidge and Edward Thomas, and in 2012, he wrote a poem, "In a Field," responding to Edward Thomas's poem "As the Team's Head Brass," for a volume entitled *1914: Poetry Remembers*, edited by the British Poet Laureate Carol Ann Duffy. "In a Field" captures several interlinked preoccupations of Heaney: his desire to connect to the earth, his interest in boundaries, his need to commune with the dead. It also enacts a conversation with earlier poems, including "Clearances," "Poet's Chair," "To Mick Joyce in Heaven," and "Route 110." And yet the most influential poetic presences hovering over the poem are Kavanagh and Dante. In the last section of "Poet's Chair," the poet sits "all-seeing / At centre field," watching his father "ploughing one, two, three, four sides / Of the lea ground . . ." (*SL* 47). Fintan O'Toole has suggested that the lines from "In a Field" in which "The long healed footprints of one who arrived / From nowhere, unfamiliar and de-mobbed, / In buttoned khaki and buffed army boots," refers to Heaney's poem, "To Mick Joyce in Heaven." Joyce was a Corkman in the British Army married to Heaney's Aunt Susan, and he once arrived on the Heaney family farm while on leave.[59] And finally, the closing lines of the poem, in which the speaker "stumble[s] from the windings' magic ring" and walks back "Through the same old gate into the yard / Where everyone has suddenly appeared, / All standing waiting,"[60] recalls the similar participial conclusion of the eleventh section of "Route 110," where the poet becomes part of the "shades and shadows stirring on the brink / And stood there waiting, watching, / Needy and ever needier for translation" (*HC* 57).

Discussing Edward Thomas's "As the Team's Head Brass," the Thomas scholar Matthew Hollis has remarked that Heaney "admired what he called its 'Homeric plane': the way a local conversation shadowed events on the world's field," noting too how Heaney "savored what he termed its apparent 'dailiness,' its lower key that disguised, in his phrase, 'a big wheel of danger' turning behind it."[61] In this regard, Heaney was thinking of Kavanagh, particularly his famous poem "Epic," when responding to Thomas's poem. In that poem, Kavanagh eventually privileges a local row between two families as more important than the rise of Nazi Germany, channeling Homer's ghost who says, "I made the *Iliad* from such / A local row."[62] In his essay, "The Sense of Place," Heaney points out "the very ordinariness of the quarrel between the Duffys and the McCabes," pointing out further how Kavanagh "cherished the ordinary, the actual, the known, the unimportant" and in so doing made the local universal.[63]

Edward Thomas wrote his poem in 1916, not long before he asked to be sent to the front, where he died at Arras in 1917. "In a Field" thus does double duty, as it were: It honors and recalls Thomas and his contribution to poetry and sacrifice on the field of battle, even as it seemingly anticipates the poet's own death, walking like the narrator into "the same old gate" where those who have gone before him wait for him. Thomas's poem begins *in medias res*—"As the team's headbrass flashed out on the turn . . ."[64]—and so does Heaney's—"And there I was in the middle of a field."[65] Heaney undoubtedly draws too on the abrupt opening of Dante's *Inferno* here, which begins, in his own translation, "In the middle of the journey of our life / I found myself astray in a dark wood / where the straight road had been lost sight of."⁶⁶ Heaney's paratactic opening and use of a liminal position thus pay homage to Dante as well, yet while that exemplar despairs at finding himself lost in a hell, Heaney's speaker, likely the poet himself, revels in his purgatorial position "in the middle of a field." There, he finds comfort in the field's having been plowed: "Last of the jobs, / The windings had been ploughed, furrows turned . . ."⁶⁷ It is difficult not to read into this description a relief on the part of the poet because he senses his life's work is finished. Heaney even described "the poet as a ploughman," drawing upon the etymology of "verse" from the Latin "*versus*," which he argues, "could mean a line of poetry but could also mean the turn that a ploughman made at the head of the field as he finished one furrow and faced back into another."⁶⁸ Finally, "In a Field" finds the poet heading home, to a heaven where those who have gone before him through the "old gate" have "suddenly appeared, / All standing waiting," an earthy, more populated recapitulation of the shining conclusion of the second sonnet from "Clearances," where he imagines his mother going to heaven and her father standing to greet her (*HL* 26).

"In Time," first published in the *New Yorker* a few months after Heaney's death and dated August 18, 2013, only twelve days before he died, also features the poet caught up in familial love and longing, this time through a dance with his granddaughter Síofra. Through its three, six-lined stanzas comprised of a series of couplets, the poet expresses his delight in dancing with his grandchild yet laments that he will not have the chance to dance with her when she is a "sure and grown woman." The triple cluster of nouns "Energy, balance, outbreak" begins the poem and feature again in the third line of stanza three, anchoring the two visions the poet has of Síofra as a grown woman and as a child. As he listens to Bach in the first stanza, he imagines "Your toddler wobbles gone," and her transformed into a confident young woman. In the present, however, the heart of the poem, "Your bare foot on the floor / Keeps me in step," and the elderly poet moves gently in time to his wobbling toddler granddaughter, feeling the "power" in the music he felt too as a young child. Continuing his brilliant usage of active verbs he employed often in his later poems, Heaney observes that that power "Palps your sole and heel / And earths you here for real." Earthed and grounded by the music, connected to his own childhood and that of his granddaughter, the poet seems truly caught in time, suspended between past and present with an eye on the future. As the poem concludes, he muses that "An oratorio / Would be just the thing for you," but "for now we foot it lightly / In time, and silently."⁶⁹ The passing reference to Yeats's "The Stolen Child," in which the sinister fairies "foot it all the night," dancing and having fun while humans are sleeping,[70] quickens these last lines with tension until we realize that Heaney is likely deploying this allusion to signify his delight in this stolen quiet time with his grandchild, a ritual finally outside of time where he recovers some of his childhood gaiety and connects deeply to Síofra.

Like "In Time," the tercet-driven poem "The Latecomers" captures a moment in, or rather outside, of time, but rather than a moment of domestic bliss, it demonstrates Heaney's hope in the miraculous that is thoroughly grounded in and springs from the grittily realistic. A third poem about the paralytic being lowered down to be healed by Jesus in Mark's Gospel, it thus responds to "The Skylight" (*ST*) and "Miracle" (*HC*) much as "In a Field" responds to earlier Heaney poems.

By casting it in tercets, Heaney suggests "The Latecomers" is a poem not just about healing but about last things, including death. Before I published "On the Gift of a Fountain Pen" as a broadside for Baylor University's Beall Poetry Festival, at which Heaney read on March 4, 2013, he sent me a letter where he ruefully pointed out his reliance upon tercets at this poet in his career, a reliance colored by his fear of writer's block that he raises in "On a Gift" as well:

> It's more tercets, I'm afraid. After the attention you gave the form, you'll probably wonder if I'm ever going to manage any other form—which is what I wonder myself. Quite simply, I find it an aid to composition. Once I was a marathon man, or better say 1000 metres, but nowadays it's a faltering 100 [metres].[71]

And yet tercets are the ideal form in many ways for a poet approaching the end of his life, as Heaney himself indicated about Yeats's sole employment of the form in "Cuchulain Comforted" when he remarked that Yeats "was preparing his own death by imagining Cuchulain's descent among the shades."[72] In much the same way, just as the subject matter of "In a Field" is finally Seamus Heaney, not Edward Thomas or his poem, "The Latecomers" employs a version of Dantean *terza rima* as a final form, signaling Heaney's sense that he was near the end of his life, a conviction that likely lies behind the series of imperative verbs that drive the injunction to heal and forgive in the poem's conclusion.

Heaney's Jesus in "The Latecomers" feels harassed, unable to help all those who seek his healing touch. He is "Hedged on every side, // Harried and responsive to their need," but

> However he assisted and paid heed,
>
> A sudden blank letdown was what he'd feel
> Unmanning him when he met the pain of loss
> In the eyes of those his reach had failed to bless.

This all-too-human Christ senses he may be inadequate to heal those who throng around him, accused by their gaze, and therefore "he was relieved the newcomers / Had now discovered they'd arrived too late / And gone away." But his relief quickly fades when he hears them on the roof, "a sound of tiles being shifted, / The treble scrape of terra cotta lifted" as they lower their friend down to him. Confronted with this "paralytic on his pallet," a tired Christ struggles, caught between "Exhaustion and the imperatives of love ..." He knows his role is "To judge, instruct, reprove, // And ease them body and soul." Heaney heightens the succession of imperative verbs with a series of end-stopped lines—five in all including the one just cited that spills over into the last tercet—to conclude the poem: "Not to abandon but to lay on hands. / Make time. Make whole. Forgive."[73] Rejecting his sense of exhaustion, reminded of his heavenly obligation, Heaney's Christ will move swiftly to heal this man, hoping as he does so to stop time as he eases his suffering.

The poem seems to issue a challenge to us as readers too. In reading the poem, we steal time and are offered a chance to be made whole in dwelling on this narrative of brokenness that gently, quietly shades into wholeness. And most disturbingly, the example of forgiveness stands before us like the paralytic's persistent friends. We cannot escape our responsibility, suggests Heaney. We too must forgive others even when we dearly wish to avoid our duty to do so. The near rhymes and full rhymes that feature earlier in this tercet-driven poem that lead it to approach Dantean *terza rima* in the first three stanzas break off in the last four stanzas, which nevertheless feature some occasional rhymes but without the *terza rima* form. In the final tercet, the last words of each line—"soul," "hands," "Forgive," do not rhyme at all, implying, perhaps, the difficulty of reaching out to others given our own broken condition. And yet those imperative verbs, those end-stopped lines, above all Christ's decision to heal and forgive, nonetheless urge us to contribute our own potentially healing words and actions to those who may be paralyzed or broken.

In 2014, after Heaney's death, both Faber and Faber, Heaney's British publisher, and Farrar, Straus and Giroux, Heaney's American publisher, republished his earlier volume, *New Selected Poems 1966–1987* as *Selected Poems 1966–1987*, along with a second volume of selected poems, what Faber and Faber now calls his *New Selected Poems 1988–2013* and Farrar, Straus and Giroux his *Selected Poems 1988–2013*. The republication of the former volume of earlier selected poems coupled with the release of the new volume suggests that Faber & Farrar, Straus and Giroux, and perhaps the Heaney estate, now see these two volumes rather than *Opened Ground: Selected Poems, 1966–1996*, as the canonical collections of his poetry. The provenance of *New Selected Poems 1988–2013* is somewhat curious. As the Publisher's Note states, "This edition reproduces selections from *Seeing Things* (1991) and *The Spirit Level* (1996) that Seamus Heaney made for *Opened Ground: Poems 1966–1996*," and then immediately points out that the selections from *Electric Light*, *District and Circle*, and *Human Chain* "were prepared by the author for a prospective edition of his works in Italian translation."[74] Two excerpts from Heaney's translation of *Beowulf* are also included in this new volume; although "he had not identified an extract" from that translation, he "had previously chosen passages from the opening and closing sections included here."[75] It is impossible to know whether the poet would have selected these same poems for a volume that Faber and FSG are now marketing as the definitive edition of Heaney's poetry for the last twenty-five years of his career, a companion volume to the earlier volume of selected poetry. The two volumes share a near symmetry of years, covering twenty-one and twenty-five years, respectively, of Heaney's career, but the latter volume includes selections from only five volumes of poetry, while the earlier one features selections from seven of them. This imbalance has occurred not only because of Heaney's premature death, but also because this new volume has the feeling of being rushed into production. It could easily have included excerpts from Heaney's *The Cure at Troy* and *The Burial at Thebes*. Even more surprising, this new selection leaves out even an excerpt from Heaney's Nobel Prize lecture, *Crediting Poetry*, the entirety of which is reproduced in *Opened Ground*. The lecture constitutes one of the major *apologias* for poetry in the twentieth century and instantly became one of Heaney's best known and most quoted works.

At least an excerpt from those translations, along with other marvelous late poems such as "Banks of a Canal," "In a Field," "In Time," "The Latecomers," perhaps the ekphrastic "Actaeon," written in response to Titian's painting *The Death of Actaeon*, and "On the Gift of a Fountain Pen," would have rounded this latter volume off and suggested, variously, the continuing importance of ancient and contemporary Italy for the poet, as well as showing the ongoing relevance of twin strands in Christianity—the miraculous and the charitable—particularly the narrative about the paralytic from Mark 2: 1–12 drawn upon in "The Latecomers" and the so-called "Golden Rule" drawn from Luke 6: 31 in "On the Gift of a Fountain Pen," respectively. *Opened Ground*'s inclusion of four fugitive poems such as "Antaeus," "The Names of the Hare," "Villanelle for an Anniversary," and "A Transgression" established a precedent for such a practice in future selections of Heaney and it is a shame that only the lovely "In Time" is republished in the recent *New Selected Poems 1988–2013*. The volume identifies "In Time" as "Seamus Heaney's last poem, [which] appears here in accordance with the wishes of his family."[76] It simply beggars belief that had Heaney lived and made choices for an English-language version of his later work, however, he would have accepted only the choices included here without complementing them with excerpts from the two Greek dramatic versions, translations beyond *Beowulf*, and recent fugitive poetry.[77]

Students, teachers, and scholars of Heaney are thus left with a dilemma. They might rely upon studying, reading, and citing from the individual volumes by the poet along with the periodical publications of fugitive poems, a procedure I have followed in this study. On the other hand, especially in the case of classroom teachers, they could choose the two volumes of *Selected Poetry*, a choice compounded by the incomplete nature of the second volume, or rely on the equally incomplete *Opened Ground*, which leaves out entirely the last three individual volumes, but has the virtue of demonstrating Heaney's excellent forays into the occasional poem and including his inimitable *apologia*, *Crediting Poetry*. One hopes for a *Collected Poems*, or even a more broadly inclusive *Selected Poems* spanning 1966–2013, but the appearance of the second collection of selected poetry suggests we may be waiting for some time for such a volume.

In the meantime, we have many of the poems readily available to us, and their staying power, drawn from Heaney's unique word-hoard and driven by his inimitable music, seems unlikely to fade.

Notes

1. McDonald, "The Clutch of Earth," n.p.
2. The phrase "rise and go" echoes the opening line of Yeats's "The Lake Isle of Innisfree": "I will arise and go now" (Yeats, 39).
3. The solidity of the kettle lid here is echoed by the stove lid later in the volume in Heaney's lyric "A Stove Lid for W. H. Auden," from his sequence "Home Fires." That "cast-iron stove lid" was a "hell-mouth stopper, flat-earth disc," which the poet would lift off his childhood stove so it could be stoked (*DC* 73).
4. Young, n.p.
5. Ibid.
6. Eliot, 203.
7. Ibid., 55.
8. Brodsky, 196. Brodsky's poem responds to Auden's "In Memory of W. B. Yeats," a touchstone poem for Heaney.

9. Heaney, *Seamus Heaney: Out of the Marvelous.*
10. Heaney, "The Whole Thing: On the Good of Poetry," 8; my emphases.
11. Heaney, "Time and Again," 20; my emphasis.
12. See Gardner, xx–xxiii, for a short but incisive discussion of inscape and instress. Heaney argues in "The Convert" that in Hopkins' poetry, thingness and words merge: "World becomes word: the volume and density of the actual has been transformed into a high linguistic voltage. To read these poems is to go through the hoops of the palpable" (15). For a thoughtfully argued review of Hopkins' influence on Heaney in the poems of *District and Circle*, see Bleakney. She argues that "Few [poets] remain as unashamedly in thrall [to Hopkins] as Seamus Heaney; as enchanted with the physicality of language; as attuned to the natural order" (29).
13. But see Muldoon, n.p., for an argument that Heaney's "engagement with the things of the world was so unadorned as to invite comparison with John Clare—yes, except a clearer John Clare."
14. Heaney, Introduction to *William Wordsworth: Poems Selected by Seamus Heaney*, viii, citing Wordsworth and Coleridge, 433.
15. Wordsworth, *Selected Poems*, 319.
16. Eliade, *Images and Symbols*, 174.
17. Heaney, "Time and Again," 20, 21.
18. Heaney, "The Door Stands Open," 28.
19. Heaney, "Time and Again," 21.
20. J. W. Foster, *The Achievement of Seamus Heaney*, 44.
21. Corcoran, "The Melt of the Real Thing," 15.
22. Roy Foster, n.p.
23. See my discussion of these paired poems in *Seamus Heaney's Regions*, 377–81.
24. Virgil, lines 158–62, p. 163
25. Ibid., lines 936–42, p. 184.
26. Heiny, 307.
27. Donne, 53.
28. Ibid., 53.
29. See Keats, *The Poems of John Keats*, 371.
30. Haughton notes that "'*In illo tempore*' echoes a phrase used in the Latin Mass, itself an allusion to the Vulgate, where, for example, it occurs in Matthew 14.1 ('*in illo tempore audit Herodes tetrarcha famam Iesu*')" (202). Taken with Heaney's last words, "*Noli timere*," themselves from the Vulgate translation of Matthew, which I discuss in the first chapter, such allusions demonstrate how the Vulgate remained a significant part of Heaney's literary and cultural memory.
31. Sidney, 114.
32. Casey, 310.
33. Heaney, "Mossbawn," 20.
34. Casey, 311–12.
35. Virgil, lines 296–8, p. 167.
36. Ibid., lines 291–3, p. 167.
37. Employing this language from Virgil, Heaney discusses in "Frontiers of Writing" how the constitutional nationalist John Hume was assailed both by physical force republicans and loyalists as a sell-out to the British and

colluder with the IRA, respectively, as he sought peace in Northern Ireland but could not find the "political equivalent of a golden bough that would guarantee him a safe return from the underground of secret talks into the daylight of the old banal repetitions" (188).

38. Heaney, "Suffering and Decision," 221.
39. For the best brief analysis of Heaney's attention to and knowledge of Virgil's Latin here, including the momentum of the sentence, see Heiny, 308–9.
40. The original version of the poem featured "butterflies" instead of bees; Heaney evidently made the change to more greatly contrast his world with Virgil's. See *The Riverbank Field*, n.p.
41. Here too, the subtle changes from the original version of the poem work better. In the later version, the "presences" have more imagistically "rolled time's wheel," rather than the flatter "done their turn," in the earlier version (ibid.), while the pithier and more mythological "underworld" replaces the original memories of "life on this side" (ibid.).
42. Virgil, *The Aeneid*, Book VI, lines 414, 421–3, p. 170.
43. Ibid., lines 272–91, pp. 166–7.
44. Joyce, 120; Joyce's emphasis.
45. Kiberd, 168 and 168–74.
46. The language of this passage was more disturbing in the version published in *The Riverbank Field*. There, he conjoins O'Neil and the thirteen dead in Derry this way: "Or of Louis O'Neill / Bomb-blasted after hours the Wednesday // The thirteen Bloody Sunday dead were buried?" (*The Riverbank Field*, n.p.). Rather than simply being "In the wrong place," this earlier version works against the original context of O'Neill's murder (and the way its accidental nature is signaled by the title "Casualty"). Instead, "Bomb-blasted" implies (wrongly) he was targeted. Moreover, the earlier version notes the bombing took place "after hours" in that pub, suggesting the illicit presence of O'Neill there. Finally, by representing the murdered civil rights marchers as "The thirteen Bloody Sunday dead" in the former version (the latter a close replication of the original phrase in "Casualty," "After they shot dead / The thirteen men in Derry," FW 22), Heaney couples their passing to a particular historical moment, giving them a more specific identity than merely "Thirteen who'd been shot in Derry."
47. Joyce, 3.
48. Heaney, "Place, Pastness, Poems," 31.
49. Heaney, "From Monaghan to the Grand Canal: The Poetry of Patrick Kavanagh," 120.
50. Ibid., 127.
51. Heaney, "Banks of a Canal," n.p.
52. Heaney, "The Latecomers," 122.
53. Heaney, "Banks of a Canal."
54. The perdurance of the canal in this sonnet is echoed by the "ongoing / Seaward rush of Tiber" in another late sonnet by Heaney set in Italy, "Du Bellay in Rome," which concludes, "O world of flux / Where time destroys what's steady as the rocks / And what resists time is what's ever flowing" (7).
55. Heaney, "Banks of a Canal"; my emphasis.

56. Keats's urn states, "Beauty is truth, truth beauty—that is *all / Ye know and all ye need to know*" (Keats, *The Poems of John Keats*, 373; my emphasis). See my essay, "The Keats and Hopkins Dialectic in Seamus Heaney's Early Poetry: 'The Forge,'" 47, for a full analysis of this phrase. Heaney first uses the word "coolth" in the second lyric, "Nights of '57" from "Bodies and Souls": "The older I get, the quicker and the closer / I hear those laboring breaths and feel the coolth" (*EL* 88). These lines in turn seem indebted to the passage in Wordsworth's *The Prelude*, Book I, when the young boy hears "Low breathings coming after me and sounds / Of undistinguishable motion," after he steals birds from others' snares (*Selected Poems* 316).
57. Heaney, "On Home Ground," 21.
58. Heaney, "The Makings of a Music," 65.
59. Heaney, "In a Field," n.p.; O'Toole, n.p.
60. Heaney, "In a Field."
61. Qtd in Mark Brown, n.p.
62. Heaney quotes Kavanagh's poem in his essay, "The Sense of Place," 139.
63. Ibid., 138–9, 139.
64. Qtd in Mark Brown.
65. Heaney, "In a Field."
66. Heaney, "Canto I," 3.
67. Heaney, "In a Field."
68. Heaney, "The Makings of a Music," 65.
69. Heaney, *New Selected Poems 1988–2013*, 218.
70. Yeats, 18.
71. Heaney, "Letter to Richard Rankin Russell."
72. Heaney, "Yeats as an Example?", 113.
73. Heaney, "The Latecomers," 122.
74. "Publisher's Note," v.
75. Ibid.
76. Ibid.
77. In reviewing the *New Selected* for the widely read British newspaper *The Guardian*, David Wheatley anticipated my argument in part by pointing out that "Only one posthumous poem, 'In Time,' is included; the failure to find a place for the beautiful 'In a Field' is much to be regretted" ("*Seamus Heaney, New Selected Poems 1966–1987* and *New Selected Poems 1988–2013*," n.p.).

Chapter 6

Prose, Drama, and Translations

First-time readers of Heaney may not be aware of his major achievement in other genres, which are so rich and deep that treating them in their entirety lies beyond the scope of this introductory study, focused as it is on his poetry. But those who teach Heaney's work or who have followed his career know that he has become one of the foremost critics and translators of our time, as well as having written some fine "versions" of Greek drama, including *The Cure at Troy*, after Sophocles' *Philoctetes*, and *The Burial at Thebes*, after the same playwright's *Antigone*. In what follows, I trace the emergence of Heaney's articulation of the role of poet as priest or shaman figure through his invigorating literary criticism that repeatedly circles round the intertwined concerns of the poet's authority and poetry's adequacy, then I turn to *The Cure at Troy* and *The Burial at Thebes*, along with his most famous translation, of *Beowulf*, and his most recent translation, of Giovanni Pascoli's *L'Ultima Passeggiata*, or *The Last Walk*. Together, these last four works not only powerfully suggest the range of Heaney's profound abilities in drama and translation, but also show his continuing facility with lineation, dialogue, rhyme, and style. They also illustrate his ongoing interest in literature's capacity to encompass otherworldly concerns such as magic and spirituality—and even to convey the eruption of the miraculous into the midst of the murderous or dully quotidian.

Criticism

Heaney's remarkable literary criticism constitutes a body of work that makes the most serious *apologia* for lyric poetry in the second half of the twentieth century. This defense has been so well made and articulated that it stakes a substantive claim to the best kind of ethical poetry criticism. If Eliot's *The Varieties of Metaphysical Poetry* recovered the voices of Donne and Herbert for readers in the modernist period, Heaney has reclaimed Dante, Wilfred Owen, Yeats, Eliot, Patrick Kavanagh, Robert Frost, and the Eastern European poets, the most important of whom is Czesław Miłosz, for contemporary readers. As Neil Corcoran has articulated, "the permeability of Heaney's critical consciousness to Wordsworth makes his basic conceptions of poetry essentially late Romantic ones," and thus "Approbation, celebration, and self-identification, rather than irony, temper, and measure, are the characteristic motives and moods of his criticism."[1] Heaney's authority as a literary critic grew out of many years of teaching the classics of literature in a variety of universities, ranging from Queen's in Belfast, to Carysfort College in Dublin, and Harvard University. In his role as an educator that includes his role as a critic, he has influenced several generations of poets, including Medbh McGuckian and Paul Muldoon in Northern Ireland and Ireland, the African-American poets Natasha Trethewey (US Poet Laureate from 2012 to 2014) and Kevin Young, and the Caribbean-born Nobel Prize winner Derek Walcott, among many others. As an educator, his criticism is inherently text-focused and perspicacious, attuned to a variety of reading audiences, always eminently readable.

Heaney's own literary criticism has often set the terms for evaluation of his own poetry, sometimes in enabling ways, but occasionally in potentially disabling ways such that the criticism mimics his own. Michael Cavanagh has located Heaney's belief in poetry's power, expressed often in his prose, in a belief "that poetry's sources run deeper than any one source can account for, and poetry therefore is more culturally sanctioned than it would be if it came from a single person, or if it were chosen from a single source." In other words, he argues, "Heaney's criticism creates a world in which his own poetry is expected and hence accepted."[2] The poetry and the prose represent two complementary, not contradictory, stances toward Heaney's art since he "often characterizes poetry as a nondiscursive, nondidactic art, as something that issues from a private contact with the world," which his "[public] prose reaches out to accompany . . . and prepare" for . . . Prose would be poetry's public face, its public relations agent."[3] And indeed, Heaney's many public addresses and orations seek to inculcate and spread his gospel about poetry's power as life-affirming, hopeful, and sometimes even redemptive of reality.

Peter McDonald, who has evinced, until relatively recently, a guarded and cautious attitude toward Heaney's poetry, fairly bursts with praise in his assessment of the prose criticism, noting, for example, in his assessment of Heaney's lectures as Oxford Professor of Poetry, collected as *The Redress of Poetry*, that "the authority of poetry itself, and the authority possessed by the writer of poetry, are twin themes in a great deal of his work, and they are explored with particular subtlety and elegance in the best of his critical writing."[4] David Wheatley also singles out Heaney's preoccupation with authority in his survey of the poet's prose, noting that for Heaney, poetic authority "is a form of truth-telling detectable in the smallest detail of voice and style," and pointing out how he often weds "signifier and signified in a seamless pre-Saussurean union" whereby "the union of sound and sign in nature is a model for the higher union again of writer and achieved poetic voice . . ."[5] And in his book-length assessment of Heaney's poetics, Cavanagh cannily suggests that "there is in his work something very much like a belief, perhaps an anxiety, that poetry needs explaining and defending, that poets and readers alike must have some sense of what poetry is *doing*, and whether it is a luxury or a necessity."[6] Indeed, Heaney has likely been the best, most profound, and most articulate contemporary advocate for poetry's authority in essays such as "Feeling into Words," "The Government of the Tongue," "The Whole Thing: On the Good of Poetry," "The Redress of Poetry," "Frontiers of Writing," and *Crediting Poetry*. And yet as John Dennison has shown in his study of Heaney and the adequacy of poetry, the poet often wonders and worries if poetry can shoulder the huge burden he and others have placed upon it. Dennison believes that

> Heaney's modestly framed claims for the sufficiency of the lyric utterance rest on a belief in its assumption of the stuff of history into a realized expression of the human spirit. It is this reified mediation of what is and what ought to be—this theologically mimetic construct—that has become central to Heaney's transcendental poetics.[7]

Dennison here identifies crucial intertwined aspects of the poet's prose criticism: its contention that lyric poetry can accommodate the hurt of history and still express the hope of the yearning of the human spirit, and thus that the achieved poem can issue forth in a theologically inflected utterance.

Such concepts as the authority of the poet and the poem as transcendental utterance spring from Heaney's conception of the poet as aesthetic priest or shaman-figure. His work is replete with such statements of the poet's role. For instance, in his rollicking "Verses for a Fordham Commencement," given at Fordham University in 1982, Heaney affirms

> . . . before the first college
> Was built on earth, the men of knowledge
>   Were sacrosanct:

> Magi, druids, seers and augurs,
> Brehons, temple priests, witch doctors
> And a thousand other characters
>   Long since defunct.[8]

Despite his tendency to look askance at the role of the academic, a role which he assumed for many years, Heaney implies here that the poet is seer, soothsayer, speaker of spells, adept above all in sacred knowledge that he is duty-bound to promulgate to the wider population.

In his unpublished essay about the appointment of Ted Hughes as the Poet Laureate of Britain, after noting how this position demonstrates "the implied message of Hughes's poetry that the instinctual, intuitive side of man's and in particular the Englishman's nature has been starved and occluded and is in need of refreshment," Heaney wrote movingly and positively of how Hughes had quickly "re-established, without sanctimoniousness, a sacerdotal function for the poet in the realm."[9] He sees another exemplar, Patrick Kavanagh, as having embodied this same role for the poet. For instance, in his early essay, "From Monaghan to the Grand Canal: The Poetry of Patrick Kavanagh," the poet describes early Kavanagh as "a postulant, full of uninitiated piety towards the office," but observes that "now he has taken orders, [he] has ordained himself and stands up in Monaghan as the celebrant of his own mysteries . . . Kavanagh's Monaghan is his pastoral care in the sacerdotal as much as in the literary sense."[10]

Because Heaney believes so strongly in what he considers the still-viable "sacerdotal function" of the poet, he invests his criticism—and the best lyric poetry—with a tremendous amount of morality and transcendent yearning. Anthony Hecht even understates the situation when he posits, "I think it is fair to say that Heaney brings to the topic of where poems come from a moral tone and ethical dignity that has about it a nobility and sense of vocation that are not far from religious."[11] In his essay, "Yeats's Nobility," Heaney casts Yeats's life and work as inhering in a quality he terms "nobility," and argues that "This nobility has nothing to do with birth or rank but concerns rather the measure of what Wallace Stevens called 'our spiritual height and depth.'" Stevens's articulation of the lyric poem's imaginative force attuned to harsh outer realities yet sufficient to hold a bulwark against them—"'a violence from within that protects us from a violence without . . . the imagination pressing back against the pressure of reality'"—describes for Heaney "what the great Yeats poems do." Such poems as the sequences "'Meditations in Time of Civil War' and 'Nineteen Hundred and Nineteen' have about them the high pitch of sacred rite."[12] The life of the best kind of lyric poem thus expresses a vivifying vision that is equal to the worst news from the world outside the poem and which can finally express a salutary hope that surpasses and outfaces the harshness of reality. Although I disagree with Neil Corcoran's contention that the trajectory of Heaney's literary criticism collected in *The Redress of Poetry* "moves into what is virtually a metaphysical, rather than an ethical dimension"—instead, Heaney recovers an ethical dimension to the metaphysical—he helpfully points out his view in that volume "of poetry as an overcoming, an outstripping, a transcending of contingent or corrupting circumstance ... His theory" of poetry's function "demands that it exceed historical contingency rather than be merely collusive with, or subject to it."[13] When Heaney affirms the "'temple inside our hearing' which the passage of the poem calls into being ... an adequacy deriving from what Mandelstam called 'the steadfastness of speech articulation,' from the resolution and independence which the entirely realized poem sponsors," he clearly privileges the sacerdotal role of the poet in establishing spiritual spaces in our minds through his concurrent deployment of the formal properties of the poem along with its "truthfulness" (*CP* 28).

Along with valuing the hope articulated by both Yeats and Auden (particularly in the English poet's "In Memory of W. B. Yeats" and its affirmation of poetry as leading us to rejoice), Heaney repeatedly turned toward the example of Czeław Miłosz to express the hope that abounds in lyric poetry. In a lengthy essay written soon after the Polish poet died, Heaney convincingly postulates that Miłosz's hope in words "was clearly related to the last Gospel of the Mass, the *In principio* of St John: 'In the beginning was the Word,'" observing that "through his pursuit of poetic vocation ... he developed a fierce conviction about the holy force of his art, how poetry was called upon to combat death and nothingness ..." With his death, Heaney laments, "the world has lost a credible witness to this immemorial belief in the saving power of poetry."[14] Poet as witness, poem as savior: Miłosz and his poetry simultaneously affirmed both these roles.

Since he holds this religious, finally hopeful role of the poet, despite clearly expressing cautions and caveats about it, Heaney therefore believes that poetry is freighted with spiritual power to potentially redress wrong. In "Frontiers of Writing," a lecture he gave as Oxford Professor of Poetry, Heaney celebrates one of several manifestations of the "redress" of poetry in the sense of re-establishing it and thus he "celebrate[s] it for its forcibleness as itself, as the affirming spiritual flame which W. H. Auden wanted to be shown forth ... as a matter of angelic potential, a motion of the soul."[15] Thus he privileges what in another lecture he terms poetry's "self-delighting inventiveness," a phrase he builds upon in "Frontiers of Writing" when he "profess[es] the pleasure and surprise of poetry, its rightness and thereness, the way that it is at one moment unforeseeable and at the next indispensable, the way it arrives as something unhindered and self-directing sweeping ahead into its full potential."[16] Because of its sheer truth in and unto itself and its unpredictability, poetry arrives sometimes when we least expect it, like a visitation of grace, and when it does, can startle with its harmonious power. For Heaney, the best poetry from Northern Ireland that dealt with its recent conflict suggests "a mode of integration, of redistributing the whole field of cultural and political force into a tolerable order."[17]

Elsewhere, Heaney has argued, resorting to medical terminology, that the poem itself can exemplify wholeness, healthiness, and that the poet can potentially bring healing to his society. In fact, the occasion for perhaps his clearest articulation of poetry and the poet's role in promoting societal health, his lecture "The Whole Thing: On the Good of Poetry" was given as a distinguished lecture to the Royal College of Surgeons in Ireland on November 5, 2001. As he states there, "The virtue of poetry, of art in general, resides in the fact that it is first and foremost a whole thing, a hale thing, a thing formally and feelingly sound, right within itself, a thing to which the ultimate response—if not always the immediate response, is 'yes.'"[18] Although at first he suggests that "the discovery of wholeness is not a mystical matter" but "a result of a worker's specialized skills and heightened intuitions being brought to bear deliberately and intently," he then quickly moots an image perhaps borrowed from Coleridge's entranced, mage-like poet in "Kubla Khan": "a poet's intelligence and cognitive faculties are never more alive than during those moments when he appears to be off in a world of his own, absorbed in the creative trance, preoccupied with the dreamwork."[19] Poetry, art in general, Heaney concludes, citing both Caliban's despair in Shakespeare's *The Tempest* and the careful pararhyme construction of Wilfred Owen's poem "Strange Meeting," gives us "a momentary sensation of resolution, a healing moment."[20] Arguing further and resorting to medical language, he claims poetry "is like the immunity [sic] system of the spirit; it works for good but it cannot always withstand assault ... poetry is a kind of drip feed, and when it works it percolates down out of its refined element into the common speech and understanding of a whole society."[21] Thus poetry can potentially—but not always—protect us from harm, and its wholeness, its haleness, can slowly insinuate itself into the larger world, spreading health.

In his reading of Heaney's criticism, Eamon Duffy judges that he "moves decisively beyond any strictly literary criteria" because he asserts "a vision of the value and worth of life, and of the affirmation of life, which I do not know how to describe except as religious ..." And yet, he ponders, "it is not obvious to me that poetry, however great, is in fact capable of bearing the redemptive weight which Heaney seeks within it."[22] This "redemptive weight" is part and parcel of the finally spiritual ground upon which Heaney stakes much of his work and criticism, but it may be too strong *always* to characterize in this way, because while at times he certainly evinced a belief that poetry contained such redemptive power, as I have just shown, at other times he took pains not to argue for poetry's redemptive value but simply for its intimation of an order or harmony to which we might aspire.

Heaney most famously signals this proleptic order with the image of the honeybee in *Crediting Poetry*, when musing upon section four of Yeats's "Meditations in Time of Civil War." Yeats's association of a mother bird feeding its young with the honeybee leads Heaney to argue how that insect suggests "the ideal of an industrious, harmonious, nurturing commonwealth" (*CP* 25). At such moments, poetry does not outstrip reality, but it maintains the possibility of an existence beyond the terrible current reality, "the need not to harden the mind to a point where it denies its own yearnings for sweetness and trust. It is a proof that poetry can be equal to *and* true at the same time ..." (26). In such moments in his criticism, Heaney intimates that it is enough for poetry to exist as the site of an alternative, sweet and truthful order over against that harsh and consequently false chaos outside the poem. By balancing his view of poetry as adequate to resisting the blandishments and temptations to despair in time of war and atrocity with his more redemptive view of poetry, his criticism affirms his spiritual role of the poet and maintains poetry's potentially transformative power, both sufficient to itself and at other times more than sufficient for redeeming reality.

No less of an authority than the poet and critic Anthony Hecht, upon the publication of Heaney's *Finders, Keepers: Selected Prose 1971–2001*, remarked that he has usually recommended to young poets "a number of texts that provoke long and lively thought, most often among them the letters of Keats," noting further that "if a young writer" would ask him what prose he would recommend to help them understand their craft, "I would now happily and gratefully add *Finders Keepers*."[23] And yet for those wanting the fullest sense of Heaney's criticism, *Finders, Keepers* remains a woefully incomplete guide to the prose. For acquiring such an understanding of this aspect of his work, it would be far better to obtain each individual volume—*Preoccupations, The Government of the Tongue, The Place of Writing, Crediting Poetry, The Redress of Poetry*—along with *Finders, Keepers*, which does include some previously unpublished essays, and to get the full versions of other essays in

Finders, Keepers, such as Heaney's wonderful essay on Dante, in their original periodical format.

Drama

Heaney's dramatic work was always attuned to this conjunction of dissonance and harmony, history and hope, which his criticism addresses so thoughtfully. He held a long interest in drama, going back to his acting in plays about the 1798 Irish Rebellion with the Bellaghy Dramatic Society in the 1950s and continuing with his BBC Northern Ireland Radio work in the 1960s and 1970s, including a play about 1798 entitled *Munro*, and his radio scripts with dramatic elements.[24]

With his version of Sophocles' *Philoctetes*, *The Cure at Troy* (1990), written for the Field Day Theatre Company, Heaney may have reached the apotheosis of his dramatic art. This nuanced and sensitive appreciation of the character who, for Heaney, was the central figure of the Trojan War, the wounded archer Philoctetes, became one of his most poignant explorations of the human condition, and it also critiqued entrenched political discourses that would see the "other" as inhuman in a much subtler way than would *The Burial at Thebes*. The initial Field Day production of the play, in the culturally, religiously, and politically divided city of Derry/Londonderry, Northern Ireland, not only spoke against the entrenched sectarianism of that city but also against that attitude in all of the province, and by extension, throughout the world. Heaney strikingly explores the condition of woundedness as both a site of suffering and potential empathy, and also as an alienating condition—for individuals and communities whereby they cut themselves off from the fellowship of others.

Despite the real sympathy that the Chorus and, by extension, Heaney feel for the wounded Philoctetes, the play nonetheless opens with the Chorus's chanting of "Philoctetes. / Hercules. / Odysseus," who they term, "Heroes. Victims. Gods and human beings. / . . . every one of them / Convinced he's in the right . . ." Worse, the Chorus then likens them to "People so deep into / Their own self-pity, self-pity buoys them up," lamenting "People so staunch and true, they're fixated, / Shining with self-regard like polished stones" (*CT* 1). As I have argued elsewhere, these lines are replete with meaning for the Catholic/Nationalist/Republican community and the Protestant/Unionist/Loyalist community in Northern Ireland, although Heaney brilliantly suggests that stereotypically assigning the self-pitying identity to the first community and the staunch identity to the second is too reductive; either description could equally apply to each community.[25]

Heaney, speaking through the Chorus in this opening section, cautiously moots poetry's power to change hearts and minds even as he qualifies that potential. Observing "my part is the chorus, and the chorus / Is more or less a borderline between / The you and the me and the it of it," he muses further, "that's the borderline that poetry / Operates on too, always in between / What you would like to happen and what will— / Whether you like it or not" (*CT* 2). He has long argued for the inherent liminality of poetry and here praises its self-sufficiency and agency. In "The Redress of Poetry," written in 1989 while he was also working on *The Cure at Troy*, Heaney anticipated this argument about the "operation" of poetry, affirming that "Such an operation does not intervene in the actual but by offering consciousness a chance to recognize its predicaments, foreknow its capacities, and rehearse its comebacks in all kinds of venturesome ways, it does constitute a beneficent event, for poet and audience alike." While he believes that poetry can create a "liberating and verifying effect upon the individual spirit," he quickly observes that "such a function would be deemed insufficient by a political activist."[26] Indeed, the play's core features not a political movement per se, but a change in heart by the crippled Philoctetes, effected in part by Neoptolemus's decision to stop being duplicitous and keep his promise to the archer, after which Philoctetes decides to go back and help the Greeks in the Trojan War. Societal change, Heaney therefore implies, will not come about by forced government policies, but by one heart at a time changing and softening toward others who have done us grievous wrongs.

As the play proceeds, Heaney's Neoptolemus tricks Philoctetes out of his magic bow in order to give it to the treacherous Odysseus, but then realizes how wrong he is and hands the weapon back to Philoctetes, who aims the bow at Odysseus, then is stopped by Neoptolemus. In these dual acts of giving, then restraining, Neoptolemus reclaims the bond of friendship with Philoctetes, but also stops this reprisal killing by the great archer, who is still angered at Odysseus's abandonment of him on the island of Lesbos ten years before (71). Shortly thereafter, Neoptolemus argues to Philoctetes in lines resonant for both the ordinary people who carried on their lives with dignity and for the killers who operated with impunity in the past conflict in Northern Ireland, "There's a courage / And dignity in ordinary people / That can be breathtaking," holding that "you're the opposite. / Your courage has gone wild, you're like a brute / That can only foam at the mouth" (72). In a stroke, our sympathy for the abused and wounded Philoctetes dissipates as we realize the truth of Neoptolemus' claim that his righteous anger has now spilled over into vengeful talk and actions. Through such scenes, Heaney consistently shows the power of words, not violence, to lead us into new solidarities with unexpected allies. Thus Neoptolemus gradually leads Philoctetes back into an alliance with Odysseus and the Greeks against the Trojans, urging him to "Stop just licking your wounds. Start seeing things," a line that recommends a halt to wallowing in self-pity and a welcoming of visionary possibilities as it adumbrates the title of his volume *Seeing Things* (74). But crucially, Philoctetes must undertake this decision freely, as Neoptolemus tells him: "You are to come / Of your own free will to the town of Troy" (72). Only then will he be healed of his suppurating foot wound by Asclepius the healer (73).

As the two men prepare to head for the waiting Greek ships, the Chorus reappears and chants what have become some of Heaney's best-known lines, although he runs the risk of their being too local in their application to both the main religious/cultural/political communities in Northern Ireland. The Chorus first reminds us of our depravity—that "Human beings suffer, / They torture one another, / They get hurt and get hard." The alliteration of the "h" sound here hammers home the hurt we inflict on others, and then Heaney quickly slips in direct references to a presumably republican "hunger-striker's father / [Who] Stands in the graveyard dumb," while a likely Protestant and unionist "police widow in veils / Faints at the funeral home" (77).

Had the Chorus continued in this vein, the last part of the play would have collapsed under the weight of such topical references to the conflict, but the very next stanza condemns all such deaths and introduces the possibility of justice for all who have lost loved ones in the conflict:

> History says, *Don't hope*
> *On this side of the grave.*
> But then, once in a lifetime
> The longed-for tidal wave
> Of justice can rise up,
> And hope and history rhyme. (77)

Now the "h" sound re-enters the choral chant, admitting the miraculous possibility, signaled in the play's title, of justice sweeping into such deadly situations like a rising tidal wave.

Hope and history can only rhyme when they coincide and the slant-rhymed couplets of the next stanza offer some rhyming affirmation of this unlooked-for potential: "So hope for a great sea-change / On the far side of revenge." Twice in a row then the Chorus asks us to have faith in that possibility: "Believe that a further shore / Is reachable from here. / Believe in miracles / And cures and healing wells" (77). These last two lines were particularly resonant for Irish audiences north and south of the border, Heaney believed. He has recalled that Field Day's touring production of *The Cure at Troy* would be reaching "audiences who wouldn't have much historical sense of the play or its place in Sophocles' *oeuvre*, so I believed a new title could work as a pointer, a kind of subliminal orientation." His titular evocation of a cure thus was drawn from "the idea of a miraculous cure" being "deeply lodged in the religious subculture, whether it involves faith healing or the Lourdes pilgrimage" (*SS* 422). Notice the ecumenical balance in this last statement: Protestant evangelicals would still subscribe to faith healing and Catholics to the Lourdes pilgrimage, which Heaney himself had gone on during the 1950s. The Chorus's words here then attempt to reach out to both Protestant and Catholic audiences and by extension to all those people groups such as those in South Africa formerly locked into combat with each other.

And yet these are not the last words of the play, much quoted as they have been by politicians. Heaney concludes the play by ushering in an ambiguity through the Chorus's admonition to "Suspect too much sweet talk," while immediately having it urge us, "But never close your mind." Now united into one person, standing for the poet himself, the Chorus muses, "I leave / Half-ready to believe / That a crippled trust might walk // And the half-true rhyme is love" (*CT* 81). Attuned to the truth, suspicious of platitudes and deception such as that practiced earlier in the play by Neoptolemus, the Chorus nonetheless keeps an open mind and is partially ready to believe that both Philoctetes might walk again, and by extension, that a new trust created through dialogue, not violence, between formerly opposed factions in Northern Ireland and elsewhere might blossom into understanding, even, possibly, love.

In 2003, Heaney wrote a version of Sophocles' *Antigone* he entitled *The Burial at Thebes* at the behest of Ireland's famous Abbey Theatre for their centenary in 2004. He knew the play well, having taught it at St Joseph's, the Belfast teacher-training college where he taught in 1963, and having read an article by Conor Cruise O'Brien about the brutality with which the Royal Ulster Constabulary met the (mostly) Catholic civil rights marchers on October 5, 1968 in the politically gerrymandered city of Derry.[27] Heaney approves of O'Brien's reading of Antigone and her sister, Isemene, who "represent two opposing impulses that often co-exist: the impulse to protect and rebel and the impulse to conform for the sake of a quiet life."[28] Despite being honored by this invitation from the Abbey Theatre, Heaney expressed his wariness of it in a public lecture he gave to the American Philosophical Society, "Title Deeds: Translating a Classic." He mused that since "the play had been translated and adapted so often, and had been co-opted into so many cultural and political arguments, it had begun to feel less like a text from the theatrical repertoire and more like a pretext for debate, a work that was as much if not more at home in the seminar room than on the stage."[29]

When he decided to undertake this project, he "wanted to do a translation that would be true to the original in so far as it would be as much musical score as dramatic script, one that actors could speak as plainly or intensely as the occasion demanded, but one that still kept faith with the ritual formality of the original."[30] Once again, to signal his distance from the drama and his desire not to do a strict translation, he called it, as he had with *Philoctetes*, a "version," not even an adaptation. Such language further indicates that Heaney's "take" on this drama is not meant to be the final word, but simply to jostle and compete for elbow room, as it were, in our collective thinking about Sophocles' rich play. Finally, by entitling his version *The Burial at Thebes*, and focusing on Antigone's desire to bury both her brothers who have fought on opposite sides in the War of the Seven against Thebes, he freighted his title with a connotation that simultaneously was subversive in an Irish postcolonial context and underscored our common humanity. For Heaney, the word "burial" not only "recalls us to our final destiny as members of the species," but also, it "reminds us, however subliminally, of the solemnity of death, the sacredness of life and the need to allow in every case the essential dignity of the human creature."[31]

Heaney, however, finally could not resist using his version of *Antigone* to score political points in a way that suggests he too finally "co-opted" it into his own "cultural and political arguments." He links Creon's intransigence and unyielding attitude toward his daughter Antigone in her desire to bury both her brothers, bizarrely, to the then American President George W. Bush's attitude toward the radical Muslim terrorists who killed many Americans and world citizens on September 11, 2001. Rather than allowing the kind of ambiguity in his language that he did, for instance, in the opening lines of *The Cure at Troy*, which suggests both sides in the Northern Irish conflict wallow at times in their woundedness, Heaney instead took the didactic low road and critiqued Bush in his version of *Antigone*, a view that he signaled to future audiences of the play in an interview in the *Irish Times* in 2004, in an essay he published in *The Guardian* in 2005, and most didactically, in a note that accompanies the American, but significantly not the British, text of the play.[32] In his note on the play, Heaney equated Creon's coercion of the citizens of Thebes "into an either/or situation in relation to Antigone," just as the Bush administration in the White House was using the same tactic to forward its argument for war on Iraq ... Bush was using a similar strategy, asking, in effect: Are you in favor of state security or are you not? If you don't support the eradication of this tyrant in Iraq and the threat he poses to the free world, you are on the wrong side in "the war on terror."[33]

The Northern Irish contexts Heaney elsewhere insisted colored the play do not appear clearly in it, but Heaney's view of Creon as a Bush figure does, appearing most prominently in a scene where Antigone confronts her father Creon, using the language of patriotism that would have been unfamiliar to the Greeks (or indeed to the nationalists and republicans in Northern Ireland). Defending her burial of her brother Polyneices, she states, "And if these men / Weren't so afraid to sound unpatriotic / They'd say the same." Then she immediately adds, "But you are king / And because you're king you won't be contradicted."[34] Shortly thereafter, Creon, who earlier, speaking of his son Eteocles, vowed to "honour patriots in life and death," again uses the contemporary language of terror, noting flatly about Polyneices, "He terrorized us. Eteocles stood by us."[35]

At least some American theater critics loved the comparison. In their reviews, published together, of the production at LaMaMa in New York City directed by Paul Harrington, both Ellen W. Lytle and Paulanne Simmons can scarcely conceal their glee at Heaney's reading of Creon as Bush, while elevating even Creon over the despised president. In stunningly bad prose and grammer, Lytle, for example, observes:

> Heaney is a poet who also eases in the message that Sophocles' Greece is an absolute metaphor for today's U.S. government. The similarity between the rigid royalty from fourth century B.C. and the Bush regime is stunningly accurate, except for the fact that King Creon finally listens to reason and acquiesces his brutal assessment of Antigone and the will of his people, while our cabinet keeps on lying.[36]

And Simmons chirpingly maintains that the play

> was commissioned in 2004 as part of the centenary celebration of the Abbey Theatre and was inspired by the war in Iraq. By his own admission (in the *Guardian*, 2005), Heaney saw in George W. Bush "a Creon figure ... a law and order bossman trying to boss the nations of the world into uncritical agreement with his edicts." That may be so, but [Frank] Anderson's Creon is far more reasonable and thoughtful than one suspect [sic] President Bush is, even on his best days. Unlike Bush, this Creon has a certain dignity, indeed a benevolence that somehow softens his stubborn refusal to listen to the sound advice of others.[37]

Putting aside Simmons's uncanny ability to know another person's mind and Lytle's supposed ability to apprehend what went on at Cabinet meetings in the White House, their elevation of Creon above Bush seems more about their hatred of Bush than their reading of the play. Taken together, Heaney's comparison of Creon and Bush in his *Guardian* essay along with his contention in "Title Deeds" that the German censors who approved Jean Anouilh's adaptation of *Antigone* in 1944 Paris "must have been dreaming that this time Creon's rule would be more perfectly realized in the ongoing dominance of the Reich" signal a reductive, even crude alignment of Creon, Bush, and Hitler, with Creon coming off best. This is what happens when art descends into propaganda.

Around this same time, Heaney had, on commission from Amnesty International, re-imagined a Horatian ode as "Horace and the Thunder," a poem he later revised and retitled as "Anything Can Happen," which I explored in the previous chapter. In his essay that accompanied the poem's publication, Heaney lamented not only the deaths of the thousands murdered by Islamic terrorists that day, but also "Stealth bombers pummeling the fastnesses of Afghanistan, shock and awe loosed from the night skies over Iraq . . ." Regardless of one's approval or disapproval over that misguided and finally disastrous invasion, equating those mass murders with an international air campaign ostensibly undertaken to liberate Iraq's populace from the murderous Saddam Hussein, startles, even shocks, and suggests the failure of Heaney's vaunted imagination. One wishes that he had not published the various statements equating Creon and President Bush and Hitler as a didactic guide to viewing and reading the American version of *The Burial*. When Heaney writes about Horace's ode that "the original is a poem of religious awe rather than any kind of political comment or coded response to events. It is the voice of an individual in shock at what can happen to the world," one wishes that he had let *The Burial at Thebes* function in a similar fashion.[38]

Heaney's *Cure* (which has no note by him that conditions our reading of it as explicitly political like *The Burial* or "Anything Can Happen" do) and his translation of *Beowulf* manifest subtly polyvalent political readings widening out from the recent conflict in Northern Ireland to World War One and Yeats's attitude toward the Easter Rising in Ireland, and Northern Ireland, Kosovo, and Rwanda, respectively. In his prose, Heaney tried valiantly to link *The Burial* to the situation in Northern Ireland, both at the beginning of the Troubles through his invocation of Conor Cruise O'Brien's use of Antigone to critique the attacks on the civil rights marchers at a low point of the Troubles, and with the burial of his former neighbor, the republican hunger striker Francis Hughes, in 1981 and to be sure, these events were important to him in apprehending and responding to Antigone's dramatic situation in the play.[39] He also pointed out that the emotion and the "drive and pitch of the Irish verse," particularly its three-beat line, of the eighteenth-century lament in Irish, *Caoineadh Airt Uí Laoghaire*, or "The Lament for Art O'Leary," helped inspire his sense of Antigone's movement from mourning to outrage.[40] But Heaney's clamorous insistence in interviews, essays, and particularly in his note attached to the American publication of the play, which were all repeated by critics, along with the suggestive language of the play itself that traffics in the idiom of the Bush administration's emphasis on patriotism amidst the mis-named "war on terror," contradict his own understanding of art's freedom and its privileging of its autonomy. *The Burial at Thebes* thus remains hampered and hindered by its finally monovalent, limiting equation of the Bush administration's engagement with terrorists and through the American invasions in Iraq and Afghanistan to Hitler's pogroms.

Translations

Through his translations from the Irish, Old English, Scots, Italian, and other languages, Heaney became one of our major translators and generally resisted propagandizing as he did in *The Burial at Thebes*. His 1983 translation of the Irish work, *Buile Suibhne*, as *Sweeney Astray*, published by Field Day in Derry in the wake of the republican hunger strikes, poignantly portrayed the lonely Sweeney flitting from treetop to treetop, suggesting to unionists that Ulster had a strong Irish identity in its original nine-county manifestation while allowing them to nonetheless identify with that region.[41] After his engagement with Dante's Canti XXXII and XXXIII from *The Inferno* in "An Afterwards" and then his translation of passages from those same canti in "Ugolino" (*FW* 44 and 61–4), Heaney employed the Florentine poet's model of Hell, Purgatory, and Paradise in *Station Island* along with his modified tercet form drawn on Dante's *terza rima*, as we have seen. He also published a major essay on Dante in 1983.[42] Beyond the persistent influence of Dante's *terza rima* form on his penchant for the tercet in the last three and a half decades of his poetic career, Heaney planned an entire translation of Dante's *Commedia*, but finally settled for translating the first three canti of *The Inferno* in the late 1980s that were published in 1993.[43]

That same year, Heaney published two translations from Ovid's *Metamorphoses*, Books X and XI, respectively—"Orpheus and Eurydice" and "The Death of Orpheus"—along with his translation from the Irish of selected lines from Brian Merriman's *Cúirt an Mheán Oíche* (*The Midnight Court*) as *The Midnight Verdict*. He noted that as he "put bits of the Irish into couplets," he thought of Merriman's poem in the context of Orpheus' death and realized that "The end of *The Midnight Court* took on a new resonance when read within the acoustic of the classical myth . . ."[44] Two years later, Heaney and Stanisław Barańczak translated the poet Jan Kochanowski's *Laments* or *Treny* about the death of that Polish poet's daughter Orszula. Kochanowski (1530–84) was the first great Polish poet to write in the vernacular and became a major influence on one of Heaney's exemplars, Czesław Miłosz. He was likely drawn to Kochanowski's work because of his own predilection for the vernacular. In 1999, Heaney published a new version of the *Diary of One Who Vanished: A Song Cycle* by Leoš Janáček of Poems by Ozef Kalda, commissioned by the English National Opera for several international performances, a further confirmation of his deep interest in Eastern European poetry. Finally, his translation of the Middle Scots poem *The Testament of Cresseid*, published with seven of Robert Henryson's fables in 2009, also continues his work of recovering regional voices and accents outside the metropole of London and across the Atlantic archipelago.[45] By virtue of his sensitivity to lineation and sound, he has popularized translations of major works that seek to recover marginal voices and promote our common humanity.

Heaney had long been drawn to what he might have termed the internal music of the sixth-century Old English epic *Beowulf* set in modern-day Scandinavia—its alliterations, assonances, and medial caesuras. Winner of the 1999 Whitbread Book of the Year Award and a bestseller in Britain and America, his translation of *Beowulf* quickly became the most commercially successful translation in years, even as some reviewers disparaged it as "Heaneywulf," noting how much the poet appropriated it into his own poetic. The medievalist Tom Shippey, writing in the influential *Times Literary Supplement*, captures the spirit of its reception in many quarters: "Like it or not, Heaney's *Beowulf* is the poem now."[46] Following J. R. R. Tolkien's landmark lecture on the poem in 1936, "*Beowulf*: The Monsters and the Critics," which Heaney felt "took for granted the poem's integrity and distinction as a work of art and proceeded to show in what this integrity and distinction inhered," he similarly sought to reclaim it as a "work of the greatest imaginative vitality, a masterpiece where the structuring of the tale is as elaborate as the beautiful contrivances of its language."[47]

He clearly sees the poem as a valuable inheritance for contemporary English-speakers and signals its value in this regard with his brief epigraph drawn from his own poem, "The Settle Bed," collected in *Seeing Things*:

> And now this is "an inheritance"—
> Upright, rudimentary, unshiftably planked
> In the long ago, yet willable forward
> Again and again and again.⁴⁸

Imagining lying in the settle bed, Heaney's speaker in that poem anticipates the framing funerals of *Beowulf*: "If I lie in it, I am cribbed in seasoned deal / Dry as the unkindled boards of a funeral ship." Just as his poem celebrates that bed's "un-get-roundable weight" and functions as a sort of vessel holding the dialects of Heaney's native Northern Ireland, "the long bedtime / Anthems of Ulster" (*ST* 30), so too, he implies, does *Beowulf*. We simply cannot avoid its bedding, its lodging in our linguistic and literary heritage; thus the poem bluntly thrusts forward, competing for our attention through the ages "Again and again and again." And yet despite its weighty presence in our minds and common history, *Beowulf*, he posits, nonetheless has a sense of beyondness like the imagined "dower of settle beds tumbled from heaven" in the second part of "The Settle Bed" (31). Heaney believed that the Anglo-Saxon epic "possesses a mythic potency," having "Like Shield Sheafson … arrive[d] from somewhere beyond the known bourne of our experience, and having fulfilled its purpose (again like Shield) it passes once more into the beyond."⁴⁹ In this regard, we can beneficially read this notion of the poem through Heaney's lyric "viii" in the "Lightenings" sequence. Just as the ghost ship hangs its anchor on the altar rails at Clonmacnoise and must be freed by human help, *Beowulf* snags on "rails" of language, past translations that may have imprisoned it, and it comes to a standstill in our busy lives, demanding our focus, even, in Heaney's case, so that he may translate it and "free" it from formerly cumbersome translations that may have reduced its buoyancy. Once we attend to it and recognize its power to transport us to another time and place, we too can, like the crewman at Clonmacnoise, climb "back / Out of the marvelous as he had known it" (*ST* 62).

However, for most of his profound and moving introduction to his translation, Heaney focuses on its quotidian qualities, including its language and sounds. As he worked on translating the poem for Norton, a project that was years in the making, he gradually realized he had been speaking and writing its music most of his life. He first tried translating it at Harvard in the early- to mid-1980s, believing that if he could carry it off, the translation would ward off the potentially dislocating effect of the "unmoored speech of some contemporary American poetry": It "would be a kind of aural antidote, a way of ensuring that my linguistic anchor would stay lodged on the Anglo-Saxon sea-floor."⁵⁰ Once he returned to the poem in the 1990s, Heaney made multiple discoveries, including that his famous poem "Digging" featured some lines that echoed the Anglo-Saxon penchant for "two balancing halves," along with alliteration, leading him to conclude, "Part of me, in other words, had been writing Anglo-Saxon from the start." He realized, too, that one of his early exemplars, Gerard Manley Hopkins, "was a chip off the Old English block," and somewhat ruefully recalled the poem with which the current study proper started, his early "October Thought," which featured lines that "were as much pastiche Anglo-Saxon as they were pastiche Hopkins . . ."[51] Even his choice to translate the opening "Hwaet" of the Old English as the weighty "So" derived from the heavy, weighty voices of his father's Scullion uncles. Musing further, he "realized that I wanted it [*Beowulf*] to be speakable by one of those relatives" and so he settled upon "So" because in the Hiberno-English spoken by those Scullion ancestors, "'so' operates as an expression that obliterates all previous discourse and narrative, and at the same time functions as an exclamation calling for immediate attention."[52] Another inheritance from his Northern Irish soundscape was its reticence and preference for unadorned speech. Thus, when Beowulf and his Geatish company sail toward King Hygelac and the Spear-Danes' land, Heaney shears articles from some nouns and delivers a pared-down, utterly effective line which, by virtue of its understatement, calls attention to time, movement, and space almost as a parenthetical pause before the weighty words and major actions begin: "Time went by, the boat was on water, / in close under the cliffs."[53] This tendency to cluster three phrases together persists throughout the poem, and allied with this reticent line, conveys the action of the poem effectively through its concision. When, to give another example, Beowulf grapples with Grendel that fateful night in Heorot, the narrator relates, "Fingers were bursting, / the monster back-tracking, the man overpowering."[54]

Heaney further realized that the Old English word that denotes suffering, *tholian*, was echoed in the use of a word with the same etymological root among the "older and less educated people . . . in the country where I grew up. 'They'll just have to learn to thole,' my aunt would say about some family who had suffered an unforeseen bereavement." Heaney grasped in this moment that "my aunt's language was not just a self-enclosed family possession but an historical heritage, one that involved the journey" that the Anglo-Saxon word *tholian* had "made north into Scotland and then across into Ulster with the planters, and then across from the planters to the locals who had originally spoken Irish," and "then farther across again when the Scots Irish emigrated to the American South in the eighteenth century."[55] The persistence of this word and its transnational journey across Britain and Ireland, arriving in America years later, clearly made Heaney feel that he could return the word (and, by extension, the poem) eastward again, resituating it in a transatlantic context that nonetheless lodged in Anglo-Saxon culture and society, yet could speak to contemporary concerns in divided societies such as Rwanda and Kosovo through the keening (derived from the Irish word for grievous lamenting) of the Geatish woman in the poem's conclusion, since "her keen is a nightmare glimpse into the minds of people who have survived traumatic, even monstrous events and who are now being exposed to a comfortless future."[56]

Certainly Heaney himself was drawn also to the poem in part through his own deep interest in exploring the troubled state of Northern Ireland and trying to ascertain what contribution literature specifically and the arts generally might make to ameliorating conflict springing from cultural and religious and political differences there. We can almost feel the evident relish with which Heaney must have written Hygelac's final speech to Beowulf after the Geatish hero has defeated the nemeses of the Spear-Dane king, the monster Grendel and his mother:

> What you have done is to draw two peoples,
> the Geat nation and us neighbouring Danes,
> into shared peace and a pact of friendship
> in spite of hatreds we have harboured in the past.[57]

Continuing his translation of the epic during and after the 1994 ceasefires declared by both the IRA and the Combined Loyalist Command must have led the poet to ponder again how ancient foes could potentially be reunited in the face of a common enemy. Because Catholics and Protestants share a common language in Northern Ireland's linguistic confluence of the remnants of Irish, Elizabethan English, and Scots, and since they worship a common God and Savior, Heaney's translation can be read as a positive affirmation of those commonalities. In this sense, the high point of the poem occurs in this passage I have just cited, but its proper conclusion in wailing and moaning in the face of invasions by multiple countries implies how internal differences and departures from codes of loyalty and family render a country vulnerable and exploitable. And yet, to his great credit, Heaney "manages to preserve the cultural and literary alterity of his original: he has not reduced the poem to a costume-drama allegory of the Ulster situation."[58]

While some medievalists disliked the liberties Heaney took with the Anglo-Saxon language, others defended Heaney. Heather O'Donoghue, for instance, went so far as to claim that "with Heaney, distinctions between the roles of scholar, critic, and poet dissolve; he combines the strengths of all three in this new text."[59] She especially praised his subtle use of alliteration in contrast to its more obvious appearance in the original: "one is surprised by how insidiously the alliteration is worked into the line; particularly attractive (and indeed authentic) is Heaney's tendency to alliterate on stressed second syllables, so that 'behind' alliterates with 'housed,' or 'beyond' with 'yield.'"[60] Having himself previously translated the poem, Howell Chickering lauded it for Heaney's treatment of the dramatic speeches, roughly 40 per cent of the poem. For Chickering, "passage after passage delivers the sense and the tone of the Old English with effortless grace. It doesn't matter which character is speaking, nor whether with enthusiasm or stoic irony: Heaney captures their verbal gestures just about perfectly."[61]

One example of such a dramatic speech comes late in the poem, when Wiglaf chastises his comrades who have broken the comitatus creed whereby they voluntarily fight for the king, noting how Beowulf always kept his end of the creed and rewarded his warriors freely: "So it is goodbye now to all you know and love / on your home ground, the open-handedness, the giving of war-swords." He suggests now that each of them "will be dispossessed, once princes from beyond / get tidings of how you turned and fled / and disgraced yourselves."[62] Always supremely generous of his own time and talents, Heaney must have silently identified with such ring-givers as Hygelac, Beowulf, and other good kings in the poem, just as he rejected the greed epitomized by Grendel, his mother, and especially the grim dragon. And once again, his turn to an epic work from the past, just as his versions of *Philoctetes* and *Antigone* do, displays his deep interest in the binding force of loyalties and how even deep loyalties can be broken by greed and pride. Generosity, receptivity to common linguistic heritages, and an open heart trump tight-fistedness, mono-lingualism, and hard hearts every time.

Often, the last poem in any Heaney volume "introduces" the next volume's concerns and thus "A Kite for Aibhín," the last poem from *Human Chain*, prepares us for the translations of *The Last Walk*, Heaney's gathering of translations from Giovanni Pascoli's *L'Ultima Passeggiata*, what Heaney's editor Peter Fallon terms a "sequence of 'madrigals' composed for Pascoli's lifelong friend and fellow poet, Severino Ferrari . . . on the occasion of Ferrari's wedding to Ida Gini in 1886. It appears in his first collection, *Myriciae* (1891)."[63] This limited edition volume features gorgeous full-color paintings and drawings by Martin Gale, who had also illustrated Gallery Press's limited edition of Heaney's chapbook, *The Riverbank Field*, in 2007. Published posthumously, *The Last Walk* reconnects Heaney to Italy in a new and sensuously natural way that differs from his love of the *Aeneid*'s Book VI, expressed so poignantly in the father/son motif from *Human Chain*.

Heaney's interest in Pascoli stemmed from a visit he made to Urbino, Italy in 2001, where Professor Gabriella Morisco introduced him to that poet's work, especially his kite poem, "*L'Aquilone*," which, in 2009, Heaney extracted and adapted and dedicated to his granddaughter Aibhín in *Human Chain*. In late 2011, he received literal translations and brief commentaries by Professor Tony Oldcorn and found a volume of English translations of Pascoli, from which he then translated the sixteen-lyric sequence *L'Ultima Passeggiata*.[64]

The translations for *The Last Walk* celebrate this landscape that Heaney felt a connection with, what he described as "Men ploughing the fields—with oxen in his case, with horses in mine; a lark in the morning rising from its nest; a housewife in the farmyard feeding her free-range hens . . ." He thought that "these scenes were rendered in lovely miniature, as if they were a book of hours."[65] The very first lyric, "Ploughing," opens in that rural world with a stanza featuring near *terza rima*, running *ab1/2a*, but then the second stanza lapses into a full triplet, *bbb*, while the last stanza, a quatrain, rhymes *cd1/4cd* (*TLW* n.p.). In his essay on Pascoli, Heaney observed that the Italian's "miniature treatment of these [natural] scenes could easily have ended up as little stimulants for nostalgia but instead they are tautly constructed artifacts." He thus suggests that these sixteen poems themselves are one with their depicted topics in their artfulness—poetry as a thing with its own integrity becomes here of a piece with its subjects. More interesting for the question of form is his contention that the poems' ten-line structure "feels like a condensed sonnet, and it possesses something of the sonnet's structure, having a *volta* after 6 lines, which allows the matter to be refocused in the next 4."[66]

With his earlier poems about plowing, such as "Follower" (*Death of a Naturalist*), several lyrics from "Glanmore Sonnets" (*Field Work*), and his own extensive experience with plowing as a boy and young man, Heaney would have been drawn to Pascoli's poetic but near-anthropological recreation of plowing, "In the field, where there's a reddish look / And shine off the trained vines . . ." In that field where "Morning mist appears to rise like smoke, // They are ploughing. One drives slow oxen with a slow / Ploughman's word; one sows; one grubs the furrows / Patiently with his hoe." The full-page reproduction of Gale's painting that prefaces this poem features a vertical golden field neatly bisected by a reddish-brown strip of a ploughed field, framed by black and dark brown tree branches. There are no human witnesses, but the concluding stanza envisions a jubilant sparrow, who "rejoices, / Spying all from the prickly mulberry tree . . ." He is joined in his singing by "the robin—you can hear him from the hedges, / His notes like gold coins jingled for pure glee" (*TLW* n.p.). These birds are anticipated by the Gale painting of a sparrow perched upon a branch that precedes the reproduction of his painting of the field.

One cannot help but hear in this last line and indeed in the poem's celebration of ploughing and birdsong the joyful tone of Heaney's own "Oysters," which concludes with the poet's eating "the day / Deliberately, that its tang / Might quicken me all into verb, pure verb" (*FW* 11). Singing for the sake of singing by the birds confirms one of Heaney's long-held affirmations of poetry—that it is for and unto itself first of all. He remarks, for instance, in "The Whole Thing: On the Good of Poetry," that incorporating his response to Sean O'Riada and his musicians' rendition of the Irish air, "*Port na bPúcai*," into his poem, "The Given Note," that "You can hear with your own ears that the language itself was disposed to come out and come down in exactly those terms, as if in obedience to some pulse or wave pattern at work not just in my ear but in the general ear, in the very life-lines of spoken English." As he holds further, "the good of poetry resides in just such a sensation of rightness, a sensation you might characterize by saying, 'It did me good to hear it.'"[67] For Heaney, Pascoli's poetry was firmly on the side of life, as he believed all good poetry should be—connected to and transmitting its quotidian, affirmative rhythms and songs.

Moreover, he believed that Pascoli's concluding quatrains in his sequence anticipated the development of the English poetry movement Imagism and its focus on an instant of complex intellect and emotion that quickly led to a liberating movement. So in his essay on Pascoli, he holds that the end of "Ploughing" enables what Ezra Pound, one of the chief architects of Imagism, would later call for: the "'direct treatment of the thing,'" and "secondly, the assertion that 'the natural object is always the adequate symbol.'" Listing the sparrow, mulberry tree, the birds, the hedges, the jingle of gold coins, Heaney posits that "all of them belong in one atmosphere, in the same imaginative climate, a pristine here and now."[68] In this sense, too, he returns in this posthumous volume to the direct treatment of things and their liberating spirituality he essayed magnificently in *Seeing Things*. *The Last Walk* itself, replete with the lovely drawings and paintings by Gale, finally becomes a luminous artistic "thing" in its own right, a "pristine here and now" that captures a time and place once and for all and ushers us into the life of it.

Other poems from *The Last Walk* affirm the rightness—of poems, of sounds, of subjects—in natural hymns to rural work and beauty. For example, lyric IV, "Washerwomen," accompanied by a Gale painting with a plowed field on the left and a washerwoman in the foreground, laden down with an overflowing basket of clothes, gives glancing credence to "men's work" with its opening image of an abandoned plow, "Forgotten looking, half-hid in a mist-cloud," but focuses its second and third stanzas on the rhythmic work of the washerwomen with their "wet slapping and surge, / . . . / "Each splish-splash keeping time with their sing-song dirge . . ." Startlingly, the last stanza retrieves the opening image of the forgotten plow and re-employs it to characterize the speaker's bereft state after being deserted by a lover:

The wind is blowing, the bush is snowing,
You've not come back to your native heath:
When you went, you left me sorrowing
Like a plough left out in a fallow field. (TLW n.p.)

Given the title of the poem and that this closing, "sing-song dirge" is sung by the washerwomen it is tempting to assume that it is narrated by a washwoman; after all, the painting features such a woman staring at the field. But the field is only "half-fallow," and partially plowed and ready for sowing (TLW n.p.). And likening herself to a plough, the instrument wielded most commonly by men then and later, makes little sense. Men who would have objectified women at the time might in fact have likened their bodies to fertile fields and themselves to plows. So the poem's dirge slips free from its seeming "ownership" by working women and instantiates an elegiac tone of lament that could be sung by a sorrowful man or woman. This song of the deserted lover balances the sprightly tunes sung by sparrow and robin in the opening lyric, but it grounds the volume in the human sphere of suffering.

By the last lyric in the volume, "O Vain Dream!," Heaney's translation achingly introduces another note of domestic sorrow, tempered at the end only by the speaker's recourse to making poetry. The longest poem in the volume at twelve lines, its structure recalls Heaney's tendency toward the twelve-liner through much of *Seeing Things* and *Human Chain*. The vain dream of the poem is quietly ushered in as the speaker sits by the fire in the opening stanza, "either nodding off or sitting with you, / Nibbling at my chicory and lettuce." After foddering "my companionable cows" with a "forkful of sweet-smelling hay" during a night-time storm, the speaker returns to "go upstairs with you—vain dream!" In an instant, this tableau of domestic tranquility vanishes and the poem seems to tilt toward horror. But reversing course again, it veers into another type of abundance other than love or cattle fodder. By line eight, it has become spring and "the brushwood blooms with cyclamen" while the student returns to his "long neglected lexicon," and the speaker hears outside "The blackbird's warbling" and the snipe's "drumming." Then, "I, in my native tongue, return to versing" (*TLW*, n.p.). Caught back up into the rhythms of the natural world's soundscape, the speaker is able to re-enter the sounds of poetry and returns to "versing" as both tribute to nature and perhaps to sing the "song" we have just perused.

Heaney's other foray into translating Pascoli's work, "The Dapple-Grey Mare," explores a son's murder and the mother's identification of that murderer through the neighing of the horse once she spoke aloud the murderer's name.[69] As Heaney muses, "To have a mare respond with recognition to a name uttered by a human voice asks us to suspend belief further than we are reasonably prepared to. . ." But he believes that "the . . . the poem . . . subvert[s] the reasonable . . . magic[s] the murder, as it were." He identifies the "metrical regularity of the quatrains [that] gives the story a haunting ballad-like appeal, but also a sense of fatality and inevitability."[70] He clearly identifies with the visionary, magical quality of this strange poem.

More important for our purposes here, even beyond how Heaney goes on to connect the mother's lament to that articulated by the widow of the Irish captain Art O Laoghaire (O'Leary) in that well-known Irish lament, concerns how he reads Pascoli through a brief conspectus of his own work. Thus he suggests that

> Country life and family grief are clearly the source of much of Pascoli's early poetry, which is characteristically lyric and often supplied with images out of childhood; but the late poems, which are more meditative and mythical, reveal a poet who is capable of dealing with the preoccupations that occur at a later stage of life, capable also of finding new creative energies to encompass the new conditions . . . The late style found in "The Sleep of Odysseus" and "The Last Voyage" is fresh and inventive, new abilities reveal themselves as new motifs present themselves.[71]

The Last Walk and "The Dapple-Grey Mare" function in many ways as a *summa* of Heaney's long career. Cast in a style that incorporates both his later habitual turn to variations on the *terza rima* and anchored in the blocky, concluding quatrains that characterized his work in the 1970s, they return to childhood images yet consistently enter a spiritual realm where transcendent truths gleam. Heaney's engagement with Pascoli's rich rural poetry, along with his new translation of Book VI of Virgil's *Aeneid*, not only suggests his trans-historical and transnational interests, but also his enduring place as poetic citizen of the world. We shall not see his like again.

Notes

1. Corcoran, *The Poetry of Seamus Heaney*, 229.
2. Cavanagh, 29.
3. Ibid., 11.
4. McDonald, "The Poet and 'The Finished Man': Heaney's Oxford Lectures," 99.
5. Wheatley, "Professing Poetry: Heaney as Critic," 124, 125.
6. Cavanagh, 45.
7. Dennison, 134.
8. Heaney, "Verses for a Fordham Commencement," n.p.
9. Heaney, "[Appointment of Ted Hughes as Poet Laureate of Britain]," n.p.
10. Heaney, "From Monaghan to the Grand Canal," 120–1.
11. Hecht, n.p.
12. Heaney, "Yeats's Nobility," 12.
13. Corcoran, *The Poetry of Seamus Heaney*, 213, 214.
14. Heaney, "The Door Stands Open: Czesław Miłosz, 1911–2004," 28.
15. Heaney, "Frontiers of Writing," 192.
16. The term "self-delighting inventiveness" draws on language from Yeats's "A Prayer for My Daughter," particularly the phrases about his desire for his daughter's soul, "The soul recovers radical innocence / And learns at last that it is self-delighting, / Self-appeasing, self-affrighting" (Yeats, 189), and is used in Heaney, "The Redress of Poetry," when he argues "Poetry cannot afford to lose its fundamentally self-delighting inventiveness, its joy in being a process of language as well as a representation of things in the world" (5). Heaney, "Frontiers of Writing," 192–3.
17. Heaney, "Frontiers of Writing," 189.
18. Heaney, "The Whole Thing: On the Good of Poetry," 8.
19. Ibid.
20. Ibid., 10.
21. Ibid., 16.
22. Duffy, "Seamus Heany and Catholicism," 180.
23. Hecht, n.p.
24. For a brief discussion of this play, see my *Seamus Heaney's Regions*, 86–94, and for a full discussion of Heaney's radio work for BBC Northern Ireland, see ibid., 66–100.
25. Ibid., 290.
26. Heaney, "The Redress of Poetry," 2.
27. Heaney, "A Greek Tragedy for Our Times," n.p. He expands much more on the O'Brien essay in "Title Deeds: Translating a Classic," 416–18.
28. Heaney, "A Greek Tragedy for Our Times."
29. Heaney, "Title Deeds: Translating a Classic," 414.
30. Ibid., 426.
31. Ibid.
32. See Heaney's interview, "A Greek Tragedy for Our Times," in which he states about his inspiration to take on a new version of the play in a post-9/11 world, "There was the general worldwide problem where considerations of state security posed serious threats to individual freedom and

human rights. Then there was the obvious parallel between George W. Bush and Creon."
33. Heaney, "A Note on *The Burial at Thebes*," 76.
34. Heaney, *The Burial at Thebes*, 32.
35. Ibid., 17, 33.
36. Lytle, n.p.
37. Simmons, n.p.
38. Heaney, "Anything Can Happen," 18.
39. Heaney, "Title Deeds," 411–14.
40. Heaney, "A Note on *The Burial at Thebes*," 77, 76–8.
41. See my discussion of *Sweeney Astray* in *Seamus Heaney's Regions*, 324–35, as a unifying regional act of cultural devolution.
42. See Heaney, "Envies and Identifications: Dante and the Modern Poet."
43. See Heaney, "Canti III," 3–15. Heaney's translation of Canto III, *Inferno*, appears as "The Crossing" in *Seeing Things*, a poem I explored earlier in this study. Homem points out that Heaney's employment of "astray" in the first line of the first canto "retroactively emphasizes the wanderings of Sweeney (rather than the madness element), while it also reminds the readers of Heaney's concern with continuity and coherence in his writing" (49).
44. Heaney, "Translator's Note," *The Midnight Verdict*, 11.
45. For a helpful overview of the context of Henryson's career in relation to the other "Scottish Chaucerians," see the review by Greggs of Heaney's translation.
46. Shippey, 10.
47. Heaney, "Introduction," *Beowulf*, xi, ix.
48. Ibid., ix.
49. Ibid., xii.
50. Ibid., xxii.
51. Ibid., xxiii.
52. Ibid., xxvii.
53. Heaney, *Beowulf*, lines 210–11, p. 9.
54. Ibid., lines 760–1, p. 25.
55. Heaney, "Introduction," *Beowulf*, xxv.
56. Ibid., xxi. But see Dennison, who argues that Heaney's emphasis in his introduction on words such as "thole" leading to his recovery of an "aboriginal consciousness" suggest that "his prose poetics are caught between an impossible metalinguistic and metaphysical 'nostalgia for the original undifferentiated linguistic home' and the unstable implications of his belief that the poet constructs (interested) 'supreme fictions'—here, the cultural politics of translation arising from Heaney's personal history, and from the preoccupations of late-twentieth-century literary theory" (206).
57. Heaney, *Beowulf*, lines 1855–8, p. 60. I have argued in *Seamus Heaney's Regions* that in other moments in the poem, by advocating Beowulf's great martial prowess, Heaney "allegorizes it so that it represents his own poetic power and poetic combat, an inner 'violence' pressing back protectively against outer violence, implicitly affirming poetry's power to offer a site of possibility where opposed 'tribes' might meet" (327).
58. Heather O'Donoghue, "Review of Seamus Heaney, *Beowulf: A New Translation*," 236.

59. Ibid., 231.
60. Ibid., 232.
61. Chickering, 162.
62. Heaney, *Beowulf*, 90–1, 91.
63. Fallon, "[Editor's Note]," n.p.
64. Heaney, "On Home Ground," 20.
65. Ibid., 21.
66. Ibid.
67. Heaney, "The Whole Thing: On the Good of Poetry," 7.
68. Heaney, "On Home Ground," 22.
69. See "The Dapple-Grey Mare."
70. Heaney, "On Home Ground," 23.
71. Ibid., 24–5.

Primary Works by Seamus Heaney

Major Archives

The Seamus Heaney Literary Papers, 1963–2010. National Library of Ireland, Dublin, Ireland.
The major collection of Heaney's diaries, drafts of poetry volumes, and notebooks, this collection is carefully dated and labeled by the poet himself and the library's presentation of the material is helpful. Somewhat limited visiting hours. Any permission to cite these papers must come from the poet's estate through Faber and Faber.
Seamus Heaney Papers, Stuart A. Rose Manuscript, Archives, Rare Book Library, Woodruff Library, Emory University, Atlanta, Georgia.
A valuable collection of Heaney's manuscripts, particularly for prose essays and occasional pieces.

Bibliography

Durkan, Michael and Brandes, Rand. *Seamus Heaney: A Bibliography, 1959–2003*. London: Faber and Faber, 2008.
An invaluable resource, it will soon be updated, perhaps in an electronic edition.

Drama

The Cure at Troy: A Version of Sophocles' Philoctetes. Produced by Field Day Theatre Company in Dublin, 1990. Derry: Field Day and London: Faber and Faber, 1990; New York: Farrar, Straus and Giroux, 1991.
The Burial at Thebes: Sophocles' Antigone. Produced by the Abbey Theatre in Dublin, 2004. London: Faber and Faber; published as *The Burial at Thebes: A Version of Sophocles' Antigone* with "A Note on *The Burial at Thebes*" by Heaney. New York: Farrar, Straus and Giroux, 2004.

Editor

With Alan Brownjohn and Jon Stallworthy. *New Poems, 1970–71: A P.E.N. Anthology of Contemporary Poetry*. London: Hutchinson, 1971.
Soundings '72: An Annual Anthology of New Irish Poetry. Belfast: Blackstaff Press, 1972.
Soundings II: An Anthology of New Irish Poetry. Belfast: Blackstaff Press, 1974.
With Ted Hughes. *Arvon Foundation Poetry Competition: 1980 Anthology*. Todmorden: Kilnhurst Publishing, 1982.
With Ted Hughes. *The Rattle Bag: An Anthology of Poetry*. London/Boston: Faber and Faber, 1982.
With Rebecca James, Miles Graham, and Raphael Lyne. *The May Anthology of Oxford and Cambridge Poetry*. Oxford: Varsity/Cherwell, 1993.
With Ted Hughes. *The School Bag*. London: Faber and Faber, 1997.
W. B. Yeats: Poems Selected by Seamus Heaney. London: Faber and Faber, 2000.
The Essential Wordsworth. New York: Ecco Press, 1988. Published as *William Wordsworth: Poems Selected by Seamus Heaney*. London: Faber and Faber, 2001.

Letters

Heaney's letters are archived as part of the Seamus Heaney Papers, Stuart A. Rose Manuscript, Archives, Rare Books Library, Woodruff Library, Emory University in Atlanta, Georgia.

Poetry

Death of a Naturalist. London: Faber and Faber; New York: Oxford University Press, 1966.
Door into the Dark. London: Faber and Faber; New York: Oxford University Press, 1969.
Wintering Out. London: Faber and Faber, 1972; New York: Oxford University Press, 1973.
Stations (prose poems). Belfast: Ulsterman Publications, 1975.
North. London: Faber and Faber, 1975; New York: Oxford University Press, 1976.
Field Work. London: Faber and Faber, 1979; New York: Noonday, 1979.
Selected Poems 1965–1975. London: Faber and Faber, 1980; published as *Poems 1965–1975*. New York: Farrar, Straus and Giroux, 1980.
Station Island. London: Faber and Faber, 1984; New York: Farrar, Straus and Giroux, 1985.
The Haw Lantern. London: Faber and Faber; New York: Farrar, Straus and Giroux, 1987.
New Selected Poems 1966–1987. London: Faber and Faber, 1990; published as *Selected Poems 1966–1987*. New York: Farrar, Straus and Giroux, 1990.

Seeing Things. London: Faber and Faber; New York: Farrar, Straus and Giroux, 1991.
The Spirit Level. London: Faber and Faber; New York: Farrar, Straus and Giroux, 1996.
Opened Ground: Poems 1966–1996. London: Faber and Faber, 1998; published as *Opened Ground: Selected Poems 1966–1996*. New York: Farrar, Straus and Giroux, 1998.
Electric Light. London: Faber and Faber; New York: Farrar, Straus and Giroux, 2001.
District and Circle. London: Faber and Faber; New York: Farrar, Straus and Giroux, 2006.
Human Chain. London: Faber and Faber; New York: Farrar, Straus and Giroux, 2010.
New Selected Poems 1988–2013. London: Faber and Faber; published as *Selected Poems 1988–2013*. New York: Farrar, Straus and Giroux, 2014.

Poetry Pamphlets and Chapbooks

This list does not include the many broadsides and private cards printed for Heaney.

Eleven Poems. Belfast: Festival Publications, Queen's University of Belfast, 1965.
Room to Rhyme. With David Hammond and Michael Longley. Belfast: Arts Council of Northern Ireland, 1968.
The Island People. London: BBC, 1968.
A Lough Neagh Sequence. Ed. Harry Chambers and Eric J. Morten. Manchester: Phoenix Pamphlets Poets Press, 1969.
A Boy Driving His Father to Confession. Farnham: Sceptre Press, 1970.
Night Drive: Poems. Crediton: Richard Gilbertson, 1970.
Bog Poems. Illustrated by Barrie Cooke. London: Rainbow Press, 1975.
Four Poems. Illustrated by Margaret McCord. Belfast: Crannog Press, 1976.
Glanmore Sonnets. Illustrated by Cecil King. Hamburg: Edition Monika Beck, 1977.
With Derek Mahon. *In Their Element: A Selection of Poems*. Belfast: Arts Council of Northern Ireland, 1977.
After Summer. Illustrated by Timothy Engelland. Deerfield, MA: Deerfield Press; Dublin: Gallery Press, 1978.
The Family Album. Nottingham: Byron Press, 1979.
Gravities: A Collection of Poems and Drawings. Drawings by Noel Connor. Newcastle-upon-Tyne: Charlotte Press, 1979.
Hedge School: Sonnets from Glanmore. Illustrated by Claire Van Vliet. Portland: Charles Seluzicki, 1979.
Ugolino. Illustrated by Louis Le Brocquy. Dublin: Andrew Carpenter, 1979.
Toome. Illustrated by Jane Proctor. Dublin: National College of Art and Design, 1980.
Poems and a Memoir. Selected and illustrated by Henry Pearson and introduced by Thomas Flanagan with a preface by Heaney. New York: Limited Editions Club, 1982.

"Verse for a Fordham Commencement." New York: Fordham University, 1982; New York: Nadja, 1984.
An Open Letter. Derry: Field Day Theatre Pamphlets, 1983.
Hailstones. Dublin: Gallery Press, 1985.
Clearances. Amsterdam: Cornamona Press, 1986.
Towards a Collaboration. Illustrated by Felim Egam. Belfast: Arts Council of Northern Ireland, 1986.
Seamus Heaney. New York: Dia Art Foundation, 1988.
The Sounds of Rain. Atlanta: Shadowy Waters Press for Emory University, 1988.
With Michael Longley. *An Upstairs Outlook.* Belfast: Linen Hall Library, 1989.
Conlán. Selected Heaney poems translated into Irish by Gabriel Rosenstock. Dublin: Coiscéim, 1989.
With John Montague. *50/60.* Dublin: Poetry Ireland, 1990.
The Tree Clock. Belfast: Linen Hall Library, 1990.
Squarings. Dublin: Hieroglyph Editions, 1991.
The Gravel Walks. Hickory, NC: Shadowy Waters Press for Lenoir Rhyne College, 1992.
Keeping Going. Illustrated by Dimitri Hadzi. Adams House, Harvard University: Bow and Arrow Press for William Ewert Publisher, Concord, NH, 1993.
Audenesque. Paris: Maeght Éditeur, 1998.
Light of the Leaves. Mexico D.F.: Imprenta de los Tropicos; Banholt, Holland: In de Bonnefant, 1999.
Ballynahinch Lake. Ballynahinch Castle, Ireland, 1999.
A Shiver. Thame: Clutag Press, 2005.
The Riverbank Field. Loughcrew, Ireland: Gallery Press, 2007.

Prose Books

This list does not include the many separately published individual lectures or essays by Heaney.
Preoccupations: Selected Prose, 1968–1978. London: Faber and Faber; New York: Farrar, Straus and Giroux, 1980.
The Government of the Tongue: Selected Prose 1978–1987. London: Faber and Faber; New York: Farrar, Straus and Giroux, 1988.
The Place of Writing. Atlanta: Scholars Press, 1989.
The Redress of Poetry: Oxford Lectures. London: Faber and Faber; New York: Farrar, Straus and Giroux, 1995.
Crediting Poetry: The Nobel Lecture. London: Faber and Faber; New York: Farrar, Straus and Giroux; Loughcrew, Ireland: Gallery Press, 1995.
Finders, Keepers: Selected Prose 1971–2001. London: Faber and Faber; New York: Farrar, Straus and Giroux, 2002.

Recordings

With Hugh MacDiarmid, Sydney Goodsir Smith, Norman MacCaig, Iain Crichton Smith, Austin Clarke, Louis MacNeice. Series: "The Poet Speaks: Record 9." London: Argo Records, 1967.

With John Montague. *The Northern Muse*. Lloyd's International, Belfast for Claddagh Records, Dublin, 1968.

A Concert for Tom Delaney. London: Audio Arts Editions, 1980 of December 7, 1979 reading at the Ulster Museum, Belfast.

Seamus Heaney and Tom Paulin. Introduced by Craig Raine. London: Faber and Faber, 1983.

For Frances Horovitz—A Celebration of Poetry. London: TalkTapes, 1985.

Seamus Heaney at Harvard: Heaney Reads His Own and Poems of Dunbar, Wyatt, Raleigh, Shakespeare, Marvell, Blake, Wordsworth, Hardy, and Yeats. Cambridge, MA: Harvard College Library, 1990 of November 18, 1987 reading.

The Poet Speaks: A Twentieth-Century Anthology Read by the Poets. London: Argo/Polygram Records, 1995.

Stepping Stones: Selected Poems. London: Faber and Faber/Penguin Audiobooks, 1995.

The Spirit Level. London: Faber and Faber/Penguin Audiobooks, 1996.

Station Island. London: Faber and Faber/Penguin Audiobooks, 1997.

Beowulf. London: Faber and Faber/Penguin Audiobooks, 1999.

With Liam O'Flynn on Uilleann Pipes. *The Poet and the Piper*. Dublin: Claddagh Records, 2003.

Collected Poems [*Death of a Naturalist, Door into the Dark, Wintering Out, North, Field Work, Station Island, The Haw Lantern, Seeing Things, The Spirit Level, Electric Light*, and *District and Circle*.] Introduced by Peter Sirr. Dublin: RTÉ, 2009.

New Selected Poems 1988–2013. London: Faber and Faber, 2014.

Translations

Sweeney Praises the Trees. Illustrated by Henry Pearson. New York: Privately printed for Henry Pearson, 1981.

Sweeney Astray: A Version from the Irish. Londonderry/Derry, Northern Ireland: Field Day, 1983; New York: Farrar, Straus and Giroux, 1984. Revised edn, with photographs by Rachel Giese, published as *Sweeney's Flight*. Winston-Salem, NC: Wake Forest University Press, 1992.

The Golden Bough. Mexico D.F.: Imprenta de los Tropicos; Banholt, Netherlands: In de Bonnefant, 1990.

The Midnight Verdict. Translations from *Cúirt an Mheán Oíche* by Brian Merriman and from the *Metamorphoses* of Ovid. Loughcrew, Ireland: Gallery Press, 1993.

Kochanowski, Jan. *Laments*, trans. by Heaney and Stanisław Barańczak. London: Faber and Faber, 1995.

Poet to Blacksmith. Hoogeveen: The Netherlands, 1997.

Beowulf: A New Translation, London: Faber and Faber, 1999; *Beowulf: A Verse Translation*, ed. Daniel Donoghue, New York: Norton, 2000; published as *Beowulf: A New Verse Translation*, bilingual edition, New York: Farrar, Straus and Giroux, 2000; published as *Beowulf: An Illustrated Edition*, illustrations ed. by John D. Niles, Norton, 2008.

Diary of One Who Vanished: A Song Cycle by Leoš Janáček of Poems by Ozef

Kalda. London: Faber and Faber; New York: Farrar, Straus and Giroux, 2000.
Hallaig by Sorley McLean. Raasay, Scotland: *Urras Shomhairle*/The Sorley Maclean Trust, 2002.
Arion by Alexander Pushkin. San Francisco: Arion Press, 2002.
Columcille the Scribe. Dublin: Royal Irish Academy, 2004.
The Testament of Cresseid by Robert Henryson. London: Enitharmon, 2004.
The Testament of Cresseid and Seven Fables by Robert Henryson. London: Faber and Faber; New York: Farrar, Straus and Giroux, 2009.
The Last Walk: Translations from the Italian of Giovanni Pascoli, with paintings and drawings by Martin Gale. Loughcrew, Ireland: Gallery Press, 2013.
Aeneid: Book VI: A New Verse Translation. London: Faber and Faber. New York: Farrar, Straus and Giroux, 2016.

Annotated Bibliography of Selected Critical Books, Book Chapters, Interviews, and Essay Collections

Selected Secondary Criticism (Books Only)

Morrison, Blake. *Seamus Heaney*. London: Methuen, 1982.
  The best shorter study of Heaney's work until the critical studies by Corcoran and Vendler, it establishes important cultural, poetic, and historical contexts for his work.

Andrews, Elmer. *The Poetry of Seamus Heaney: All the Realms of Whisper*. London: Macmillan; New York: St. Martin's Press, 1988.
  Replete with solid close readings of the poetry from a veteran teacher and scholar.

Burris, Sidney. *The Poetry of Resistance: Seamus Heaney and the Pastoral Tradition*. Athens: Ohio University Press, 1990.
  The only critic to treat Heaney's engagement with the natural world extensively in a monograph until Russell's *Heaney's Regions* nearly twenty-five years later, Burris articulates the history of pastoral going back to its classical roots and situates Heaney's poetry in that and other, more contemporary pastoral contexts.

Hart, Henry. *Seamus Heaney: Poet of Contrary Progressions*. Syracuse: Syracuse University Press, 1992.
  The most sophisticated earlier study of Heaney, it argues for a Blakean reading of the poetry that proceeds by contraries and is especially helpful on the early poetry and the prose poems published as *Stations*.

Parker, Michael. *Seamus Heaney: The Making of the Poet*. University of Iowa Press; Dublin: Gill & Macmillan, 1993.
  Still the definitive early biography of the poet.

O'Donoghue, Bernard. *Seamus Heaney and the Language of Poetry*. Hemel Hempstead, England: Harvester Wheatsheaf, 1994.
  A penetrating account of Heaney's particular sense of language, including his use of Irish and Irish rhyme schemes, it remains the standard on the topic.

Molino, Michael. *Questioning Tradition, Language, and Myth: The Poetry of Seamus Heaney*. Washington, DC: Catholic University Press, 1994.
  A still-valuable guide to the poetry, comprehensive and well-argued.

Foster, John Wilson. *The Achievement of Seamus Heaney*. Dublin: Lilliput, 1995.

A brief but intellectually bracing account of Heaney's development by one of his earliest and best critics.

Corcoran, Neil. *The Poetry of Seamus Heaney: A Critical Study*. London: Faber and Faber, 1998.

A revised and much-expanded edition of his earlier *A Student's Guide to Seamus Heaney* (London: Faber and Faber, 1986), it is simply the best and most perspicacious introduction to Heaney's work through the mid-1990s. Along with convincing readings of many major poems, it also contains an authoritative chapter on Heaney's prose criticism and a very helpful biography.

Vendler, Helen. *Seamus Heaney*. Cambridge, MA: Harvard University Press, 1998.

A fine introduction to Heaney's work through the mid-1990s, offers stimulating close readings of emblematic poems but also their relevant cultural, political, and religious contexts.

Andrews, Elmer. *The Poetry of Seamus Heaney: Essays, Articles, Reviews*. New York: Columbia University Press; Cambridge: Icon Books, 1998.

A valuable reprinting of relevant secondary criticism with running commentary divided by topic.

Tobin, Daniel. *Passage to the Center: Imagination and the Sacred in the Poetry of Seamus Heaney*. Lexington: University of Kentucky Press, 1999.

A seminal book in Heaney studies because it takes seriously Heaney's spirituality by engaging both Derrida's notion of the center and Foucault's "return to origins" to show how Heaney often returns to the center as a sacred space.

O'Brien, Eugene. *Seamus Heaney and the Place of Writing*. Gainesville: University Press of Florida, 2002.

Argues powerfully for Heaney's aesthetic as inherently ethical in terms articulated by Derrida and Levinas.

Tyler, Meg. *A Singing Contest: Conventions of Sound in the Poetry of Seamus Heaney*. Studies in Major Literary Authors. New York: Routledge, 2005.

An under-appreciated study of the poet's acoustics by an accomplished poet-critic who worked under Vendler.

Desmond, John. *Gravity and Grace: Seamus Heaney and the Force of Light*. Studies in Christianity and Literature. Waco: Baylor University Press, 2009.

A compelling brief study, particularly in its employment of French philosopher Simone Weil to read Heaney theologically, but limited mainly to Heaney's *Seeing Things*.

Cavanagh, Michael. *Professing Poetry: Seamus Heaney's Poetics*. Washington, DC: Catholic University of America Press, 2009.

An excellent and thorough book on the topic—particularly good on Heaney's engagements with T. S. Eliot, Robert Lowell, Dante, Larkin, and Yeats.

McCarthy, Conor. *Seamus Heaney and Medieval Poetry*. Cambridge: D. S. Brewer, 2008.

The best treatment of the subject; particularly compelling on Heaney's use of Lough Derg's setting as the actual medieval site of Purgatory for *Station Island*.

Hall, Jason David. *Seamus Heaney's Rhythmic Contract*. New York: Palgrave, 2009.

The only such book of its kind—short but penetrating on rhythm and form.

Murphy, Andrew. *Seamus Heaney*. Writers and Their Work Series. Tavistock: Northcote House/British Council, 3rd edn, 2010.
   A judicious short overview of the work with helpful bibliographies of secondary criticism.
Kay, Magdalena. *In Gratitude for All the Gifts: Seamus Heaney and Eastern Europe*. Toronto: University of Toronto Press, 2012.
   The definitive treatment of the topic by a comparative literary scholar—with the exception of her neglect of Heaney's engagement with Miroslav Holub.
Russell, Richard Rankin. *Seamus Heaney's Regions*. Notre Dame: Notre Dame University Press, 2014.
   The first book on Heaney published after his death, it is also the most comprehensive, offering an account of the three interlinked "regions" of Heaney's work: the actual region of Northern Ireland, an imagined future region of harmony, and the spirit region. Also retrieves and explores many neglected works by Heaney, putting them in helpful contexts.
Dennison, John. *Seamus Heaney and the Adequacy of Poetry*. Oxford: Oxford University Press, 2015.
   A very thoughtful, reasoned consideration of Heaney's poetics through the issue of poetry's adequacy by an Anglican priest and poet who takes seriously how poetry became a sort of substitute for or "after-image" of religion for the poet.
O'Brien, Eugene. *Seamus Heaney as Aesthetic Thinker: A Study of the Prose*. Syracuse: Syracuse University Press, 2016.
   The first study to read Heaney's prose in the context of European aesthetics and critical theory, including the work of Heidegger, Adorno, Lacan, and Derrida.

Selected Chapters in Books

There are hundreds of essays on Heaney; this section simply lists and annotates several of the most influential book chapters on his work outside of the essay collections cited below.

Brown, Terence. "A Northern Renaissance: Poets from the North of Ireland 1965–1980." *Ireland's Literature: Selected Essays*. Mullingar: Lilliput Press; Totowa, NJ: Barnes & Noble, 1988, pp. 203–22. Originally published in a slightly different form as "An Ulster Renaissance: Poets from the North of Ireland." *Concerning Poetry* 14.2 (Fall 1981): 5–23.
   An early and discerning essay that rejects Thomas Kinsella's influential contention that a Northern Irish poetic renaissance was "largely a journalistic entity" (qtd on 203) and shows how the well-made poem exemplified by Philip Larkin's poetry flourished in the province since the mid-1960s yet was "charged" with a "tense astringency" by Heaney, Michael Longley, Derek Mahon, and Paul Muldoon that reinvigorated that type of poetry (215).
Longley, Edna. "*North*: 'Inner Emigré' or 'Artful Voyeur'?". Shorter version first published in *The Art of Seamus Heaney*, ed. Tony Curtis. Bridgend: Poetry Wales Press, pp. 65–95. *Poetry in the Wars*. Newcastle: Bloodaxe, 1986, pp. 140–69.
   A harsh (and unfair) attack on Heaney, focusing on *North* because it departs

from the earlier volumes' "hovering suggestiveness of thresholds" and "comes to or from political conclusions" (142). Insists that he neglects "the intersectarian issue, warfare between tribes, by concentrating on the Catholic psyche as bound to immolation, and within that immolation to savage tribal loyalties" (154).

Donoghue, Denis. "The Literature of Trouble." Abridged version published in *Hibernia*, May 11, 1978. *We Irish: Essays on Irish Literature and Society*. New York: Knopf, 1986, pp. 182–94.

A crucial essay written in the wake of the IRA murders of twelve people at the La Mon Hotel near Comber, County Down on February 17, 1978, treating responses to violence in Ireland by mainly Yeats and Heaney. Argues the reverse of Edna Longley's position and posits that Heaney's *North* gives us both the "consolation of hearing that there is a deeper, truer life going on beneath the bombings and torture" and "a present moment still in touch with its depth" (193) that "release the reader's mind from the immediacy of his experience" (194) at such moments as the La Mon bombing because of Heaney's archaeological perspectives on violence.

Deane, Seamus. "Seamus Heaney: The Timorous and the Bold." *Celtic Revivals: Essays in Modern Irish Literature*. London: Faber and Faber, 1985; Winston-Salem, NC: Wake Forest University Press, 1987, pp. 174–86.

Deane, a long-time friend of Heaney since St Columb's College and through their joint involvement in the Field Day Theatre Company, analyzes Heaney's work in the context of the continuing British imperial presence in Northern Ireland and Heaney's "Wordsworthian idea of poetry as a healing..." (176). Memorably suggests that Heaney "is indentured, finally, to the idea of poetry itself and is awed to see it become tactile as poems in his own hands" (175).

Coughlan, Patricia. "'Bog Queens': The Representation of Women in the Poetry of John Montague and Seamus Heaney." *Gender in Irish Writing*, ed. Toni O'Brien Johnson and David Cairns. Milton Keynes and Philadelphia: Open University Press, 1991, pp. 88–111.

A seminal feminist essay that holds Heaney's women are overly archetypal and stereotypical, stripped of agency and never role models as his rural masculine craftsmen are.

Lloyd, David. "'Pap for the Dispossessed': Seamus Heaney and the Poetics of Identity." *Anomalous States: Irish Writing and the Post-Colonial Moment*. Dublin: Lilliput Press; Durham, NC: Duke University Press, 1993, pp. 13–40.

A late deconstructionist argument, already dated by the time of its appearance, that draws on the work of Frantz Fanon and Antonio Gramsci to attack Heaney's use of mythology. Further argues, ignoring Heaney's dwelling on the condition of the wound, that his "poetic offers constantly a premature compensation, enacted through linguistic and metaphorical usages which promise a healing of division simply by returning the subject to place..." (20–1).

Ramazani, Jahan. "Seamus Heaney." *Poetry of Mourning: The Modern Elegy from Hardy to Heaney*. Chicago: University of Chicago Press, 1994, pp. 349–75.

Explores the bog poems from *North* in the context of the ethics of the elegy and while praising them, nonetheless observes that "To make sense of these atrocities, he risks making them seem sensible" (337).

McDonald, Peter. "Poetry, Narrative, and Violence." *Mistaken Identities:*

Poetry and Northern Ireland. Oxford: Oxford University Press, 1997, pp. 41–80.

A stirring defense of poetry's autonomy in the context of the Northern Irish conflict, it criticizes Heaney's "The Toome Road" for seeking coherence, but suggests later poems are more open to bewilderment and resist consoling narratives in their specificity—just as the best poetry from Northern Ireland by fellow poets such as Michael Longley and Ciaran Carson does.

Clark, Heather. "The Belfast Group." *The Ulster Renaissance: Poetry in Belfast, 1962–1972*. Oxford: Oxford University Press, 2006, pp. 43–71.

Offers the definitive account of Philip Hobsbaum's Belfast writing group that helped confirm and make Heaney as a poet.

O'Brien, Peggy. *Writing Lough Derg: From William Carleton to Seamus Heaney*. Syracuse: Syracuse University Press, 2006, pp. 153–257.

Helpfully situates Heaney's *Station Island* in a tradition of Irish writing about the Lough Derg pilgrimage going back to the nineteenth century. Contains four chapters on Heaney and terms his treatment of the pilgrimage the "most self-referential and intertextual" (153).

Russell, Richard Rankin. *Poetry and Peace: Michael Longley, Seamus Heaney, and Northern Ireland*. Notre Dame: Notre Dame University Press, 2010, pp. 1–43, 167–290, 291–9, 302–10.

Reads Heaney's work through literary singularity and recovers the ethical dimensions of beauty in it. Also shows how Heaney has imagined peace in the province.

Selected Interviews

Heaney himself has said he was probably over-interviewed; certainly he was one of the most interviewed writers ever. This list gives several of the most compelling of these interviews.

"Unhappy and at Home: Interview with Seamus Heaney by Seamus Deane." *New York Times Book Review* 84:48 (1979): 79–101; reprinted in *The Crane Bag Book of Irish Studies (1977–1981)*, ed. Mark Patrick Hederman and Richard Kearney. Dublin: Blackwater Press, 1982, pp. 66–72.

Likely the most important of Heaney's early interviews, conducted by Heaney's St Columb's classmate and fellow intellectual Deane, who was an important force for the Field Day Theatre Company and major critic.

"An Interview with Seamus Heaney." Conducted by James Randall. *Ploughshares* 5.3 (1979): 7–22.

Another important early interview with Heaney that is helpful in apprehending his own sense of the 1970s poetry especially.

"The Art of Poetry: Interview with Seamus Heaney." Interviewed by Henri Cole. *Paris Review* 75 (Fall 1997): 88–138.

A comprehensive and thoughtful interview, the longest conducted to that date.

Seamus Heaney in Conversation with Karl Miller. London: Between the Lines, 2000.

Important for Heaney's candor with Miller, an old friend.

Stepping Stones: Interviews with Seamus Heaney. Conducted by Dennis O'Driscoll.

London: Faber and Faber; New York: Farrar, Straus and Giroux, 2008.
The closest Heaney ever came to an autobiography, these interviews both cover familiar territory and break new ground in his revelations to his trusted friend, fellow poet, and critic.

Essay Collections

Broadbridge, Edward, ed. *Seamus Heaney*. Copenhagen: Denmark Radio, 1977.

Curtis, Tony, ed. *The Art of Seamus Heaney*. Bridgend: Poetry Wales, 1982; revised edn 1985; 3rd rev. edn 1994; 4th edn 2001. Chester Springs: Dufour Editions, 1985.

Bloom, Harold, ed. *Seamus Heaney*. New Haven, CT: Chelsea House, 1988.

Andrews, Elmer, ed. *Seamus Heaney: A Collection of Critical Essays*. London: Macmillan; New York: St. Martin's Press, 1992.

Garratt, Robert F., ed. *Critical Essays on Seamus Heaney*. New York and London: G. K. Hall, 1995.

Malloy, Catherine and Carey, Phyllis, eds. *Seamus Heaney: The Shaping Spirit*. Newark: University of Delaware Press; London: Associated University Presses, 1996.

Allen, Michael, ed. *Seamus Heaney*, Macmillan Casebook Series. London: Macmillan; New York: St. Martin's Press, 1997.

Crowder, Ashby Bland and Hall, Jason, eds. *Seamus Heaney: Poet, Critic, Translator*. Basingstoke: Palgrave, 2007.

O'Donoghue, Bernard, ed. *The Cambridge Companion to Seamus Heaney*. Cambridge: Cambridge University Press, 2009.

O'Brien, Eugene, ed. *"The Soul Exceeds Its Circumstances": The Later Poetry of Seamus Heaney*. Notre Dame: Notre Dame University Press, 2016.

Works Cited

Alighieri, Dante. *The Comedy of Dante Alighieri, The Florentine. Cantica II: Purgatory*, translated by Dorothy L. Sayers. London: Penguin, 1980 rept. of 1955 edn.
Anonymous. "Heaney deserves place among the pantheon, says Dorgan." http://www.irishtimes.com/culture/books/heaney-deserves-place-among-the-pantheon-says-dorgan-1.1510770 (last accessed August 30, 2013).
Auden, W. H. *Selected Poems*. Ed. Edward Mendelson. Expanded edition. New York: Vintage, 2007.
———. "Yeats as an Example." *The Complete Works of W. H. Auden: Prose, Vol. II*, ed. Edward Mendelson. Princeton: Princeton University Press, 2002, pp. 384–90.
Bleakney, Jean. "Gear and tackle and trim: *District and Circle*, Seamus Heaney." *Fortnight* 445 (June/July 2006): 29.
Boland, Eavan. "Seamus Heaney, 1939–2013." *The New Republic*, August 30, 2013. http://www.newrepublic.com/article/114560/obituary-seamus-heaney-1939-2013 (last accessed August 31, 2013).
Brandes, Rand. "Seamus Heaney's Working Titles." *The Cambridge Companion to Seamus Heaney*, ed. Bernard O'Donoghue. Cambridge: Cambridge University Press, 2009, pp. 19–36.
Brandes, Rand and Durkan, Michael J. *Seamus Heaney: A Bibliography, 1959–2003*. London: Faber and Faber, 2008.
Brewer, John D. and Higgins, Gareth I. *Anti-Catholicism in Northern Ireland, 1600–1998: The Mote and the Beam*. New York: St. Martin's Press, 1998.
Brodsky, Joseph. "Verses on the Death of T. S. Eliot." Trans. George L. Kline. *Russian Review* 27.2 (April 1968): 195–8.
Brown, Jeffrey. "Poet Seamus Heaney, 74, Explored the 'Wideness of Language.'" NewsHour, Public Broadcasting System, August 30, 2013. http://www.pbs.org/newshour/bb/remember-july-dec13-heaney_08-30/ (last accessed September 1, 2013).
Brown, Mark. "New Seamus Heaney Poem Published." *The Guardian*, October 25, 2013. http://www.theguardian.com/books/2013/oct/25/seamus-heaney-last-poem-published (last accessed October 26, 2013).
Brown, Terence. "Seamus Heaney's Tender Yeats." *Eire-Ireland* 49. 3–4 (Autumn/Winter 2014): 301–19.

Carey, John. "The Most Sensuous Poet to Use English since Keats." *Sunday Times*, April 3, 1998: G9.
Carson, Ciaran. "'Escaped from the Massacre?'" *The Honest Ulsterman* 50 (Winter, 1975): 183–6.
Casey, Edward. *Getting Back into Place*. Bloomington: Indiana University Press, 1993.
Chickering, Howell. "*Beowulf* and 'Heaneywulf': Review of *Beowulf*, translated by Seamus Heaney." *Kenyon Review* 24.1 (Winter 2002): 160–78.
Christie, Douglas E. *The Blue Sapphire of the Mind: Notes for a Contemplative Ecology*. Oxford: Oxford University Press, 2013.
Corcoran, Neil. *English Poetry since 1940*. London: Longman, 1993.
———. "The Melt of the Real Thing." *Irish Review*: "Seamus Heaney," 49–50 (Winter 2014/Spring 2015): 5–18.
———. *The Poetry of Seamus Heaney: A Critical Study*. London: Faber and Faber, 1998.
———. "Seamus Heaney Obituary." *The Guardian*, August 30, 2013. http://www.theguardian.com/books/2013/aug/30/seamus-heaney (last accessed August 30, 2013).
Crowder, Ashby Bland. "Seamus Heaney's Revisions for *Death of a Naturalist*." *New Hibernia Review* 19.2 (Summer 2015): 94–112.
Cunningham, John. *Lough Derg: Legendary Pilgrimage*. Monaghan, Ireland: R. and S. Printers, 1984.
de Bréadun, Deaglán. "Comfortable Image Belies the Serious Poet." *Irish Times*, September 13, 1984, p. 13.
Deane, Seamus. "The Artist and the Troubles." *Ireland and the Arts: A Literary Review Special Issue*, ed. by Tim Pat Coogan. London: Namara Press, 1983, pp. 42–50.
Delaney, Paul. *Brian Friel in Conversation*. Ann Arbor: University of Michigan Press, 2000.
Dennison, John. *Seamus Heaney and the Adequacy of Poetry*. Oxford: Oxford University Press, 2015.
Des Pres, Terrence. "Emblems of Adversity." *Harper's Magazine*, March 1, 1981, pp. 73–7.
Donne, John. *The Complete English Poems*. Ed. A. J. Smith. New York: Penguin, reprint of corrected 1976 edition with revised Further Reading, 1996.
Donoghue, Denis. "Teaching Literature: The Force of Form." *New Literary History* 30 (1999): 5–24.
Duffy, Eamon. "Seamus Heaney and Catholicism." *The Present Word: Culture, Society, and the Site of Literature: Essays in Honor of Nicholas Boyle*. Ed. John Walker. Oxford: Legenda, 2013, pp. 166–83.
———. *The Stripping of the Altars: Traditional Religion in England, 1400–1580*. 2nd edn. New Haven: Yale University Press, 2005.
Dunlop, John. *A Precarious Belonging: Presbyterians and the Conflict in Ireland*. Belfast: Blackstaff Press, 1995.
Durkan, Michael J. and Brandes, Rand. *Seamus Heaney: A Bibliography, 1959–2003*. London: Faber and Faber, 2008.
Eliade, Mircea. *Images and Symbols: Studies in Religious Symbolism*. Trans. Philip Mairet. Princeton: Princeton University Press, 1991 rpt. of 1952 edn.

———. *The Sacred and the Profane: The Nature of Religion.* Trans. Willard R. Trask. New York: Harcourt, Brace, &World, 1959.

Eliot, T. S. *Collected Poems 1909–1962.* San Diego, CA: Harcourt, 1991.

Fallon, Peter. "Conversation with Richard Rankin Russell." November 16, 2014. Ireland.

———. "[Editor's Note]." Seamus Heaney, *The Last Walk: Translations from the Italian of Giovanni Pascoli*, with paintings and drawings by Martin Gale. Loughcrew, Ireland: Gallery Press, 2013, n.p.

Ferriter, Diarmaid. *The Transformation of Ireland.* Woodstock, NY: Overlook Press, 2007.

Filkins, Peter. "*The Haw Lantern* by Seamus Heaney; *The Arkansas Testament* by Derek Walcott; *Archer in the Marrow* by Peter Viereck." *Iowa Review* 18.2 (Spring–Summer, 1988): 184–203.

Flood, Alison. "Seamus Heaney Chooses Two Poems to Sum Up His Lifetime Achievement." *The Guardian*, March 19, 2009. http://www.theguardian.com/books/2009/mar/19/david-cohen-seamus-heaney (last accessed June 10, 2009).

———. "Seamus Heaney's Last Poem Published in Irish Gallery's Anthology." *The Guardian*, October 3, 2014. http://www.theguardian.com/books/2014/oct/03/seamus-heaney-last-poem-national-gallery-ireland-anthology (last accessed October 14, 2014).

Foster, John Wilson. *The Achievement of Seamus Heaney.* Dublin: Lilliput Press, 1995.

———. "Seamus Heaney: *Electric Light.*" *Canadian Journal of Irish Studies* 27.2/28.1 (Fall, 2001/Spring, 2002): 117–20.

Foster, Roy. "Seamus Heaney Remembered." *The Observer*, August 31, 2013. http://www.theguardian.com/books/2013/sep/01/seamus-heaney-roy-foster-appreciation (last accessed September 1, 2013).

Frazier, Adrian. "Anger and Nostalgia: Seamus Heaney and the Ghost of the Father." *Eire-Ireland: A Journal of Irish Studies* 36.2 (Fall–Winter 2001): 7–38.

Gardner, W. H. "Introduction." *The Poems of Gerard Manley Hopkins.* 4th edn, revised and enlarged. Ed. W. H. Gardner and N. H. MacKenzie. Oxford: Oxford University Press, 1970, pp. xiii–lxvi.

Gillis, Alan. "Heaney's Legacy." *Irish Review*: "Seamus Heaney," 49–50 (Winter 2014/Spring 2015): 141–6.

Girard, René. *The Scapegoat.* Trans. Yvonne Freccero. Baltimore: Johns Hopkins University Press, 1986.

———. *Violence and the Sacred.* Trans. Patrick Gregory. Baltimore: Johns Hopkins University Press, 1977.

Greggs, Jeffrey. "Northern Transfusions." Review of Seamus Heaney, translator, Robert Henryson's *The Testament of Cresseid and Seven Fables.*" *New Criterion* 28.9 (May 2010): 74–6.

Griffin, Dan. "'When All the Others Were Away at Mass' Tops Favourite Poem Poll." *Irish Times*, March 11, 2015. http://www.irishtimes.com/culture/when-all-the-others-were-away-at-mass-tops-favourite-poem-poll-1.2135284 (last accessed March 15, 2015).

Halbertal, Moshe. *On Sacrifice.* Princeton: Princeton University Press, 2012.

Harrison, Stephen. "Virgilian Contexts." *A Companion to Classical Receptions.*

Ed. Lorna Hardwick and Christopher Stray. Malden, MA: Blackwell, 2011, pp. 113–26.

Hart, Henry. *Seamus Heaney: Poet of Contrary Progressions*. Syracuse: Syracuse University Press, 1992.

———. "Seamus Heaney and Ted Hughes: A Complex Friendship." *Sewanee Review* 120.1 (Winter 2012): 76–90.

Haughton, Hugh. "Seamus Heaney: First and Last Things." *Irish Review*: "Seamus Heaney," 49–50 (Winter 2014/Spring 2015): 194–207.

Heaney, Mick. "My Father's Famous Last Words." *Irish Times*, September 12, 2015. http://www.irishtimes.com/life-and-style/people/mick-heaney-my-father-s-famous-last-words-1.2348525 (last accessed September 13, 2015).

Heaney, Seamus. Commonly cited works are given in the Primary Bibliography.

———. "Above the Brim." *Homage to Robert Frost: Joseph Brodsky, Seamus Heaney, Derek Walcott*. New York: Farrar, Straus and Giroux, 1996, pp. 61–88.

———. "Anything Can Happen." *Anything Can Happen: A Poem and Essay by Seamus Heaney with Translations in Support of Art for Amnesty*. Dublin: TownHouse, 2004, pp. 8–18.

———. "[Appointment of Ted Hughes as Poet Laureate of Britain]." Springback notebook, containing manuscript and typescript drafts of poems and prose, n.d. Seamus Heaney Literary Papers, National Library of Ireland, MS 49,493/79.

———. "Aran." *Seamus Heaney: The Incertus Years*. The Pirate Press, 1985, p. 5. Seamus Deane Collection, Stuart A. Rose Manuscript, Archives, Rare Book Library, Emory University.

———. "Banks of a Canal." Alison Flood, "Seamus Heaney's Last Poem Published in Irish Gallery's Anthology." *The Guardian*, October 3, 2014. http://www.theguardian.com/books/2014/oct/03/seamus-heaney-last-poem-national-gallery-ireland-anthology (last accessed October 5, 2014).

———. "Belfast." *Preoccupations: Selected Prose 1968–1978*. London: Faber and Faber, 1980, pp. 28–37.

———. "Broadcast of *North* Poems: 6th June 1975." Manuscript draft of a script for a radio broadcast concerning the poetry collection "North," June 1975. Seamus Heaney Literary Papers, MS 49,493/46, National Library of Ireland.

———. "Canticles to the Earth: Theodore Roethke." *Preoccupations: Selected Prose 1968–1978*. London: Faber and Faber, 1980, pp. 190–4.

———. "Canto I," "Canto II," "Canto III." *Dante's Inferno: Translations by Twenty Contemporary Poets*, intro. by James Merrill and ed. Daniel Halpern. Afterword by Giuseppe Mazzotta. Hopewell, NJ: Ecco Press, 1993, pp. 3–6, 7–11, 12–15.

———. "Cessation—1994." *Finders, Keepers: Selected Prose 1971–2001*. New York: Farrar, Straus and Giroux, 2002, pp. 48–50.

———. "Civil rights, not civic weeks." *Gown*, Queen's University Belfast, October 22, 1968, n.p.

———. "The Convert." *Alpha*, June 8, 1989, p. 15.

———. "Counting to a Hundred: On Elizabeth Bishop." *The Redress of Poetry: Oxford Lectures*. London: Faber and Faber, 1995, pp. 164–85.

———. "Current Unstated Assumptions about Poetry." *Critical Inquiry* 7.4 (Summer 1981): 645–51.

———. "The Dapple-Grey Mare." *Peter Fallon: Poet, Publisher, Editor, and Translator*, ed. Richard Rankin Russell. Sallins, Ireland: Irish Academic Press, 2014, pp. 241–3.

———. "The Diviner." *Poetry Supplement*, Christmas, 1965, p. 5.

———. "The Door Stands Open: Czesław Miłosz, 1911–2004." *New Republic*, September 13 and 20, 2004, pp. 27–31.

———. "Du Bellay in Rome." *New England Review* 34.2 (2013): 7.

———. "Earning a Rhyme." *Finders, Keepers: Selected Prose, 1971–2001*. New York: Farrar, Straus and Giroux, 2002, pp. 63–70.

———. "Eclogues *in Extremis*: On the Staying Power of Pastoral." *Proceedings of the Royal Irish Academy* 103C.1 (2003): 1–12.

———. *Eleven Poems*. Belfast: Festival Publications, 1965.

———. "Envies and Identifications: Dante and the Modern Poet." *Irish University Review* 15.1 (Spring/Summer 1985): 5–19.

———. "Feeling into Words." *Preoccupations: Selected Prose 1968–1978*. London: Faber and Faber, 1980, pp. 41–60.

———. "From Monaghan to the Grand Canal: The Poetry of Patrick Kavanagh." *Preoccupations: Selected Prose 1968–1978*. London: Faber and Faber, 1980, pp. 115–30.

———. "Frontiers of Writing." *The Redress of Poetry: Oxford Lectures*. London: Faber and Faber, 1995, pp. 186–203.

———. "Funeral Elegy for Ted Hughes." Typescript. Seamus Heaney Papers, Stuart A. Rose Manuscript, Archives, and Rare Book Library, Emory University.

———. "The Government of the Tongue." *The Government of the Tongue: Selected Prose 1978–1987*. New York: Farrar, Straus and Giroux, 1988, pp. 91–108.

———. "A Greek Tragedy for Our Times." Interview with Eileen Battersby. *Irish Times*, April 3, 2004. http://www.irishtimes.com/news/a-greek-tragedy-for-our-times-1.1138235 (last accessed October 31, 2015).

———. "Heaney Tells of His Stroke Ordeal." Interview with Henry McDonald. *The Observer*, July 18, 2009. http://www.theguardian.com/books/2009/jul/19/seamusheaney-ireland (last accessed on August 14, 2009).

———. "On Home Ground." Address to Pascoli e l'immaginario degli italiani," Convegno Internazionale di Studi, Bologna, Italy, April 2–4, 2012. *Rivista Pascoliana* 24–25 (2012–13): 19–26.

———. "The Home Place: The Mud Vision." *Irish Times*, September 28, 2013. http://www.irishtimes.com/culture/the-home-place-the-mud-vision-seamus-heaney (last accessed September 28, 2013).

———. "In a Field." Mark Brown, "New Seamus Heaney Poem Published." *The Guardian*, October 25, 2013. http://www.theguardian.com/books/2013/oct/25/seamus-heaney-last-poem-published (last accessed October 26, 2013).

———. "The Indefatigable Hoof-taps: Sylvia Plath." *The Government of the Tongue: Selected Prose 1978–1987*. New York: Farrar, Straus and Giroux, 1988, pp. 148–70.

———. "Interview with Melvyn Bragg." ITV: *The South Bank Show*, October 1991.

———. "Interview with Michael Silverblatt." October 15, 1991. Lannan Literary Videos #27. Video-recording, 1991.

———. "An Interview with Seamus Heaney." Conducted by James Randall. *Ploughshares* 5.3 (1979): 7–22.

———. "An Interview with Seamus Heaney." Conducted by Eleanor Wachtel. *Brick Magazine* 86 (Winter 2011), n.p. http://brickmag.com/interview-seamus-heaney (last accessed December 31, 2015).

———. "Interview with Seamus Heaney." Conducted by J. J. Wylie and John C. Kerrigan. *Nua: Studies in Contemporary Irish Writing* 2.1–2 (Autumn 1998–Spring 1999): 125–37.

———. "Introduction." *Beowulf*, trans. Heaney. London: Faber and Faber, 1999, pp. ix–xxx.

———. "Introduction." *The Redress of Poetry: Oxford Lectures*. London: Faber and Faber, 1995, pp. xiii–xviii.

———. Introduction. *W. B. Yeats: Poems Selected by Seamus Heaney*. London: Faber and Faber, 2000, pp. xi–xxv.

———. "Introduction." *William Wordsworth: Poems Selected by Seamus Heaney*. London: Faber and Faber, 2001, pp. vii–xii.

———. "The Irish Quest." *The Guardian*, November 2, 1974, n.p.

———. "John Clare's Prog." *The Redress of Poetry: Oxford Lectures*. London: Faber and Faber, 1995, pp. 63–82.

———. "Joy or Night: Last Things in the Poetry of W. B. Yeats and Philip Larkin." *The Redress of Poetry: Oxford Lectures*. London: Faber and Faber, 1995, pp. 146–63.

———. "Joyce's Poetry." *Finders, Keepers: Selected Prose 1971–2001*. New York: Farrar, Straus and Giroux, 2002, pp. 422–4.

———. "King of the Dark." *The Listener*, February 5, 1970, pp. 181–2.

———. "The Latecomers." *Poetry Ireland Review*: Special Issue on Responses to Christ, "Name and Nature: 'Who Do You Say That I Am?'" 112 (2014): 122.

———. "Learning from Eliot." *Finders, Keepers: Selected Prose 1971–2001*. New York: Farrar, Straus and Giroux, 2002, pp. 28–41.

———. "Lenten Stuff." Unpublished holograph poem. Hardback notebook containing manuscript drafts of poems and some prose pieces, 1966–1972. Seamus Heaney Literary Papers, National Library of Ireland, MS 49,493/5.

———. "Letter to the *Irish News*." Qtd in David McKittrick, Seamus Kelters, Brian Feeney, Chris Thornton, and David McVea. *Lost Lives: The Stories of the Men, Women, and Children Who Died as a Result of the Northern Ireland Troubles*. Rev. and updated edn. Edinburgh: Mainstream, 2007, p. 1408.

———. "Letter to Richard Rankin Russell." December 23, 2012.

———. "Letter to Jon Stallworthy." March 6, 1980. "The Poet as Archaeologist: W. B. Yeats and Seamus Heaney." *Review of English Studies*, N.S., 33.130 (May, 1982): 158–74.

———. "A Life of Rhyme." Interview with Robert McCrum. *The Observer*, July 18, 2009. http://www.theguardian.com/books/2009/jul/19/seamus-heaney-interview (last accessed August 14, 2009).

———. "Lux Perpetua." *The Guardian*, June 16, 2001, Review, 9. Orig. published in *The Poetry Book Society Bulletin*, Summer 2001: 5–6.

———. "The Makings of a Music: Reflections on Wordsworth and Yeats." *Preoccupations: Selected Prose 1968–1978*. London: Faber and Faber, 1980, pp. 61–78.

———. "The Man and the Bog." Opening Speech to the Exhibition of Bog Bodies: "Face to Face with Your Past," Silkeborg Museum, Denmark, August 2, 1996. Seamus Heaney Papers, Stuart A. Rose Manuscript, Archives, Rare Book Library, Emory University.

———. "Meeting Seamus Heaney: An Interview." Conducted by John Haffenden. *Viewpoints: Poets in Conversation with John Haffenden*. London: Faber and Faber, 1981, pp. 57–75.

———. "From Monaghan to the Grand Canal: The Poetry of Patrick Kavanagh." *Preoccupations: Selected Prose 1968–1978*. London: Faber and Faber, 1980, pp. 115–30.

———. "Mother Ireland." *The Listener*, December 7, 1972, p. 790.

———. "New Staves." *Threepenny Review* 79 (Autumn 1999): 6–7.

———. "The North: Silent Awarenesses with Seamus Heaney." Interview with Monie Begley. Begley, *Rambles in Ireland and a County-by-County Guide for Discriminating Travelers*. Old Greenwich, CT: Devin-Adair, 1977, pp. 159–70.

———. "A Note on *The Burial at Thebes*." *The Burial at Thebes: A Version of Sophocles' Antigone*. New York: Farrar, Straus and Giroux, 2004, pp. 75–8.

———. "October Thought." *Seamus Heaney: The Incertus Years*. The Pirate Press, 1985, p. 3. Seamus Deane Collection, Stuart A. Rose Manuscript, Archives, Rare Book Library, Emory University.

———. "Old Derry's Walls." *The Listener*, October 24, 1968, pp. 521–3.

———. "Orpheus and Eurydice." *The Midnight Verdict*. Translations from the Irish of Brian Merriman and from the *Metamorphoses* of Ovid. Loughcrew, Ireland: Gallery Press, 1993, pp. 11–19.

———. "Out of London: Ulster's Troubles." *New Statesman*, July 1, 1966, pp. 23–4.

———. "PENAL STATIONS" Sketch. Hardback notebook containing manuscript drafts of poems and some prose pieces, 1966–1972. Seamus Heaney Literary Papers, National Library of Ireland, MS 49,493/5.

———. *Place and Displacement: Recent Poetry of Northern Ireland*. Grasmere, England: Trustees of Dove Cottage, August 2, 1984.

———. "Place, Pastness, Poems: A Triptych." *Salmagundi*: "The Literary Imagination and the Sense of the Past," 68–9 (Fall 1985–Winter 1986): 30–47.

———. "The Poet as a Christian." *The Furrow* 29.10 (October 1978): 603–6.

———. "A Poet's Childhood." *The Listener*, November 11, 1971, pp. 660–1.

———. "The Poet's Perspective." Interview conducted by Adam Kirsch. *Harvard Magazine*, November–December, 2006. http://harvardmagazine.com/2006/11/the-poets-perspective-html (last accessed December 12, 2015).

———. "Preface." *The Penguin Book of Irish Poetry*. Ed. Patrick Crotty. New York: Penguin Classics, 2010, pp. xliii–xlvi.

———. "Reading at Baylor University." Baylor University, Waco, Texas, March 4, 2013. http://www.baylor.edu/beall/index.php?id=93429 (last accessed October 24, 2014).

———. "Reaping in Heat." *Seamus Heaney: The Incertus Years*. The Pirate Press, 1985, p. 3. Seamus Deane Collection, Stuart A. Rose Manuscript, Archives, Rare Book Library, Emory University.

———. "The Redress of Poetry." *The Redress of Poetry: Oxford Lectures*. London: Faber and Faber, 1995, pp. 1–16.

———. "The Regional Forecast." *The Literature of Region and Nation*, ed. R. P. Draper. New York: St. Martin's Press, 1989, pp. 10–23.

———. *The Riverbank Field*. Loughcrew, Ireland: Gallery Press, 2007.

———. "Seamus Heaney." *Desert Island Discs*. BBC Radio 4, November 19, 1989. http://www.bbc.co.uk/radio4/features/desert-island-discs/castaway/8b fd36b2 (last accessed November 11, 2014).

———. "Seamus Heaney." *Metre* 3 (1997): 15–16.

———. "Seamus Heaney." *Reading the Future: Irish Writers in Conversation with Mike Murphy*. Ed. Clíodhna Ní Anluain. Dublin: Lilliput Press, 2000, pp. 81–97.

———. "Seamus Heaney's 70th Birthday Speech." April 13, 2009. http://www.youtube.com/watch?v=kcBq2ULmsw (last accessed June 10, 2014).

———. "Seamus Heaney Writes . . ." *The Poetry Book Society Bulletin*, Summer 1969, 1.

———. "The Sense of Place." *Preoccupations: Selected Prose 1968–1978*. London: Faber and Faber, 1980, pp. 131–49.

———. "Sixth Sense, Seventh Heaven." *Dublin Review* 8 (Autumn 2002): 115–26.

———. "Small Fantasia for W. B." *Times Literary Supplement*, January 27–February 2, 1989, p. 76.

———. "Something to Write Home About." *Finders, Keepers: Selected Prose 1971–2001*. New York: Farrar, Straus and Giroux, 2002, pp. 51–62.

———. *Station Island* Notebook. Hardback minute book containing drafts and notes relating to the composition of poems collected in "Station Island," 1968–1983. Seamus Heaney Literary Papers, National Library of Ireland, MS 49,493/57.

———. "The Strand at Lough Beg." *Threshold* 30 (Spring 1979): 34–5.

———. "Suffering and Decision." *Ted Hughes: From Cambridge to Collected*. Ed. Mark Wormald, Neil Roberts, and Terry Gifford. New York: Palgrave, 2013, pp. 221–37.

———. ["Talk on Field Day."] Incomplete manuscript draft of a speech concerning both the Field Day Theatre Company and W. B. Yeats, n.d. Seamus Heaney Literary Papers, MS 49,493/155, National Library of Ireland.

———. "Time and Again: Poetry and the Millennium." *European English Messenger* 10.2 (2001): 19–23.

———. "Title Deeds: Translating a Classic." *Proceedings of the American Philosophical Society* 148.4 (December 2004): 411–26.

———. "Translator's Note." *The Midnight Verdict*. Loughcrew, Ireland: Gallery Press, rev. paperback edn [1993], 2000, p. 11.

———. Typescript note appended to "October Thought," 1959. Springback notebook containing manuscript and typescript drafts of poems and prose, n.d. Seamus Heaney Literary Papers, MS 49,493/79, National Library of Ireland.

———. "Unidentified Fragments." Seamus Heaney Papers, Stuart A. Rose Manuscript, Archives, Rare Book Library, Emory University.

———. "Verses for a Fordham Commencement." New York: Fordham University, May 23, 1982. http://fordhamnotes.blogspot.com/2013/08/seamus-heaneys-verses-for-fordham.html (last accessed September 1, 2013).

———. "The Whole Thing: On the Good of Poetry." *The Recorder: A Journal of the American Irish Historical Society* 15.1 (Spring 2002): 5–20.

———. "Worksheets for 'Funeral Rites,' 'Punishment,' 'Act of Union,' 'A Constable Calls.'" *Quarto: Magazine of the Literary Society of the New University of Ulster* 2.1 (November 1975): 3–17. Seamus Heaney Papers, Stuart A. Rose Manuscript, Archives, Rare Book Library, Emory University.

———. "Writer and Righter." Fourth Irish Human Rights Commission Annual Human Rights Lecture, December 9, 2009. Dublin: Irish Human Rights Commission, 2010.

———. "Writer at Work." *The Honest Ulsterman* 8 (December, 1968): 13–14.

———. "Yeats as an Example?". *Preoccupations: Selected Prose 1968–1978*. London: Faber and Faber, 1980, pp. 98–114.

———. "Yeats's Nobility." *Four Quarters* 3.2 (1989): 11–14.

———. "III." [Originally the third lyric in an early draft of "Station Island."] Manuscript and typescript drafts of poems for possible inclusion in the collection "Station Island," ca. 1982. Seamus Heaney Literary Papers, MS 49,493/68, National Library of Ireland.

——— and Hass, Robert. *Sounding Lines: The Art of Translating Poetry*. Ed. Christina M. Gillis. Occasional Papers Series No. 20. Berkeley: Doreen B. Townsend Center for the Humanities, University of California, Berkeley, 2000.

Hecht, Anthony. "Knowing the Score: Rev. of *Finders, Keepers: Selected Prose 1971–2001* by Seamus Heaney." *New York Review of Books*, December 5, 2002. http://www.nybooks.com/articles/archives/2002/dec/05/knowing-the-score/ (last accessed September 15, 2013).

Heidegger, Martin. *On the Way to Language*. Trans. Peter D. Hertze and Joan Stambaugh. New York: Harper, 1971.

Heiny, Stephen. "Virgil in Seamus Heaney's *Human Chain*: 'Images and Symbols Adequate to Our Predicament.'" *Renascence* 65.4 (Summer 2013): 305–18.

"Helicon." *Oxford English Dictionary* Online.

Higgins, Charlotte and Henry McDonald. "Seamus Heaney's death 'leaves breach in language itself.'" *The Guardian*, August 30, 2013. http://www.theguardian.com/books/2013/aug/30/seamus-heaney-death-breach-language (last accessed September 3, 2013).

Holy Bible. King James Version. Nashville: Thomas Nelson, 1977.

Holy Bible. New King James translation. Nashville: Thomas Nelson, 1982.

Homem, Rui Carvalho. *Poetry and Translation in Northern Ireland: Dislocations in Contemporary Writing*. New York: Palgrave, 2009.

Hopkins, Gerard Manley. *The Poems of Gerard Manley Hopkins*. Ed. W. H. Gardner and N. H. MacKenzie. 4th edn, revised and enlarged. Oxford: Oxford University Press, 1970.

Hughes, Ted. "To Seamus Heaney." October 8, 1989. *Letters of Ted Hughes*. Selected and ed. Christopher Reid. New York: Farrar, Straus and Giroux, 2007, pp. 564–5.

Jantzen, Grace M. *Violence to Eternity: Death and the Displacement of Beauty*. Vol. 2. Ed. Jeremy Carrette and Morny Joy. New York: Routledge, 2009.
Joyce, James. *Finnegans Wake*. Ed. Robbert-Jan Henkes, Erik Bindervoet, and Finn Fordham. Oxford: Oxford University Press, 2012.
Kavanagh, Patrick. "The Parish and the Universe." *Collected Pruse*. London: Macgibbon & Kee, 1967, pp. 281–3.
Keats, John. "Letter of December 22, 1818 to George and Tom Keats." *Selected Letters of John Keats*. Ed. Grant F. Scott. Rev. edn. Cambridge, MA: Harvard University Press, 2002, pp. 59–61.
———. *The Poems of John Keats*. Ed. Jack Stillinger. Cambridge, MA: Harvard University Press, 1978.
Kiberd, Declan. *Synge and the Irish Language*. Totowa, NJ: Rowman & Littlefield, 1979.
Laxton, Edward. *The Famine Ships: The Irish Exodus to America*. New York: Henry Holt, 1996.
Lowell, Robert. *Collected Poems*. Ed. Frank Bidart and David Gewanter. New York: Farrar, Straus and Giroux, 2003.
Lytle, Ellen W. "It's a Wrap." Review of Seamus Heaney's *The Burial at Thebes*, LaMaMa, New York City, dir. Alexander Harrington. *New York Theatre Wire*, February 6, 2007. http://www.nytheatre-wire.com/el07011t.htm (last accessed October 31, 2015).
McConnell, Gail. "Catholic Art and Culture: Clarke to Heaney." *The Oxford Handbook of Modern Irish Poetry*. Ed. Fran Brearton and Alan Gillis. Oxford: Oxford University Press, 2012, pp. 437–55.
McDonald, Peter. "The Clutch of Earth." Review of *Electric Light*. *Literary Review* 331, April 2006, n.p. https://literaryreview.co.uk/the-clutch-of-earth (last accessed November 15, 2014).
———. "Heaney's Implications." *Irish Review*: "Seamus Heaney," 49–50 (Winter 2014/Spring 2015): 71–89.
———. *Mistaken Identities: Poetry and Northern Ireland*. Oxford: Oxford University Press, 1997.
———. "The Poet and 'The Finished Man': Heaney's Oxford Lectures." *Irish Review* 19.1 (Spring/Summer 1996): 98–108.
McGrath, Alister. *The Reenchantment of Nature: The Denial of Religion and the Ecological Crisis*. New York: Doubleday, 2002.
McGuckian, Medbh. *Horsepower Pass By! A Study of the Car in the Poetry of Seamus Heaney*. Coleraine: Cranagh Press, 1999.
McKittrick, David, Kelters, Seamus, Feeney, Brian, Thornton, Chris and McVea, David. *Lost Lives: The Stories of the Men, Women, and Children Who Died as a Result of the Northern Ireland Troubles*. Rev. and updated edn. Edinburgh: Mainstream, 2007.
Marlowe, Lara. "The End of Yeats: Work and Women in His Last Days in France." *Irish Times*, January 28, 2014. http://www.irishtimes.com/culture/the-end-of-yeats-work-and-women-in-his-last-days-in-france-1.1669759 (last accessed January 29, 2014).
Martens, Lorna. *The Promise of Memory: Childhood Recollection and Its Objects in Literary Modernism*. Cambridge, MA: Harvard University Press, 2011.

Massie, Alan. "Seamus Heaney Was the Greatest Irish Poet since Yeats, and a Nicer Man." *Daily Telegraph*, September 1, 2013. http://blogs.telegraph.co.uk/culture/allanmassie/100070512/seamus-heaney-was-the-greatest-irish-poet-since-yeats-and-a-nicer-man-than-yeats/ (last accessed on September 1, 2013).

Mendelson, Edward. "Digging Down." Review of Seamus Heaney, *Opened Ground: Selected Poems 1966–1996* and of Helen Vendler, *Seamus Heaney*. New York Review of Books, December 20, 1998. https://www.nytimes.com/books/98/12/20/reviews/981220.20mendelt.html (last accessed November 21, 2015).

Meyer, Robinson. "How So Many People Got Seamus Heaney's Last Words Wrong." *The Atlantic*, September 4, 2013. http://www.theatlantic.com/technology/archive/2013/09/how-so-many-people-got-seamus-heaneys-last-words-wrong/279330/ (last accessed November 4, 2013).

Milton, John. *The Complete Poetry of John Milton*, ed., intro., notes, and variants by John T. Shawcross. New York: Doubleday, 1971.

Molino, Michael. *Questioning Tradition, Language, and Myth: The Poetry of Seamus Heaney*. Washington, DC: Catholic University of America Press, 1994.

Monroe, Jonathan. *A Poverty of Objects: The Prose Poem and the Politics of Genre*. Ithaca: Cornell University Press, 1987.

Morrison, Danny. "In the Simplicity of His Defiance—Kieran Nugent." http://www.dannymorrison.com/wp-content/dannymorrisonarchive/085.htm (last accessed December 12, 2015).

Muldoon, Paul. "Paul Muldoon on Seamus Heaney: The Mark of a Great Poet." *Daily Beast*, August 30, 2013. http://www.thedailybeast.com/articles/2013/08/30/paul-muldoon-on-seamus-heaney-the-mark-of-a-great-poet.html (last accessed September 2, 2013).

"The Nobel Prize in Literature 1995." http://www.nobelprize.org/nobel_prizes/literature/laureates/1995/ (last accessed November 27, 2015).

O'Brien, Brendan. *The Long War: The IRA and Sinn Féin*. Syracuse: Syracuse University Press, 2nd rev. edn, 1999.

O'Brien, Eugene. "'Any Catholics among you . . .?': Seamus Heaney and the Real of Catholicism." *Breaking the Mould: Literary Representations of Irish Catholicism*. Ed. Eamon Maher and Eugene O'Brien. Oxford: Peter Lang, 2011, pp. 159–77.

O'Brien, Peggy. *Writing Lough Derg: From William Carleton to Seamus Heaney*. Syracuse: Syracuse University Press, 2006.

O'Donoghue, Bernard. *Seamus Heaney and the Language of Poetry*. Hemel Hempstead: Harvester Wheatsheaf, 1994.

O'Donoghue, Heather. "Review of Seamus Heaney, *Beowulf: A New Translation*." Translation and Literature 9.2 (2000): 231–6.

O'Driscoll, Dennis. "Seamus Heaney: 'The Biretta.'" *Troubled Thoughts, Majestic Dreams: Selected Prose Writings*. Loughcrew, Ireland: Gallery Press, 2001, pp. 142–9.

O'Neill, Charles L. "Violence and the Sacred in Seamus Heaney's *North*." *Seamus Heaney: The Shaping Spirit*. Ed. Catharine Malloy and Phyllis Carey. Newark: University of Delaware Press, 1996, pp. 91–105.

O'Toole, Fintan. "Echoes of Violence in a Rural Idyll Revisited." *Irish*

Times, October 26, 2013. http://www.irishtimes.com/culture/books/echoes-of-violence-in-a-rural-idyll-revisited-1.1573720 (last accessed October 27, 2013).

Owen, Wilfred. *The Poems of Wilfred Owen*. Ed. Jon Stallworthy. New York: Norton, 1986.

Parker, Michael. *Seamus Heaney: The Making of the Poet*. Iowa City: University of Iowa Press, 1993.

Paulin, Tom. "Political Anxiety and Allusion: Seamus Heaney." *Crusoe's Secret: The Aesthetics of Dissent*. London: Faber and Faber, 2005, pp. 349–73.

Piering, Julie. "Diogenes of Sinope (*c*.404–323 B.C.E.)." *Internet Encyclopedia of Philosophy*. http://www.iep.utm.edu/diogsino/ (last accessed December 22, 2014).

Potts, Robert. "The View from Olympia." Review of *Electric Light*. *The Guardian*, April 7, 2001. http://www.theguardian.com/books/2001/apr/07/poetry.tseliotprizeforpoetry2001 (last accessed September 14, 2014).

"Publisher's Note." *Seamus Heaney: New Selected Poems 1988–2013*. London: Faber and Faber, 2014, p. v.

Rafferty, Oliver P. *Catholicism in Ulster, 1603–1983: An Interpretative History*. Dublin: Gill & Macmillan, 1994.

Regan, Stephen. "Seamus Heaney and the Modern Irish Elegy." *Seamus Heaney: Poet, Critic, Translator*. Ed. Ashby Bland Crowder and Jason David Hall. New York: Palgrave, 2007, pp. 9–25.

Ricks, Christopher. "Lasting Things." Review of Seamus Heaney's *Door into the Dark*. *The Listener*, June 26, 1969, pp. 900–1.

Ricœur, Paul. *Memory, History, Forgetting*. Trans. Kathleen Blamey and David Pellauer. Chicago: Chicago University Press, 2004.

Rowse, Christopher. "Why Seamus Heaney's Last Words Weren't the Last Laugh." *Daily Telegraph*, September 3, 2013. http://www.telegraph.co.uk/culture/books/10283710/Why-Seamus-Heaneys-last-words-werent-the-last-laugh.html (last accessed September 3, 2013).

Russell, Richard Rankin. "'Deep down Things': The Inner Lives of Things in Later Heaney." *The Soul Exceeds Its Circumstances: Essays on the Later Poetry of Seamus Heaney*. Ed. Eugene O'Brien. Notre Dame: Notre Dame University Press, 2016, pp. 239–60.

———. "The Keats and Hopkins Dialectic in Seamus Heaney's Early Poetry: 'The Forge.'" *ANQ* 25.1 (January–March 2012): 44–50.

———. *Poetry and Peace: Michael Longley, Seamus Heaney, and Northern Ireland*. Notre Dame: Notre Dame University Press, 2010.

———. *Seamus Heaney's Regions*. Notre Dame: Notre Dame University Press, 2014.

Seamus Heaney: Out of the Marvelous. Documentary. Dir. Charlie McCarthy. Prod. Clíona Ní Bhuachalla. Dublin: Icebox Films Production for RTÉ Television, 2009.

"Seamus Heaney Poem Chosen as Ireland's Best-Loved." *Irish Times*, March 11, 2015. http://www.rte.ie/news/2015/0311/686370-poem/ (last accessed November 27, 2015).

Scruton, Roger. "The Sacred and the Human." *Prospect Magazine* 137, August 2007. http://www.prospectmagazine.co.uk/features/roger-scruton-on-religion (last accessed November 17, 2014).

Shippey, Thomas. "*Beowulf* for the Big-Voiced Scullions." *Times Literary Supplement*, October 1, 1999, pp. 9–10.
Shakespeare, William. *Complete Works of William Shakespeare*. Glasgow: Collins Classics, 1994.
Shelley, Percy Bysshe. "A Defence of Poetry." *Shelley's Poetry and Prose*. Selected and ed. by Donald H. Reiman and Sharon B. Powers. New York: W. W. Norton, 1977, pp. 478–508.
Sidney, Sir Philip. *An Apology for Poetry or The Defence of Poesy*. Ed. Geoffrey Shepherd. London: Thomas Nelson, 1967.
Simmons, Paulanne. "A Familiar Tragedy." Review of Seamus Heaney's *The Burial at Thebes*, LaMaMa, New York City, dir. Alexander Harrington. *New York Theatre Wire*, February 6, 2007. http://www.nytheatre-wire.com/el07011t.htm (last accessed October 31, 2015).
Sperry, Stuart M. *Keats the Poet*. Princeton: Princeton University Press, 1994. Rpt. of 1974 edn. Bloomington: Indiana University Press.
Stallworthy, Jon. "The Poet as Archaeologist: W. B. Yeats and Seamus Heaney." *Review of English Studies*, NS, 33.130 (May, 1982): 158–74.
Stevens, Wallace. *The Collected Poems of Wallace Stevens*. New York: Vintage, 1982.
Tobin, Daniel. *Passage to the Center: Imagination and the Sacred in the Poetry of Seamus Heaney*. Lexington: University of Kentucky Press, 1999.
"Tourbillon." *OED* online.
"Turfman Piece Marks Heaney Poem." BBC News, April 2, 2009. http://news.bbc.co.uk/2/hi/uk_news/northern_ireland/7980136.stm (last accessed April 3, 2009).
Tyler, Meg. *A Singing Contest: Conventions of Sound in the Poetry of Seamus Heaney*. New York: Routledge, 2005.
Vendler, Helen. *Seamus Heaney*. Cambridge, MA: Harvard University Press, 1998.
Virgil. *The Aeneid*. Trans. Robert Fitzgerald. New York: Vintage, 1983.
Weir, John. "The Troubles I've Seen." *Harper's Magazine*, September 1999, pp. 30–5.
Welch, Robert. "Sacrament and Significance: Some Reflections on Religion and the Irish": "The Endless Knot: Literature and Religion in Ireland," *Religion and Literature* 28.2–3 (Summer–Autumn 1996): 101–13.
Wheatley, David. "Professing Poetry: Heaney as Critic." *The Cambridge Companion to Seamus Heaney*. Ed. Bernard O'Donoghue. Cambridge: Cambridge University Press, 2009, pp. 122–35.
———. "Seamus Heaney, *New Selected Poems 1966–1987* and *New Selected Poems 1988-2013*." *The Guardian*, December 12, 2014. http://www.theguardian.com/books/2014/dec/12/seamus-heaney-new-selected-poems-1966-1987-1988-2013-review (last accessed December 15, 2015).
Woodham-Smith, Cecil. *The Great Hunger: Ireland, 1845–1849*. New York: Harper & Row, 1962.
Wordsworth, William. *William Wordsworth: Selected Poems*, ed. John O. Hayden. London: Penguin, 1994.
Wordsworth, William and Coleridge, Samuel Taylor. Preface to *Lyrical Ballads*, with *Pastoral and Other Poems* [1802]. *William Wordsworth: Selected Poems*, ed. John O. Hayden. London: Penguin, 1994, pp. 431–59.

Yeats, W. B. *The Collected Poems of W. B. Yeats: A New Edition.* Ed. Richard J. Finneran. New York: Macmillan, 1989.

Young, Kevin. "Handkerchief Sandwich." Poetry Society of America. http://www.poetrysociety.org/psa/poetry/crossroads/on_poetry/poets_on_form_kevin_young/ (last accessed April 12, 2015).

Index

1798 Rebellion, 52–3, 240

Abbey Theatre, 243, 245
Aeschylus, 166
Afghanistan, 246
Alighieri, Dante, 8, 18, 21, 46, 91, 92, 106, 107, 108–9, 111, 112, 116–17, 118, 122, 127, 138n7, 142–3, 144, 147, 152, 159, 165, 185, 203, 213, 217, 219, 220, 224–5, 226, 227, 234, 240, 247, 258n43
alliteration, 30, 35, 43, 192, 217, 242, 248, 250, 252
Amnesty International, 191, 246
Anahorish, 1, 7, 12, 58–9, 182, 218, 219–20
Anglo-Saxon, 35–6, 86n23, 103, 166, 173, 181–4, 192, 248–52
Anouilh, Jean, 246
Aquinas, Thomas, 154
Aran Islands, 30–1, 32, 180, 214
Aristotle, 154
Armagh, 7, 92, 95, 218
Armstrong, Sean, 107
Auden, W. H., 5, 22, 23–4, 25, 28n64, 70, 86n28, 168, 181, 184–5, 189n65, 229n3, 229n8, 237

Barańczak, Stanisław, 248
BBC, 16, 103, 240, 257n24
Beckett, Samuel, 20, 152
Belfast, 11, 13, 14–15, 16, 17, 18, 32, 44–5, 52, 53, 55, 58, 84, 109, 116, 165, 175, 186, 213, 215, 234, 243
Belfast Festival, 15, 32
Belfast Group, 14–15, 47
Bellaghy, 1, 7, 22, 25, 36, 118, 119, 175, 178, 190, 207, 215

Bellaghy Dramatic Society, 240
Berryman, John, 194
biblical allusion/inspiration, 24–5, 44, 48, 60–1, 66, 75, 77–9, 112, 117, 121, 126–7, 141n77, 145–6, 149, 157, 159, 161–3, 164, 175, 176, 199, 200–1, 208, 216, 223, 226–7, 228, 230n30, 237
birth imagery, 46–7, 48, 49, 62, 174, 175–7, 216
Bishop, Elizabeth, 49–50, 105
Bleakney, Jean, 230n12
Brandes, Rand, 76, 85n14
Breen, Bobby, 193
Brewer, John D., and Gareth I. Higgins, 87n44
Broagh, 1, 58–9
Brodsky, Joseph, 173, 184–5, 189n63, 196, 229n8
Brown, Jeffrey, 86n32
Brown, Sean, 177–8
Brown, Terence, 22, 105
Brueghel, 70
Bush, George W., 244–7, 257n32

caesura, 35, 43, 101, 150, 155, 164, 173, 176, 183, 184, 192, 248
Caillebotte, Gustave, 222–3
Carleton, William, 109, 113, 114–16, 122, 140n46
Carson, Ciaran, 15, 64, 69
Casey, Edward, 210–11
Catholic community/Catholic minority, 2, 4, 6, 7, 11–12, 13, 14, 15–16, 20, 32, 45, 52, 53, 55, 57, 59, 61–2, 65, 76–7, 79, 80, 81, 82, 83, 87n44, 90, 92, 93, 98, 99, 107, 108, 109, 114, 117, 119, 122–3,

131–2, 135, 154, 156, 175–6, 177, 178, 214, 240, 243, 251
Catholicism, 11, 61–2, 71, 77, 103, 108, 115, 128, 136, 138, 148, 151
  sacrament, 11, 44, 114
Cavanagh, Michael, 139n39, 234–5
Chaucer, Geoffrey, 186
Chickering, Howell, 252
Christie, Douglas E., 163
Church Island, 93–5
Clare, John, 230n13
Clinton, William, 21, 24
Coleridge, Samuel Taylor, 154, 197, 238
Corcoran, Neil, 1, 3, 10, 26n2, 56, 88n99, 107, 113, 131, 140n63, 142, 203, 234, 237
Crowder, Ashby Bland, 86n29
Cuchullain/Cuchulain, 96, 218, 226

Davies, John, 59
de la Cruz, Juan,/St John of the Cross, 121, 127
Deane, Seamus, 12, 30, 110
Delaney, Tom, 118
Dennison, John, 235, 258n56
Derry, 7, 8, 11, 15–16, 19–20, 22, 24, 29–30, 31–2, 36, 55–6, 57–8, 60, 86n26, 92, 95–6, 101, 114, 117, 129, 148, 150, 174, 205, 207, 215, 216, 231n46, 240, 243, 247
Des Pres, Terrence, 91
Devlin, Barney, 50
Devlin, Denis, 109
Diodorus Siculus, 79, 89n124
Diogenes, 130–1
disenchantment and re-enchantment, 31, 85n9
Donne, John, 66, 206–7, 208, 234
Donoghue, Denis, 158
Dublin, 4, 11, 13, 17, 21, 52, 69, 73, 81, 84, 92, 122, 138n14, 151, 164, 165, 180, 185, 218, 221–2, 234
Duffy, Carol Ann, 223
Duffy, Eamon, 10, 238–9
Dunlop, John, 60–1
Durkan, Michael J. and Rand Brandes, 88n71, 139n26

Easter Rising, 52, 65–6, 100, 171, 215, 246
Ebbeler, Jennifer, 24
ecumenism, 12, 53, 87n45, 243
elegy, 6, 12, 23–4, 77, 84, 90, 92–101, 103–4, 107, 129, 159, 173, 178, 181–6, 189n63, 190, 198, 203, 215, 219, 255
Eliade, Mircea, 9–10, 49, 50, 70, 96, 128–9, 135–7, 141n95, 199–200
Eliot, T. S., 3, 8, 34, 123, 151, 155, 177, 195–7, 233–4
Elizabeth I, 59, 83
Emmerson, Michael, 32
Epic of Gilgamesh, 80, 185

Faber and Faber, 3, 15, 32, 50, 54, 161, 227–8
Fallon, Peter, 63, 252
Farrar, Straus and Giroux, 227–8
Ferrari, Severino, 252
Ferry, David, 174
Field Day Theatre Company, 18–19, 110, 240, 243, 247
Filkins, Peter, 127
Fitzgerald, Robert, 143, 187n3, 203–4
Flanagan, T. P., 53, 87n60
Foster, John Wilson, 44, 87n43, 173, 202, 212
Foster, Roy, 24, 203
Frazier, Adrian, 33
Friel, Brian, 12, 18, 86n26, 110, 174, 208
Frost, Robert, 8, 95–6, 139n16, 181, 234
Fry, Stephen, 24

Gale, Martin, 252, 253–4
Gardner, W. H., 230n12
Gillis, Alan, 23
Girard, René, 70–1, 72, 75, 77, 80, 88n100, 88n101
Glanmore, 16, 90, 101, 149, 153, 164, 179–80, 218
Glob, P. V., 17, 63, 65, 67, 200
Government of Ireland Act, 7
Grauballe Man, 63
Great Famine of 1845, 39–42, 70, 106, 119–20
Greggs, Jeffrey, 258n45
gun imagery, 33–4, 36, 82, 93, 94, 131, 157, 195, 198

Halbertal, Moshe, 75
Hall, Jason David, 50, 68, 87n57
Hammond, David, 55, 203, 219
Hámundarson, Gunnarr, 71–2
Hardy, Thomas, 8, 164
Harrington, Paul, 245
Harrison, Stephen, 175

Hart, Henry, 117, 124, 189n56
Haughton, Hugh, 230n30
Havel, Václav, 171
Heaney, Marie Devlin, 4, 7, 9, 15–17, 24, 25, 46–7, 53, 69, 73, 105, 111, 117, 149, 164, 177–8, 179, 206–8
Heaney, Seamus
  BIOGRAPHY
  agnosticism, 25, 85n9
  awards and honors, 2, 3, 15, 17, 18, 19–20, 25, 84, 111, 156, 159, 160–1, 172, 178, 190, 228, 248
  birth, 8, 174
  Buddhist influences, 110, 128
  Catholic influences, 10–11, 16, 21, 32, 35, 37, 65, 71, 72, 75, 77, 79, 89n124, 103, 108, 109, 115, 116, 127, 135, 136, 137, 138, 143, 148, 157, 217
  Catholicism, 6, 7, 10–11, 12, 13–14, 15, 20, 32, 35, 37, 45, 61–2, 66, 68, 72, 75, 76–7, 80, 83, 84, 85n12, 90, 114, 116, 127, 132, 137, 138, 143, 148, 151, 154, 157, 158, 217
  death, 1, 3, 4, 21–5, 225
  family, 8–9, 12, 15–17, 25, 32, 34, 38, 115, 133–5, 140n63, 173, 186, 205, 220, 224, 225–6, 229, 250
  Incertus, 14, 31, 35, 113, 180, 221
  leaving Northern Ireland, 15–16, 17–18, 67, 111
  Mossbawn, 1, 8, 9, 10, 12, 59, 82, 83, 157, 160, 168, 210–11, 222
  national identity, 4, 12, 20, 68, 83, 115
  parents, 8–9, 12, 18–19, 34, 38, 69, 80, 103–4, 127–8, 132–5, 142–3, 146, 157, 173, 183–4, 185, 187n3, 196, 203, 204–6, 208, 220–1, 225, 252
  poetry sales, 2–3
  professor at Harvard, 17, 18, 164, 172, 187n3, 211, 234, 249
  professor at Oxford, 19, 119, 132, 234, 237
  professor at Queen's University, 15, 73, 234
  rejection of "British" label, 18
  rural life, 6–7, 8–10, 11, 13, 14, 15, 32, 42, 44, 101, 153, 190, 203, 256
  stroke, 21, 203, 206–9, 218, 220
  student at Anahorish School, 12, 116, 129
  student at Queen's University, 13–14, 29, 30, 34
  student at St Columb's College, 12–13, 30, 129, 205, 207
  teacher at Carysfort College, 17, 234
  teacher at St Joseph's School, 243
  teacher at St Thomas's School, 14
  trained as a teacher at St Joseph's School, 14, 116
  transnationalism, 4, 236
  year at University of California, Berkeley, 15, 16, 66
  DRAMA
  Burial at Thebes: Sophocles' Antigone, The, 3, 19, 228, 233, 240, 243–7, 252
  Cure at Troy: A Version of Sophocles' Philoctetes, The, 19, 166, 172, 228, 233, 240–3, 244, 246, 252
  ESSAYS
  "Above the Brim," 95–6, 139n16, 139n21
  "Anything Can Happen," 191, 246
  ["Appointment of Ted Hughes as Poet Laureate of Britain"], 236
  "Belfast," 58
  "Canticles to the Earth: Theodore Roethke," 35, 42, 87n39
  "Cessation—1994," 171
  "Civil rights, not civic weeks," 85n12
  "Convert, The," 230n12
  "Counting to a Hundred: On Elizabeth Bishop," 50
  Crediting Poetry, 19, 25, 84, 145, 156, 159, 161, 163, 164, 172, 187n9, 202, 220–1, 228–9, 235, 237–9
  "Current Unstated Assumptions about Poetry," 136
  "Door Stands Open: Czesław Miłosz, The," 201, 237
  "Earning a Rhyme," 86n23
  "Eclogues *in Extremis*: On the Staying Power of the Pastoral," 175, 176, 179, 188n54
  "Envies and Identifications: Dante and the Modern Poet," 108, 247
  "Feeling into Words," 35, 38, 49, 53, 64, 103, 235
  Finders, Keepers: Selected Prose, 3, 19, 239–40
  "From Monaghan to the Grand

Canal: The Poetry of Patrick
   Kavanagh," 221, 236
"Frontiers of Writing," 119, 120,
   132, 156, 230n37, 235, 237, 238,
   257n16
"Government of the Tongue, The,"
   4, 37, 77–8, 123, 235
Government of the Tongue, The, 19,
   239
"Home Place: The Mud Vision,
   The," 135, 141n92
"Indefatigable Hoof-taps: Sylvia
   Plath, The," 36, 37
"Irish Quest, The," 16
"John Clare's Prog," 58
"Joy or Night: Last Things in the
   Poetry of W. B. Yeats and Philip
   Larkin," 101, 102, 152–3
"Joyce's Poetry," 122
"King of the Dark," 50–1
"Learning from Eliot," 34, 123, 155
"*Lux Perpetua*," 172, 186
"Makings of a Music: Reflections on
   Wordsworth and Yeats, The," 68,
   223, 225
"Man and the Bog, The," 64
"Mossbawn," 9, 10, 93, 94, 96,
   211
"Mother Ireland," 87n64
"New Staves," 5
"Old Derry's Walls," 85n12
"On Home Ground," 222–3, 253,
   254, 256
"Out of London: Ulster's Troubles,"
   85n12
*Place and Displacement: Recent
   Poetry of Northern Ireland*, 113
"Place, Pastness, Poems: A Triptych,"
   33, 220
Place of Writing, The, 19, 239
"Poet as a Christian, The," 14
"Poet's Childhood, A," 7
*Preoccupations: Selected Prose
   1968–1978*, 18, 239
*Redress of Poetry: Oxford Lectures,
   The*, 19, 234–5, 237, 239
"Redress of Poetry, The," 74, 235,
   241, 257n16
"Regional Forecast, The," 27n35
"Seamus Heaney's 70th Birthday
   Speech," 48–9
"Seamus Heaney Writes...," 32, 90
"Sense of Place, The," 31, 224,
   232n62
"Sixth Sense, Seventh Heaven," 149,
   151, 153, 154, 156
"Something to Write Home About,"
   7, 177
"Suffering and Decision," 175, 181,
   212
["Talk on Field Day"], 110
"Time and Again: Poetry and the
   Millennium," 197, 200, 201
"Title Deeds: Translating a Classic,"
   243–4, 246, 257n27
"Whole Thing: On the Good of
   Poetry, The," 197, 235, 238,
   254
"Writer and Righter," 26
"Writer at Work," 56
"Yeats as an Example?," 226
"Yeats's Nobility," 236
INTERVIEWS
"Art of Poetry: Interview with
   Seamus Heaney, The," 14, 17, 20,
   65, 78, 90
"Greek Tragedy for Our Times, A,"
   243, 257n27, 257n32
"Heaney Tells of His Stroke Ordeal,"
   21
"Interview with Melvyn Bragg,"
   138n13
"Interview with Michael Silverblatt,"
   10
"Interview with Seamus Heaney, An"
   [Randall], 174
"Interview with Seamus Heaney, An"
   [Wachtel], 10, 42
"Life of Rhyme, A," 16, 17
"Meeting Seamus Heaney: An
   Interview," 88n99, 182
"North: Silent Awarenesses with
   Seamus Heaney, The," 11, 63
"Poet's Perspective, The," 97
"Seamus Heaney" [*Metre*], 144
"Seamus Heaney" [Murphy], 22,
   143–4
*Seamus Heaney in Conversation with
   Karl Miller*, 7, 18, 109, 119
Stepping Stones, 3, 6, 7, 8, 9, 10, 11,
   12, 14, 15, 16, 18, 21, 34, 54, 57,
   61, 67, 73, 84, 86n26, 109, 127,
   128, 129, 131, 135, 136–7, 147,
   148, 152, 155, 159, 165, 170, 174,
   183, 195, 210, 243
POETRY
"Act of Union," 80
"Actaeon," 228

Heaney, Seamus (*cont.*)
POETRY
"Advancement of Learning, An," 7, 42, 44, 85n14
"Aerodrome, The," 191
"Afterwards, An," 106, 247
"Album," 204, 205, 220
"Alphabets," 129–30, 131
"Anahorish," 55, 57, 58–9, 129
"Ancestral Photograph," 204
"Antaeus," 48–9, 80, 172, 228
"Anything Can Happen," 190, 191–3, 219, 246
"Aran," 30–1, 32
"At a Potato Digging," 39–41, 48, 70, 119
"At Toomebridge," 173–4
"Audenesque," 173, 181, 184–5, 189n63
"Augean Stables, The," 177
"Backward Look, The," 55
"Banks of a Canal," 221–3, 228, 231n54
"Bann Valley Eclogue," 174–7
"Barn, The," 42, 44
"Basket of Chestnuts, A," 147
"Beyond Sargasso," 49
"Biretta, The," 147–8
"Blackberry-Picking," 7, 42, 43–4
"Blackbird of Glanmore, The," 190–1, 199, 202
"Bodies and Souls," 231n56
Bog Poems, 63
"Bog Queen," 71
"Bogland," 31, 49, 51, 53–4, 56, 67, 121
"Bookcase, The," 173
"Broagh," 16, 55, 59, 61, 212
"Butts, The," 206, 208
"Cana Revisited," 49
"Canopy," 211–12
"Cassandra," 166–7
"Casualty," 2, 6, 12, 27n56, 72, 81, 91, 97–101, 102, 107, 110, 123, 139n26, 188n30, 196, 201, 215, 231n46
"Chanson d'Aventure," 206–8, 209, 218
"Churning Day," 42
"Clearances," 3, 19, 53, 69, 115, 127, 132, 141n77, 193, 223, 225
"Cleric, The," 125
"*Colum Cille Cecinit*," 217–18
"Constable Calls, A," 82, 83
"Conway Stewart, The," 205
"Crossing, The," 142, 160, 213, 258n43
"Crossings," 150, 159
"Dapple-Grey Mare, The," 256
"Dawn Shoot," 30
Death of a Naturalist, 2, 7, 15, 29, 30–49, 51, 56, 58, 70, 71, 82, 85n9, 85n14, 86n29, 119, 120, 172, 179, 195, 196, 204, 207, 210, 253
"Death of a Naturalist," 32, 33, 42–3, 44
"Digging," 2, 4, 32, 33–6, 38, 39, 42, 43, 44, 54, 82, 86n32, 101, 120, 124, 131, 137, 195, 196, 198, 200, 217, 250
"Disappearing Island, The," 127, 137
District and Circle, 3, 13, 19–20, 175, 190–202, 219, 221, 228, 229n3, 230n12
"District and Circle," 194–6, 199
"Diviner, The," 32, 36–9, 86n26, 86n29, 86n32
"Docker," 32, 44–6, 87n45
Door into the Dark, 15, 29, 31, 38, 39, 44, 49–54, 56–7, 62, 73, 99, 172, 174, 222
"'Door Was Open and the House Was Dark, The,'" 219
"Drifting Off," 125
"Du Bellay in Rome," 231n54
"Early Purges, The," 7, 46
Electric Light, 3, 19, 63, 142, 172–86, 190, 203, 228, 231n56
"Electric Light," 172–4, 185–6
"Elegy for a Still-born Child," 49
Eleven Poems, 15, 32–3
"England's Difficulty," 68
"Exposure," 71, 83–4, 91
Field Work, 2, 6, 9, 17, 27n56, 29, 53, 58, 71–2, 73, 81, 84–5, 90–107, 110, 120, 127, 139n28, 139n39, 165, 178, 188n30, 196, 203, 215, 213n46, 247, 253, 254
"Field Work," 105–6
"First Flight, The," 125
"First Gloss, The," 124–5
"Fisher," 85n14
"Flight Path, The," 163–6
"Fodder," 57–8, 66, 88n71
"Follower," 32, 58, 207, 253

"For the Commander of the *Eliza*," 32, 39, 41–2, 70, 119
"Forge, The," 38, 39, 44, 49–51, 56, 72, 83, 87n51, 174, 222, 231n56
"Fosterage," 116
"Fosterling," 149–50, 152
"From the Canton of Expectation," 132
"From the Frontier of Writing," 127, 131–2
"From the Republic of Conscience," 81, 127, 132, 191
"Funeral Rites," 70, 71–2
"Gifts of Rain," 55
"Given Note, The," 254
"Glanmore Eclogue," 178–9
"Glanmore Revisited," 149, 151, 203, 208, 226
"Glanmore Sonnets," 53, 84, 101–3, 253
"Golden Bough, The," 142–4, 187n3, 203
"Grauballe Man, The," 71
"Guttural Muse, The," 58
"'Had I Not Been Awake,'" 202
"Harvest Bow, The," 91, 101, 103–6, 139n35
Haw Lantern, The, 3, 6, 18–19, 53, 69, 81, 90, 115, 127–38, 141n77, 156, 191, 225
"Haw Lantern, The," 130–1
"Helmet," 192–3
"Herbal, A," 209–11, 212
"Hercules and Antaeus," 80, 84, 91, 107
"Hermit, The," 125
"Hermit Songs," 217, 218–19
"His Dawn Vision," 167
"His Reverie of Water," 168
"Home Fires," 229n3
"Honeymoon Flight," 47
Human Chain, 2, 3, 20, 29, 46, 53, 57, 127, 190, 202–22, 224, 226, 228, 252–3, 255
"Human Chain," 206, 209
"In a Field," 221, 223–5, 226, 228, 232n77
"In Gallarus Oratory," 49, 51
"*In Illo Tempore*," 125
"In the Attic," 203, 212, 218
"In Time," 221, 222, 225–6, 228–9, 232n77
"*Is Scíth Mo Chrob Ón Scríbainn*," 217–19

"Journey Back, The," 152
"July," 82
"King of the Ditchbacks, The," 112, 126
"Kite for Aibhín, A," 219–21, 252–3
"Kite for Michael and Christopher, A," 111, 198, 220
"Known World," 173
"Latecomers, The," 221, 222, 226–7, 228
"Lenten Stuff," 107
"'Lick the Pencil,'" 217, 219
"Lightenings," 150, 151–7, 194, 216, 249
"Loughanure," 216–17
"Lough Neagh Sequence, A," 49, 53
"Lovers on Aran," 30, 32, 46, 179
"Maighdean Mara," 66
"Man and Boy," 143
"Markings," 191
"Mid-Term Break," 12, 32, 46
"Ministry of Fear, The," 29–30, 131–2, 214
"Miracle," 203, 206, 208–9, 226
"Mother," 49
"Mud Vision, The," 128, 135–7, 138, 218
"Mycenae Lookout," 53, 166–9
New Selected Poems 1966–1987, 19, 32, 48, 51, 68, 142, 172, 189n63, 227, 232n77
New Selected Poems 1988–2013, 189n53, 227–9, 232n77
"New Song, A," 55, 58
"Night-Piece," 51
"Nights of '57," 231n56
North, 8, 17, 21, 29, 31, 40, 48, 54, 56, 64, 66–84, 88n99, 88n100, 100, 101, 103, 104, 106, 110, 114, 116, 120, 121, 127, 132, 139n28, 168, 173, 174, 181, 214
"North," 71, 72–4, 75, 79, 84, 103, 104, 106, 120, 151
"Northern Hoard, A," 53, 62
"Nostalgia in the Afternoon," 31
"Ocean's Love to Ireland," 80
"October Thought," 31, 150, 250
"On His Work in the English Tongue," 173, 181–4
"On the Gift of a Fountain Pen," 1, 2, 4, 221, 226, 228
"On the Road," 125–7
Open Letter, An, 18, 121, 27n49

Heaney, Seamus (*cont.*)
  POETRY
  Opened Ground: Selected Poems, 1966–1996, 32, 48, 51, 68, 172, 228–9
  "Orange Drums, Tyrone, 1966," 82
  "Other Side, The," 16, 56, 57, 60–2
  "Out of the Bag," 174
  "Out of this World," 13, 198
  "Outlaw, The," 49
  "Oysters," 91, 254
  "Parable Island," 127
  "Peninsula, The," 49, 51–2, 172
  "Personal Helicon," 32–3, 47–8, 85n14, 110, 210
  "Peter Street at Bankside," 32
  "Pitchfork, The," 147, 198
  "Poem," 46–7
  "Poet to Blacksmith," 198
  "Poet's Chair," 223–4
  "Poor Women in a City Church," 32, 44–6, 71
  "Postcard from North Antrim, A," 107
  "Postscript," 52, 161, 171–2
  "Punishment," 69, 71, 72, 74–9, 81, 120–1, 167, 168
  "Railway Children, The," 112
  "Rain Stick, The," 161–2
  "Real Names, The," 173
  "Reaping in Heat," 29–30, 31
  "Requiem for the Croppies," 49, 50, 52–3, 65
  "Riddle, The," 137–8
  "Rilke: After the Fire," 193–4
  "Riverbank Field, The," 212, 231n40, 231n41, 231n46, 252
  "Road to Derry, The," 56
  "Route 110," 53, 212–16, 217, 223–4
  "Saint Francis and the Birds," 46
  "St Kevin and the Blackbird," 162–3
  "Scaffolding," 32, 47
  "Seed Cutters, The," 69–70, 79
  "Seeing the Sick," 173, 181, 183, 185
  Seeing Things, 18, 19, 29, 30, 46, 53, 57, 127, 138, 142–60, 161, 164, 173, 174, 191, 194, 198, 203, 208, 213, 216, 218, 226, 228, 242, 248–9, 254, 255, 258n43
  "Seeing Things," 144–6
  Selected Poems 1965–1975, 18, 32
  "Servant Boy," 55, 131
  "Settings," 150, 157–9
  "Settle Bed, The," 148–9, 187n12, 203, 248–9
  "Singing School," 8, 29–30, 71, 81–4, 91, 116, 132, 214
  "Sinking the Shaft," 188n38
  "Skunk, The," 105, 139n39
  "Skylight, The," 149, 151, 203, 208, 226
  "Sofa in the Forties, A," 196
  "Song of My Man-Alive," 31
  "Sonnets from Hellas," 173, 177
  Spirit Level, The, 3, 19, 52, 53, 63, 142, 160–72, 187n8, 196, 199, 224, 228
  "Squarings" [48 poem sequence], 53, 150–60, 164, 187n5, 191, 216
  "Squarings" [fourth part of entire "Squarings" sequence], 150, 160
  Station Island, 9, 13, 17, 18, 21, 29, 37, 46, 53, 67, 90, 102, 106, 107–27, 128, 142, 155, 178, 187n19, 195, 198, 202, 220, 247
  "Station Island," 53, 112–24, 125, 126, 127, 132, 134, 140n46, 144, 178, 187n19, 194–5
  Stations, 17, 37, 67–8, 82, 107, 142, 172, 188n38
  "Storm on the Island," 30
  "Stove-Lid for W. H. Auden, A," 229n3
  "Strand at Lough Beg, The," 91–7, 102, 107, 120, 138n10, 139n23, 178, 203
  "Strange Fruit," 69, 71, 74, 79–80, 81, 89n124, 106, 139n28, 140n46
  "Sunlight," 69, 83
  "Sweeney Redivivus," 124–5, 128
  "Synge on Aran," 30, 179
  "Terminus," 6, 130, 131
  "To George Seferis in the Underworld," 194, 196–7
  "To Mick Joyce in Heaven," 223–4
  "Tollund," 63, 168, 169–71, 187n8, 199, 221
  "Tollund Man, The," 16, 31, 54, 56, 62–6, 67, 199
  "Tollund Man in Springtime, The," 63, 190, 199–202
  "Toome," 55, 59
  "Toome Road, The," 9
  "Traditions," 55, 59–60

"Transgression, A," 172, 228
"Trout," 33
"Turnip-Snedder, The," 190
"Ugolino," 91, 106–7, 120, 165, 247
"Unacknowledged Legislator's Dream, The," 81
"Uncoupled," 205
"Underground, The," 111
"Unwinding," 125
"Verses for a Fordham Commencement," 235–6
"Villanelle for an Anniversary," 172, 228–9
"Visitant," 107
"Watchman's War, The," 166
"Waterfall," 32, 46
"Wedding Day," 66
"Westering," 66
"Whatever You Say Say Nothing," 81, 114
"Wheels within Wheels," 147
Wintering Out, 13, 16, 29, 31, 51, 53, 54–67, 69, 74, 80, 87n68, 100, 129, 197, 199, 212
"Wool Trade, The," 13
"Wordsworth's Skates," 198
RADIO SCRIPTS
Munro, 240
TRANSLATIONS
The Aeneid: Book VI, 19, 21, 142–3, 203–4, 211–13, 215–16, 252, 256
Beowulf, 3, 19, 25, 35–6, 86n23, 138n11, 173, 182–3, 184, 193, 228–9, 233, 246, 248–52, 258n56, 258n57
"Death of Orpheus, The," 247–8
Diary of One Who Vanished: A Song Cycle, 248
Laments, 248
Last Walk: Translations from the Italian of Giovanni Pascoli, The, 3, 20, 233, 252–6
Midnight Verdict, The, 247–8
"Names of the Hare, The," 172, 228
"O Vain Dream!," 255–6
"Orpheus and Eurydice," 111, 247
"Ploughing," 253–4
Sweeney Astray, 18, 121, 124, 142, 172, 202, 247, 258n41
"Sweeney in Flight," 172
Testament of Cresseid and Seven Fables, The, 248
"Washerwomen," 254–5

Heaney, Seamus and Robert Hass, 187n3
Hecht, Anthony, 236, 239
Heidegger, Martin, 55
Heiny, Stephen, 231n39
helicon, 47–8
Henryson, Robert, 248, 258n45
Herbert, George, 156, 234
Hesiod, 47–8
Hewitt, John, 14
Higgins, Gareth I., 87n44
history and historical allusion/imagery, 39–42, 52–3, 70, 71–3, 74–81, 108, 119, 135, 180, 217–18, 235, 240, 242–3, 250
Hitler, Adolf, 224, 246–7
Hobsbaum, Philip, 14–15, 44
Holiday, Billie, 79
Hollis, Matthew, 224
Homem, Rui Carvalho, 258n43
Homer, 224
hope, 19, 25–6, 48, 53, 54, 55, 71, 73, 84, 95–6, 97, 107, 110, 111–12, 163–6, 168, 169–71, 176, 177, 178, 187n19, 194, 208–9, 215, 220, 226, 234, 235, 237, 240, 242–3
Hopkins, Gerard Manley, 13, 14, 22, 29–31, 35, 42–3, 49, 85n5, 86n23, 87n51, 150, 181, 183–4, 197, 230n12, 250
Horace, 191, 246
Hughes, Francis, 119–20, 123, 246
Hughes, Olwyn, 63
Hughes, Ted, 14, 33, 63, 151, 173, 174–5, 181–4, 185, 187n5, 189n56, 189n60, 189n63, 236
human condition, 6, 26, 49, 128, 170, 200, 240
Hume, John, 12, 230n37
Hussein, Saddam, 246

Inishbofin, 144
Iraq War, 245–7
Italy, 21, 180, 186, 213, 222–3, 228, 231n54, 252–3

Janáček, Leoš, 248
Jantzen, Grace M., 72
Joyce, James, 8, 13, 18, 27n35, 27n49, 60, 110, 113, 119, 121–4, 127, 200–1, 205, 214, 218
Junkin, Johnny, 57, 60–2

Kalda, Ozef, 248
Kavanagh, Patrick, 10, 14, 34–6, 86n35, 109, 115, 116, 181, 221–2, 223–4, 232n62, 233–4, 236
Keats, John, 1, 13, 21–2, 49, 87n51, 113, 122, 123, 132, 143–4, 207, 208, 222, 231n56, 239
Keenan, Terry, 115–16
kenning, 35, 103, 182
Kenny, Enda, 24
Kerouac, Jack, 125–6
Kiberd, Declan, 214
Kochanowski, Jan, 248
Kosovo, 246, 251

"Lament for Art O'Leary, The," 246–7, 256
language, 6, 8, 9, 10, 16, 22, 23, 24–5, 26, 49, 54–5, 56, 57–62, 77–8, 83, 85n12, 87n68, 103, 122–3, 153, 157–8, 169, 179, 180, 181–2, 185, 187n9, 214, 217, 230n12, 247–56
Larkin, Philip, 14, 15, 101, 102, 151, 152, 173
Lavery, John F., 214–15
Lawless, Matthew, 148
Lawrence, D. H., 8
Laxton, Edward, 86n36
Ledwidge, Francis, 223
Lerner, Laurence, 30
liminality, 34, 68, 78, 83, 130, 131, 156, 160, 163, 171, 210, 225, 241
literary allusions see individual authors
London, 15, 20, 111, 129, 170, 190, 194, 248
London Underground, 11, 20, 190, 194–6, 198
Long, Richard, 135
Longley, Edna, 69
Longley, Michael, 14, 47, 55, 159–60
Lough Beg, 92–5, 99, 118,
Lough Derg, 37, 107–9, 111, 140n46, 144, 187n19
Lough Neagh, 98–100, 135, 144, 173, 196
Lowell, Robert, 21, 105, 139n39
Lytle, Ellen W., 245

McCartney, Colum, 92–6, 99, 107, 117, 118–19, 120, 123, 138n13, 138n14, 178, 203
McConnell, Gail, 44
McDonald, Peter, 190, 234
McGrath, Alister, 31, 85n9

McGuckian, Medbh, 15, 234
McKittrick, David, et al., 139n28, 140n66
McLaverty, Michael, 116
McLuhan, Marshall, 103
Mahon, Derek, 110
Maritain, Jacques, 154
Martens, Lorna, 187n10
Marvell, Andrew, 97
Massie, Alan, 24
Mendelson, Edward, 19
Meredith, George, 169
Merriman, Brian, 247–8
Meyer, Robinson, 24–5
Middleton, Colin, 216–17
Miłosz, Czesław, 13, 84, 181–3, 198, 200–1, 234, 237, 248
Milton, John, 22, 92, 94, 184
Monroe, Jonathan, 67
Montague, John, 57, 112
Morisco, Gabriella, 253
Morrison, Blake and Andrew Motion, 18
Morrison, Danny, 165, 166, 188n35
Muldoon, Paul, 15, 230n13, 234
Mulholland, Michael, 214
Murphy, Andrew, 3
Murphy, Barney, 116
Murphy, Mike, 22
mythology/allusions to mythology, 19, 47–9, 54, 57, 63, 64, 66, 71–2, 80–1, 84, 92, 93, 96, 109, 111, 113, 117, 124, 130–1, 137–8, 142–4, 155, 166–9, 173, 174, 177, 179–80, 186, 192, 203–4, 207, 208, 210, 211–12, 213, 215, 216, 217, 218, 219, 226, 228, 240–5, 247–8

nationalism, 6, 12, 20, 53, 60, 98, 100, 115, 119, 123, 132, 168, 170, 240, 245
nature imagery, 7, 26, 31–2, 33, 42–4, 48, 53, 85n9, 117, 129, 130, 162, 180, 184, 187n5, 201, 210, 253–6
Ni Houlihan, Kathleen, 63
Nietzsche, Friedrich, 70, 88n101
Northern Ireland conflict see Troubles
Nugent, Kieran, 165, 188n35

O'Brien, Conor Cruise, 69, 243, 246, 257n27
O'Brien, Eugene, 55
O'Brien, Flann, 179

O'Brien, Peggy, 109
O'Donoghue, Bernard, 56, 58, 87n68
O'Donoghue, Heather, 251–2
O'Driscoll, Dennis, 3, 6, 57, 148, 210: *see also* Seamus Heaney, interviews: *Stepping Stones*
O'Faolain, Sean, 109
O'Neill, Charles L., 88n100
O'Neill, Louis, 2, 6, 27n56, 72, 97–101, 107, 123, 139n28, 188n30, 196, 215, 231n46
O'Riada, Sean, 107, 254
Ó Suilleabháin, Eoghan Rua, 198
O'Toole, Fintan, 224
Oldcorn, Tony, 253
omphalos, 9, 129, 168
orality/aurality, 17, 34, 74, 81, 249
Ormsby, Frank, 15
Ovid, 111, 247
Owen, Wilfred, 181–3, 189n59, 223, 234, 238

Paisley, Ian, 45, 109
Parker, Michael, 26n2, 85n12, 86n35, 87n39, 87n60
parochialism, 35
partition, 108, 132
Pascoli, Giovanni, 3, 20, 21, 219–23, 233, 252–6
Patmore, Coventry, 104–5
Paulin, Tom, 85n5
pen and writing imagery, 1, 4, 32–6, 38, 43, 54, 82, 124–5, 195, 203, 205, 217, 218
Perrault, Charles, 43–4
Petrarch, 223
Pettigo, 108, 165
pilgrimage, 26, 37, 64, 93, 107–9, 112–16, 122–3, 128, 166, 243
place, 1–2, 6–7, 9, 12–13, 16, 31, 47–8, 49, 56, 57, 58–9, 66, 81, 87n68, 92, 94, 95–6, 99, 110, 120–1, 126–7, 132, 136–7, 150, 163, 187n9, 193–4, 209, 210–12, 220, 223, 249, 254
Plath, Sylvia, 37, 182
Plato, 217
Plunkett, Oliver, 79
"poet as witness," 8, 91, 107, 110, 237
poetic authority, 233–5
poetic forms
    blank verse, 223
    pastoral, 23, 31, 39, 42, 47–8, 52, 70, 85n9, 95, 175–6

prose poems, 17, 37, 67–8, 81, 82, 107, 142, 172, 188n38, 258n56
sonnet, 3, 15, 23, 50–3, 69, 70, 74, 79, 84, 87n57, 101–3, 115, 127, 130, 133, 141n77, 149–51, 177–8, 193–5, 199–201, 219, 223, 225, 231n54, 253: Petrarchan, 50, 130, 133, 149, 177–8, 223; Shakespearean, 70, 102, 133–4, 149
tercet, 23, 34, 46, 97, 106, 109, 112, 114, 115, 118, 122, 124, 125, 127, 139n23, 140n67, 149, 151, 155, 159, 161, 162, 166–7, 174, 192–3, 203, 204, 205, 215, 219–21, 226–7, 247
terza rima, 46, 106, 109, 118, 122, 125, 140n67, 161, 219, 220, 221, 226–7, 247–53, 256
poetic metaphor, 54, 55, 102–3, 137, 149
poetic punctuation, 35, 36–7, 44, 61, 65, 93, 101–2, 145, 157–8, 164, 176, 182, 206–7, 209, 221
poetic rhyme/rhythm, 15, 31, 34, 36, 38, 46–7, 50, 53, 71, 79, 100, 101, 103, 104, 106, 109, 114, 118, 121, 122, 125, 133–4, 140n67, 149, 151, 159, 161, 166, 167, 169–70, 171, 178, 186, 200, 221, 223, 227, 238, 242, 253, 254, 255, 256
rhyme scheme, 30, 46, 50, 70, 106, 133, 134, 149, 161, 169, 178, 223, 253
poetic structure, 21, 30, 34, 38–9, 92, 100, 109, 130, 144, 149, 169, 225, 253, 255
poet's vocation, 1, 17, 34, 38–9, 54, 83, 90, 103, 107, 110, 112, 113, 116, 143, 181, 186, 236–9
postcolonialism, 4, 181, 244
postmodernism, 4, 136, 137, 181
Potts, Robert, 173
Pound, Ezra, 254
Protestantism and Protestant majority, 4, 7, 11–13, 15–16, 20, 32, 44–5, 46, 52–3, 55, 57, 59, 60–2, 65, 80, 81, 82–3, 87n45, 107, 108, 114, 118, 119, 122, 136, 168, 175–7, 178, 240, 242, 243, 251
provincialism, 35, 60

Rea, Stephen, 18
Regan, Stephen, 94, 138n13

Ricks, Christopher, 15
Ricœur, Paul, 104
Rilke, Rainer Maria, 193–4
ritual, 10, 31, 39–41, 63–4, 66, 70, 74, 114, 203, 226
Roethke, Theodore, 35, 42, 87n39
Rowse, Christopher, 25
RTÉ Radio, 16, 176
Russell, Richard Rankin, 27n28, 27n35, 27n49, 56, 87n39, 87n51, 87n59, 87n65, 88n81, 88n91, 88n101, 89n108, 89n124, 139n16, 139n23, 140n67, 141n83, 187n12, 226, 230n23, 257n24, 258n41
Rwanda, 246, 251

Saddlemyer, Anne, 16, 101, 164, 179–81
St Jerome, 24–5
St Patricks's Purgatory, 37, 102, 107–9
Sands, Bobby, 119
Scruton, Roger, 88n101
sectarianism, 21, 32, 40, 53–4, 65–8, 74, 80–2, 84, 108, 110, 112, 114–15, 149, 170, 175–6, 177, 178, 221, 240
September 11, 2001, 190–4, 198, 219, 244, 257n32
sexual imagery, 43, 47, 51, 53, 74–9, 105, 214
Shakespeare, William, 22, 60, 63, 74, 129, 170, 186, 238
Shaw, George Bernard, 20
Shelley, Percy Bysshe, 81
Shippey, Thomas, 248
Sidney, Sir Philip, 208
Simmons, Paulanne, 245
solidarity, 5, 58, 90, 99, 119, 220
solitude, 6, 73, 81, 90, 98, 99, 101, 123–4, 179, 196, 201, 221
Sophocles, 3, 19, 166, 233, 240–7, 252
space, 9, 12, 70, 78, 94, 105, 110, 113, 115, 126, 128–9, 131–2, 133–5, 136–7, 160, 163, 170–1, 177, 190, 193–4, 201, 210, 218, 237
Sperry, Stuart M., 113
Spenser, Edmund, 59
Stevens, Wallace, 145, 236
Strathearn, William, 117–19, 140n66, 178
Strindberg, August, 117
Sweeney, 92, 93, 107, 109, 113, 120, 124–6, 138n10, 155, 179, 198, 247, 258n43

Sweeney, Simon, 113–16
Swift, Jonathan, 18
Swir, Anna, 37, 123
symbols and symbolism, 10, 44, 47, 53–4, 62–3, 85n9, 104, 105, 110, 111–12, 113–15, 122, 129, 131, 132, 134, 137, 144–5, 147–8, 149, 159, 174, 185–6, 199–200, 202, 219, 254
Synge, John M., 31, 32, 179–81, 214

Thatcher, Margaret, 119
Theocritus, 176
Thomas, Dylan, 29, 31
Thomas, Edward, 223, 224–5, 226
Titian, 228
Tobin, Daniel, 70, 80
Tolkien, J. R. R., 248
Trethewey, Natasha, 234
Troubles, 2, 6, 9, 15–16, 17, 19, 20, 22, 23, 26, 32, 39, 45, 53, 54, 55–6, 62, 65–6, 67, 68, 69, 71, 74–80, 81, 83, 84, 85n12, 90, 91–101, 105, 106, 107, 109, 110, 113, 114, 117–19, 120, 121, 131, 132, 140n66, 149, 165, 166, 168–70, 171, 173–8, 178, 180–1, 191, 199, 214–15, 221, 230n37, 238, 240–2, 243, 246, 251
  Bloody Friday, 55
  Bloody Sunday, 2, 6, 55–6, 97–9, 100, 101, 215, 231n46
  British Army, 9, 15–16, 59, 83, 97, 131, 173, 215
  ceasefires, 19, 168, 169–70, 177, 251
  Combined Loyalist Command, 19, 251
  Good Friday Agreement, 20, 176, 181
  Irish Republican Army, 16, 19, 55, 77, 84, 98–9, 106, 119, 120, 165, 169–70, 171, 215, 230n37, 251
  Royal Ulster Constabulary, 16, 117, 140n66, 214, 243
  Sinn Fein, 165, 166, 170, 221
  Ulster Volunteer Force, 92
Truagh Mo Thuras Go Loch Dearg ("Vain My Journey to Lough Derg"), 109
Tyler, Meg, 189n60

Ulster, 10, 16, 57, 59, 69, 80, 114, 124, 175, 247, 251
Ulster Plantation, 11, 57, 59

Vendler, Helen, 3, 18, 97, 128, 131, 135, 137, 141n83, 160, 167, 218
violence, 16, 17, 19, 20, 31–2, 36, 53, 54, 55–6, 62, 64, 65–6, 67, 68–9, 70–1, 72, 73, 74–5, 76, 77, 79, 80, 82, 83, 88n101, 90, 91, 101, 105, 108, 114–15, 119–21, 131, 167, 170–1, 173, 195, 199, 236, 242, 243, 258n57
Virgil, 19, 21, 92, 122, 127, 142–3, 173, 174–7, 178, 179, 181, 186, 188n54, 203, 204, 208, 211–12, 213, 215–16, 230n37, 231n39, 231n40, 256

Walcott, Derek, 234
Weir, John, 140n66
Welch, Robert, 11
Wellesley, Dorothy, 159
Wheatley, David, 189n63, 232n77, 235
Wicklow, 16, 17, 57, 67, 73, 83, 90, 101, 103, 164, 179–80

Woodham-Smith, Cecil, 40–1, 86n37
Wordsworth, William, 7–8, 9, 22, 26n6, 29, 36, 42, 82, 142, 154, 187n1, 197–8, 211, 223, 231n56, 234
World War One, 46, 182, 223, 246
World War Two, 190, 191
writing and audience, 1–2, 4, 32–4, 36, 37–8, 47, 50–1, 74–5, 77–9, 124–5, 127, 132, 156–9, 217–18, 241–4
Wyatt, Sir Thomas, 97

Yeats, William Butler, 5, 8, 10, 20, 21, 22–4, 25, 28n64, 29, 37, 53, 63, 65–6, 68, 81–2, 93, 97, 100, 101, 102, 104, 107, 121, 122, 141n72, 151–3, 156, 157–8, 159, 161, 171, 178–9, 181, 182–3, 184, 185, 187n9, 188n29, 188n30, 215, 225–6, 229n2, 229n8, 234, 236–7, 239, 246, 257n16
Young, Kevin, 194–6, 234